The Roots of French Imperialism in Eastern Asia

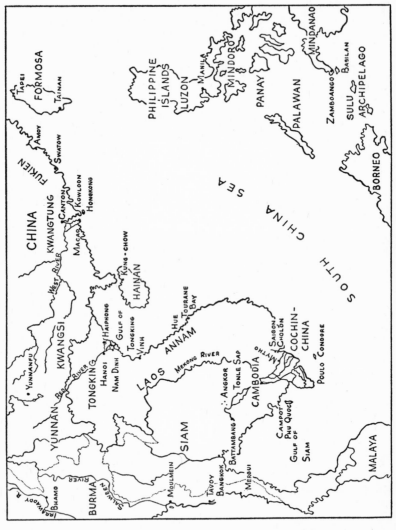

Map 1. The Coast of Southeast Asia

The Roots of
French Imperialism
in Eastern Asia

JOHN F. CADY

PROFESSOR OF HISTORY, OHIO UNIVERSITY

PUBLISHED FOR

THE AMERICAN HISTORICAL ASSOCIATION

Cornell University Press

ITHACA, NEW YORK

CORNELL UNIVERSITY PRESS
LONDON: GEOFFREY CUMBERLEGE
OXFORD UNIVERSITY PRESS
FIRST PUBLISHED 1954

THIS VOLUME IS PUBLISHED FROM A FUND CON-
TRIBUTED TO THE AMERICAN HISTORICAL ASSOCIATION
BY THE CARNEGIE CORPORATION OF NEW YORK.

PRINTED IN THE UNITED STATES OF AMERICA BY THE
VAIL-BALLOU PRESS, INC., BINGHAMTON, NEW YORK

Preface

THE policy pursued by France in the Far East during the mid-nineteenth century was the expression of a tradition of national interest in eastern Asia dating from the reign of Louis XIV and associated in large measure with Catholic missions in that area. The principal episodes connected with the development of this tradition are reviewed in the introductory chapter. Since French activity in eastern Asia during the period of the July Monarchy continued to be largely missionary in character, it was necessary in Chapter II to describe the rise of the liberal Catholic movement in France and to explain its relations with Premier Guizot, a Protestant and an anticlerical. This same theme of the political interrelations between the French clerical party and the government of the Prince-President Louis Napoleon is treated again in Chapter VII.

French activities in eastern Asia were also closely connected with the vicissitudes of the mid-century entente between Britain and France, which extended with periodic interruptions (notably in 1840, 1846–1848, and 1859) from 1830 to 1860. The entente found expression in cooperative allied action in Belgium, Spain, Texas, and the Rio de la Plata area during the thirties and forties. It was also operative during the revolutions of 1848, later in the Balkans, Turkey, the Crimean War, and finally in China in 1857–1860. The political instability of successive Paris regimes during the period of the entente, coupled with the vulner-

v

ability of France to hostile continental influences, made Great Britain easily the dominant partner in the alliance. In the Far East especially, entente co-operation was marred by Anglo-French rivalry, for the French were jealous of Britain's leadership and were trying persistently to develop a balancing influence of their own. French imperialist policies in eastern Asia have also been considered in the broader context of the interrelated policies pursued by Britain, America, and Russia in the same area. Internal political developments within China and Annam are treated only incidentally insofar as they throw light on French policy itself.

The final chapter of the book is in the nature of an epilogue, which is designed to bridge the two decades between 1861 and the eventual commitment of the French in the 1880's to conquer all of Annam. The more substantial contributions of the study based on the author's own archival research are to be found in Chapters II through XV, which cover the period between 1840 and 1861.

My interest in French imperialist policy in eastern Asia was aroused while I was serving as a lecturer in history at the University of Rangoon, Burma, prior to World War II. At that time I discovered that there was no thoroughgoing account of the activities of France in the Far East during the mid-nineteenth century and likewise no study in French which utilized systematically the manuscripts of the diplomatic archives relating to China and Annam. Prior to my return to America in 1938, I arranged to obtain access to the diplomatic correspondence on the Far East which was available at the Quai d'Orsay depository in Paris and in the Record Office in London. During the summer of 1938, I spent several months in Europe examining archival material and collecting bibliographical data on the published sources. Unfortunately, I was unable to gain access to the archives of the French Ministry of Marine and Colonies, which were needed for the period after 1860 in particular. I concluded my basic researches in the United States during the summer of 1940 with the assistance of a grant-in-aid from the Social Science Research Council.

The first and until now the only published result of my study has been a bibliographical article in the *Journal of Modern History* for March, 1942, entitled "The Beginnings of French Imperialism in the Pacific Orient." The drafting of the full study was interrupted by diversions connected with World War II. It was not until 1952, therefore, during the course of my year's tenure as visiting professor of history at Cornell University, that I was able to reassemble my notes, amplify them by additional research, and put together the completed draft. I am particularly indebted to the Southeast Asia Program at Cornell for a special research grant and for typing assistance in the final preparation of the manuscript.

An annotated bibliographical appendix covers all works actually cited in the footnotes and supplements in various particulars the previously mentioned article appearing in the *Journal of Modern History*.

JOHN F. CADY

Athens, Ohio
February, 1954

Contents

ix

MAPS

The Roots of French Imperialism in Eastern Asia

I

French Activities in

the Far East, 1662-1830

FRENCH imperialist policy in the Far East, which found ultimate expression in the acquisition of French Indo-China, was rooted in traditions extending back to the reign of Louis XIV. The one continuous thread in this tradition was the perennial activity of French Catholic missionaries in Annam (including southern Cochin-China, northern Tongking, and the connecting coastal strip), sponsored for the most part by the Société des Missions Etrangères, which was organized in Paris in 1663. These French missionaries from the outset were the bearers and representatives of French culture as well as of Catholicism; their zeal attested their confidence in the superiority of things French as well as the vitality of their religious convictions. The French East India Company of 1664, sixth of such companies in a series dating from 1600, was sponsored by Louis XIV himself, who personally subscribed one-fifth of the initial capital assets. The company developed its principal bases in India, but the China seas were part of its privileged area of operation.[1] The political and commerical threads of the tradition of French interest in eastern Asia were interrupted by circumstances at-

[1] J. Chailley-Bert, *Les Compagnies de Colonisation sous l'Ancien Régime* (Paris, 1898), 22–27, 170–171. The Compagnie des Indes Orientales of 1664 was formed from a combination of the remnants of the Compagnie de la France Orientale of 1642 and the Compagnie de Chine of 1660. The 1664 company was never prosperous, but it continued to be fairly active until 1698.

1

tending the wars of Louis XIV; they were completely broken off following the collapse of the French position in India in 1763.

Except for the activities of private adventurers, French political interest in eastern Asia was not revived until the reign of Louis Philippe. Under Louis Napoleon, the enhancement of national and dynastic prestige in the Far East became an important objective in French policy. The persecution and other difficulties which French missionaries had encountered meanwhile in various countries of eastern Asia provided convenient but incidental justification for policy decisions. Commercial considerations played a very minor part in the nineteenth-century revival of French interest in the Far East.

The first part of this story, up to 1830, needs only a brief summary, for it has been told repeatedly elsewhere.[2] This study is concerned primarily with the development of French policy in eastern Asia, under Louis Philippe and Louis Napoleon in particular, during the two decades from 1840 to 1860.

Seventeenth-Century French Activity in Southeast Asia

The first important impetus for French national activity in eastern Asia came from Catholic missionary interests following the end of the Thirty Years' War. During that war French diplomacy and military might humbled all rivals and made France the dominant state in Europe. The Roman Congregation for the Propagation of the Faith (dating from 1622), which was attempting at the time to improve the opportunities presented in eastern Asia for promoting the Christian cause, wanted to enlist the support of the powerful French monarchy and church in that task. Portugal's Catholic empire in the Far East had been virtually destroyed during the first half of the 1600's by the Protestant Dutch and British, while Spain's foothold at Manila was only an extension of its American holdings. Neither Catholic state possessed the requisite resources to support an expanding missionary operation. The decadent Iberian powers could nevertheless be counted upon to oppose any French intrusion in eastern Asia, especially in the area of ecclesiastical patronage, which was about all that remained in the Orient of their

---

[2] See K. S. Latourette, *A History of Christiain Missions in China* (New York, 1929); P. Cultru, *Histoire de la Cochinchine Française, des Origines à 1883* (Paris, 1910); T. E. Ennis, *French Policy and Development in Indòchina* (Chicago, 1936); Virginia Thompson, *French Indo-China* (New York, 1937).

2

alleged colonial monopoly dating from the papal Line of Demarcation and the Treaty of Tordesillas of 1493–1494. If the missionary cause in the Far East was to keep pace with the extensive opportunities afforded, the Portuguese "Right of Patronage" in particular must be circumvented, and the support of the influential French monarchy and church must be enlisted in the task.[3]

The initial impetus came from one Alexander of Rhodes, a French Jesuit missionary scholar interested particularly in Annam, who returned to Europe in 1649 after having spent more than a quarter century in the Far East. In 1653 Rhodes gained the approval of the College of Propaganda at Rome for his scheme to recruit from the French clergy a missionary society which would be dedicated to the task of providing manpower and funds for training an indigenous Catholic hierarchy for the church in eastern Asia. Rhodes was able to elicit a positive response from a group, both lay and clerical, living at the University of Paris under a set of religious rules drawn up by its leader, Monsignor François Pallu. Leading missionaries to be selected under Rhode's scheme for service in the Far East were designated by Rome as vicars apostolic, enjoying the rank and title of bishops of extinct sees but functioning under the authority of the Pope. The first vicars apostolic from the Paris group were designated in 1658. Pallu was himself named Bishop of Heliopolis and vicar apostolic of Tongking;[4] another of the group was designated Bishop of Berythe. These two and several others departed for the Far East in 1662 and 1663. In the latter year, the training seminary set up at Paris joined with the supporting group and the missionaries in the field to form the Société des Missions Etrangères (hereafter called the Society). It enjoyed the solid backing of both the French ecclesiastical authorities and the court of Louis XIV, and its missionaries acted in the early period as emissaries of France.[5]

[3] Latourette, 84, 109–112. Spanish religious orders entered Japan after 1600 and China in 1621.

[4] A. A. Dorland, "A Preliminary Study of the Role of the French Protectorate of Roman Catholic Missions in Sino-French Diplomatic Relations" (Cornell University thesis, 1951), 9–10.

[5] Latourette, 112–114; Chailley-Bert, 30–31. Although in 1655 the Paris government ruled that missionary activity was not intended to serve political ends, the dual goals were clearly co-ordinated during the majority rule of Louis XIV.

Activities in Siam

From the outset the French vicars apostolic were particularly interested in the countries of southeast Asia, partly because the Portuguese authorities at Macao and the regular clergy strongly opposed the efforts of the French priests to enter China. Siam was at first the most promising field. The Bishop of Berythe gained entry into Siam in 1662, and Pallu himself visited that country in 1664–1665. In return for services rendered to the Siamese King, including the preparation of fortress defenses at key cities against an expected Dutch attack, Pallu gained for the vicars permission to reside and to teach religion in the country. When Pallu returned to France in 1665 bringing an account of his encouraging reception in Siam, he was able to interest Louis XIV in his proposal to make that country a Christian stronghold and a center of French influence in eastern Asia. Rome's formal support of the French project was given in a papal bull, issued in 1669, placing Siam and neighboring states under the jurisdiction of the new church at Ayuthia, then the capital of Siam.[6]

The French mission in Siam prospered moderately during the 1670's. Pallu obtained a grant of land at Lopburi in 1673, where, three years later, the French missionaries had a Catholic seminary in operation with more than one hundred students in attendance. A female community called the Votaries of the Cross was also founded in Siam. The Siamese King gave support and allegedly promised to build a church for the mission at his own expense. The assignment in 1676 of a French medical missionary to the post of Governor of Puket, on the isthmus, foreshadowed the vigorous political role played by the French during the next decade. Following the end of the Dutch war in 1678, the government of Louis XIV attempted to establish political contact with Siam, only to have the lavish presents intended for the Siamese King captured en route by the Dutch.[7] French support was welcome at Ayuthia at this time as a makeweight against the pressure of the Dutch and subsequently against that of the British.

The arrival in Siam, in 1680 of the first French East India Company ship from Surat, India, for the purpose of setting up a French trading

[6] W. A. R. Wood, A History of Siam (London, 1933), 195–196.

[7] Ibid., 197–198. Louis XIV became interested in the Far East partly through the influence of his confessor, Père de la Chaise.

4

center in Ayuthia coincided with the appointment of a young Levantine adventurer of Greek parentage named Constantine Phaulkon [8] to the post of Superintendent of Siam's foreign trade. In this capacity, Phaulkon found himself in a key position to play off one European group against another, to the aggrandizement of his own political and personal fortunes. He favored French influence, and at the end of 1680 he assisted in sending an ill-fated Siamese embassy to Europe carrying letters to the French King. The transporting ship sank off Madagascar. A subsequent embassy, sent in 1684, proceeded first to London, where an agreement (unrecorded) was allegedly signed, and thence to Paris.

On the return trip in 1685, an impressive French embassy, escorted by two warships, accompanied the Thai emissaries. The French mission was headed by the Chevalier de Chaumont and included, besides other gentlemen of quality, the Abbé Choisy and Father Tachard, a learned Jesuit. In a treaty signed at Ayuthia in December, 1685, France was accorded commercial and religious concessions on the basis of a tacit understanding that the French would assist Siam in case of a Dutch attack.[9]

Meanwhile, Phaulkon and the Siamese court had a falling out with the British over the burning of British factories in Ayuthia in 1682, an event for which Britain blamed Phaulkon. Another cause of friction was the piratical activities along the Tenasserim coast of the Bay of Bengal of one Samuel White, a renegade Briton, claiming under authority of the King of Siam to be Governor of Mergui. British residents in Siam were also roughly treated. The controversy became critical in 1687, when the British presented Ayuthia with a £65,000 claim for damages. The outcome was a massacre of all British residents at Mergui and their expulsion from Siam proper.[10] This action against the British was approximately contemporaneous with the arrival at Ayuthia of a second French embassy, this time including three war vessels, 1,600 French troops, and 300 engineers, accompanied by religious and commercial contingents. The French troops were immediately posted as security forces at Mergui, Bangkok, and other strategic points. A treaty signed in late 1687 augmented France's commercial privileges. The French

[8] Phaulkon had first come to Siam in 1675 as cabin boy on a British ship.
[9] Wood, 200–204; Maurice Collis, *Siamese White* (London, 1936), 200–201.
[10] Collis, 111–112, 303–307; Wood, 208.

embassy recognized Phaulkon's services by making him a Count of France and a Chevalier of St. Michael and St. Peter.[11]

But French ascendancy proved to be shortlived. Jealousy on the part of the nobles of Phaulkon's power at court, coupled with fear that a French coup was impending following the conversion to Christianity of the princely heir to the ailing ruler, precipitated a revolution in June, 1688. Phaulkon was seized and executed, and all French missionary and commercial personnel were either detained or exiled. The besieged commander of the French forces was eventually obliged to sign a truce calling for the transfer to Pondicherry, on Siamese ships, of all French military contingents. The Siamese rebels seized the throne and quickly made friends with the Dutch, as insurance against possible retaliation by France.[12]

The Dutch continued for a time to trade with Siam in a meager way. Except for this trade, Siam broke off almost all European contacts for almost a century and a half, so that Catholic missionaries were not again permitted to enter the country until around 1830.

British and French prisoners were released in 1689 after the Thai ships returned from India. At the close of the War of the League of Augsburg in Europe, the French Jesuit Father Tachard made a final abortive effort in October, 1698, to negotiate for the establishment of a French factory in Siam and a fort on Siam's Tenasserim coast. The first episode of French imperialist activity in southeast Asia thus came to an inglorious end. The French East India Company managed to raise some new capital in 1701, but it was completely ruined during the course of the exhausting Spanish War which ensued.[13]

French Interest in China

Monsignor Pallu [14] meanwhile had been making disappointingly slow progress in his effort to circumvent the opposition of the Portuguese authorities and the regular clergy in the Far East to the entry of the French vicars apostolic into China. After failing to gain access by direct methods, Pallu found at Manila, to which port he had accidentally been

[11] Wood, 211–215; Collis, 56, 281.   [12] Wood, 215–216.
[13] *Ibid.*, 216–221; Chailley-Bert, 170–171.
[14] For a full-length biography of Pallu, see Louis Baudiment, *Un Mémoire Anonyme sur François Pallu, Principal Fondateur des Missions Etrangères* (Paris, 1934).

driven by a storm in 1674, an outstanding Chinese Christian leader named Gregory Lopez, whom he proposed to consecrate as the first Catholic Bishop of Nanking. Rome supported Pallu by designating Lopez a vicar apostolic in 1674, by directing him in 1679 to proceed to Nanking, and by ordering the regular clergy to recognize the authority of the vicars apostolic. The College of Cardinals in 1680 overruled Portugal's complaint that France was infringing on its patronage, whereupon Lisbon attempted to force all missionaries leaving for the Orient to take an oath to respect its control of ecclesiastical patronage. When Lisbon in 1690 obtained from Rome the right of presentment to three Chinese bishoprics,[15] those of Macao, Nanking, and Peking, the Portuguese then declared the limits of the three to be coextensive with all of China, leaving no room for the vicars apostolic. Pallu's candidate was never installed as Bishop of Nanking. Lopez was eventually consecrated at Manila in 1685 and appointed to Nanking in 1690, but he died in 1691 before he could take his post.[16]

But the French clergy and Rome were not to be blocked by Portuguese intransigence. Seven members of the Paris Society managed to enter China by 1695, and six years later the group numbered fifteen. In 1696 the papacy limited the extent of the Portuguese-patronage bishoprics to three Chinese provinces each. The remaining nine provinces Rome divided into eight vicariates, which were to be entirely independent of Portuguese authority.[17]

As an additional means of countering Portuguese presumption and of gaining French access to Peking, in 1685 Louvois, chief minister in the government of Louis XIV, persuaded the reluctant Jesuit General in France to send a number of learned French Jesuits to the Far East without clearing them through Lisbon. Two of them, including Father Tachard, stopped in Siam, while five others entered China via Ningpo. Father Verbiest, a Belgian Jesuit at Peking, facilitated their entry.[18] Two of the group, Bouvet and Gerbillon, gained high favor at the court of K'ang Hsi, partly by assisting the Chinese in the negotiations with the Russians at Nerchinsk in 1689. In 1692 they obtained an imperial decree of religious toleration, and in 1699 they enlisted the co-operation of the Emperor of China himself along with that of Louis XIV in build-

---

[15] Dorland, 13. Pope Clement X in 1673 had limited the authority of the Archbishop of Goa to Portuguese-held territory.
[16] Latourette, 122–126.   [17] Ibid., 126–129.   [18] Dorland, ch. i, n. 34.

ing the first Christian church in Peking. On Bouvet's second outward trip to China in 1699, he took with him ten additional Jesuit missionaries accompanied by a representative of the court of Louis XIV. By the action of Rome in 1700, French Jesuit missionaries in the Far East were removed from the jurisdiction of the Portuguese and placed under the direction of Gerbillon, who acted as a vice-provincial officer.[19]

The growth of French missionary influence in China was halted during the course of the famous Rites Controversy, which raged during the early decades of the eighteenth century. Jesuit advocacy of making generous accommodation to Confucianist practices was sharply challenged not only by certain elements of the regular clergy,[20] but also, and significantly, by the French vicars apostolic. The vicars were more interested in training a responsible native Chinese priesthood than in seeking favor at Peking, which was the objective of Jesuit policy. The intra-French controversy began in 1693, when Monsignor Maigrot, vicar apostolic of Fukien, forbade priests under his jurisdiction to accept Confucianist ritualistic practices sanctioned by local Jesuit missionaries. Maigrot carried the dispute to the Papal Inquisition in 1697, and by 1704 the Dominicans and the Paris Society together had obtained a ruling condemning Jesuit practices.[21] Thus the two French groups found themselves arrayed on opposite sides of a crucial issue of missionary policy.

A papal legate of French nationality, de Touran, who was sent to China in 1705 to resolve the controversy, had a difficult time. The Jesuits resisted with strong backing from the Chinese court, while the Portuguese authorities dragged their feet in supporting Rome's policy until they obtained a partial reaffirmation of their traditional "Right of Patronage." After two years of futile negotiations, de Touran and three intransigent vicars apostolic were banished from the empire.[22] When the controversy was reopened in 1715 by the issuance of a papal bull condemning the practices condoned by the Jesuits, the K'ang Hsi Emperor forbade Chinese converts to respect the bull. A final and definite ruling prohibiting Confucianist practices in the church came from Rome in 1742.[23]

[19] Latourette, 120–122.   [20] By the Spanish Dominicans in particular.
[21] Dorland, 16–17; Latourette, 139–141.
[22] Latourette, 141 ff. De Touran was imprisoned for a time by the Portuguese at Macao, where he became involved in a quarrel with the bishop.
[23] Dorland, 18–19.

The net result of the long-fought Rites Controversy was the virtual elimination of all overt missionary activity from the Celestial Empire. The propagation of Christianity was proscribed; only clandestine activities persisted. A few Jesuits serving the government in scientific capacities continued to live at Peking. After the Jesuit Society was abolished by papal action in 1773–1774, French Lazarists were confirmed as receivers and successors of the Jesuit mission at Peking.[24] The missionaries expelled from China tended to move southward, the Portuguese clergy and the Jesuits concentrating in Tongking and the priests of the Paris Society in Annam proper and Cochin-China.[25]

Early French Influence in Annam

French efforts during the time of Louis XIV to establish an area of missionary and commercial influence in Annam were at first less successful than they were in neighboring Siam. Whereas peninsular Siam could be reached from the Bay of Bengal side, seaborne access to Annam required threading the Straits of Malacca, which were under the control of the hostile Dutch. The initial move of the French East India Company to set up a factory trading base in southern Annam (Cochin-China) in 1664–1665 aroused immediate and effective Dutch resistance. Two European wars intervened before the French company made a second abortive commercial *démarche* in 1682, this time at the urgent solicitation of the Paris missionaries who were already on the ground. In 1684 a company agent visiting Tongking obtained local authorization to establish a factory. Explorations made in Cochin-China two years later produced results equally favorable. But Dutch opposition again prevented the improvement of these opportunities.[26] Then followed the collapse of the French position in Siam and, after the accession of William and Mary in 1689, the addition of Britain to the enemies of France in the Far East. During the last two exhausting wars of the reign of Louis XIV, the resources of the French Company were de-

[24] A. Thomas, *Histoire de la Mission de Pékin* (Paris, 1925), I, 320–321. The Missions Etrangères declined the invitation of Louis XVI to take over Jesuit operations in Peking.

[25] Ennis, 18–19. Louis Eugène Louvet, in *Les Missions Catholiques au XIXᵉ Siècle* (Lille, 1898), 161–175, indicates that only five Catholic missions were operating, feebly, in China by 1800: The Lazarists at Peking and Nanking, the Franciscans in Shansi, the Dominicans in Fukien, the Portuguese at Macao and Canton, and the Missions Etrangères in Szechuan-Yunnan-Kweichow.

[26] Cultru, 1–4; Chailley-Bert, 171.

pleted, so that all possibility of political and commercial support to missionary activities in Annam was eliminated. Not until several years after the revival of the French Company in 1719 was it able even to resume trading from India to China, and then only in a desultory way.[27]

The Paris Foreign Mission Society had more success in Annam than did the company. The area from the outset was a focus of French interest, partly because of the early contacts made by Alexander of Rhodes.[28] The first French missionary contacts with southern Annam, made from Siam in 1663, were discouraging. The Portuguese Jesuits, who themselves were already suffering persecution in the country, opposed French entry. Not until 1669 did a French vessel succeed in landing three representatives of the Paris Society on the coast adjacent to the Annamite capital. They managed with difficulty to obtain royal permission to remain. This group was reinforced in 1670 by six recruits brought out by Pallu on his second trip.[29] But Dutch hostility and the failure, cited above, of successive efforts to establish French commercial relations with the area prevented the expansion of French missionary influence. The operations of the Paris Society priests enjoyed no support from the homeland during the final decade of the reign of Louis XIV.

French national interest in Annam continued at low ebb for more than a score of years following the death of Louis XIV in 1715. The arrival in the area of missionaries excluded from China during the third and fourth decades of the century intensified the rivalry of Portuguese and Italian elements toward French missionaries. The vicariate system was headed by an Italian from 1728 to 1739, a circumstance which entailed a sharp falling off of French interest.[30] The revival of French mercantile operations between India and China during the 1720's aroused some interest in establishing a French base at Poulo Condore Island (lying fifty miles off the Mekong delta) and on the mainland

---

[27] Cultru, 16–17. The revival of the French company from 1719 to 1725 was accomplished under the promotional leadership of John Law. Until 1731 the new company included within its privileged monopoly the West Indies as well as the East Indies and China. It reached its peak of prosperity in 1740 and declined after 1745.

[28] Between 1650 and 1652, Rhodes published a map of Annam, a Latin-Portuguese-Annamese dictionary, and a history of Tongking.

[29] Ennis, 13–18; Latourette, 117–119.   [30] Ennis, 18–19.

itself, but financial depression and renewal of war in Europe intervened.[31]

Near the end of the War of the Austrian Succession (1740–1748) a genuine opportunity for obtaining a French foothold in Annam developed. Dupleix's amazing triumph in India during the 1740's, including the capture of the principal British post of Madras, gave to the French for the first time a temporary dominance in the Far East. Even though Paris agreed in the peace treaty of 1748 to return Madras in exchange for Louisburg on Cape Breton Island, thus sacrificing the decisive French advantage in India, the situation afforded opportunity for a French advance in Annam. The initial move was made by one Captain Friel, a nephew of Dupleix, who visited Annam in 1747 in a vessel chartered by de Rothe, a French trader at Canton. Friel found the Annamite King willing to permit trade and accordingly proceeded to Pondicherry to seek support from Dupleix. The French Company, however, dared not act at the moment in the face of British opposition.

A year later (in 1748) an ex-missionary of the Paris Society now turned colonial promoter, one Pierre Poivre,[32] prepared and led an expedition to Annam as a representative of the French East India Company. In 1749–1750 he negotiated a formal trading treaty with the King of Annam providing for French commercial access to the area. While in Hué, the capital of Annam, he obtained from French missionaries precise information about opportunities in Tongking as well. But Poivre antagonized the ruler upon his departure by abducting an interpreter, and the King responded by driving out all twenty-seven French missionaries. Dupleix managed to get the mission restored, but subsequent French efforts to trade were unprofitable.[33] Pondicherry again lacked the resources for a serious political venture in Indo-China, and feverish activity on the part of both missionary and commercial agents in India and at Paris failed to elicit the additional support required.[34] Dupleix himself was recalled to France in 1754, and during the course of the ensuing Seven Years' War the French empire in India

[31] Cultru, 1–8.

[32] Poivre had been held captive by the British from 1741 to 1744.

[33] Ennis, 20–24; Virginia Thompson, *Dupleix and His Letters* (New York, 1933), 719–722.

[34] Ennis, 6–8; Cultru, 4–8; Jean Ajalbert, *L'Indochine, par les Français* (Paris, 1931), 24–27; Henri Cordier, *Le Conflit entre la France et la Chine* (Paris, 1883), 6–8.

collapsed. France was to wait a century before so promising an opportunity in the Far East again presented itself.

The French shipbuilding and trading agency at Syriam in Burma, which dated from 1688, also came to grief during the 1750's. The Talaing allies of the French were overwhelmed at their capital, Pegu, by the Burmese army in 1756. Several French war vessels were captured and stripped of guns and ammunition. The officers were executed, but the two hundred gunners, too valuable to kill, were detained to form a *corps d'élite* in the Burman army.[35]

France was never reconciled to being excluded from Asia by the British in 1763. Pierre Poivre, who served as French intendant on Mauritius (Isle de France) from 1767 to 1773, together with Chevalier de Rothe and representatives of the Paris Missions Etrangères, continued to agitate for vigorous action in Annam, which they insisted was the only opening in Asia left for France.[36] Adventurous plans formulated by Foreign Minister Choiseul in the late 1760's came to naught with the disappearance of the French East India Company in 1769 and Choiseul's own displacement in 1770. Another flurry of interest in Annam developed in 1774–1775, after papal action in abolishing the Jesuit Society eliminated the principal rival of the vicars apostolic in Annam and brought new Roman support for French missionary activities.[37] French Foreign Minister Vergennes in 1775 assisted in equipping a secret armed expedition destined for Annam to be commanded by de Rothe. The scheme was thwarted by contrary advices at court[38] and by the immediate diversion of French interest to revolutionary developments in Britain's American colonies. Active French involvement in the American War of Independence after 1778 ended the possibility of attempting serious ventures in Asia.

Pigneau de Behaine in Annam

The final episode of eighteenth-century French imperialism in Annam developed around the colorful figure of the missionary statesman, Pigneau de Behaine. Pigneau was sent by the Paris Society to Siamese Cambodia in 1765, when he was twenty-five. At Pondicherry, in 1774,

[35] G. E. Harvey, *History of Burma* (New York, 1925), 203, 229–231.
[36] Ennis, 24–25; Cultru, 8–10.   [37] Ennis, 18–19.
[38] *Ibid.*, 25–26. The Annamite ruler in the 1770's was less friendly to the French than the one in 1749 had been.

12

he was consecrated Bishop of Adran and designated vicar apostolic to Cochin-China, Cambodia, and Tongking. As leader of a persecuted minority of Christians in Cochin-China, Pigneau allied himself in 1782 with a fugitive prince, Nguyen Anh (later Emperor Gia Long), who was ambitious to regain the throne.[39] The two friends eventually took refuge on Poulo Condore Island, where they developed their plans to enlist French assistance. Pigneau, accompanied by the young son of the pretender and a retinue of twoscore soldiers, returned to France in 1787. The mission was well received at Paris, where the aged Pierre Poivre assisted Pigneau in obtaining a hearing at court.[40] Acting as the diplomatic agent of the pretender to the Annamite throne, Pigneau, on November 28, 1787, at Versailles, obtained the signature of the French government to a treaty of alliance.[41]

Although the pre-revolutionary financial embarrassments of the French government, coupled with the termination of France's alliance with the Dutch, ruled out any serious intention that Paris may have entertained to honor the Pigneau treaty, its terms nevertheless constituted an important landmark in the growing tradition of French relations with Annam. France agreed to assist Nguyen Anh by sending 1,200 infantry, 200 artillerymen, and 250 caffres (Indian slave troops), and asked to be granted in return sovereignty over Poulo Condore Island and control over Tourane harbor (Hoi-nan), including facilities for commerce, shipbuilding, and repair. French subjects would enjoy liberty of commerce in Annam to the exclusion of other European traders and were to be given protected access to the interior on the strength of passports issued by the French commander at Tourane. Native troops could be enlisted for the defense of French establishments, but these could not be transported beyond the Straits of Malacca.[42]

Pigneau's party was accompanied by French war vessels on its return journey via Mauritius and Pondicherry, but it obtained little assistance beyond that point. Governor Conway at Pondicherry, acting under

---

[39] Cultru, 6–28.   [40] Thompson, 22–23.

[41] Ennis, 26–28; A. A. Thomazi, *La Conquête de l'Indochine* (Paris, 1934), 15–20.

[42] E. Courtambert and Léon de Rosny, *Tableau de la Cochinchine* (Paris, 1862), 190–195; Albert Septans, *Les Commencements de l'Indochine* (Paris, 1887), 79–104.

discretionary orders from Paris, denounced the proposed adventure as expensive, romantic, and dangerous. He foresaw inevitable British hostility and the almost certain closing of the Malacca Straits in time of war. Conway finally provided the frigate *Méduse* and another vessel to repatriate the mission, but no amount of argument could persuade him to implement the treaty alliance.[43] Pigneau nevertheless managed at his own expense to organize and equip a private force numbering more than one hundred men, recruited mainly from French officers in India. This group accompanied him to Cochin-China in early 1789, where it was augmented by some 125 crewmen from the *Méduse* and several score other French adventurers who drifted in later from northern Annam and the China coast. The total French group approximated 360 men. On his arrival in Cochin-China, Pigneau found Nguyen Anh, now titled Emperor Gia Long, already in possession of Saigon and preparing to conquer the rest of Annam. It was not until after 1800 that the conquest was completed.

The exploits of the French volunteers in Annam during the ensuing decade constituted a saga of daring achievement.[44] Pigneau himself excelled as organizer, administrator, and military leader. His followers established a mint, organized a navy, built fortifications, and made the most of their bluff that more French assistance was on the way. The struggle was nevertheless prolonged. Pigneau himself was killed in 1799 while leading an assault. His death was greatly mourned by the Emperor, who buried him with high honors.[45] Several others of the French groups gained high mandarin rank in Gia Long's government. On the occasion of the visit to Cochin-China in 1804 of the British supercargo at Canton bringing presents and news of French revolutionary excesses in Europe, the French mandarins persuaded Gia Long to resist the British pressure and to return the offered presents. All in all, the followers of Pigneau staged a remarkable performance.[46]

[43] Septans, 83–89, 135–136; Hoang-van-Thuy, "Introduction à l'Histoire Abrégée de l'Etablissement du Protectorat Français en Annam," *Revue Indo-chinoise* (1906), 1533–1537.

[44] For a full-length account of Pigneau's career, see Charles B. Maybon, *Histoire Moderne du Pays d'Annam, 1592–1820* . . . (Paris, 1919), chs. v–ix.

[45] Ennis, 28–29. Puymanel built fortifications; Dayot, Vannier, Chaigneau, and de Forcant commanded the navy. See Thomazi, 21–24.

[46] Septans, 105–111; Cultru (p. 28) asserts that the French cause in Annam was set back a century by the government's inability to aid Pigneau.

14

The French Revolution and After

During the turmoil of the French Revolution, the successive Paris governments were too preoccupied in Europe to do anything about the Far East. They were openly hostile to missionary endeavor. Governmental allowances previously paid to missionary personnel lapsed.[47] In the autumn of 1795 (16 Fructidor, an III) the Directory considered the remote possibility of exploiting an alliance with Spain as a means of reaching the China Sea via the Philippines. Napoleon's Egyptian campaign and his anti-British intrigues in India marked the limit of France's capabilities in eastern Asia. The French consulate at Macao closed in 1800. In 1802, when Napoleon heard of Pigneau's death, he contemplated appointing a successor as Bishop of Adran, but again nothing came of it. In 1805 Napoleon allocated 25,000 francs to assist in sending French Lazarist recruits to reinforce the mission at Peking, but war made it impossible to carry out the project.[48] The question of Annam was examined for the final time and without decision by Napoleon's Ministry of Marine in 1812.[49] Meanwhile missionary interest in France reached a low ebb. The directors of the Paris Missionary Society had fled the country in 1792. The Society was revived only temporarily from 1805 to 1809, and not until 1820 was it permanently re-established, along with the re-establishment of the Paris Seminary in 1823. The Propaganda at Rome was itself inoperative from 1808 to 1814.[50]

French Efforts to Re-establish Relations with Annam after 1815

Repeated efforts of French naval vessels to re-establish political contact with Annam in 1816–1818 were unsuccessful.[51] A private shipping firm trading with China, Balguerie Sarget et Cie of Bordeaux, had better success, for Gia Long was willing to trade. In connection with a fairly profitable trading visit in 1819, a merchant of the company obtained permission to transport Chaigneau,[52] one of the surviving French

---

[47] W. Devine, *The Four Churches of Peking* (London, 1930), 86.

[48] Dorland, 28–29.

[49] Cultru, 29–31; Septans, 105–110; P. Adrien Launay, *Histoire Générale de la Société des Missions Etrangères* (Paris, 1894), III, 22–32.

[50] Latourette, 163–180.

[51] Cultru, 31–34. The initiative was taken by the Duc de Richelieu and by Baron Portal of the Ministry of Marine.

[52] Jean Baptiste Chaigneau came from Brittany. His father had been captain of

mandarins, back to France on a leave of absence. The visit aroused French hopes that treaty relations might be established with Gia Long. Chaigneau was accordingly named agent and consul for France and was authorized on his return to negotiate a treaty of commerce between France and Annam. He brought back with him considerable merchandise, including presents for the court at Hué. His nephew, Eugène Chaigneau, accompanied him.[53]

French prospects at Hué were quickly dashed. By the time the two Chaigneaus returned in 1821, Gia Long had died and had been succeeded by King Minh Mang, a man of Confucianist training who personified the hatred and jealousy of the Chinese party at court against the French. The new ruler rejected the proffered French treaty and refused to recognize Chaigneau as French consul. He subsequently declined to communicate with the commander of a French frigate which visited Tourane harbor in 1822. In 1824 the two remaining French mandarins, Chaigneau and Vannier, returned to France on board a trading vessel. Subsequent efforts on the part of Eugène Chaigneau to negotiate with Hué, from 1826 to 1830, were equally unsuccessful.[54]

After Chaigneau's departure Minh Mang's hostility was directed against native converts and the Catholic missionaries, who began in the late twenties to receive new recruits from Europe in increasing numbers. After the last mandarin friend of the missionaries died in 1832, the King comanded that all missionaries, including new arrivals, come to his court, where he could keep an eye on them. On the pretext that he needed their services as translators and interpreters, he retained them as virtual prisoners; they were denied permission to return to their former fields of labor on pain of death. One bishop fled in 1833, and a priest was executed. Persecution was extended to native Christians after 1835, when a French priest, Marchand, was executed for alleged implication in a revolt engineered by a high official in Saigon.[55] Other

---

an East India Company vessel prior to 1789. The naval vessel on which Jean Baptiste was serving was disarmed at Macao in 1791, from which place he proceeded to Annam. He attained mandarin rank of the second order. See Henri Cordier, *Le Consulat de France a Hué sous la Restauration* (Paris, 1884), 1–3.

[53]Ennis, 30–32; Cultru, 33–40; Cordier, *Le Conflit*, 10–11. While in France, Chaigneau was made Chevalier de St. Louis.

[54] Cultru, 36–40; Ennis, 31–32; Cordier, *Le Consulat*, 116–122. Hué refused to accept a French consul for fear that the British and others would also demand one.

[55] Septans, 121–124. The revolt, which began over the defiling of a mandarin's tomb, was drowned in blood.

banishments and executions of missionaries and Christian converts followed. At least ten foreign priests (seven French and three Spanish) lost their lives between 1833 and 1840.[56] Catholic missionary interests in Annam had ample reason to complain of harsh treatment at the hands of Minh Mang. In 1840, the latter, fearful of possible retaliation, attempted to establish diplomatic contact with Paris.

After almost two centuries of desultory activity on the part of French missionaries, traders, diplomats, and adventurers in the Far East (from Louis XIV to Louis Philippe), France had very little to show in the way of tangible achievement. Traditional missionary connections in China and Annam were being maintained on a precarious footing and at considerable sacrifice. Paris authorities in 1840 were neither willing nor able to lend support to the missionaries. French commercial and diplomatic influence in the area was virtually nonexistent. Even though French pride did refuse to concede that the flag had been driven permanently from the Orient, the state possessed no point of support from which a naval venture could be projected after the British annexed Mauritius permanently in 1815. British naval and commercial hegemony in the Far East, based on India, was unchallengeable, so that any move which France might contemplate within the area would have to fall within the bounds of British consent. Except for occasional measures taken in scattered island clusters of the Pacific by adventurous naval officers, there seemed in 1840 little prospect for aggressive political action by France in the Far East.

There were nevertheless two factors on the positive side of the French ledger. One was the vigorous religious revival, centering in France, which swept across Catholic Europe following the downfall of Napoleon. The other was the well-nigh desperate concern on the part of the Orleanist and Napoleonic dynasties, which ruled France from 1830 to 1870, to recover at least a measure of the international prestige that had so long been associated with the name of France. These two elements united to revive the imperialist tradition of France in the Orient during the mid-century decades. It is the story of this revival which is the principal concern of this book.

[56] P. R. Delvaux, "L'Ambassade de Minh Mang à Louis Philippe, 1839 à 1841," *Bulletin des Amis du Vieux Hué*, XV (15 Decembre, 1928), 257–264; Henri Cordier, "La Politique Coloniale," *T'oung Pao*, 2d ser., X (1909), 20–21; Ennis, 32–33; Cultru, 42–46.

II

France under Louis Philippe

ASIDE from the abortive French efforts already described to salvage a commercial treaty from the influence which followers of Pigneau de Behaine had acquired in Annam, French interest in the Far East during the quarter century following the downfall of Napoleon was confined almost entirely to the promotion of Catholic missions. The ground swell of religious enthusiasm and activity which characterized Restoration France was part of the European-wide reaction against the philosophical and political radicalism of the eighteenth century. The French writer and statesman, Chateaubriand,[1] was for many years Europe's leading champion of the traditional faith. The French church especially demonstrated remarkable activity in the missionary field, perhaps because missions afforded for national religious enthusiasm an outlet which was temporarily denied to the country in political and diplomatic spheres. For many patriotic Frenchmen, the nation's idealized role in world affairs was reinterpreted meaningfully in terms of the medieval concept of the "eldest daughter of the Church," the chosen champion to establish God's kingdom on earth.[2]

[1] Chateaubriand's classic *Génie du Christianisme* (1802) stamped him as the leader of the new romanticist-Catholic literary movement. He served under Louis XVIII as Minister of Interior, was successively French Ambassador at Berlin and London in 1821 and 1822, and was spokesman for France at the Congress of Verona.

[2] H. F. Stewart and Paul Desjardins, *French Patriotism in the Nineteenth Century, 1814–1833* (Cambridge, 1933), xiv–xv.

18

Religious Revival in Restoration France

From the beginning the returned Bourbon dynasty contributed substantially to the religious and missionary revival. It restored the Altar and placed the Throne squarely upon it. The legitimist Louis XVIII was King by the Grace of God. One of Louis's first moves following the re-establishment of the episcopal hierarchy was to reconstitute, in 1816–1820, the Société des Missions Etrangères and the Lazarist Society, the two groups most directly interested in missionary activity in the Far East.[3] The famous Seminary at Paris was re-established in 1823. L'Oeuvre pour la Propagation de la Foi was organized in 1822, with the help of French laymen, as an international agency of the church to enlist prayers and contributions for the promotion of missions. The strongest support of the agency came from France.[4]

Co-operation between the more reactionary religious groups and the French government increased markedly after Charles of Artois took over the direction of governmental policy in the early twenties. This led to French intervention in Spain in 1823 and to the studied medievalism of Charles X's coronation ceremonies in 1824. The new King winked at the illegal activities of returned Jesuits, who were permitted to operate under the cloak of the ultrareactionary Congrégation de la Rue du Bac, the spearhead of the clerical effort to restore the prerevolutionary property and privileges of the clergy.[5] The official clerical hierarchy was itself strongly Gallican in spirit and allegiance, firmly wedded to absolutism, and not inclined to recognize papal authority in matters affecting the French church.

But the vitality of the French religious spirit was too great to be smothered by the blanket of the reactionary regime of Charles X. Large elements of French public opinion, including many loyal Catholics, were not content to see the church become the mere tool of Metternich (à la Chateaubriand) in Spain. The "eldest daughter" had come of age and was not inclined to be the dupe of designing priests or politicians.[6] Both political conservatives (such as Montlosier) and liberals (such

[3] Louis XVIII did not remove the eighteenth-century ban on the Jesuits, presumably because of popular opposition to the Society. Some Jesuit operations were begun in clandestine fashion, but the order played little part in the revival of French missions in the Far East prior to 1843. See John R. Hall, *The Bourbon Restoration* (London, 1909), 285–291.

[4] Latourette, 203–204.   [5] Hall, 288–291.   [6] Stewart and Desjardins, xxiv–xxxv.

19

as Guizot and Broglie) saw in the alliance between altar and throne a clerical threat to secular government. From 1826 to 1828 the anticlerical opposition conceived the bogey of a Jesuitical plot to subvert the interests of the state. On this point Charles bowed to pressure in 1829 and decreed the dissolution of French Jesuit establishments.[7] But the anticlerical opposition continued to grow. Bourgeois elements objected strenuously to the efforts of the *emigré* episcopacy to recover confiscated church property at the expense of the holders of liberation bonds. French Catholics generally were not ready to repudiate entirely the principles of the Revolution, and they were increasingly disturbed over the false dichotomy presented between religious convictions and liberal political principles. The religious revival in Restoration France clearly outgrew the reactionary framework of Chateaubriand and the Bourbons.

Abbé Lamennais and the Liberal Catholic Movement

That liberalism and religion in France did not entirely part company was due in considerable measure to the influence of a group of youthful ultramontane clergymen, whose most articulate spokesman was the brilliant and courageous Félicité Robert Lamennais. Abbé Lamennais became concerned as early as 1822 over the growing indifference in France to the spiritual aspects of religion. He came to see in the alliance between the absolutist court and the political-minded hierarchy an insidious combination that threatened not only the independence of the church but its future influence and vitality. Before the church could undertake to save mankind, he insisted, it must free itself from political compromises and regenerate its own purity and power.[8] Instead of courting another debacle on the pattern of 1789 by continuing the church's alliance with the discredited absolutism of Charles X, Lamennais called upon Christianity to oppose political tyranny everywhere and to set its hand to the inevitable, and in his view not impossible, task of Catholicizing democracy. Despairing of the reactionary Gallican bishops of France, Lamennais and his followers looked to the ultramontane leadership of Rome to regenerate the church and to lead it forward under its own sacred mandate, asking neither permissions nor

[7] Hall, 407–408.

[8] John M. S. Allison, *Church and State in the Reign of Louis Philippe* (Princeton, 1916), 2–3, 168.

20

favors from governments.[9] Among the earnest group attracted to Lamennais's school at La Chesnai during the twenties was Eugène Boré, the famous Orientalist and editor of the *Journal Asiatique,* who later became Superior of the Order of Missions.[10]

Upon the overthrow of Charles X in July, 1830, Lamennais moved to Paris. In October, 1830, he began the publication of his liberal ultramontane paper *L'Avenir,* which carried his views to a much wider audience. *L'Avenir* was in some respects considerably to the left of the cautious King, especially in its advocacy of French intervention in Ireland, Belgium, Poland, and even Italy against the alleged agents of tyranny.[11] In 1831 he organized the Agency for the Defense of Religious Liberty as a kind of ultramontane *internationale.*[12] The French hierarchy denounced him as a dangerous radical.

Lamennais broke with the cautious Orleanist monarchy in 1831 and came to his inevitable and disillusioning clash with the papacy in the following year. Pope Gregory XVI's encyclical, *Mirari Vos,* of August, 1832, reflecting pressure from conservative influences now recovered from their fright of 1830, condemned Lamennais's affirmations that the church needed regeneration and that religious liberty supported the right of resistance to government.[13] The abbé was effectively silenced, and *L'Avenir* was discontinued. Two years later Lamennais was hounded out of the church by his inveterate enemies.[14]

But the spirit of Lamennais and many of his ideas did not die. He had bridged the revolutionary chasm for two critical years and had laid the foundation for the amazingly vital Catholic revival based on liberal premises which persisted throughout the reign of Louis Philippe. A number of his youthful followers, more tactful than he in their dealings with ecclesiastical authorities and attempting less ambitious objectives, rose to positions of recognized leadership within the French church. Under their stimulating influence, the church sloughed off the incubus of reaction and political compromise and manifested enormous vitality. For the Catholic religion in France, 1830 was a blessing in disguise. The Orleanist period exhibited what some have characterized as one of the "brightest and most noble" episodes of the Catholic church

[9] *Ibid.,* 20; Nora E. Hudson, *Ultra-Royalism and the French Restoration* (Cambridge, 1936), 115–124.
[10] Allison, 85.   [11] *Ibid.,* 26–27.   [12] *Ibid.,* 34, 38, 41–46.
[13] *Ibid.,* 66–67.   [14] *Ibid.,* 70.

in modern times.[15] Not the least of its accomplishments was the revival of missionary activity in eastern Asia.

Domestic Political Problems of the Orleanist Regime

It is one of the ironies of nineteenth-century French history that Louis Philippe's ultracautious anticlerical regime should have laid the foundation for French colonialism in the Far East by establishing the presumption that France was the protector of Catholic missions. The July Revolution repudiated abruptly the alliance between throne and altar. It not only reduced the church to a condition of mere tolerance, but it even came near to repudiating Catholic Christianity entirely. Because of considerations of domestic politics, Louis Philippe dared not ask for papal benediction of his regime, which would probably have been denied in any case. He was King more properly by the "will of the people" than by the "Grace of God." Although the public treasury continued to pay the salaries of the clergy, both Protestant and Catholic, and the state was committed to freedom of religion and instruction, the anti-Catholic bias of most Orleanist leaders was unconcealed. Education was placed under the control of the secularist Council of the University of Paris, and the influence of the legitimist-minded bishops was strongly resisted. Until 1836 the liberal ultramontane clergy were also strongly opposed.[16] The Protestant Guizot, historian and political opportunist, became the characteristic personality of the Orleanist regime.

From the very outset the July Monarchy was beset by domestic political unrest. The reactionary Bourbonist-clerical party was contemptuously hostile but largely impotent. Political elements of the Left, however, who felt that they had been robbed of the fruits of their revolution, made plenty of trouble. The first five years in particular were punctuated by repeated barricade revolts, which were suppressed with considerable difficulty by the bourgeois National Guard. This was followed by a number of attempts to assassinate the King.[17] Successive governments accordingly shifted to the Right in search of support from elements of order. It was in this contest with disorder that the government after 1836 softened its hostility toward the liberal Catholic party.

[15] *Ibid.*, 168. [16] *Ibid.*, 8–15. [17] *Ibid.*, 75–77.

After 1840, when France fell under the personal rule of Guizot, the support of the government accorded by the middle-class elements slowly ebbed away. The country eventually became bored and apathetic when it contemplated Guizot's lackluster performance, for he depended on political manipulation to keep himself and the dynasty in power. The only remarkable thing about the regime was that it managed to last as long as it did in the face of attacks from republicans, nationalists, economic radicals, and liberal Catholic elements. Guizot's government certainly provided a most unpromising medium for the revival of France's colonial tradition in the Far East.

Dependence of France on Britain's Support Internationally

An equally serious element of weakness of the July Monarchy was its almost abject dependence on British support in the international field. The legitimist dynasties of Europe, under the leadership of Metternich, regarded revolutionary Paris as a political plague center. They refused to welcome into the royalist fraternity a monarch like Louis Philippe, who, allegedly, had plucked his crown from the gutter at the end of a street brawl. Orleanist France did not dare challenge conservative Europe by assisting liberal political risings in Belgium, Poland, and Italy, as both Lafitte and Lamennais urged it to do. Louis Philippe's only possible course was to follow a moderate policy in unwelcome alliance with Britain. This policy added to France's security but permitted very little freedom of movement.[18] London (especially Palmerston) proved to be quite as capable as Metternich of curbing French adventures in the foreign field, especially when they exceeded the bounds of British permission.

The Anglo-French entente began over the Belgian question in 1831–1832; it was formalized by the Quadruple Alliance of 1834, which included the quasi-liberal regimes of Queen Isabella of Spain and Donna Marie of Portugal as the two other parties. It found expression during the late thirties and early forties in the effort of Paris and London to support the independence of Texas. It was interrupted briefly when Lord Palmerston in July, 1840, joined with reactionary Europe to force

---

[18] *Ibid.*, 80. The French completed the conquest of Algiers in 1856 although resistance continued to the 1870's. Belgium's independence was confirmed and Louis' daughter became the wife of King Leopold, all with British backing.

Thiers to abandon his venturesome support of Egyptian Mehemet Ali's war against the Sultan of Turkey.[19] France emerged from the 1840 ordeal deeply humiliated, but Louis Philippe had no alternative except to dismiss the sputtering Thiers and to acknowledge again the need for British support.

It was Guizot's difficult task as Foreign Minister following the fall of Thiers's government in October, 1840, to find a basis for French co-operation with Britain [20] which would at the same time recover a modicum of France's lost prestige. French naval ventures at Tahiti, not specifically authorized by Paris (to be described below), embarrassed Guizot's efforts. The accession of Britain's Peel and Lord Aberdeen to power in 1841 afforded an opportunity to revive the Franco-British entente. Joint support of Texan independence was revived for a time, until the election of President Polk in the fall of 1844 forced abandonment of that objective. One conciliatory move on London's part at this juncture was to assure Guizot that England would not oppose a French mission to the Far East to obtain a treaty with China along the lines of Britain's Treaty of Nanking. In 1845 at London's suggestion a tangible, overt basis of co-operation was arranged in the joint Anglo-French naval intervention in the Rio de la Plata, designed to open the Paraná River as well as other tributaries of the Plata to European trade. Anglo-French co-operation in South America lasted until 1847.[21]

The entente was finally broken in late 1846, when Palmerston returned to the Foreign Office following the collapse of the Peel Ministry over repeal of the corn laws. Anticipating an eventual break with the overbearing Palmerston, Guizot made an abrupt move to align France with conservative Europe by his unilateral repudiation of the 1834 agreement with London in regard to the Spanish marriage question. Palmerston retaliated by withdrawing the British fleet from the Argentine intervention area in such a manner as to leave French forces in a most embarrassing position, from which they were unable to escape

[19] This Near Eastern policy of Thiers was accompanied by a decision to return the ashes of Napoleon to France, done with British consent, as a symbol of renascent French nationalism. Thiers's policy of supporting liberalism in Spain was repudiated by Molé in 1836 and by Soult in 1837.

[20] Allison, 84–85.

[21] John F. Cady, *Foreign Intervention in the Rio de la Plata, 1838–1850* (Philadelphia, 1929), chs. iv and v.

24

without loss of prestige.[22] The tottering July Monarchy, bereft of both domestic and international support, fell in early 1848, an event which proved to be the signal for the collapse of the entire Metternich system.

Guizot's policies in the Far East inevitably reflected the limitations imposed by his domestic and international problems. High policy considerations forbade any break with England during his entente with Aberdeen from 1842 to 1846, and after that time Guizot's government was fighting for its life against mounting domestic opposition. The July Monarchy found few opportunities in the international field for bolstering its prestige. Minor moves were made in Mexico, Morocco, and the Pacific islands. France was blocked by conservative enemies in Europe, while any vigorous move overseas undertaken without prior British permission encountered hostility from London.

The eventual French policy initiated during the 1840's of extending protection over Catholic missionaries in the Far East was not the result of any deliberate decision on the part of authorities at Paris. It was rather the product of circumstances. The missionary program was the only important activity in which France was engaged in that part of the world. Guizot, even though he was Protestant and anticlerical, saw no useful end to be achieved in renouncing an opportunity for a diplomatic coup turned up by French negotiators at Canton. He also had in mind the possible bearing of a promissionary policy in moderating the opposition of liberal Catholic elements in France to the tottering Orleanist regime. It is to the evolution of the relations between church and state after 1834 that brief attention must now be given.

The Development of the Liberal Catholic Program

In 1834, two years after the silencing of Abbé Lamennais, a number of his youthful disciples revived the liberal Catholic movement in France. They were an intelligent, sincere group, tactful in their methods and moderate in their aims. Prominent among them was the young scholar Ozanam, who organized the Society of Saint Vincent de Paul, which became in time the foremost charitable organization of the French church. Associated with Ozanam was a former editor of *L'Avenir*, Lacordaire, who in 1835 gained access to the pulpit of Notre Dame

[22] *Ibid.*, ch. viii; Allison, 157–162.

itself for the purpose of challenging the secularist policy of the Council of the University of Paris in educational matters. The political leader of the group, Montalembert, a peer of France, was an able and determined defender of Catholic rights, especially in the educational field. Eugène Boré, an early disciple of Lamennais, supported the missionary cause.[23] Thè group won the support of influential members of the religious hierarchy, and eventually the respect of elements of the government as well. By 1836, after six years of harried struggle against street barricades, even the anticlerical members of the government began to perceive that some political advantage might be realized by placating nonlegitimist Catholic groups who were not overtly hostile to the Orleanist regime. The first major concession to the liberal Catholics was made by the relatively conservative governments of Premiers Moulé and Soult (1836–1839), who saw in religion a useful barrier to republicanism and socialism. Moulé in particular permitted the liberal Catholics to extend their organization widely into the provinces. He allowed the regular clergy (Trappists, Carthusians, and even the Jesuits) to return to France in large numbers. Lacordaire entered the Dominican order. No fewer than four hundred Lazarist establishments were functioning in France by 1837. Louis Philippe himself began to toy with the idea of using the nonhostile clergy as a means of lessening the opposition of conservative Europe to his dynasty. The contemplated shift of French affiliation away from England and in the direction of Metternich's Europe proved premature, however, for Soult was forced out of office in 1839, following the election victory of the nationalist, anticlerical coalition.[24]

The Catholic missionary revival made remarkable progress during the decade following 1839. The annual income of L'Oeuvre pour la Propagation de la Foi was almost two million francs in 1839, with France the largest contributor.[25] Papal recognition of the primacy of the French in Far Eastern missionary operations came in 1839, when Gregory XVI concluded a concordat with Portugal formally abolishing Lisbon's traditional "Right of Patronage." The Paris Société des Missions Etrangères was assigned a number of new Chinese vicariates: Che-

---

[23] Allison, 85–95.   [24] Ibid., 80–81, 97–101.

[25] Latourette, 203–204, 233–234. L'Oeuvre de la Sainte Enfance for the support of orphanages in foreign lands was established in 1834. Some 300,000 francs from its funds were set aside for China annually from 1843 to 1854.

kiang and Kiangsi (1838), Hunan-Hupeh (1839), North of the Wall (1839), Shantung (1839), Yunnan (1843), Kweichow and Tibet (1846), and Kwangsi (1849), plus prefectures at Hongkong (1843) and in Kwangtung (1856). In addition the Society was placed in charge of a half-dozen vicariates in Indo-China and also of missions in Korea and Manchuria. In 1850 the bishopric of Peking, hitherto invariably filled by a Portuguese appointee, was entrusted to a French Lazarist.[26] A revival of Jesuit missions in the Shanghai area (Kiangnan), with headquarters at Zikawei, began in 1841–1842, and from 1843 to 1848 some fifty-eight members of the Society entered China.[27] Jesuit personnel was not entirely French, of course. All of these allocations were made without regard to the fact that travel by Europeans in the interior of China (outside the treaty ports) was forbidden by Chinese law and by the terms of international treaties. The ultramontane missionary program in the Far East was moving forward under its own momentum, accepting no limitations by the Paris government but ready to accept any support that might be forthcoming.

The trend which relations between Guizot's faction and the Liberal Catholics took needs only to be briefly described. The two were not bitter antagonists because Montalembert did not attack the Orleanist regime directly. Beginning with March, 1843, the liberal Catholics centered their attacks on one clear-cut issue, the right of Catholic schools to exercise freedom of instruction under Article 69 of the Charter of 1830. The eclecticism of the University group was denounced, and its monopolistic control of education became the target of Catholic attacks not only in the Parliament, but also through the newspaper L'Univers and through the Association Catholique, both of which supported Montalembert's policy.[28] This tactic succeeded eventually in driving a wedge between the King and Guizot on the one hand and the more radical supporters of the secular educational policy of the University Council on the other.

The stock rejoinder made by spokesmen of the University Council,

[26] Louvet, 161–175. Six vicariates in Annam in 1850 were under the Paris Society, an increase of two since 1839; two were under the Spanish Dominicans. See also Latourette, 232–233, 239–240, and Chinese Repository, VIII (1840), 601–615.

[27] Latourette, 235–237. The Jesuit mission of Kiangnan had 78 schools with 1260 pupils operating in 1852. They also worked in Shantung and, after 1856, in Hopeh provinces.

[28] Allison, 106–115.

that Montalembert's attack was part of a reactionary Jesuitical plot, was completely unconvincing. Guizot was inclined to make minor educational concessions, while republican elements in the Chamber and Thiers, as opposition leader after 1845, tended to take the side of the University.[29] In an attempt to quiet the furor over the Jesuits, Guizot undertook in 1845 to obtain their voluntary recall from France through diplomatic negotiations in Rome. A premature announcement of the success of these negotiations backfired, so that Guizot succeeded only in offending the neoliberal Catholics without satisfying his opposition critics. Not even Guizot's break with Britain over the Spanish marriage issue in 1846 brought him any Catholic support.

The liberal Catholic cause in France was strengthened in 1846 with the accession of Pius IX to the Holy See. Thereafter Montalembert steadfastly refused to accept any compromise from Guizot on the educational question. The liberal Catholics thereafter sustained their opposition to the regime and found themselves in a favorable position, following the downfall of the July Monarchy, to come to terms with the government of President Louis Napoleon on the famous *Loi Falloux* (March, 1850), which ended the University monopoly.[30] Catholic influence in the new Napoleonic regime was much stronger, but the vitality and independence which had characterized the liberal Catholic movement under the Orleanists began to ebb away.

[29] *Ibid.*, 119–134.　　[30] *Ibid.*, 136–155.

III

The Revival of

French Political Interest

in the Far East, to 1844

THE French Ministry of Marine and the naval officers operating under its direction played a conspicuous role in sustaining French prestige in the distant Pacific area. Sometimes war vessels did no more than show the flag in foreign ports; occasionally their presence was utilized to support negotiations; [1] often they protected French nationals. The Ministry of Marine and the professional navy seem on the whole to have been very little affected by the anticlerical leanings of the Orleanist regime. In the absence of any French Far Eastern commerce to protect, the missionaries constituted the only tangible aspect of national interest with which naval officers could concern themselves. They intervened repeatedly, therefore, to protect adventurous French missionaries who had courted danger by penetrating remote and forbidden areas, such as Korea, Annam, China, and the islands of the Pacific.

[1] Cordier, *Le Consulat,* 123–125. Eugène Chaigneau here attributed his own failure in negotiating with Annam (1827–1831) to the lack of support of a French war vessel in the vicinity.

Naval Adventure in the Far East: Tahiti

A series of incidents which took place from 1836 to 1843 on the Pacific Island of Tahiti illustrated the close rapport which obtained between missionary personnel and the navy. Following Rome's assignment in 1835 of a vicariate apostolic in the Pacific islands to the French Société de Marie,[2] two French missionaries, accompanied by an artisan-carpenter, landed secretively on Tahiti in late 1836 for purposes of missionizing.[3] They were forcibly expelled on order of the Tahitian Queen, who acted on the advice of the Rev. George Pritchard, her British missionary adviser. A second attempted entry by members of the same order was thwarted by the Queen in early 1837.[4] Approximately two years later a visiting French naval captain, Dupetit Thouars, exacted an apology and an indemnity from the Queen for alleged violence and insult suffered by the missionaries. At the same time the highly partisan American consul, a Dutch Catholic trader by the name of Moerenhaut, was designated French consul.[5] Partly as the result of Moerenhaut's influence, the Queen was obliged in 1839 to repeal her laws barring Catholic missionaries. By 1841 several enemies of the Queen, including an unprincipled Governor in league with Moerenhaut,[6] were influenced to ask for French protection. The French navy again went into action in September, 1842, when Dupetit Thouars, now an admiral, declared the establishment of a French protectorate over the island group.[7]

The "Pritchard affair," as London termed it, became the subject of diplomatic controversy between London and Paris. An armed clash at

[2] J. M. Brooks, *International Rivalry in the Pacific Islands, 1800–1875* (Berkeley, Calif., 1941), 39–40.

[3] The Frenchmen came from Gambiers Island on an American ship and found temporary asylum in a house owned by the American consul (State Department, Tahiti, Consular Letters 1 [hereafter cited as SD, Tahiti, CL 1], from Moerenhaut, Dec. 24, 1836).

[4] *Ibid.*, March 25, 1837.

[5] J. R. Baldwin, "England and the French Seizure of the Society Islands," *Journal of Modern History*, X (1938), 212–214. Moerenhaut served as American consul from 1836 to 1838 and as French consul from 1838 to 1846, when he was shifted to California to become the first French consul there. See A. P. Nasitir, *The French and the California Gold Rush* (New York, 1934), 9–12.

[6] SD, Tahiti, CL 1, June 5, 1841.

[7] Dupetit had just completed the annexation, not without bloodshed, of the nearby Marquesas Islands, where missionaries had also prepared the way.

the island was narrowly averted in January, 1843, when the Queen, in the presence of a British war vessel and a slightly more powerful French one, declared her preference for British protection. To end all doubt about the matter, Admiral Dupetit Thouars appeared for a third time in October, 1843, with four heavily gunned vessels. He landed several hundred French troops, deposed the recalcitrant Queen, dismissed Pritchard (whom he later arrested), and declared the islands annexed outright to France.[8]

These unauthorized actions on the part of Admiral Dupetit Thouars were a source of acute embarrassment to Premier Guizot. He was sensitive to London's protests but dared not disavow the *fait accompli*, for Baron Mackau, the Minister of Marine, refused to recall the aggressive admiral. Guizot at first attempted to mollify Foreign Minister Aberdeen by assuring him that France did not contemplate any further island acquisitions in the Pacific. When news reached Europe in 1844 that the French authorities on the island had arrested Pritchard, the controversy was magnified into a minor war crisis. Guizot's eventual agreement in September, 1844, to pay an indemnity to the British was approved in the French Chamber by the narrow margin of only five votes, even though under the agreement France kept the islands.[9] Both Aberdeen and Guizot were determined not to let the incident upset their entente and were greatly relieved when a settlement was reached, but the clash of national prestige associated with religious and naval rivalry made the situation a delicate one. In no other area of the Pacific did Orleanist France dare flout the interests of Great Britain so flagrantly.

The Question of Protecting Missionaries in Annam

In the meantime, the new situation on the Asiatic mainland growing out of the Opium War was brought sharply to the attention of Paris authorities. An early proposal made by a government counselor in the spring of 1840 that a diplomatic mission be sent to China was not

---

[8] SD, Tahiti, CL 2, Sept. 26, 1842, Feb. 11 and Nov. 23, 1843, and Jan. 12, 1845. In January, 1845, Admiral Hamelin of France revived the Tahitian monarchy under a hand-picked Regent and re-established the protectorate.

[9] Baldwin, 215–231. The new American consul on Tahiti, S. R. Blackler, took an anti-British stand, partly from his dislike of Pritchard and partly as reflecting strained U.S.–British relations at the time, particularly concerning Oregon.

acted on.[10] Thiers, the nationalist Premier at the time, was too busy with other matters, including his Egyptian venture and his plans to return Napoleon's ashes to Paris. The Near Eastern diplomatic crisis of the summer and fall then intervened.

In November, 1840, following the resignation of Thiers's government, France was surprised by the arrival at Brest of an official Annamite embassy, consisting of two mandarins and two interpreters. The aging King Minh Mang had apparently become frightened over what the British were doing in China and had decided by a peaceful gesture to try to forestall any similar punitive action by the French.[11] The appearance of the embassy caused quite a stir. The Seminary of the Missions Etrangères used the occasion to publicize the harsh treatment which missionaries in Annam had been undergoing during the previous decade. The Pope and several French bishops appealed publicly to Louis Philippe to use his influence to end the persecutions. Clerical pressure was sufficiently strong to influence Louis Philippe to refuse an audience to Minh Mang's representatives.[12]

The policy adopted by Foreign Minister Guizot in 1840–1841 toward the plight of missionaries in Annam was nevertheless firmly negative. He admitted no obligation on the part of France to protect missionaries, even those of French nationality, from the perils to which they gratuitously and recklessly exposed themselves. But the issue did not die. Public pressure was so strong by 1843 that the French Foreign Office finally authorized chiefs of naval divisions in China waters to afford protection to French missionaries threatened with personal violence or death, if it could be done without involving the French flag in any altercation.[13] When persecutions were resumed in Annam shortly thereafter by the antiforeign Thieu-Tri, following Minh Mang's death in January, 1841, periodic visits to Annamite ports became part of the

[10] Angelus Grosse-Aschhoff, *The Negotiations between Ch'i-ying and Lagrené, 1844–1846* (Allegany, N.Y., 1950), 15; A. S. Bellé, *Programme d'un Mission en Chine, Fait et Addressé . . . à M. Thiers le 19 Mars et le 16 Avril, 1840* (Paris, 1842).

[11] Delvaux, 257–259; Cultru, 42–46.

[12] Delvaux, 260–264; Cultru, 42–46. The Annamite embassy proceeded to England after leaving France.

[13] Delvaux, 264; Cultru, 45–46; Cordier, "La Politique Coloniale," *T'oung Pao,* X, 21–22. Cordier's assertion that only the death of Minh Mang in January, 1841, prevented France from intervening in Annam is not confirmed by anything in the French Foreign Office archives.

established routine of French naval vessels assigned to Far Eastern waters.[14]

Preliminaries of the Jancigny-Cécille Mission to China

It was not until the spring of 1841, when the furor in France over the Near Eastern crisis had begun to subside, that Foreign Minister Guizot dispatched a French observation mission to Canton.[15] The objective of the expedition was threefold: (a) to obtain firsthand information on the political situation in China and on the prospects of extending French trade in the Far East; (b) to formulate recommendations respecting the role which France might play in the area; and (c) to show the French flag in the midst of the British Far Eastern squadron as a contribution to national prestige. The members of the mission carried no diplomatic credentials or specific instructions and were not authorized to enter into negotiations. The senior member of the mission in point of years was Captain Cécille of the frigate *Erigone*. The civilian observer was Dubois de Jancigny, who reportedly had seen service in French India and had spent much of the preceding decade as a private adventurer in southeast Asia.[16] The selection of such an untried representative as Jancigny is testimony to the limited number of qualified persons available in France for such assignments.[17] Jancigny's two principal aides were the apprentice consul at Canton (since 1839), Charles Alexander Challaye, the twenty-five-year-old son of a former Minister of Foreign Affairs, and the Polish-born Henry de Chonski, who represented the Ministry of Agriculture and Commerce. The small

[14] King Tu-Duc succeeded Thieu-Tri in 1847. Courtambert and Rosny, 218–232; Hoang-Van-Thuy, 1537–1539. Thieu-Tri had Fathers Berneux and Galy arrested in April, 1841, Charrier in October, 1841, and Miche and Duclos in February, 1842. All were maltreated and sentenced to death, but Thieu-Tri postponed the executions. See *Chinese Repository*, XII (1843), 537–540.

[15] Prior to 1841 the only regularly commissioned representative of the French government in the Far East had been the consul at Manila, a post established in July, 1839. Charles Alexandre Challaye came to Canton in October, 1840, as representative of the Manila consulate (*Chinese Repository*, IX [1840], 425).

[16] Grosse-Aschhoff, 15. Cécille was forty-four years old, Jancigny, thirty-six. During the 1830's Jancigny had reportedly entered the service of a minor southeast Asian ruler, one King Aough, who had sent him on a mission to Europe in 1834–1835. He attracted attention in France through a series of articles on the Far East appearing in the *Revue des Deux Mondes*.

[17] In comparable situations the British could command the services of responsible members of the India service and of merchants long experienced in the China trade.

33

squadron sailed from Brest harbor on April 28, 1841, and reached China waters in the following December.[18]

Presumably because Jancigny lacked diplomatic status, no formal record of his mission was preserved in the French Foreign Office archives. The fullest secondary treatment of the mission, that by Cordier, leaves many gaps and unanswered questions.[19] Cécille and Jancigny acted independently of each other, and toward the end of the mission, in 1843, the two chiefs were pursuing policies quite contradictory in character. The significance of the episode in terms of the revival of French imperialism is twofold: (a) it demonstrated the personal liberties which French representatives in distant areas were wont to take, and (b) it illustrated the alacrity with which resident French missionaries endeavored to influence political decisions. French missionaries from Macao served as interpreters for the mission, and the procurator of the Lazarist mission, Father Guillet, took an active role in managing the negotiations.

The first meeting arranged by Father Guillet was a highly secret one between Captain Cécille and ranking Chinese mandarins held on January 30, 1842, at P'an-t'ang, three miles distant from Canton. Guillet and another missionary acted as interpreters. Cécille apparently understood that the Chinese had offered to make unusual but unidentified concessions to France if assistance could be afforded China in the war with Britain.[20] The Chinese, on the other hand, were reportedly told by Guillet that Cécille had requested a personal meeting to discuss military matters in strictest secrecy with only French interpreters present.

During the course of the conference, the Chinese spokesmen asked Cécille for direct military assistance and promised in return that they would petition the Emperor to secure for the French "unusual kindness and special favors"[21] (presumably for Catholic missions). The

[18] Henri Cordier, *Histoire Générale de la Chine* (Paris, 1920), IV, 22–24; *Chinese Repository*, X (1841), 688.

[19] Henri Cordier, "La Mission de Dubois de Jancigny dans l'Extrême Orient, 1841–1846," *Revue de l'Histoire des Colonies Françaises*, IV (1916), 140–179.

[20] Cordier, *Histoire Générale*, IV, 22–24; Adolph Dubois, *Les Accords Franco-Chinois* (Paris, 1928), 23; Earl Swisher, *China's Management of the American Barbarians* (New Haven, 1953), 79–80.

[21] Swisher, 79–81. The Chinese memorial speaks of "officers" in the plural, suggesting that Cécille was accompanied by persons other than priests.

French account indicates that Cécille pled complete lack of authority to deal with such questions. He proposed, in rejoinder, that if China wanted to pursue the matter of an alliance with France, Peking should send a special envoy to Paris to present the request in regular fashion. He and his associates thereupon returned to Macao.[22] The Chinese memorial, by contrast, reported that Cécille proposed only that China send to France an envoy who would inquire into the art of shipbuilding and the making of munitions. It stated also that Cécille explained that he could not act rashly against the English without a pretext. He nevertheless offered to negotiate with the English in the interest of an early settlement without requiring as a condition that a memorial be previously sent to the Emperor in behalf of French interests. The Chinese memorialists hoped that the prospective negotiations might provide Cécille with the necessary pretext. The Frenchmen reportedly returned to Macao after presents were distributed.[23]

The French report is obviously incomplete, and the Chinese report was apparently doctored for Peking's benefit. Several years later Cécille told American Minister Everett, probably correctly, that on the occasion in question he had expressed to the Chinese his disapproval of Britain's warlike actions but had indicated the difficulty of giving aid at so late a date. He had therefore advised the Chinese to make peace as quickly as possible.[24] It is not clear whether the Chinese officials or Father Guillet were the most disappointed with Cécille's performance. In late February, Guillet reported to Canton authorities through a Chinese magistrate at Macao that Captain Cécille and the British chief at Hongkong, Henry Pottinger, had conferred on two occasions, but that the results would be reported by M. Jancigny, since Cécille had departed on February 25 for Manila. The still-hopeful Chinese thereupon invited Jancigny to come to Canton for secret talks.[25]

---

[22] Grosse-Aschhoff, 15–16; Cordier, "Jancigny," *Revue de l'Histoire des Colonies Françaises*, IV, 157–158.

[23] Swisher, 80–81, 143.

[24] SD, China 3, dispatch no. 3, Feb. 28, 1847.

[25] Swisher, 81. Cécille's correctly neutral policy with respect to the war is attested by the high regard in which he was held by the British at Hongkong. They distrusted Jancigny as an officious troublemaker.

Jancigny's Conversations of March–April, 1842

Jancigny's indiscreet dealings with the Chinese at Canton were apparently designed to obtain, among other things, protection for Chinese Christians and free access to the interior for the missionaries, in return for merely arousing Chinese expectations of eventual French military aid. Jancigny began by being coy. He waited two weeks before responding to the invitation to come to Canton. At his first conversation held at the trading factory area on March 13,[26] Jancigny presented a simple request for a minor commercial concession and for the release of a Chinese Christian who had been arrested in the company of a French missionary attempting to penetrate into the interior. It was only in response to considerable Chinese urging that Jancigny agreed to return a week later for secret conferences covering political matters, but then only on condition that the meetings be held at a private residence and that the highest Chinese officials stationed at Canton be present. The Chinese apparently did not ask for any diplomatic credentials, and Jancigny was silent concerning his own lack of authority to discuss political questions.

The conferences lasted from March 20 to April 7. They were held at the summer retreat of a wealthy member of the *Co-hong,* one P'an Shih-ch'eng, located outside of Canton. Here Jancigny met Imperial Commissioner I-shan and other ranking Chinese officials. I-shan's participation was brief, but Jancigny met his host and other officials in daily conferences, while being entertained in lavish fashion. When he returned to Macao on April 7, he was laden with presents.

What happened at these meetings was never fully reported by the French and was even more sketchily reported by the Chinese.[27] The harried Chinese spokesmen sought both assistance and advice, in spite of their distrust of Jancigny and their suspicion that France wanted to share in the territorial concessions which the British were expected to demand. In reply to the Chinese request for French military aid, Jancigny gave vague promises, but he refused to make clear just what

[26] Swisher, 81. The Chinese report gives this date as March 16.

[27] The Paris archives contain very little. Cordier's "Jancigny," *Revue de l'Histoire des Colonies Françaises,* IV, 163–179, is summarized by Grosse-Aschhoff, 18–20. P. C. Kuo's *Critical Study of the First Anglo-Chinese War* (Shanghai, 1935), 157–158, asserts that Jancigny offered in February, 1842, to conclude an alliance with China. Swisher's documents do not bear out Kuo's claims, nor do the French.

36

he would do to disperse the English rebels. If, as alleged by French reports, he reaffirmed Captain Cécille's recommendation that a Chinese envoy carry their request for aid to Paris, the Chinese accounts give no hint of it.[28] When queried concerning the probable peace terms to be demanded by Britain, Jancigny outlined the commercial demands which he knew the English negotiators were shortly to make at Nanking.

The Chinese account of the conversations implies that the French spokesman and Father Guillet asked for free missionary access to the interior in return for promises of future military assistance. The memorial reflected suspicion that the French intended to spy out the interior and commented that contact at Canton was sufficient.[29] It concluded by feigning lack of interest in immediate French aid because the developing military operations against the British at Ningpo obviated the necessity for haste in making a treaty at Canton. This report was a fairly obvious attempt to shift the responsibility for obtaining a settlement to the efforts of the armies in Chekiang Province. The tone of the Chinese conversations with Jancigny became markedly more friendly, however, after March 31. P'an acknowledged to him that peace with Britain must be made immediately, although China would still be prepared to make great sacrifices in order to obtain French aid.[30] Actually the changed tone was probably caused by receipt of the news prior to March 31 that the long-prepared Chinese attack against Ningpo had been disastrously defeated.[31]

Later Phases of the Jancigny Mission

The influence of the French on the negotiation of the Treaty of Nanking was negligible. Regardless of Jancigny's promises, the Chinese knew that the French had neither the power nor the will to intervene.

[28] Swisher, 81.

[29] *Ibid.;* Launay (*Histoire Générale,* III, 154) asserts that during the Opium War an imperial edict was issued explaining that the faith of the Chinese Christians differed from that of the English. Father Guillet's efforts may have been directed toward this end.

[30] Grosse-Aschhoff, 21–22.

[31] John K. Fairbank, "Chinese Diplomacy and the Treaty of Nanking, 1842," *JMH.,* XII (March, 1940), 4–10. Since the news of the Ningpo defeat reached Peking on March 23, where it caused a reshuffling of high government officials in the interests of peace and the perservation of the dynasty, it could easily have reached Canton by March 31. The Chinese memorial concerning Jancigny was dated April 13, 1842. See Swisher, 82.

They may have attributed the unexpected moderation of the British demand to the presence of the French, but of this also there is no tangible evidence. The overriding objective of the Chinese court was to get the British ships to withdraw quickly so as to obviate the danger of fomenting antidynastic rebellions in the coastal provinces. The negotiators Ch'i-ying and I-li-pu paid little attention to the phraseology of the treaty terms, some of which were in direct violation of Peking's edicts. The importance of dynastic survival made the commercial and (subsequently) the religious concessions demanded by the Europeans seem of minor significance.[32]

For almost a year following the conclusion of the Nanking treaty in August, 1842, there was little that Jancigny could do. During much of that time (October to May), Chi'-ying was in the Yangtse area working to develop its defenses against possible future naval attack. The ailing I-li-pu was left in charge at Canton, where he fumbled confusedly with commercial negotiations until his death in March, 1843. Ch'i-ying returned to Canton in May and immediately began the execution of his scheme to "subdue" the foreigner psychologically by removing their suspicions and by cultivating intimate personal relations. The corollary to this policy was to accede to all reasonable demands. It was not until the end of June that the round of official Chinese visits to Hongkong was completed, first by Ch'i-ying's subordinates, Huang En-t'ung and Hsien-lui, and then by Ch'i himself.[33]

Under the circumstances, Jancigny had to go to considerable lengths to attract Ch'i's attention, especially since the appointment in September, 1842, of a regular French consul for Macao, the Comte de Ratti-Menton, had officially ended his mission. He began by sending his subordinates, Challaye and Chonski, to Canton to offer their services to the Chinese for the repair of cannon.[34] Jancigny then caught Ch'i's approving attention by proposing on July 5, 1843, that he proceed to work out, with the co-operation of the imperial authorities, the general principles which would govern future treaty relations between France

[32] Fairbank, "Chinese Diplomacy," *JMH.*, XII, 19–34. Captain Cécille appeared in the Yangtse on July 31, 1842, and made a quixotic offer to aid the Chinese in concluding peace if Peking would agree to set up a Foreign Office at the capital. He was not taken seriously (Swisher, 89–93).

[33] John K. Fairbank, "The Manchu Appeasement Policy of 1843," *Journal of the American Oriental Society*, LIX (1939), 471–484.

[34] Grosse-Aschhoff, 17, 23.

and China. Meanwhile Father Guillet, who acted throughout as interpreter and translator for Jancigny, requested personally of Ch'i-ying the revocation of the law forbidding the practice of Christianity in China.[35]

The draft of Jancigny's "Provisional Project of a Convention between France and China" was completed on July 31, twenty days after the actual arrival of Consul Ratti-Menton at Macao. The proposed treaty contained fifteen articles, the fifteenth to remain secret. In disregard of "open door" principles, several articles proposed to grant special import privileges to items of French manufacture and also to make provision for the export of raw silk to France outside of regular Chinese tariff requirements. Article 15 provided that arms and ammunition of war of all sorts carried to China by French ships would be exempt from duty.[36] Chinese sources allege that Jancigny was actually commissioned to purchase warships, guns, and torpedoes for China and to assist in organizing a Chinese naval defense for Canton.[37] There is ample reason to believe that Ch'i-ying was seriously interested in the Jancigny proposals, for he spoke feelingly at the time about the long friendship between France and China.[38] He was certainly interested in acquiring arms if they could be procured in return for such minor sacrifices as the proposed trade concessions and Guillet's request to legalize the Catholic religion. It is understandable why both Ch'i-ying and the French principals directly responsible for the proposal were not happy to abandon the negotiations.

The presence in Macao of Ratti-Menton, bearing official credentials and claiming to be sole French negotiating agent, precipitated an unseemly quarrel. Jancigny refused to yield office to the newcomer. Both Captain Cécille and Challaye broke with Jancigny but acted also quite independently of the new consul. The Lazarist Fathers Guillet and Durran sided with Jancigny, whereas Father Libois of the Missions Etrangères, whom Cécille had recently rescued from Tongking, supported the naval captain. The angry and frustrated Ratti-Menton lost

---

[35] *Ibid.*, 25–26.

[36] J. M. Callery, *Journal des Opérations Diplomatiques de la Légation Française en Chine* (Macao, 1845), 30.

[37] Kuo, 157–158. Kuo cites as his source the *Sheng wa-Chi* (Shanghai, 1888), 74–76.

[38] Grosse-Aschhoff, 25.

his temper and published in the local press the full details of his quarrel with Jancigny. The Chinese officials at Canton became understandably confused over the fact that virtually every Frenchman in Macao seemed bent on negotiating independently. The British at Hongkong were highly amused. All negotiations covering the Jancigny treaty, denounced by Ratti-Menton as unauthorized, were naturally suspended, but neither the French nor the Chinese lost interest in the terms which Jancigny and Guillet had formulated.[39]

When news of the discreditable state of affairs at Canton reached Paris in October, 1843, Ratti-Menton was removed as consul and Jancigny was abruptly recalled. The youthful and inexperienced Charles Lefèbvre de Bécour, who had been the French consul at Manila since March, 1843, eventually arrived to take over the consulate at Macao on March 10, 1844,[40] to await the arrival of the special French mission then on the way. Despite all the confusion of the previous summer, de Bécour found French prestige still high at Canton and Chinese spokesmen extremely friendly.

Captain Cécille's conduct alone received the commendation of the French government. His relations with both the Chinese and the British had been correctly neutral. He had also utilized the time at his disposal in 1843 to visit Tourane and other Annamite ports, from which his ships had rescued five condemned French missionaries besides Father Libois.[41] A subsequent visit of one of Cécille's vessels to the coast of Annam, following his return from Europe in 1844, set up the channels for future naval communications with missionaries in the area.[42] When his squadron returned to France in late 1843, Cécille was raised to the

[39] Grosse-Aschhoff, 26; Cordier, *Histoire Générale*, IV, 23–24; Swisher, 123–124, 132–134. The *Chinese Repository*, XIII (1844), 336, listed Jancigny not as a member of the consulate but as a French agent on a special mission.

[40] Grosse-Aschhoff, 29.

[41] Cultru, 46–48. This was in anticipation of actual authorization of such activities by Guizot given at the end of 1843. Five were rescued by Capt. Favin-Levêque in October, 1842. Captain Levêque refused the request of the vicar apostolic for southern Cochin-China to repatriate to Annam the five rescued from Hué. He took them instead to Singapore, where Miche and Duclos were released; but Berneux, Galy, and Charrier were transferred to a ship en route to France. See note 14, this chapter.

[42] Charles Lavollée, *France et Chine; I, Traité de Whampoa (1844): Correspondance Diplomatique de M. de Lagrené* (Paris, 1900), 164–166; Callery, *Journal*, 64–65.

40

rank of rear admiral and was immediately sent back to China with five additional war vessels under his command.[43]

Ratti-Menton's Consulship, 1843–1844

Ratti-Menton's brief consulship at Macao was noteworthy for two things, aside from his quarrel with Jancigny. He found out that Ch'i-ying was fully ready to concede, in view of China's long and peaceful relations with France, all the privileges contained in the English treaty,[44] so that when the Lagrené mission arrived in August, 1844, it had virtually nothing to negotiate on this score. The second action of Ratti-Menton was an astute policy recommendation sent to Paris on July 29, 1843, shortly after his arrival at Macao. He observed that in view of England's tendency constantly to enlarge the circle of her dominion in Asia, the intensification of rivalry between England and Russia, extending from Turkey to China, was inevitable. Such a development, he argued, would afford France an opportunity to undertake aggressive measures in that part of the world. Recent French actions in Tahiti, the Marquesas, and Madagascar were, in his view, fore-runners of such a policy. The essential preparation for a long-term French policy of aggrandizement in eastern Asia would be the establish-ment of a shorter and more secure line of communications with the homeland. He defined his proposal in the following terms:

This re-enforcement would consist, for example, of the occupation of a port or an island in the Red Sea, the seizure of one or two islands in the Gulf of Siam and that of Tongking, and the acquisition from the Chinese govern-ment, as a counterweight to the cession of Hongkong, of one of the numerous islands which border the immense littoral of the Celestial Empire. The project would require necessarily the assembling of numerous steamboats, which would become at an opportune time the nucleus of a French fleet ready to act according to the exigencies of the moment. They would also serve, if need be, to transport via the Red Sea the French troops to which the Egyptian government would accord, either from inclination or from necessity, the privilege of crossing its territory. If established immediately under the pretext

---

[43] Grosse-Aschhoff, 25.

[44] Dubois, 24–25. Ch'i-ying's reply, dated Sept. 6, 1843, included a cordial letter to Guizot (*Chinese Repository*, XIII [1844], 270–273).

of the requirements of our new establishments, that service [via Suez] could not carry, as far as I know, any serious umbrage to England.[45]

Although the government of Guizot was in no position to undertake such a bold policy as that outlined by Ratti-Menton, the perceptive proposal anticipated subsequent policy. It foresaw the Anglo-Russian rift, sought to utilize French friendship with Egypt, and foreshadowed the eventual French-supported project of de Lesseps' canal at Suez. But fulfillment was delayed. The opportunity for aggrandizement in the Far East did not come to France until after the Crimean War.

[45] *Ministère des Affaires Etrangères, Chine* (hereafter, AEC), 1, pages 182–187.

IV

The Lagrené Mission:

First Phase, 1844

HE French mission which departed for China in December, 1843, was headed by Théodose de Lagrené, an experienced diplomat who had previously served as French ambassador to Greece.[1] The embassy was impressive,[2] consisting of two secretaries, seven attachés, specialists from the Ministries of Commerce and Finance, an interpreter, a historiographer, a doctor, representatives from various textile and other industries, and delegates from the Chambers of Commerce of Paris, Lyons, Mulhouse, Reims, and Saint-Etienne.[3] The naval escort consisted of six vessels: two fifty-gun frigates commanded by Admiral Cécille and Captain Charner, three corvettes,

[1] Dubois, 25.

[2] Cordier (*Histoire Générale*, IV, 24) indicates that Chambers of Commerce and publicists had urged the government to send an impressive embassy. Lagrené's party included three unsalaried attachés and four delegates representing commerce and industry. The religious party apparently had little to do with sending the mission, although a number of outgoing missionaries were accorded free passage on its ships.

[3] The most important of Lagrené's aides, seventeen all told, were Ferrière Le Vayer, Bernard d'Harcourt, the secretaries, and J. M. Callery, interpreter and translator. Callery was a naturalized Frenchman, born at Turin, who had studied Chinese at Macao under the Portuguese Father Gonzalvez during the 1830's. He had resigned as a missionary in 1840 and returned to France. His connections appear to have been with the Paris Society. Callery had returned to China as interpreter for the consulate ahead of Lagrené. One of the salaried attachés, M. de Montigny, later distinguished himself as French consul to Shanghai. Charles de Lavollée, sec-

43

and one steamer, with Captain Rigault de Genouilly in command of the smallest of the corvettes. The vessels carried no armed forces apart from their crews.[4]

Objectives of the Mission

The principal objectives of the mission, according to Guizot's instructions of November 9, 1843, were commercial. Lagrené was directed to negotiate a treaty with China following the British model, but was accorded some leeway with respect to any special additional claims which he might wish to advance. His mission was also ordered to collect commercial and shipping data which might be useful to French commercial interests.

Supplementary secret instructions of the same date emphasized a need, which had apparently been brought to Guizot's attention by Admiral Cécille,[5] to acquire a territorial foothold for France somewhere in the vicinity of China. Such a base was required, according to Guizot, to free French vessels from dependence on the hospitality of the Portuguese, British, or Spanish-held ports and to provide facilities for extending political and commercial contacts with the peoples of the area.[6] The base should possess a large and enclosed harbor, be easy to defend, and have a healthful climate with abundant supplies of stores and water at hand. A number of islands in the South China Sea were considered and rejected by Guizot as being either unattractive in themselves or too vulnerable because of their nearness to British and Dutch establishments.[7] Tourane, the port nearest the Annamite capital of Hué, was

retary of M. Ytier of the customs service, later became the editor of the correspondence of the mission (*Chinese Repository*, XIII [1844], 447).

[4] Charles Maybon and Jean Fredet, *Histoire de la Concession Française de Changhai* (Paris, 1929), 5, 10; Cordier, *Histoire Générale*, IV, 24.

[5] Hippolyte Gautier, *Les Français au Tonkin, 1787–1883* (Paris, 1884), 16–17.

[6] In a public statement to the Chamber of Deputies, Guizot explained that the wide extension of French ports of call throughout the world and the resulting enhancement of French prestige would serve to stimulate commercial activity. He declared that if national interest demanded it, France should do in the seas of China what she had recently done off the African coast (Madagascar), namely take possession of two or three islands. See Baron de Bazancourt, *Les Expéditions de Chine et de Cochinchine . . .* (Paris, 1861–1862), I, 11–12. Also reported by SD, China, Cushing from Macao, no. 85, Aug. 16, 1844.

[7] AEC, 1, 217–221. Anambas, Natuna, Poulo Condore, and Cham-Colao Islands were considered and rejected.

adjudged adequate as a harbor but unsatisfactory on grounds of health. Guizot also concluded that commercial possibilities in Annam were too meager to compensate for the difficulty of defending Tourane's continental position. The instructions finally directed Lagrené to explore the possibilities of acquiring a base in the Sulu Archipelago, situated between Spanish Mindanao and Borneo, and to consider in particular the island of Basilan.[8]

Guizot enjoined the most scrupulous secrecy in the Basilan affair, pointing out to Lagrené that every move of the French forces in China waters would be jealously watched by the British at Hongkong. Only Lagrené himself or officers directly under his command should undertake the preliminary reconnaissance. If Basilan was found to be satisfactory as a base and if it appeared practicable to take possession of it without difficulty, Lagrené could proceed to negotiate its provisional cession either with the local chieftains or with the sovereign whose authority they recognized. Any arrangements which he might make would be conditioned on the subsequent approval by the Paris authorities.[9] It apparently did not occur to Guizot that the Spanish, who were only ten miles distant from Basilan at Zamboanga, would claim title to the island.

Lagrené's mission reached Macao in mid-August, 1844. The French were received cordially by both the American negotiator, Caleb Cushing, and by the British representative at Hongkong, J. F. Davis. Cushing had delayed his departure to await the French arrival. He was relieved to learn that Lagrené had no intention of proceeding to Peking, as persistent rumors circulated at Macao had suggested that he intended to do.[10] Davis, who was under express orders from Aberdeen to promote friendly relations, felicitated Lagrené on the fact that the negotiations were "a co-operation and not a rivalry." Other British officials did not share Davis' confidence in the intentions of Lagrené and Cécille.[11] Cushing

[8] *Ibid.* Guizot's instructions are fully reproduced by Charels Lavollée, historian of the expedition, in his *France et Chine,* I, 1–17.

[9] AEC, 1, 219–221.

[10] SD, China 2, from Macao, Aug. 16, 1844. Lagrené took over the quarters that the American had just vacated. In Cécille's correspondence with Ch'i-ying earlier in 1844, the latter had refused as unnecessary the Admiral's request for the establishment of regular diplomatic relations and had proposed instead that the French pledge military assistance to China in case the greedy English merchants should again make trouble. See Cordier, "Jancigny," *Revue de l'Histoire des Colonies Françaises,* IV, 214–225.

[11] Foreign Office (FO), 17, vol. 88, from Davis, Aug. 19, 1844; vol. 89, Oct. 21

too thought that the size of the French fleet was unnecessarily large if its objective were merely to negotiate a treaty with China which had already been promised by Peking. He recalled Guizot's public statement concerning the need for an island base and thought it probable that the French intended to acquire a colonial establishment in China.[12]

The Problem of Missionary Interference

One of the immediate problems which Lagrené encountered grew out of the jealous rivalry between Father Guillet, the Lazarist chief, and J. M. Callery as to which of the two would occupy the key role of interpreter in the forthcoming negotiations. The feud between them dated from their earlier relations at Macao, before Callery had resigned from the Missions Etrangères in 1840 and had returned to France. Callery had been recommended to Guizot as an able Sinologist by the head of the Paris Society. Father Guillet had the backing of both Consul de Bécour and Admiral Cécille for the translator's role, and the Lazarist leader apparently assumed that he would take over where he left off at the end of the Jancigny negotiations. Guillet was apparently the source of information reaching the worried Ch'i-ying in July that Lagrené would proceed directly to Tientsin. Callery on his part strongly opposed the participation of the missionaries in the negotiations, and especially Fathers Guillet and Durran, for whom he professed to have no respect.[13]

Lagrené attempted at first to take a middle path. He threatened to deny Guillet any participation in the negotiation when the missionary communicated, privately and quite erroneously, to local mandarins that the French emissary intended to go to Peking. On the other hand, Lagrené esteemed the missionaries generally, felt that they could be useful to him, and wanted to remain on good terms with them. Although he resented their meddling and refused to follow their suggestions, he was not antagonistic to missionary interests.[14]

---

and 30, 1844. The British consul at Ningpo entertained the officers of a French corvette which blundered into the port without an interpreter.

[12] SD, China 2, from Macao, Aug. 16, 1844. Cushing was nevertheless obligingly helpful to Lagrené. See Lavollée, 24–26, 30–31.

[13] Callery, Journal, 12. Callery's Journal refers derisively to Durran as a former opium merchant. The basis of the accusation is not disclosed (Swisher, 164–166, in memorial dated July 28, 1844).

[14] Callery, Journal, 24–25.

Callery gained an initial advantage when he demonstrated to Lagrené's satisfaction that the Jancigny treaty, with which Guillet had had much to do, was not only an ill-advised and mischievous diplomatic gesture but also that it had been miserably translated into Chinese by Guillet.[15] Another count against Guillet was his prejudiced hostility toward both the Chinese and the British. Guillet recommended quite recklessly at the outset that Lagrené force the tardy Chinese to recognize his presence by moving war vessels toward Canton in a kind of armed ultimatum. When Lagrené, following Callery's alternative proposal, addressed a friendly letter to Ch'i-ying, the Lazarists and Admiral Cécille tried to intercept the message. Lagrené was finally forced to conclude that if he wanted to keep control of the negotiations he would have to exclude the missionaries and put his confidence in Callery.

Subsequent events strengthened him in this conviction. On several occasions he was even obliged to bar members of his personal staff from participating because they became too intimate with the missionaries.[16] Apparently the only missionary who supported Callery was Father Libois of the Missions Etrangères. He confided to Lagrené that he much preferred that Callery rather than Guillet handle any negotiations concerning Catholic rights in China.[17] Lagrené's two able secretaries, Ferrière Le Vayer and Bernard d'Harcourt,[18] participated actively in the negotiations, but Callery carried the major burden. The Lazarists at Macao never ceased their efforts to undermine Callery's influence.[19]

[15] *Ibid.*, 35–38, 42, 52, 79–80, 109. When Lagrené in conversation praised the Lazarist order in France for supporting the July Revolution, Callery replied that they had indeed managed to exploit their genuine or fictitious partisanship for Louis Philippe with great ability.

[16] *Ibid.*, 64–65, 110. On September 10, local Chinese mandarins complained to Callery that Guillet and Durran had approached them independently. In mid-September, Lagrené reprimanded two attachés, de Montigny and de la Haute, for nosing into matters not entrusted to them and for communicating with Father Durran. Lagrené threatened to ship Haute home, bag and baggage.

[17] *Ibid.*, 125, 162.

[18] Théopile de Ferrière Le Vayer published *Une Ambassade en Chine* (Paris, 1854) and two articles in the *Revue des Deux Mondes*, V (1854), covering his experiences in China. Bernard d'Harcourt's "La Première Ambassade Française en Chine" appeared in the *Revue des Deux Mondes*, XIII (June 1, 1862), 654–673.

[19] Callery, *Journal*, 138–139, 142, 156–162. The missionaries spread rumors that Lagrené intended to demand a money indemnity for offenses against Frenchmen, plus an island opposite Canton, an embassy at Peking, the free exercise of the Christian faith, and the return of former Christian properties in Peking. They blamed

Lagrené and Callery Lay Their Plans

Although Lagrené felt obliged to deny the missionaries any role in the negotiations, he selected from their numerous proposals the one which appeared most feasible and made it the principal objective of his negotiation. He informed Callery on September 1 that he intended to ask the Chinese government, as a voluntary gesture indicative of its friendliness toward France, to legalize the practice of Christianity within the empire.[20] His motives were mainly personal and political. He was ambitious to achieve some striking accomplishment which would redound to his personal credit and to the glory of France. He saw an opportunity to exploit the obvious concern of the Chinese to court the friendship of France and at the same time to soften, both in China and in France, the hostility of the missionary community, which he was offending by refusing it any part in the negotiations. He told Callery that in view of the strong criticism advanced by the religious party in France against the anti-Catholic principles of the Paris government, it would be gratifying to demonstrate the solicitude of the government for Christian interests on the opposite side of the world. He pointed out that success in such an endeavor would also enable Callery to silence effectively his clerical enemies.[21]

Plans for the negotiations were carefully laid during the month of September, while Lagrené awaited Ch'i-ying's convenience for the opening of formal conferences.[22] Callery approached the task with both enthusiasm and realism. He saw in it an opportunity to obtain for France a moral ascendancy in the Far East comparable to that which it had

---

Callery when all these objectives were not obtained. Just prior to the start of formal negotiations on October 1, M. Ytier, the representative of the customs service of the embassy, was detected attending an unscheduled meeting with Huang En-t'ung in the company of Fathers Guillet and Durran.

[20] Grosse-Aschhoff, 37–42; Callery, *Journal*, 197. The Bishop of Besi at Kiangnan (Missions Etrangères) had prepared earlier a formal petition requesting Lagrené to endeavor to legalize Christianity in China. It was strongly supported by the Macao Lazarists. Father Libois signed it with some reluctance. The idea had been rejected by Guizot, according to Callery, because of the difficulties it might entail for France.

[21] Callery, *Journal*, 65–66.

[22] Lagrené at first chafed over the delay in starting negotiations. After he determined to ask for religious concessions, he needed the extra time to perfect his plans (Callery, *Journal*, 70–71).

long enjoyed in the Levant, an achievement which would go far to counterbalance Britain's commercial and political ascendancy. He confided to Lagrené, however, that they would probably not be able to interest Huang En-t'ung, the provincial treasurer who was in charge of detailed negotiations, in making the desired concession to Christianity unless the matter could be made monetarily profitable to him. Callery thought that it would be easy to buy off Huang if only one could find his price, but his official position afforded him such an enormous income that the mission might not be able to offer enough to tempt him. Lagrené replied as follows: "All right, we will buy off Huang. If money alone is required to entice him, I will place a sum at your disposal; offer it to him provided he does what we wish." [23]

But Lagrené did not depend on bribery alone. He had Callery examine the history of early missionary activity in China to find everything good that preceding Emperors had said about the Christian faith. K'ang Hsi's toleration edict of 1692, a copy of which had been provided by Guillet, proved to be an especially important item. It was decided to avoid any mention of the missionaries themselves in order to obviate any embarrassing counterdemand on the part of the Chinese that France accept responsibility for preventing furtive missionary penetration into the interior of China. Lagrené clearly could make no such pledge because the ultramontane Catholic spirit was not subject to political control. And yet under the circumstances of his making a plea on behalf of the missionaries themselves he would have no plausible grounds on which to refuse it. Similar considerations counseled avoiding any demand for the right to establish mission schools in the interior. He and Callery agreed, instead, to stress the values which China could derive from closer political and cultural relations with France but to stop short of any pledge of alliance and not to require that the religious toleration concession be incorporated into the regular treaty. Callery argued that the cession of an island to France could be obtained, if at all, only on the pretext that it would afford a base from which France could assist China in the event of another war, a commitment which Lagrené was likewise not authorized to make. This and other collateral demands were to be advanced for bargaining purposes only. Callery's draft of the terms of the commercial treaty and of the proposed memorial by Ch'i-ying to the Emperor respecting the legalization of Christianity were

[23] *Ibid.*, 66–67.

completed on September 25. Formal negotiations got under way on October 1.[24]

Lagrené's Official Report of the Negotiations of October, 1844

Only after the negotiations were completed and the treaty signed did M. de Lagrené inform Guizot that he was endeavoring to obtain Peking's consent to the legalization of Christianity within the empire. He had assured Guizot in an earlier dispatch that he would not compromise the success of his mission by making impossible demands.[25] The full report covering the negotiations (including nine enclosures) was dated November 1; it was carefully tailored to meet the anticipated objections of the Foreign Minister.

According to Lagrené's official account, the idea of exploring the possibility of obtaining Peking's voluntary legalization of Christianity had been suggested to him by statements in Ch'i-ying's early correspondence, which indicated China's awareness that France was a nation which made much of religion. The idea was allegedly strengthened by an examination of Cécille's previous correspondence and by noting the deference paid to former missionary interpreters by high functionaries of Canton. He reported that he had then sounded out the French missionaries resident at Macao concerning the possibility that legalization of Christianity might impair their opportunities to enter the interior of China and had found them prepared to accept the risks involved. He had therefore taken advantage of the opportunity afforded by his first meeting with Ch'i-ying on October 1 to point out that it would be difficult for France, a civilized country with cultivated tastes and with little interest in the commercial aspects of the treaty, to be convinced of China's friendship as long as the religion professed by Frenchmen was proscribed as a criminal offense in China. He would not presume to tell the Chinese what they should do, except to point out that it might be to China's advantage to cultivate the friendship of Occidental maritime powers which would be in a position to render material or mediatorial aid should China again find itself in trouble with the commerce-hungry nations. He had reminded Ch'i-ying that the latter had requested such aid from Cécille in 1842.[26] Lagrené had then explained that France

---

[24] *Ibid.*, 74–77, 89, 126, 129.

[25] AEC, 1, to Guizot, Sept. 1, 1844; Lavollée, I, 35.

[26] Lagrené here made no mention to Guizot of Jancigny or of the Jancigny treaty.

asked for no indemnity and that he had orders not to proceed to Peking
provided the ministers of the Emperor would afford convincing proof
of China's friendliness.[27]
Lagrené stated that the question of religious policy had been referred
to again incidentally on October 6. On October 7 Ch'i-ying, accepting
the hint, had assured the French negotiator that China would not expect
the embassy to return home from so long a journey with nothing more in
hand than the bagatelle of a useless commercial treaty.[28] Accordingly,
on October 13, Huang En-t'ung had presented for French comment a
draft of a memorial which Ch'i-ying proposed to transmit to the Tri-
bunal of Rites at Peking. Lagrené allegedly had suggested a few minor
changes and then had asked that he be informed of the status of the
matter at the time of the exchange of treaty ratifications. He had also
promised at the time to afford personal protection to the Chinese commissioners if the prejudice and fanaticism of Peking should expose them
to personal danger because of the memorial. He closed the story by stating that Callery had assisted in drawing up the final draft, which contained a reservation, not entirely satisfactory to Lagrené but eventually
accepted, concerning China's right to punish Christians for criminal
acts.[29]
Lagrené concluded his dispatch with the observation that since his
instructions could not have foreseen the nature of his relations with the
imperial commissioner, he had not hesitated to follow along the promising path that Ch'i-ying himself had opened. In the absence of any difficulties in the negotiation of a commercial treaty, he had deemed it
worthy of France to signalize its influence in the sphere of civilization
and moral concern. He expressed the belief that the French success in
achieving the legalization of Christianity in China would constitute a
diplomatic feat equal to the opening of the five treaty ports. Only a diffusion of the two civilizations would in the end suffice to break down
partisanship and afford opportunity for Chinese *rapprochement* with
the West. He added, "These are dreams perhaps, but at least they do
not lack grandeur." The voice of France had been "listened to, its influence recognized, its sympathies understood."[30]

[27] Lavollée, I, 69–83.
[28] *Ibid.*, 122–125; J. M. Callery, *Correspondance Diplomatique Chinoise Relative
aux Négociations du Traité de Whampoa . . . (1844)* (Paris, 1879), 33–34.
[29] Lavollée, I, 122–130.   [30] *Ibid.*, 129–133.

51

Lagrené's report put much less stress on the Treaty of Whampoa itself, which contained three articles going beyond the terms of the British and American treaties. In Article 22, China conceded the right of foreigners in the treaty ports to establish schools and asylums. Article 23 provided that Frenchmen arrested for illegal penetration into the interior of China should be conducted to the nearest consulate but should not be physically mistreated or harmed. Article 24 permitted foreigners at the treaty ports to hire teachers, buy and sell books, and engage in scientific and literary work.[31]

Callery's Version of the Negotiations of 1844

Callery's account in his *Journal* of his day-to-day negotiations with his Chinese counterpart, Huang En-t'ung, which Ch'i-ying's reports to Peking generally substantiate, presents a far different picture from that which Lagrené gave to Guizot. The dickering over religious toleration was actually fought out on a realistic basis. In pursuit of their basic demand, the French proposed two false issues for bargaining purposes. The first was a request for a French territorial foothold on Chinese soil, which could serve as a means of implementing their potential alliance.[32] The argument was that if France was expected to be of any assistance to China, possession of a nearby base would be required. China did not stand to gain, argued Callery, by letting its enemies into its house (at Hongkong) and by keeping outside those friends who were in a position to aid her. The proposal was not pressed actively, partly because Lagrené admittedly feared (albeit groundlessly) that the Chinese might embarrass him by actually offering to cede to France Chusan Island, which the British were occupying at the time as security for payment of the indemnity fixed in the Nanking treaty.[33] On October 11 Huang proposed an alliance agreement, entirely unsatisfactory to Lagrené, under which France would mediate in case China again found itself in

[31] *Ibid.*, 132–133.

[32] Taiping (Humen) Island near Canton was first proposed, later the Ryukyu Islands.

[33] Callery, *Journal*, 182–185, 199–200. Since August, 1844, the British community at Hongkong had been concerned over the reported statements of two underofficers of the French corvette *Alcmène*, anchored at Chusan, and allegedly confirmed by Father Dannicourt, a French missionary on the island, that France intended to occupy the place. Distrust of French intentions was one of the reasons for the British refusal to evacuate the island until after the French fleet had departed for Europe early in 1846. See FO, 17, 89, August, 1844.

difficulty, while China in turn would permit the free exercise of Christianity by Frenchmen living in the treaty ports. Callery immediately shifted the discussion to the possible cession of the Ryukyu Islands, a maneuver which had the desired effect of sidetracking the alliance proposal.[34] Thus the territorial cession issue served the French as an effective rebuttal to Chinese alliance proposals.

The second bargaining proposal made by Lagrené concerned the exchange of diplomatic embassies and the setting up of cultural institutes at the respective capitals of the negotiating countries. Lagrené was well aware that this proposal was unacceptable in view of China's traditional isolationist concepts of relations with outer barbarian states, and he himself admittedly had no genuine interest in the matter.[35] This issue was designed as a shield for the more feasible objective of the free grant by the Emperor of toleration of the practice of Christianity within China as an earnest of Peking's friendly regard for France. This latter objective was pursued with vigor. Callery even threatened that without it France would sign no treaty at all. The bluff came near being called, for on one occasion Lagrené was on the verge of giving up the effort to do something for the missionaries.[36] French bluster ran the gamut of simulated temper outbursts on the part of Lagrené (Chi'i-ying described him to Peking as a violent and unreasonable man) to thinly veiled threats that the French might resort to punitive naval action.[37] These tactics must have gone far to dissipate any real expectation on the part of the Chinese that the French intended to befriend China.

Whether and when the bribing of Huang took place can only be inferred from the context of the sources. If a bargain was struck, it must have occurred in private sessions between Huang and Callery on October 13 or 14, when Huang's previously stubborn objections abruptly melted away.[38]

[34] Callery, *Journal*, 210–215. Huang replied that the Ryukyu Islands were only nominally under Chinese control. He refused also to accept the alternative suggestion that China agree never to surrender the islands to anyone except to France.

[35] *Ibid.*, 65–67, 89, 161–162. Lagrené confided to Callery that he had no desire to establish an embassy in Peking for the missionaries to run.

[36] *Ibid.*, 199–200, 215–218.

[37] Lagrené on October 6 predicted calamity for China if his suggestions concerning the need for French friendship were disregarded.

[38] Huang had insisted that imperial edicts and ancient custom could not be arbitrarily changed, that Chinese Christians really had nothing to fear, and that the French were already free to practice Christianity in the treaty ports.

53

Serious negotiations began on October 12, when Ch'i-ying urged the conclusion of an alliance pledging French mediation in return for a declaration by Peking that Christianity was no longer to be considered a false sect. Lagrené feigned insult over the meagerness of the Chinese concession, and Callery demanded that Huang consider, instead, the French-prepared draft of an imperial edict, on pain of inviting serious trouble which might involve military operations.[39] On October 13 Huang agreed to submit to Peking Callery's proposed edict concerning the toleration of Christianity if the French would pledge to advance no additional demands. On October 14 he asserted categorically that the toleration issue would be settled to the satisfaction of the French. Callery and Huang collaborated throughout October 15 on drafting a formal letter of agreement which Ch'i-ying then transmitted to Lagrené on the following day.[40] Lagrené's acknowledgment of Ch'i-ying's acceptance of the French proposal included as an enclosure, by prearrangement, the copy of K'ang Hsi's edict of toleration of 1692. Lagrené asked that he be informed at the time of the exchange of treaty ratifications that the imperial consent had been duly granted in compliance with the agreement reached, so that he could return to France confident that no future obstacle would mar the peace and harmony between the two countries.[41]

Callery's *Journal* reflects the negotiator's jubilance at having completed the agreement. He wrote, "What an event! What a victory! What glory for the church! . . . What happiness for me!"[42] But another round of acrimonious discussion was still in store. The French objected strenuously to Ch'i-ying's requirements advanced on October 21 that the memorial include statements explicitly prohibiting foreigners from penetrating beyond the treaty ports and affirming China's unrestricted criminal jurisdiction over the Christian Chinese. Tempers again reached the breaking point.[43] Ch'i-ying threatened to return all the gifts (previously unmentioned) which Lagrené had presented him in appreciation of his co-operation in obtaining toleration for Christianity, alleg-

[39] Callery, *Journal,* 207–208, 213–221.
[40] *Ibid.,* 223–226; Callery, *Correspondance,* 48–52.
[41] Callery, *Correspondance,* 55–56, dated Oct. 17, 1844.
[42] Callery, *Journal,* 232–241.
[43] *Ibid.,* 236–262; J. K. Fairbank, *Trade and Diplomacy on the China Coast . . . 1842–1854* (Cambridge, 1953), II, 197. French-Chinese dealings were far less pleasant than Chinese sources suggest.

54

ing that Peking might charge that he had been motivated in his action by reasons of personal reward or profit.[44]

Callery's *Journal* closes uncompleted on page 276 in the midst of an account of his violent argument with Huang in which the Frenchmen threatened to reopen earlier demands for a territorial concession and access to Peking.[45] In this instance Ch'i won out, for he was convinced that he could not persuade Peking to accept the memorial without including the two qualifications. Lagrené had no choice but to concede the points in dispute. Despite the effusion of personal compliments and simulated cordiality which characterized the final exchange of letters between the two chief negotiators and despite Ch'i-ying's subsequent elaborate entertainment of Lagrené outside Canton (November 14–16), it is obvious that the negotiations were not concluded in any atmosphere of friendship and trust.[46]

Sequel to the Callery Negotiations

Ch'i-ying's confidential reports to Peking covering the negotiations do not support the conclusion that he really expected to purchase by China's legalization of Christianity any assured assistance in the form of a French alliance. He characterized Lagrené as shrewd and uncompromising, the agent of a proud nation that was capable of provoking serious incidents if all of its requests were refused. Ch'i was not unaware of the rivalry and distrust obtaining between the British and the French

[44] Callery, *Correspondance*, 63–64; Swisher, 175. Ch'i-ying's memorial to Peking of Nov. 23, 1844, explained that it had seemed politic for Huang to accept trifling presents from the French.

[45] Callery, *Correspondance*, 68, 69, 72; Callery, *Journal*, 262–276. In the course of this quarrel Ch'i-ying deprecated any thought that France wanted to be the protector of Chinese who intended to use religion as a cover for evil-doing or that French citizens coming to China to preach religion intended to disturb the customs of the empire and to cause disagreements by penetrating into the interior. All copies of Callery's *Journal* end abruptly with page 276. It was published in Macao in 1845, but was suppressed by the French authorities, according to a note in the Harvard College library. The reason for the action is fairly obvious.

[46] Callery, *Correspondance*, 81–105; Grosse-Aschhoff, 90. Ch'i-ying's letters of Nov. 18 and Dec. 1, 1844, praised Lagrené's generosity, hoped that they would again be able to "converse joyously together," and declared that he carried in his heart a lively memory of their cordial relationship. Lagrené reciprocated. Even after Lagrené on December 8 delivered a sharp warning against using the character meaning "barbarian" in the text of the French treaty, Ch'i-ying responded with the same effusive protestations of friendship and affection.

forces in the Far East, and he naturally tried to make the most of it. But his policy appears to be more a continuation of the bankrupt methods of appeasement and personal ingratiation employed with respect to the British in the previous year than an attempt to achieve an alliance. He simply did not dare leave France unappeased.[47]

It required the sending of no less than three successive memorials to Peking before Ch'i-ying obtained the Emperor's approval of the agreement which had been made with the French emissary. Imperial approval was accorded on December 28 to the effect that Chinese who accepted the religion of the Lord of Heaven for good purposes would thereafter be exempt from legal culpability.[48] The first phase of the mission had been completed.

In early November Lagrené sent his first secretary, Ferrière Le Vayer, back to France carrying copies of the formal Treaty of Whampoa with covering dispatches. Lagrené also directed the emissary to transmit to Guizot relevant oral explanations not included in the written correspondence. Ratification of the treaty as well as approval of Lagrené's religious policy was promptly accorded by Guizot. Ferrière returned to Macao in August, 1845. Meanwhile Lagrené devoted his efforts to carrying out other phases of his instructions.[49]

[47] *Ibid.;* also Grosse-Aschhoff, docs. I and II, 137–142. Ch'i-ying's repeated reference to the fact that he was incurring personal risks in following his policy of friendship was not without some validity, as was demonstrated in 1848 by his abrupt dismissal from office. But he had made the same pretense in dealing with Pottinger in 1842–1843.

[48] Callery, *Correspondance,* 114–121, 154. Ch'i finally argued simply that failure to placate the French would cause endless trouble for China. The *Chinese Repository* (XIV, 587–589) of 1845 reproduced Ch'i-ying's communication to U.S. Consul Forbes announcing toleration of the religion of the Lord of Heaven in English and in Chinese.

[49] Grosse-Aschhoff, 90; Gabriel Hanotaux, *Histoire des Colonies Françaises* (Paris, 1932), V, 374–376. Hanotaux says that Lazarist interests and Cécille forced Lagrené's hand at Macao and that pressure of Catholic patriots in France forced Guizot to approve the actions of Lagrené, neither of which statements is strictly true. The full text of the Treaty of Whampoa in French and in Chinese is given in the *Chinese Repository,* XV (1846), 10–38.

V

The Lagrené Mission:
Second Phase, 1845

AVING concluded the negotiation of the Treaty of Whampoa, Lagrené turned his attention to the second aspect of his instructions, the possible acquisition for France of the island of Basilan. Two corvettes had been sent ahead under the command of Captain Guérin of *La Sabine* in October to reconnoiter the place. The main French fleet left Macao for Manila on December 21, 1844, arriving at the Spanish port on December 27. There Lagrené learned to his chagrin that difficulties had already arisen which had attracted the jealous concern of the Spaniards.

The Basilan Adventure

A party of five French sailors venturing ashore on Basilan Island had disappeared, and Captain Guérin had sailed to nearby Zamboanga, ten miles distant on Mindanao Island, to enlist the aid of the Spanish authorities in obtaining their release. The payment of a ransom of three thousand piasters had produced the surrender of three only, for the other two had been killed. To avenge their deaths, the *Sabine* had sailed up the river in Basilan at high tide on November 27 and had bombarded the palisaded town, only to be obliged to return without achieving a decisive victory when the water level fell at low tide. Captain Guérin nevertheless had announced the annexation of the island in the

57

name of France. He had then returned to Manila to build the flat-bottomed boats needed for the conquest of Basilan and to rendezvous with Lagrené and Admiral Cécille.[1]

When the main French fleet left Manila for Basilan on January 8, 1845, it was preceded to that destination by a Spanish frigate. This did not prevent the stronger French force from taking punitive action during its nearly seven weeks stay at the island. Cécille sent ashore a force of sailors, who exacted from the Sultan under duress a convention acknowledging French proprietorship over the island in return for the promised payment within six months of $100,000. The French fleet then proceeded from Basilan to Singapore and thence to Batavia, where it awaited favorable winds for the return to Macao. The latter port was again reached on July 14, 1845.[2]

The Basilan affair was a complete fiasco as far as French prestige was concerned. A Sultan of Zulu had defied the might of France, had exacted ransom for prisoners, and had finally signed only a conditional acknowledgment of French proprietorship in return for a considerable money payment. The French could designate no force to occupy the island. The Spanish Governor at Manila forwarded to Madrid his protest that Basilan was a dependency of the Philippines, and the settlement of the affair was shifted to Europe. The British at Hongkong were astonished as well as perturbed that so prudent a person as they knew Admiral Cécille to be would attempt to annex a Spanish dependency. They were also more than slightly amused at the outcome.[3] It is not surprising that the frustrated French mission was in an angry and aggressive mood when it returned to China in July.

Guizot's Repudiation of Imperialistic Objectives

Difficulties between Paris and Madrid about the Basilan episode were resolved in favor of Spain's assertion of prior claim to the island, for Guizot was interested at the time in promoting a *rapprochement* with

[1] *Revue des Deux Mondes*, 5th ser., X (May 31, 1845), 1033–1036; Lavollée, I, 176–177. The informed reporter in the *Revue* commented as follows: "Perhaps the island is going to be seized; at least the pretext is good, and it only remains to learn if it is worth the trouble. What is certain is that we . . . are seeking to found a colonial establishment or a military post in that part of the China Sea."

[2] Lavollée, I, 180; FO, 17, 98 and 99, from Davis, March 12 and April 9, 1845.

[3] FO, 17, 98 and 99, from Davis, March 12 and April 9, 1845.

Madrid on the Spanish marriage question. On August 5, 1845, the Paris government issued a face-saving announcement that France had decided not to occupy Basilan Island because its value to France would not compensate for the effort required to conquer the natives, overcome climatic difficulties, and suppress piracy. Even if a port were developed on the island, Guizot concluded, the base would profit foreign ships more than French ones, which could not be expected to play an important role commercially in that part of the world.[4]

Guizot's repudiation of the Basilan adventure, which he himself had proposed, was accompanied by his equally emphatic veto of an alternative proposition to obtain a French foothold in Tongking. The suggestion originated from French missionary circles in touch with Admiral Cécille, who transmitted it in late 1844 to the Minister of Marine, and he in turn to Guizot. Lagrené learned about it through Father Libois, who shared the doubts of the French emissary as to its wisdom. The Tongking missionaries had reported that a sustained French naval demonstration at Tourane or off the coast of Tongking would lend encouragement to the numerous partisans of the old dynasty of Lê, whose representative was friendly to the missionaries and desired to detach Tongking from the rule of Annam. Cécille proposed that a representative of Lê journey to Macao or even to Paris to negotiate for French aid in behalf of his cause. Once the new ruler was installed in Tongking, France could obtain from him a naval base on the coast and concessions in favor of missions.

Lagrené was far from enthusiastic over the proposal. He foresaw that difficulties would arise with the British and that the enterprise, if unsuccessful, might react disastrously for both the missionaries and the native Christians. He indicated to Paris, nevertheless, that if the Basilan venture should fail and Guizot should decide to undertake further action, Tongking offered a possible alternative.[5] Guizot's reaction was more emphatically negative. In a statement transmitted to the Minister

---

[4] Launay, *Histoire Générale*, III, 155–156; Lavollée, I, 176–179. Guizot admitted in 1860 that the Spanish marriage issue was the principal reason for the decision.

[5] Lavollée, I, 164–167; Hanotaux, V, 376–377. Admiral Cécille, acting on a tip from Captain Percival of the U.S.S. *Constitution*, who visited Tourane in May, 1845, sent the *Alcmène* to that port in June and rescued the condemned French missionary, Monsignor Lefèbvre. Percival had previously used force to attempt the rescue. See SD, Singapore, CL 70, from Balestier, April 7, 1847.

of Marine, he explained that France was incapable at the moment of undertaking an imperialistic effort in Tongking. His statement ran in part as follows:

We have sufficiently grave and complicated questions to manage in Europe . . . , an oversight to exercise in the [Near] East, a difficult task to complete in Algeria, and interests of considerable importance to care for in America [Rio de la Plata] without throwing ourselves into other hazardous enterprises somewhere else, without undertaking . . . in the seas of India and China, a new source of preoccupation, embarrassment, and expense for France.[6]

Lagrené's Negotiation of July–August, 1845

When Lagrené returned to Macao in mid-July, 1845, he found Ch'i-ying persisting in his labored effort to cultivate cordial personal relations. Ch'i's friendly notes had, in fact, followed Lagrené to Manila. In a series of letters filled with protestations of friendship, Ch'i-ying had informed the French leader that the petition regarding Christianity had been approved by the Emperor and that Peking had also ratified the Treaty of Whampoa. Upon his return to Macao, Lagrené reciprocated Ch'i's friendly advances, but he adopted a rigidly formal tone in explaining his disappointment that the edict had not canceled the previous anti-Christian laws but had merely suspended their application on the ground that Christianity was now adjudged to be a moral religion. The reply of the Chinese spokesmen, still profuse in protestations of friendship, indicated that they dare not antagonize the Peking mandarins by again raising the subject of religious toleration.[7]

After Ferrière Le Vayer arrived at Macao, on August 3, with the French ratification of the treaty in hand and the more important news that Guizot had approved the efforts of the mission in the previous year to legalize Christianity in China, Lagrené adopted a much more peremptory tone. He declared that the failure of the recent toleration edict to define precisely what was meant by the "law-abiding" observance of the Christian religion left wide open the possibility of the persecution

6 Septans, 128.

7 Callery, *Correspondance*, 124–125, 128, 131–133, 138–142, 145–146, 151, 154, 167, 172–173, 177–178, 209–210. Lagrené took advantage of Ch'i-ying's ingratiating posture to ask that copies of a rare government-published edition of collected Buddhist writings in Chinese, Manchu, Mongolian, and Tibetan languages dating from K'ang Hsi's time be obtained for him. Lagrené offered French books in exchange, if requested. Ch'i agreed to comply but pointed out the difficulties involved.

of Christians for allegedly illegal activities. He declared that the edict was worthless unless clarified, and he demanded full toleration as contained in the 1692 decree. He also asked that enforcement of the edict be strengthened and that Christian offenders under the old law be pardoned. After a week or more of bitter argument, during which Lagrené alleged that he would suffer ridicule and shame if he returned to Europe empty-handed, and Callery threatened to hold up indefinitely the exchange of treaty ratifications, Chinese resistance was beaten down. Ch'i-ying accepted a statement drafted by Callery which identified as legal certain characteristic aspects of Catholic worship, such as veneration of the cross and images, the singing of liturgical songs, assembling for purposes of exhortation to moral conduct, and the building of churches. All but the demand for amnesty was conceded. Lagrené accepted the clarifying statement on condition that it be sent out immediately to all provinces of the Empire.[8]

Ch'i-ying handled the matter with Peking not as a supplementary memorial but as a clarifying statement regarding the earlier edict already approved by the court. In his official report of the episode dated September 20, he explained that Lagrené surpassed all other foreigners in arrogance and cunning, that his mood turned quickly from shame to rage, and that unless the French had obtained this further concession they would probably have broken off relations, and China's policy of pacification would have been wrecked. He also announced that the exchange of ratifications had been completed on August 25 and that the negotiation (he hoped) had been completed.[9] Toward the French, Ch'i-ying continued to pose as the personification of accord and friendliness. On September 2 he presented valuable presents to the four principal negotiators and to Guizot as marks of the profound esteem of the Ch'ing dynasty for statesmen of such rare wisdom.[10]

There was nothing in Lagrené's official reports to Paris following the exchange of ratifications to indicate that he was disappointed with the result of his mission. He did complain that the meddlesome opportunism

[8] Grosse-Aschhoff, 90–103; Ferrière Le Vayer, 351.

[9] Grosse-Aschhoff, document VIII, 148–151; Callery, *Correspondance*, 217–219, 223–224. Lagrené's official report to Paris explained only that he had informed Ch'i-ying of the satisfaction of France over the news of the imperial edict, and that he had obtained from the Chinese further clarification of its meaning.

[10] Callery, *Correspondance*, 233. The presents were necklaces (*colliers*) of golden amber.

61

of Father Guillet had again occasioned him unnecessary difficulty.[11] Otherwise he reported that information from missionary sources and native priests throughout China indicated that the toleration edict had been widely published, even as far inland as Szechuan Province and the borders of Tibet. Imprudent enthusiasm on the part of native Christians and missionaries to reopen churches, especially in the Jesuit mission at Nanking, had caused difficulties and several arrests, but such misunderstandings, he commented, would be unavoidable for some time to come.[12] Here is the first hint that French diplomacy had prompted aggressive missionary operations which Paris was committed by implication to support but could not control.

The Final Episode of Lagrené's Mission

In mid-September Lagrené and others of his mission started on a tour of the treaty ports. His ostensible objective was to examine the possibilities for expanding French trade. Several of this group, notably the indefatigable M. de Montigny, collected voluminous commercial data of presumed value to France. A second concern was to have a look at Chusan Island, particularly the port of Ting-hai, where the British forces were still in occupation and where a French missionary, Father Dannicourt, was available for conference. Sections of the French fleet remained for a time at Ting-hai, where Lagrené later rejoined them after a visit to nearby Ningpo. At Ningpo the taotai took no notice of the French visitors. The French emissary was much impressed by the commercial possibilities of Shanghai, where he remained for several weeks. Lagrené also stopped at the Fukien ports on his way back to Macao, which he reached in early December. His summary commercial report held out little hope of developing French trade.

The only political report of any importance which developed from the northern trip concerned Chusan Island. Lagrené found there no evidence to justify the fears current at Macao that the British intended permanently to occupy the place. All facilities were improvised, no new buildings had been erected, and preparations for evacuation were already in progress. The occupation, he concluded, might be prolonged to buttress current British negotiations concerning the right of entry into Canton, but Lagrené was convinced that England would not use the issue as a pretext for refusing to honor the treaty pledge (made at

[11] Lavollée, I, 226, Aug. 30, 1845.   [12] Ibid., 264, Sept. 10, 1845.

the Bogue, 1843) to withdraw from Chusan as soon as the indemnity was paid. He observed also that the commercial possibilities of Chusan seemed not to justify the effusive regrets of English merchants at Hongkong over the British decision to abandon the island. Chusan, he concluded, had some advantages over Hongkong with respect to climate and productivity, but very little from a political or military point of view.[13] These comments concerned the undercover Anglo-French rivalry over Chusan, which will be treated in the final section of this chapter.

During the course of his tour of the port cities, Lagrené also made contact with French missionary personnel and investigated the extent to which the toleration decree had been brought to the attention of the mandarin officials and the people. He also acceded to the request of British and American missionaries at Shanghai that the toleration edicts be made to apply to all Christians. Whether he became genuinely aroused by missionary complaints over the inadequacy of previous concessions and the alleged failure of the government to implement the imperial toleration decree or whether he simply seized on the issue as a pretext for advancing a final series of demands is not clear. It is significant that Lagrené's return to Macao in early December, 1845, coincided with the arrival of seven or eight additional French war vessels. For whatever reason, Lagrené plunged vigorously into a third round of acrimonious negotiations.

The exchanges began on December 8. Lagrené complained through Callery that in the port cities he had visited he found almost no posting of the imperial proclamation exempting the law-abiding Catholic Chinese from prosecution. Inquiries addressed to local mandarins had elicited only evasive replies. Lagrené had thereby suffered both ridicule and loss of prestige, and he was intensely angry for having been grossly deceived by Chinese promises. Callery predicted that if the news should reach France that an expedition costing an estimated million silver taels had been barren of tangible results, Lagrené would be recalled for punishment and another sent to replace him. The French leader demanded, therefore, that a supplementary sacred edict be issued explaining the toleration policy and that it be sent to the local officials in all provinces. Callery also added the new requirement, long advocated by the missionaries, that old church buildings dating from K'ang Hsi's time, if still

[13] *Ibid.*, 269–273, 288–292; Callery, *Correspondance*, 266–271.

63

standing and not otherwise in use, should be restored to Christian ownership.[14]

Ch'i-ying saw in the new French demand, coupled as it was with the appearance of a greatly augmented French fleet, an ominous threat to China. Although he recognized that the British were also somewhat concerned over French intentions, he did not credit Callery's explanation that additional war vessels had been sent to enable France to assist China in case the British should refuse to evacuate Chusan. Apparently convinced that the only way he could rid himself of the annoying presence of the French was to accede to their requirements, Ch'i-ying agreed on December 22 to petition the Emperor as Callery demanded. Callery himself drafted the proposed sacred edict.

Obtaining Peking's approval of the edict was far from easy. No fewer than four successive memorials were required. When persuasion failed, Ch'i-ying finally told the Emperor bluntly that he feared that France harbored treacherous designs. French war vessels had been brought to China at great cost to support Lagrené's demands, and China could not afford, in the face of British hostility, to sacrifice the friendship of France as well. Wider publication of the toleration edicts, he added, would also please the English and Americans, especially since all Christian groups were now to be included within its provisions. He was sure in any case that relatively few church properties would have to be returned.[15] Peking finally consented to Ch'i's importunate pleas in February, 1846.

Lagrené left China on January 9. The rest of his party, including most of the naval force, departed for Europe on January 11, before the second of Ch'i-ying's four memorials to Peking had been dispatched. Lagrené left word with Callery that if the Chinese should again raise the embarrassing subject of French aid against the British at Chusan, he should counter the move by proposing the sending of a French embassy to Peking.[16] Lagrené returned to France via Suez, as Ferrière Le Vayer

---

[14] Grosse-Aschhoff, 110–120, 153–156, document X, dated Dec. 21, 1845; Callery, *Correspondance*, 282–284.

[15] Grosse-Aschhoff, 153–162, 169–172, documents X, XII, XIV, XVIII, from December, 1845, through February, 1846. Ch'i-ying accepted Lagrené's interpretation that the absence of characteristic aspects of Catholic worship would not exclude other Christians from the toleration decree (Callery, *Correspondance*, 266–271, 291–296).

[16] Grosse-Aschhoff, 118–119; *Chinese Repository*, XV (1847), 158.

had done the previous year, and reached Marseilles on May 27.[17] The government on the whole was pleased with the results of his mission, but approval was far from unanimous. From the religious party in France came a veritable chorus of criticism alleging that Lagrené had failed to accomplish any substantial results. In this outburst was reflected the inveterate opposition of the Lazarists at Macao to Callery's influence. Only the Société des Missions Etrangères acknowledged Lagrené's helpful efforts in behalf of the cause of Christianity in China.[18]

The Chusan Island Evacuation

It remains to examine the Chusan Island episode as an element in the triangle of Anglo-French-Chinese relations. In an earlier connection it was noted that some of the British at Hongkong became greatly perturbed in August, 1844, over rumors that the French intended to annex Chusan if and when the British evacuated the island.[19] Lagrené was fully aware of British sensitivity on the question, and he had actually become worried at one stage of his October, 1844, negotiations over the prospect that Ch'i-ying might offer him the island and thus confront the French with the embarrassing dilemma of either declining the Chinese proposal or of incurring the wrath of the British.[20] In November, 1844, Lagrené, sensing Ch'i-ying's anxiety with respect to British intentions, assured the imperial commissioner that Britain would honor its pledge to withdraw from Chusan provided other aspects of the Nanking treaty were scrupulously observed.[21] British suspicions regarding French imperialist designs died down following Lagrené's departure for Manila, only to be revived on the receipt of the news of the Basilan episode.

British Minister Davis himself seems never to have believed that the French harbored intentions of occupying Chusan. His relations with both Lagrené and Cécille were cordial, and their conversations were invariably reassuring.[22] Lord Aberdeen, British Foreign Secretary, was also fairly confident as to the objectives of the Lagrené mission, for he had received quieting comments from Guizot concerning it, transmitted by the British Ambassador at Paris.[23] Nevertheless, the episode at Ba-

[17] Maybon and Fredet, 11–12.   [18] Launay, Histoire Générale, III, 159–160.
[19] See Chapter IV, n. 33.   [20] Ibid.
[21] Lavollée, I, 153–154, Nov. 26, 1844.
[22] FO, 17, 90, from Davis, Dec. 4, 1844.
[23] FO, 27, 701, from Lord Cowley, Dec. 9, 1844. Guizot's assurances followed directly the settlement of the "Pritchard affair." See Chapter III.

silan, coupled with the temporary French naval superiority over the British in the Far East in 1845, aroused considerable anxiety in British circles.[24] The situation became the subject of voluminous correspondence between Hongkong and London.

Two members of Davis' staff at Hongkong, Gutzloff and Martin, the treasurer of the colony, prepared long memoranda on Chusan with which Davis did not fully agree but which he nevertheless saw fit to transmit to London. Martin was convinced that the French would seize Chusan just as soon as the British forces withdrew, and he advocated permanent British retention of the island because of its intrinsic commercial and political importance.[25] Gutzloff argued similarly for retention on the ground that Ch'i-ying's anti-European enemies at court were gaining the upper hand and that Chusan, potentially a second Malta, must be retained by Britain against the inevitable event of renewal of warfare.[26] On the heels of the news of the Basilan episode, Martin prepared another dissertation for London's examination. This time he denounced England's failure in China to pursue its manifest destiny as the great civilizing agency in the world and criticized especially London's virtual prohibition of British missionary activity within China. He now urged that Britain should not only annex Chusan but should also press for a legation at Peking, for free access to the interior, and for the opening of the Yangtse to trade.[27]

Lord Aberdeen entertained no intention of refusing to restore Chusan to China, but he was also concerned not to see France profit from Britain's scrupulously correct conduct in the affair. His instruction to Davis of May, 1845, ruled that as a matter of political necessity Chusan must not be allowed to fall into the hands of a foreign power either through voluntary cession by China or through forcible occupation. He had no reason to believe that either China or France entertained such inten-

---

[24] In April, 1845, Britain had only two frigates and a war steamer in China waters as compared with the six-vessel French fleet (FO, 17, 99, April 2, 1845).

[25] FO, 17, 89; the Martin manuscript was prepared in August, 1844, and submitted to London in October. It was fifty pages long and covered descriptively all aspects of the island, which Martin regarded as in every way superior to Hongkong.

[26] FO, 17, 90, December, 1844.

[27] FO, 17, 99, April 19, 1845. Davis on this occasion (FO, 17, 100, June 24, 1845) criticized Martin for meddling, for misstating the facts about Chusan, and for mistakenly predicting a renewal of warfare. Aberdeen's comments were equally caustic, and Martin eventually resigned his post.

tions. He directed, nevertheless, that Ch'i-ying should be informed of Britain's determination to resist by arms any move to alienate Chusan and of the British intention to postpone withdrawal from the island if there were at the time any danger of such a development taking place. Davis was ordered, without making further reference to London, to defend the island by every means in his power whenever he obtained indisputable evidence that another foreign power had designs upon it.[28]

In subsequent instructions, sent in the fall of 1845, Aberdeen ordered Davis to attempt to obtain before surrendering the island both a written pledge from China not to cede Chusan to any foreign power and also assurances that English aid would be accepted to expel any invader, all on the understanding that the island would revert to China when the hazard had passed. Aberdeen included in his political calculations the possibility that from vindictive motives the Chinese might consider ceding Chusan in order to raise up a rival to Britain's leadership in the Far East. He also granted Davis full power to negotiate the purchase of the island in the improbable contingency that China could be induced to sell it.[29]

When Lagrené returned to Macao in July, 1845, Davis convinced himself that no rational grounds existed for supposing that France had designs on Chusan. He pointed out that the French war vessels carried not a single marine or sailor beyond their respective crews and that they had not left a person in occupation of Basilan. The Chinese firmly opposed surrendering Chusan to anybody, he added, and a quixotic French attempt to seize it in the presence of a British garrison and naval force was out of the question. Lagrené, in fact, had assured Davis that the French fleet would quit China waters before the time came for Britain to restore Chusan.[30]

British doubts concerning French intentions may have been revived in December, 1845, when the additional French war vessels appeared at Macao for no ascertainable reason. Ch'i-ying did not credit Callery's allegation that the vessels had come to enable France to assist China if trouble arose over Chusan, but he still thought that the presence of the

[28] FO, 17, 96, Aberdeen's instructions dated May 6, 1845. Aberdeen on August 8 stated that Martin would do better to confine himself to the duties he was appointed to perform.

[29] FO, 17, 96, instructions dated Oct. 23 and 24, 1845.

[30] FO, 17, 100, from Davis, Aug. 6, 1845.

French vessels might give the British pause if the rumor of Callery's assertion got around.[31] Actually the French entertained no intention of becoming involved in the Chusan affair, and their fleet departed for Europe, as Lagrené had promised, long before Britain withdrew from the island.[32] The episode illustrated the intensity of Anglo-French rivalry in the Far East and also the influence of the Aberdeen-Guizot entente as a check to any serious imperialist adventure on the part of the French forces. The British were interested in extending commercial opportunities rather than in annexing additional territory, so long as their dominant position was not challenged by the acquisitions of others. France waited another decade before she again dispatched a powerful fleet to the Far East, that time with definitely aggressive intent.

Interpretation of the Mission

An analysis of Lagrené's mission must start with an appreciation of the limitations within which he was obliged to operate. Both he and his principal negotiator, Callery, were under constant harrassment locally from missionary groups in China, especially the Lazarists, who were determined to make maximum use of the presence of the French mission and naval forces in the area, and who were grievously offended over being denied an active role in the negotiations. The fact that the missionaries had influential political friends in France who would echo

[31] John Jacob Nolde, "The Canton City Question, 1842–1849" (Cornell University thesis, 1950), 119–120. Citing the *I Wu Shi Mo* (chuan 75, p. 19b), Nolde quotes from Ch'i-ying's report of his settlement of the Chusan issue with Davis on April 3, 1846, explaining to Peking that his plan was to rely on French influence to oblige the British to return Chusan to China and to use the British, once the island was returned, to forestall reckless acts by others. Barbarian would thus control barbarian to the benefit of China. Ch'i-ying also approached U.S. Commodore Biddle with the complaint that the British were demanding a pledge of nonalienation for Chusan and were refusing to accept the final installment of the indemnity (SD, China, DD, from Com. Biddle at Canton, Jan. 8, 1846). Ch'i-ying's basic concern was probably to avoid collusion between the British and the French, whose hostility to China arose from differing but simultaneous grievances. Hence his willingness to meet Lagrené's demands in order to get the French naval force to leave.

[32] Article III of the Convention signed by Davis and Ch'i-ying on April 4, 1846, stated that Chusan after its evacuation "shall never be ceded to any other foreign power" (Sir Godfrey Edward Hertslet, *Treaties, etc., between Great Britain and China* [London, 1896], 15–16). China would not incur any expense by reason of England's possible aid in defense of Chusan. The British evacuation of Chusan took place on July 25, 1846.

their grievances had an undoubted bearing on the conduct of the later phases of the negotiations. As a second limitation, Lagrené was obliged to stay within the bounds of his instructions from Guizot and to conform to the generally Anglophile orientation of French foreign policy at the time. The French government was reluctant to accept any obligation to safeguard French missionaries who deliberately exposed themselves to danger, and yet Guizot was seeking to soften clerical opposition in France. A third limitation stemmed from the jealous watchfulness of the British at Hongkong, a situation which carried with it the corollary incentive to accomplish something unobjectionable to the British but designed to bolster French prestige.

Virtually the only leeway afforded Lagrené came from Ch'i-ying's policy of appeasement, and of this the French negotiator took full advantage. The labored efforts of the Manchu commissioner to ingratiate himself personally and his obvious readiness to make concessions in order to please the French denied him any opportunity to exact from Lagrené a tangible *quid pro quo* in return for Chinese concessions. The probable bribery of Huang in 1844 was an exception. Lagrené and Callery successfully evaded all Chinese requests for French assistance either by suggesting the cession of a territorial foothold or by urging an exchange of diplomatic representatives. They then overcame Chinese reluctance by threatening overt reprisals if minimum concessions were not made. Ch'i-ying was probably never very hopeful of obtaining a French alliance. At the end he was quite prepared to forgo the chance possibility of French assistance in order to be free from the annoying presence of the French forces on the China coast. The concessions he made may have bought time for the tottering dynasty, but they mortgaged heavily China's political integrity without realizing any compensatory advantages. On the other hand, the Lagrené mission committed France to the protection of missionary activities which Paris could not control and which would afford provocation for subsequent imperialist adventures.

VI

French Activities

in the Far East, 1846-1851

URING the first half decade following the termination of the Lagrené mission, French activities in the Far East were very largely associated with the aggressive surge of the Catholic missionary movement and with naval and other measures taken in its support. Political policy was by comparison extremely cautious, and commercial interests were almost nonexistent.

Increased Missionary Activity

The groups most active in the missionary movement continued to be the Societé des Missions Etrangères and the Lazarist Society, the first being an exclusively French group and the second largely so. The Missions Etrangères manned six of the eight vicariates in southeast Asia, and assumed wide responsibilities with respect to fourteen new vicariates established in China between 1844 and 1860. Its assignments covered portions of eleven provinces of China proper, plus operations in peripheral Tibet, Manchuria, and Korea. French Lazarists also expanded their operations during the same period, adding more than fifty Chinese and foreign priests to their staffs.[1] French Jesuit activities also

[1] Lazarist efforts were concentrated in the two Kwangs, in Chekiang and Kiangsu, in Honan and Hopeh Provinces. They also penetrated Mongolia (Latourette, 237–242; Henri Cordier, "La France et la Cochinchine, 1852–1858," *T'oung Pao*, 2d ser.

70

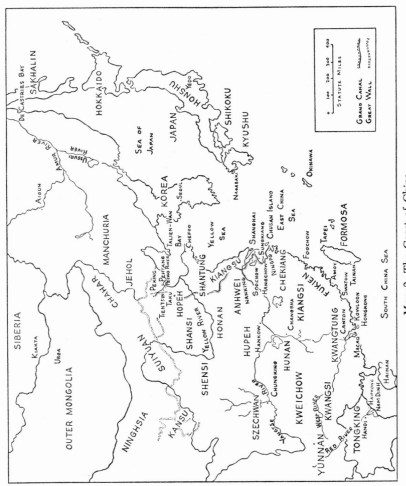

Map 2. The Coast of China

71

were resumed in 1842 in the areas of Shanghai and Nanking (Kiang-nan), where they achieved remarkable success.[2]

An aggressive ultramontane spirit characterized the entire French missionary program. Heedless of personal risks and paying little attention to contrary royal decrees or to treaty regulations, the missionaries penetrated the interior of eastern Asia wherever an opening could be found. Dressed in native garb and subsisting on native fare, they worked unostentatiously and unremittingly. As voluntary exiles, they entertained no intention of returning home. Both Protestant missionaries and non-French diplomatic officials testified to their devotion and effectiveness.[3]

The reception accorded the French missionaries varied widely from place to place. In areas peripheral to China, especially Annam and Korea, they suffered severe persecution and hardship. Within China proper, they fared better on the whole. Enforcement of both the Christian toleration edicts and the almost contradictory prohibition of foreign penetration into the interior depended in large measure on the attitude of local Chinese officials and gentry in any given area. In the vicinity of Shanghai, the mandarins ignored illegal missionary residence outside the port. They avoided granting positive permission for penetration by foreigners but regularly winked at it and even permitted the settlement by consular agents on the spot of disputes involving missionaries or native Christians. French operations in this connection will be described later. Even in areas where the local population and the mandarins were hostile to the presence of missionaries, officials usually found it more convenient to ignore them or to work out a local compromise than to escort the offending foreigner to some distant treaty port.

VII [1906], 481, 483). The Missions Etrangères withdrew from Fukien in 1850, leaving the province to the Spanish Dominicans (Latourette, 238).

[2] R. B. Broullion, *Missions de Chine: Mémoire sur l'Etat Actuel de la Mission du Kiang-nan, 1842–1855* (Paris, 1855), 45–50, 112–127. No less than twelve Jesuit mission centers developed in the vicinity of Shanghai. Their college of Zikawei was across the Woosung, six kilometers east of the city.

[3] W. H. Medhurst, *The Foreigner in Far Cathay* (London, 1872), 33–35; Theodore Walrond, ed. *Letters and Journals of James, Eighth Earl of Elgin* (London, 1872), 241–242. Lord Elgin contrasted the vigor of the Catholic operations with the relative ineffectiveness of the Protestant missionaries. The latter lived with their families at the treaty ports, were largely absorbed in translation work and tract distribution, and returned home periodically.

When a missionary offender was delivered to a French consul, the latter was in possession of no legal code under which to try the surrendered person, who usually returned to his previous post at the earliest opportunity.[4] The French missionaries encountered determined hostility only in Hopeh Province, especially in the vicinity of Peking, where were located former Catholic church properties which the Lazarists wished to recover.

French Naval Support of Missionaries

The relations between French missionaries and the antiforeign King Thieu-Tri of Annam (1841–1847) were uniformly hostile. Most of the missionaries within the kingdom were obliged to go into hiding on pain of suffering imprisonment or death. The ruler's vindictive mood was aggravated by the periodic French naval forays at Tourane, the harbor nearest the capital of Hué. It has already been noted that Captain Levêque of the *Heroine* in October, 1842, achieved the release of five condemned missionaries[5] and that in June, 1845, Captain Fournier Duplan of the *Gloire*, acting on a tip from an American naval officer, rescued the imprisoned Bishop Lefèbvre.[6] But despite the persecution, French and other Catholic missionaries continued to enter Tongking in particular, where Thieu-Tri was himself not universally popular. From Tongking in 1844 through missionary channels came the specific proposal mentioned earlier for French intervention in behalf of the Lê pretender to the Annamite throne,[7] in the pattern of Pigneau de Behaine's tactics in the eighteenth century.[8] Thieu-Tri's inveterate distrust of the political designs of the French were not without some foundation.

Bishop Lefèbvre's subsequent conduct generated a measure of international rivalry over Annam. While the Bishop was being accorded temporary asylum at Singapore in early 1846, awaiting an opportunity to return to Annam, the resident British Governor allegedy offered to

---

[4] AEC, 2, 96–97, 118, 135, dated respectively June 19, Sept. 20, Oct. 24, and Dec. 31, 1846. In 1846, one Lazarist was conducted afoot and in chains from Hopeh Province to Macao. Two others, who proved to be Dutch, were brought all the way from Tibet to Macao. In both instances, Consul de Bécour declined to protest, conceding that the Chinese acted within their treaty rights. See Latourette, 231.

[5] Chapter III, n. 35.

[6] Captain Percivall of the U.S.S. *Constitution* visited Tourane in May, 1845, learned of Lefèbvre's imprisonment, and tried to rescue him (*Chinese Repository*, XVI [1847], 310–314).

[7] Chapter V, n. 5.   [8] Chapter I, nn. 39–46.

73

repatriate him by steamer if he would await the outcome of British negotiations with Annam for the free exercise of the Christian faith and the right of entry for missionaries. Lefèbvre refused the British offer, and shortly thereafter, in May, 1846, in the company of Father Duclos (one of the five who had been rescued in 1843), he re-entered Cochin-China by bribing the frontier guards. The two priests were nevertheless promptly arrested and imprisoned. Lefèbvre died of illness at Saigon in June, 1846, and Duclos was again taken to Hué as a prisoner.[9]

French Catholic writers subsequently made much of the patriotic spirit of Lefèbvre's rejection of British aid, alleging that Annam was prevented by his decision from falling into British hands. Launay commented, "England penetrating into Annam under color of protecting missions would be England master of the country, with all of her ability to augment prestige and to conquer through incidental means."[10]

The French feud with Thieu-Tri entered a new phase in March, 1847, when two naval vessels commanded respectively by Lapierre and Rigault de Genouilly appeared at Tourane, presumably to deliver a letter addressed to the King of Annam and to rescue a missionary (possibly Duclos, who had meanwhile escaped). The letter demanded among other things that Thieu-Tri cease persecuting Christians. The French overcame the reluctance of the local prefect to accept delivery of the letter by stripping the sails from several Annamite war vessels found in the harbor. When the King's reply came on April 12, the French commodore refused to go ashore to receive it and the mandarin official, in turn, declined to deliver it aboard a French vessel. Deadlock ensued. Meanwhile the King had assembled a defense force. A clash occurred on April 15, when the French guns destroyed both the Annamite fleet and the harbor forts. But as the French commanders had no

[9] Launay, *Histoire Générale*, III, 179–182; L. E. Louvet, *La Cochinchine Religieuse* (Paris, 1885), II, 162–163. Cordier ("La Politique Coloniale," *T'oung Pao*, 2d ser., X, 22) asserts, apparently mistakenly, that Duclos died at Saigon and that Lefèbvre was exiled.

[10] Launay, *Histoire Générale*, III, 163, 182–183; Louvet, *La Cochinchine*, 163. Launay also quoted Bishop Puginier of Tongking to the effect that French missionaries worked "for God, for *la patrie*, and for the country to which they dedicated themselves." Louvet praised Lefèbvre: "The noble exile remembered that he was French. . . . He wished to leave to our country the exclusive honor of intervening in favor of its nationals and the possibility of establishing some day our influence over that rich peninsula."

74

means to force Hué to negotiate, they could only issue a threat and depart without achieving their declared objectives.[11] The King, now furiously angry, denounced the missionaries as accomplices of his foreign enemies, placed a price of thirty bars of silver on the head of each, and authorized the killing of Europeans on sight. These orders were not fully executed, however, and shortly thereafter the King contracted a fever which eventually brought on his death in early November, 1847.[12]

British interest, dating from 1845, in the opening of Siam and Annam to European trade was stimulated by the news that the French had bombarded Tourane and were in the bad graces of Thieu-Tri. Acting on direct authorization from London, Davis proceeded to Tourane in October, 1847, accompanied by two British war vessels.[13] Davis hoped that a friendly British approach in the interest of commerce alone, contrasting with the harsh methods used by the French, would provide a basis for successful negotiation.[14] He nevertheless met with little success. He talked with mandarins on friendly terms both on shipboard and ashore, but they refused his request for permission to proceed to Hué to deliver his letter to the King in person. The two parties did not even get around to exchanging presents. Davis attributed his lack of suc-

[11] Launay, *Histoire Générale*, III, 216–218. The clash was precipitated by the news, furnished by a *catechiste cochinchinoise*, that the Annamites planned to assassinate the French leaders while they were guests ashore. This warning was allegedly confirmed by a note found aboard an Annamite boat ordering that the French be attacked if they acted without due respect. In response to a later inquiry from Davis at Hongkong, Lapierre denied that his action at Tourane had been prompted by any political motive. See FO, 17, 125, April 25, 1847; *Chinese Repository*, XVI (1847), 310–314.

[12] Cordier, "La Politique Coloniale" *T'oung Pao*, 2d ser., X, 21–22; Hanotaux, V, 377.

[13] The original British proposal made in 1845 was in the form of a long memorandum prepared by Gutzlaff of the Hongkong legation and sent to London by Davis (FO, 17, 100, from Davis, Aug. 1). It recommended that Britain take advantage of the military prestige gained in the recent China war to obtain trade treaties with Siam, Annam, Korea, and Japan. Annam was regarded as the most promising opportunity. On March 18, 1846 (FO, 17, 108), Davis was sent a full power to negotiate treaties with Annam and Japan. Authorization to visit Hué came in a later instruction of Jan. 25, 1845 (FO, 17, 121).

[14] FO, 17, 130, from Davis, Oct. 4, 1847. Wrote Davis: "We at least have not been the subjects of jealousy and disagreement which brought on that [French] collision. The vicinity of our Indian empire and our successes in China are additional reasons why we should be treated with respect and consideration."

cess to the unfortunate impression made by the French. British interest in the commercial possibilities of the area did not wane, however.[15]

King Thieu-Tri died within ten days after Davis' departure. The new Annamite ruler known under the reign title of Tu-Duc was no improvement as far as the status of the French missionaries was concerned.

Meanwhile, French naval vessels had also been active in Korean and Japanese waters, acting there as in Annam without specific authorization. Admiral Cécille appeared off the Korean coast in September, 1846, and sent to Seoul a peremptory letter demanding the release of an imprisoned Korean priest named André Kim.[16] Cécille declared that the French Minister of Marine had charged him with protecting French nationals in the Far East. The effect was to cause the immediate execution of the unfortunate Kim.[17] Two months later Cécille brought a French frigate and corvette into Nagasaki harbor, ostensibly to request from the Japanese better treatment for French vessels in distress, but actually to show the French flag and to gain information concerning harbor defenses. On their arrival, the French vessels were immediately surrounded by Japanese warcraft, and Cécille was denied opportunity to communicate with port officials. He departed twenty-four hours later, highly displeased and talking about returning to demand satisfaction.[18]

A subsequent adventure of the French fleet off the Korean coast in the late summer of 1847 proved disastrous. Commander Lapierre and Captain Genouilly with the frigate *La Gloire* and the corvette *La Victorieuse*, the same vessels which had participated earlier in the year in the bombardment of Tourane, were attempting to land some missionaries on the coast.[19] On August 10 both ships ran aground on an offshore

[15] FO, 17, 130, from Tourane, Oct. 26, 1847, and from Hongkong, Oct. 30, 1847. Palmerston (152, Dec. 18, 1849) authorized Sir James Brooke to negotiate with Cochin-China, and subsequently (Jan. 17, 1851) he directed Bonham to get information about Cambodia.

[16] Kim had served as one of the interpreters for Cécille and Jancigny in 1842–1843 while he had been in training for the priesthood at Macao.

[17] Launay, *Histoire Générale*, III, 212–215.

[18] SD, China, DD, no. 12, Oct. 26, 1846; no. 14, Nov. 9, 1846. The British Captain Paulding had made a similarly unsuccessful attempt to negotiate at Nagasaki shortly before Cécille's visit. American reports concerning Cécille's trip said that he also intended to call at the Ryukyu Islands to pick up a Frenchman who had been left there in 1845 to study the language. See SD, Hongkong, CL 10, from Bush, July 24, 1846.

[19] SD, Hongkong, CL 11, Sept. 25, 1847. One of the missionaries attempting to land was Father Lamaitre.

island and were hopelessly wrecked. The two crews, numbering 560 men, evacuated to a nearby island with some food and small arms. Two small boats manned by ten men each managed to carry to Shanghai their plea for rescue. Three British vessels were sent to pick up the stranded mariners, and they brought the entire force to Shanghai by the end of September. The French crewmen were grateful for timely British succor, but lacking vessels to man, they were obliged to return to Europe as passengers. The wreck of the two vessels and the inability of the distraught revolutionary regime of 1848–1849 in France to interest itself seriously in the Far East brought an end for the time being to active French naval support of missionary operations in eastern Asia.[20]

Official French Policy, 1847–1851

Foreign Minister Guizot made no formal effort to define French policy in China until his appointment of a diplomatic official early in 1847.[21] Baron Forth Rouen, who had previously been secretary of the French legation at Lisbon, was accredited as the first resident diplomatic envoy and chargé d'affaires for China. The establishment of the new legation was undertaken to afford better protection for French nationals and to raise French representation at Canton to the level of the British and American agents. The French action involved the suppression of consulates at Manila and Canton and the creation of a new vice-consulate post of Shanghai.[22]

Forth Rouen's instructions of April 15, 1847, were mostly negative. He was ordered to make no effort to communicate with Peking and also to divorce France from the British effort, currently being pressed on Foreign Minister Palmerston's orders, to gain right of foreign entrance into the city of Canton. In more general terms he was directed to gather commercial data, to enhance the dignity and authority of France, and to consolidate French relations with China, already so happily established, in the interest of cultural exchange between the Far East and the Christian nations of western Europe. Guizot cautioned Forth Rouen, however, not to allow the aggressive spirit of the French missionaries,

[20] FO, 17, 130, from Davis, Sept. 22 and 28, 1847.
[21] AEC, 2, 167. Guizot on April 7, 1847, ordered de Bécour to honor the request of the Superior of the Missions Etrangères to assist in carrying the mail of both the Lazarists and the Jesuits in China.
[22] Dubois, 31; Henri Cordier, "La Première Légation de France en Chine (1847) Documents Inédits," T'oung Pao, 2d ser., VII (1906), 351–364; AEC, 2, 138–141.

77

who were inclined to exceed their treaty privileges, to involve France in difficulties with the Chinese government.[23] Tact would be required because under the imperial edicts the protection of missionary nationals could be accomplished only by the awkward method of reminding the Peking government of its promises. Forth Rouen was therefore ordered to grant full respect to the rights of the imperial government and to give no support either diplomatically or through the action of national vessels to missionary activities in China notoriously contrary to the terms of the treaty. Guizot commented that unfortunately there existed no French law under which French violators of the treaty limitations could be tried, whereas British consuls, by contrast, were empowered to inflict punishments of increasing severity with each repetition of the offense. He added that a French legal code designed to fill this gap was in preparation and would be submitted shortly for the approval of the Chambers.[24]

Guizot's policy of denying the positive protection of his government to those nationals who became involved in difficulties from actions in violation of treaty regulations was never actually applied. The Orleanist monarchy itself fell in February, 1848, shortly after the new officials reached their posts in China (in January, 1848) and before the promised legal code had been completed. At Canton, where local mandarins and gentry opposed British efforts to enter the old city, Forth Rouen maintained correct relations with the Chinese authorities in line with Guizot's instructions. But Vice-Consul Montigny at Shanghai, when left to shift for himself, resorted to procedures and policies of his own devising, which had no relevance to the wishes of Guizot. Paris was far away, and the political leaders of France following the collapse of the July Monarchy in 1848 were concerned with matters of greater moment at home. In fact, the entire French legation in China narrowly escaped being liquidated in 1849 as an economy measure.[25]

[23] The following paragraph of Guizot's instruction was particularly relevant: "The stipulation which compels the surrender to our agents of those French who would have gone outside the [treaty port] limits could excite the hostility of the Chinese government against those agents themselves, if they do not hinder, as far as it is in their power to do so, their nationals from exceeding the privileges which are assured to them" (AEC, 2, 170).

[24] AEC, 2, 170–171; Cordier, "La Première Légation," T'oung Pao, 2d ser., VII (1906), 364–366.

[25] Dorland, 123.

Missionary pressure to obtain governmental assistance in both Annam and China continued despite adverse sentiment at Paris. In late 1847 the Superior of the Seminary of the Missions Etrangères appealed through the Ministry of Marine and with the backing of the papal legate for the application of punitive measures to end the persecution policy of King Thieu-Tri.[26]

A year later a memorial from the two French bishops in Tongking complaining of the anti-Christian policy of King Thieu-Tri's successor, Tu-Duc, reached the authorities of the Seminary in October, 1848. The authors argued that the fleeting appearances of French men-of-war at Tourane had done more harm than good. What was needed was a sustained diplomatic action under the direct authorization of the King of France. They declared that by utilizing the co-operation of a disgruntled minority in Tongking headed by the King's older brother, France could realize liberty of religion as well as national glory and political advantage in a country coveted by others through an action "as glorious in the eyes of men as it was meritorious before God." [27] So discouraging was the political outlook at Paris at the time of the receipt of the memorial in late 1848 that it was not even delivered to the interim government. France at that moment was absorbed in preparations for the election of President Louis Napoleon, who was destined a decade later to play a crucial role in reviving the imperial tradition of France in the Far East.

If Tu-Duc's barbarous anti-Christian edicts of 1848 and 1851 had been systematically enforced, they would have ended all European contact with Annam, both missionary and commercial. The half-mad King destroyed European-made palace furniture and offered a reward for the capture of Christian priests. The missionaries were to be killed and the Annamite priests were to be branded and exiled. The Christian movement in Annam perforce went underground. Entry and operations came to be limited pretty largely to Tongking, whose mandarins could be bribed and whose borders were less well guarded than were the entry points in the south.[28] Persecution was intensified in 1851, follow-

[26] Launay, *Histoire Générale*, III, 218. Monsignor Forçade, the papal representative, prolonged his stay in France in order to support this appeal. He affirmed: "His Holiness would not disapprove rigorous measures which France could employ against the Annamite King."

[27] *Ibid.*, 219–223. The memorial was signed by Pierre André and Charles Hubert, Bishops of Acanthe and of Pentacomie respectively.

[28] Cultru, 49–50; Ennis, 34–35.

ing an abortive Tongking rebellion led by the King's dissatisfied brother in which Christians were accused of being implicated.[29] The youthful Father August Schoeffler (twenty-nine years old) of Nancy was executed on May 1, 1851, and a year later the same fate befell Father Bonnard of Laon.

Such was the discouraging situation in Annam when M. de Bourboulon, the first accredited minister to China under President Louis Napoleon, arrived at Canton in 1851. Early dispatches from Bourboulon contained information, furnished by Abbé Libois, procurator of the Missions Etrangères at Hongkong, that more rigorous persecutions by Tu-Duc were in prospect.[30]

M. de Montigny and the French Concession at Shanghai

The arrival of Vice-Consul de Montigny at Shanghai in January, 1848, initiated a new and unofficial aspect of French policy with respect to missionary operations in China.[31] Montigny was selected by Guizot for the Shanghai post on the basis of an extended report, published in 1846, containing detailed commercial information covering China and Annam, which Montigny had prepared for the Ministry of Agriculture and Commerce following the return of the Lagrené mission to France.[32] Montigny was a tall man of striking appearance, a person of energetic action rather than of calm judgment and deliberation. He was noted particularly for his industry and personal daring as well as for his ardent patriotism and his jealous concern for the enhancement of the honor and prestige of France.[33]

[29] Launay, *Histoire Générale*, III, 266–269. Monsignor Retord, a prisoner of the Viceroy of Tongking, talked himself to freedom in early 1851 by insisting that missionaries had no interest in political affairs.

[30] Cordier, "La Politique Coloniale," *T'oung Pao*, 2d ser., X, 24–25.

[31] Louis Charles . . . de Montigny was born in 1805 of emigré French parents living at Hamburg. He fought in the Greek war during the eighteen twenties, worked at Paris for a time with the Ministry of Marine, and in 1835 or soon thereafter went to Athens as attaché to the embassy of Lagrené. In 1843 he was selected by the Chambers of Commerce of Elboeuf and Mulhouse to accompany Lagrené to China, as chancellor of the mission (Maybon and Fredet, 16–18).

[32] Charles de Montigny, *Manuel du Negociant Français en Chine; ou, Commerce de la Chine Considéré au Point de Vue Française* (Paris, 1846). This is the second part (pp. 185–502) of *Chine et Indo-Chine: Faits Commerciaux* no. 10, published by the Ministère de l'Agriculture et du Commerce.

[33] It will be recalled that Lagrené in 1844 (Chapter IV, n. 16) had been obliged to reprove Montigny for his undue loquaciousness and intimacy with Fathers Guillet

With characteristic independence, Montigny proceeded directly to Shanghai in January, 1848, not bothering to confer at Macao with Baron Forth Rouen, who had preceded him to China. At the time of Montigny's arrival, he was the only French resident at Shanghai, aside from one lone merchant residing in the British Concession.[34] Since the consul had virtually no French commerce to care for, he found an outlet for his abundant energies in other activities. His most remarkable political achievement was the establishment in 1849 of the French Concession in the area lying between the canal adjacent to the native city and the Yang king pang Creek, which marked the southern boundary of the International Settlement.

Montigny immediately refused to live in the British-administered area under the British flag. On the second day after his arrival, he moved into a ruined Chinese house, which he eventually rebuilt, located on Catholic mission property near the native city. It was near the house occupied by the Catholic bishop for the Shanghai area, Father Moresca, the successor to Monsignor Besi. Here Montigny proudly raised the French flag, remarking that although the place was small it was nevertheless France.[35] The house was located in an unattractive locality at the end of a muddy lane leading back from the river. It had to be abandoned for a month or two each spring when the Woosung River was in flood.

Montigny's acquisition of the Concession seems not to have been planned officially or even to have been sought as a deliberate objective. In any case he did not bother to consult Forth Rouen about the matter. It developed out of Montigny's request, first made in August, 1848, and renewed in October, that the taotai of Shanghai allocate a plot of land on the right (south) bank of the Yang king pang Creek to meet the needs of the newly arrived French wine merchant, M. Remi. When the

---

and Durran. According to Charles Meyniard (*Le Second Empire en Indo-Chine* . . . [Paris, 1891], 105–109), Montigny's interests before going to Shanghai were essentially commercial, not religious. Personally inclined toward skepticism, Montigny regarded religious factors as instruments of French political and moral influence. He was also interested in zoological problems.

[34] Maybon and Fredet, 15–16. Eighty-seven of the one hundred foreigners resident at Shanghai in 1847 were British. The French merchant was M. Aroné of Bac, Aroné et Cie.

[35] By these tactics, Montigny avoided the difficulty that U.S. Consul Griswold had encountered when he attempted to raise the American flag in the British concession.

taotai demurred and suggested that Montigny make application instead to the British consul, who was at the time presuming to exercise jurisdiction over the major foreign concession area lying opposite the best river anchorage, Montigny protested violently. He denounced the refusal of his request as a breach of Article 22 of the Whampoa treaty and threatened that the Grand Mandarin of France would carry his demand to Peking if it were not promptly satisfied. The taotai accordingly consented, in January, 1849, to the sale of a portion of the original area requested by Remi. Kleczkowski,[36] Montigny's translator, undertook to draft the formal agreement.

The idea of the separate French Concession germinated during the course of the ensuing negotiations. The agreement granting to the French consul jurisdiction over a considerable area of unoccupied real estate (mostly mud flats) was signed in March, 1849, and was announced on April 16. The decision was confirmed shortly thereafter by the arrival of Forth Rouen in May, 1849, on board the French corvette *Bayonnaise,* commanded by Captain Jurien de la Gravière.[37] Forth Rouen approved the *fait accompli,* but he was nevertheless angry over Montigny's failure to refer so important a matter to him for prior confirmation.

The action of the French consul did not pass without eliciting a protest from his British and American colleagues. But since Montigny's coup duplicated previous British tactics and was accepted by the Canton Viceroy, and since the area involved was not desirable for business purposes, the agreement was permitted to stand.[38]

The commercial development of the French Concession was very

[36] Count Michael Alexandre Kleczkowski was a native of Galicia, born in 1818, and naturalized as a French citizen in 1850. See Swisher, 273.

[37] Maybon and Fredet, 27–38, 408–409; Jurien de la Gravière, *Voyage en Chine . . . pendant les Années 1847–1848–1849–1850* (Paris, 1854), I, 277–278. La Gravière described traversing the muddy lane leading to Montigny's humble retreat, where he encountered an atmosphere at once pious and naïvely gay. He described also an imposing array of twenty sedan chairs, with porters, which Montigny put at the disposal of his visitors.

[38] Tyler Dennett, *Americans in Eastern Asia* (New York, 1922), 194–202; SD, China, DD, 15 from J. W. Davis, May 21, 1949. The American representative argued that U.S. nationals should be able to obtain land which they required at Shanghai directly from the Chinese without reference either to the British or the French consuls. On this ground he had challenged the exclusive use of the British flag in 1848. U.S. Consul Griswold also claimed that the area obtained by Montigny had previously been offered to him by the Chinese.

slow, and it continued for a number of years to be economically unimportant. In late 1850 the French colony contained only ten persons, five of them being members of Montigny's family. Montigny himself made one abortive attempt to develop a trade in French cloth on the basis of several thousand samples which he acquired through the aid of missionary friends. The project aroused no local interest and was later vetoed by Forth Rouen. When the arrangement for the collection of customs revenue at Shanghai by the Europeans was entered into in August, 1851, the French area could be ignored as commercially unimportant. At the end of 1853, the French Concession included a cathedral, newly constructed and in operation, as well as a collegiate building and a residence for those connected with the Catholic propagandist agencies.[39] The motivation behind Montigny's achievement had little to do with economic considerations.

Montigny and the Protection of Catholic Missionary Operations

The pattern of Protestant missionary operations around Shanghai contrasted sharply with the bold penetration of the interior by the Catholic missionaries. The former lived with their families at the treaty ports and only occasionally made journeys into the interior. British consular officials were instructed, furthermore, to curb the tendency of missionaries to wander outside the treaty ports not only by suasion but also by the assessment of penalties under the consular court code. No exception was made in favor of missionaries in dealing with wandering Englishmen whom the Chinese might apprehend and surrender to consular custody. The adverse economic and political results which might attend such expressions of "injudicious zeal" on the part of British missionaries outweighed in London's view any religious imperative.[40]

Official British policy became somewhat less insistent after the Reverend Medhurst, the interpreter for the Shanghai consulate, ventured into the interior during the summer of 1845. The trip was undertaken against the wishes of the consul, but Medhurst found that he was not

[39] Maybon and Fredet, 39–40, 42–43. W. C. Milne, *Life in China* (London, 1857), 472–494.

[40] FO, 17, 99, May 28, 1845, Davis to Col. Balfour at Shanghai; 96, from Aberdeen, Oct. 10, 1845. Aberdeen wrote: "It is in vain that we may expect to reap the full advantages which we have obtained by our treaties with China unless not only the government but the individual subjects of Great Britain scrupulously adhere . . . to the stipulations of those treaties."

molested by Chinese officials. The Chinese intendant at the port, although fully informed concerning Medhurst's journey, connived at the affair and reported to his superior, quite incorrectly, that the Englishman had gone to Chusan Island only.[41] Trouble did arise in 1848, however, when three English missionaries were attacked by a mob near Shanghai. On that occasion Consul Alcock demanded redress and went so far as to hold up the departure of several hundred junks laden with tribute rice in order to obtain it. The situation caused a mild panic among both Chinese and foreign traders, who feared that war might ensue.[42] Palmerston applauded Alcock's action but cautioned against any repetition of the incident, partly because revolutionary explosions in Europe during 1848 made war out of the question.[43] British policy favored pressure for increased commercial access to the interior, but Palmerston opposed provocative action either by merchants or missionaries at the risk of impairing British prestige and the legal trade at the treaty ports. American consuls generally followed the same policy, and all had reason to be concerned about worsening relations between foreigners and the Chinese population.[44]

Montigny's methods came close to being the reverse of those of the British and American consuls. He had no reason to restrain Catholic missionaries from entering the interior because France had no commercial interests to jeopardize. No doubt the missionaries would have defied any attempted restraints in any case. Instead, Montigny developed a pattern of active personal intervention with local mandarins extending over a wide radius around Shanghai in behalf of both native Christians and Catholic missionaries. He was convinced that by such

[41] FO, 17, 100, from Davis, July 25, 1945; also Aberdeen's instructions, Nov. 4, 1845.

[42] SD, China DD, Parker no. 40 and 41, Jan. 25 and 27, 1848.

[43] Alexander Michie, *The Englishman in China . . . Sir Rutherford Alcock* (Edinburgh, 1900), I, 129–134; H. B. Morse, *The International Relations of the Chinese Empire* (London, 1910), I, 392–398.

[44] FO, 17, 139, from Palmerston, Oct. 18, 31, and Dec. 19, 1848; 152, Nov. 2, 1849. Davis and the American Forbes at Canton complained that foreign merchants paid no attention to Chinese laws and were difficult to control. Forbes wrote as follows: "As there is no adequate provision for the collection of debts due by Americans, contracts may be broken with impunity and the Chinese, unprotected by, or afraid to apply to their own [greedy] officers, submit to injustice without a murmur" (SD, Canton, CL 3, no. 38, Dec. 1, 1845; En-sai Tai, *Treaty Ports in China* [New York, 1918], 35).

84

tactics he could enhance not only his personal prestige but also the long-run political and commercial interests of France.[45] Whenever news of difficulty came to his attention, Montigny mounted his junk or his sedan chair and hurried to the spot, traveling night and day. In a personal confrontation of the local mandarin he obtained sometimes by argument, sometimes by intimidation, satisfaction for the offense and a promise that in the future Christians resident in that district would not suffer annoyance.[46] His repeated overland trips to Ningpo, where he also claimed consular jurisdiction, were made after prior announcement of intention to the Chinese officials en route and invariably without challenge.

Montigny was particularly solicitous for the welfare of the French Jesuit establishments in the Shanghai area. His relations with non-French missionaries, such as Monsignor Maresca and his coadjutor, Monsignor Spelta, at Shanghai, who did not share Montigny's patriotic sentiments, were by comparison co-operative and correct rather than intimate and cordial.[47] Montigny's enormous popularity within missionary circles was not echoed by Forth Rouen and his French diplomatic successors at the Canton legation. The Shanghai consul operated independently under his own patriotic mandate and invariably justified his methods on the basis of his own estimate of the results obtained. He was convinced that French missionaries in China would in the future serve the interests of France both politically and commercially, and he boasted of his own achievement in acquiring a unique position of prestige among the mandarins in the vicinity of Shanghai. His religious sentiments seem to have been distinctly subordinate to his patriotic enthusiasm to enhance the prestige and honor of France.[48]

---

[45] Meyniard, in describing the work of Montigny (105–108) comments: "The missionaries became in his hands as much the docile and devoted instruments of French policy as [they were] . . . agents to inculcate . . . love for France throughout a numerous Catholic clientele." The author estimated that Montigny's protective influence extended for 200 to 300 leagues around Shanghai and over some 70,000 native Christians.

[46] Marquis de Moges, *Recollections of Baron Gros's Embassy to China and Japan in 1857–58* (London, 1860), 195–196.

[47] Broullion, 226–228; Joseph de la Servière, *Histoire de la Mission du Kiangnan* (Shanghai, 1914), II, 167–168.

[48] La Servière, I, 168–169. In reply to Forth Rouen's protests, Montigny replied that the missionaries would contribute much to the role of France when "soon or late, the Occident will intervene seriously in the affairs of China."

Several examples of Montigny's exploits can be cited by way of illustration. He played a heroic role during the Woosung floods of May and June, 1849. Later in the same year, when famine developed, he cowed a band of brigands who were threatening to plunder the Jesuit school of Zikawei by his sheer personal daring and bravado, bearding the brigand leader in his very headquarters. On this and other occasions when police protection was unavailable during the troubled times of the Taiping rebellion, he repeatedly assumed responsibility for the protection of French citizens and native Christians. On one occasion at Ningpo, Montigny and his interpreter held off a mob for two hours until officials arrived. He allegedly terrorized local Chinese officials with his burning ardor, a capacity demonstrated so convincingly later by the leaders of the Ever Victorious army.[49] Other feats included the rescue of some twenty shipwrecked French seamen of the whaler *Narwal* off the Korean coast, in April and May, 1851. Although his zeal repeatedly attracted the criticism of his immediate diplomatic superiors and involved him in numerous unauthorized expenditures, he escaped censure because of religious support at Paris. His success in establishing French prestige around Shanghai was directly attributable to these very qualities of independence, intransigence, and lack of regard for conventional diplomacy.[50]

When the new regime of the Prince-President Louis Napoleon eventually got around to formulating a considered policy for the Far East, Montigny's performance at Shanghai was one of the few shining examples of the enhancement of French prestige in that part of the world.[51]

[49] This situation will be clarified in Chapter VII.

[50] Maybon and Fredet, 20–23, 405; La Servière, I, 168–170. For a full account of the rescue off Korea see *Chinese Repository*, XX (1851), 500–506. One sympathetic observer described Montigny as follows: "He was of tall stature, of haughty appearance, of exceptional vigor, and of very irascible temperament. . . . He was convinced that God had created him for struggle and for conquest. . . . He believed himself possessed of the gift of charming by his glance both men and animals. In reality his eyes, hard and piercing, were not exactly in accord, and when anger inflamed them, which was frequently, their divergence produced an impression almost terrifying. A man endowed with such temperament and such a character was not made to follow the advice of prudence" (Marie-René Roussel de Courcy, *Souvenirs* [Paris, 1900], II, 175–176).

[51] Baron Forth Rouen was succeeded by a new chargé named Codrika in late 1850, but no formal policy was delineated until France's first minister, M. de Bourboulon, was sent to China in 1851. See AEC, 11, 153–167, 211.

VII

French Policy under
Louis Napoleon, 1848-1853

I
T WAS more than four years after the revolutionary upheavals of
1848 in Europe before France was able to resume an aggressive
posture in the Far East. Within France, the republican system, improvised in 1848 to replace the monarchy, was betrayed after three
years by the Napoleonic adventurer who became the first President.
Until 1852 the country lacked the political stability requisite to any forward policy overseas. Religious interests were directly involved in the
forming of such a policy because Louis Napoleon's assiduous courting
of Catholic support was an important aspect of his preparation for the
successful *coup d'état* of December 2, 1851. Once he was firmly established in control, clerical support rendered the Prince-President vulnerable to clerical pressure in behalf of the protection of missionary interests in the Far East. The other principal ingredient of Bonapartism,
its commitment to the re-establishment of nationalist prestige and empire as a condition of the survival of the dynasty, also contributed to the
inevitable emergence of an imperialist adventure in the Orient. But
numerous events intervened, so that these developments required some
time to take place.

A New Context for French Policy

Louis Napoleon's policy in the Far East had first of all to be fitted
into the context of altered European relationships. France after 1848

enjoyed considerably more freedom of movement internationally than it had under the preceding regime because the cohesion of conservative Europe under the Metternich system disappeared in the smoke of the multiple revolutions which convulsed central Europe. France no longer faced the concerted opposition of reactionary Europe to its every move on the continent. Prussia and Austria became rivals for the leadership of Germany. Hapsburg influence in Italy was so weakened that Vienna could not crush the constitutional regime in Sardinia-Piedmont and did not dare challenge the French action taken at Rome in 1849 to restore the temporal rule of the Pope. Differences between Russia and the Hapsburg empire about the future of the Balkans, which eventually came to the surface during the Crimean War, constituted another rift in the conservative ranks.

The foreign policy of postrevolutionary France was still largely dependent on British acquiescence, especially in French overseas ventures distant from Europe, but Paris no longer had to pay the same almost abject deference to London that had been required of the Orleanist regime. During the first decade of Louis Napoleon's rule, he managed to keep French foreign policy synchronized with that of Britain, notably in central Italy, in the Crimean War, and in the war in China. It was after he decided to cut adrift from London in 1859 that he ran into the disastrous difficulties and compromises which finally wrecked his regime.

Louis Napoleon and the Clerical Party in France

Among the domestic factors which had a bearing on French policy in the Far East, none was more directly relevant than the urgency with which the President courted the support of the party of religion in France.

The zeal with which the liberal Catholic leadership in France, acting from its inveterate opposition to Orleanist rule, hailed the principles of republicanism and social reform expressed at the outset of the revolution of 1848 earned for the church a position of considerable political influence in the early stages of the provisional regime. Pulpits all over France rang in favor of the revolution. The cause of Christian socialism was acclaimed by a new religious periodical, the *Ere Nouvelle*, of which Lacordaire, Ozanam, Abbé Muret, and Bishop Dupanloup became the

88

editors. Even the conservative *Univers* for a brief time championed the right of laborers to associate together.[1]

Clerical liberalism began to fade during the course of the elections of April, 1848, to the Constitutional Assembly. Active participation of Montalembert's Parti Catholique was responsible for the widespread participation of rural voters in support of selected lists of delegates dedicated to the principles of religion, liberty (of education), family, and property. Few provincial candidates whom the church opposed were elected. Clerical liberalism declined sharply, however, in the frightened stampede to conservatism which followed the subsequent disorders of May and June.[2] At the end of 1848 the liberal minority within the Catholic party, which still favored social reform as an antidote for popular unrest, was denounced as an accomplice of the enemies of religion. The original editors of *Ere Nouvelle* were all forced to resign their posts in April, 1849. By the end of 1849, the church was committed to the cause of political and social reaction.[3]

Both of the leading candidates for the presidency in the elections of December 10, 1848, General Cavaignac and Louis Napoleon, bid for the support of the Catholic party. Cavaignac's gesture miscarried when his belated decision to dispatch troops to Rome to protect the person of the pope had to be canceled following receipt of the news that Pius IX had already fled to Gaeta. Among the clergy only the editors of *Ere Nouvelle* and its limited liberal readership gave active support to Cavaignac.[4]

Louis Napoleon was much freer with his promises to the clergy than was Cavaignac. To satisfy demands presented by Montalembert, Louis issued a manifesto on November 27, 1848, acclaiming religion, family, and property as the basis of society and pledging his support from free-

[1] Ross William Collins, *Catholicism and the Second French Republic, 1848–1852* (New York, 1923), 45–58, 79–99.

[2] The Comte de Falloux of the Catholic party was chairman of the Assembly's commission of inquiry which reported adversely on the national workshops (C. S. Phillips, *The Church in France, 1789–1848* [London, 1929], 22–30).

[3] Collins, 111–135. The *Univers*, in February, 1849, declared that the proper adjustments to conditions of poverty were abstemious living, acceptance of one's lot, and refuge in the solace of religion; society's needs dictated that some must work much and live little. Frightened liberals like Adolphe Thiers as well as the clericals joined the party of "order."

[4] Collins, 153–170.

89

dom of worship and liberty of instruction and for the restoration of papal authority at Rome. He promised Montalembert that, if elected, he would make Falloux his Minister of Public Instruction. He also repented of ever having opposed the Holy See and flatly denied having been a *Carbonaro*. The liberal Catholics were too wary to credit Napoleon's promises, but the candidate's representations went far to neutralize the distrust of the more conservative readers of the *Univers* and the *Ami de la Religion*.[5] As a result, Louis got his share of the religious vote, although religion was not the determining factor in the outcome of the presidential election of 1848. The Catholic forces were not unified in their support of any candidate, and the issues of Bonapartist nationalism and order were far more potent factors.

After his election triumph, Louis Napoleon moved to bind the church closely to his cause. The reluctant Falloux was persuaded to join the new ministry when the President threatened to turn to the Left and then enlisted clerical pressure to overcome Falloux's hesitance. Falloux was subsequently accorded wide influence in fashioning the new education bill, which was finally passed in March, 1850. In the French military action in 1849 to restore Pius IX to the control of the papal state, Louis Napoleon acted primarily to check Austrian influence in Italy. In the end, the French President accepted the restoration of Pius IX on the pontiff's own terms. He suppressed his own sympathies for Italian nationalist ideals and moderate reform proposals in order to keep from alienating Catholic political leaders like Falloux and Montalembert, who objected strenuously to coercing the Pope.

It became one of the new ruler's cardinal political principles, successfully maintained until the fateful French invasion of Italy in 1859, to make whatever concessions were required to keep on friendly terms with the French clergy. During the three years of the Republic, the bishops of the French church reciprocated the flattery accorded them by Louis Napoleon and hailed him enthusiastically as the benefactor of religion and the bulwark of social order.[6] This policy gained support for the government and also ensured against the development within the church of any legitimist monarchial leanings.

Clerical backing was an important element in obtaining popular acquiescence in Napoleon's *coup d'état* of December, 1851. The action

[5] *Ibid.*, 171–186; Phillips, *1789–1848*, 30–31.
[6] Collins, 187–194, 205–259, 292–317.

was strongly defended by conservative Catholic political elements as necessary to save France from the disaster and chaos of a socialist republic. Napoleon's twelve-to-one victory in the plebiscite vote (7,100,-000 to less than 600,000), which extended the President's term for ten years, was partly attributable to clerical exhortation of the faithful to vote affirmatively. The Bishop of Poitiers declared that a negative vote favored those who would burn the churches and assassinate priests. Pius IX himself also backed Louis Napoleon's cause in the plebiscite. French Catholic churches celebrated the victory with Te Deums, and the vast majority of the bishops gave prompt adhesion to the new order.

Liberal Catholics, on the other hand, were not enthusiastic; a few like Lacordaire saw in the overthrow of the constitution a public calamity. Second thoughts were still more in evidence at the time of the second coup d'état of December, 1852. Bishop Dupanloup, Falloux, and Montalembert himself joined with the former editors of the Ere Nouvelle in deploring the loss of popular esteem involved in the sacrifice of liberty and the chaining of religion to the idol of despotism. But the liberal elements of the clergy lacked organization and unity, so that they acted timorously and ineffectively as individual dissenters only. On the other hand, the ultra-Catholic following of the Univers, which seemed bent on proving the socialist allegation that liberalism and Catholicism were incompatible, was a powerful and closely knit group.[7] Thus clerical reaction and political opportunism temporarily joined hands.

But since the new Emperor was more dependent on the church than it was on him, the price which he paid for clerical support became steadily more burdensome, a kind of "dragging chain . . . endowed with the live quality of some great tropical creeper." The honeymoon was beginning to wane by the end of 1853, and the rift slowly widened until the divorce of 1859.[8] The Empress Eugénie, however, was always susceptible to clerical influence.

Louis Napoleon was eventually caught in the dilemma of an Italian

[7] Ibid., 313–337. Antonin Debidour, in his Histoire des Rapports de l'Eglise et de l'Etat en France de 1789 à 1870 (Paris, 1898), 524–525, commented on the perfect accord prevailing during the 1850's between the church and the new Emperor: "The church had not seen in France a government more desirous of pleasing it. If the soverign pontiff blessed Napoleon III, if the bishops flattered him, if the vicars vied in glorifying his sacred person, it was only right."

[8] C. S. Phillips, The Church in France, 1848–1907 (New York and London, 1936), 41–57.

policy in which his personal sympathy for Italian nationalism canceled out the policy of supporting the papacy as a means of retaining Catholic backing in France. Cavour challenged Austria at the Congress of Paris in 1856; his meeting with Louis Napoleon at Plombières came in July, 1858; Napoleon's intervention in the war between Sardinia and Austria followed in May, 1859. Thereafter events passed from his control. The Italian war turned all French Catholics, except, interestingly enough, a few with liberal convictions, against the Emperor. He felt obliged to suppress the *Univers* in January, 1860, for publishing a papal encyclical praising the role of the French clergy in resisting Napoleon's policies.[9]

The bearing of these European political developments on French policy in the Far East derived from the important fact that the only tangible French activity and interest in the area was the Catholic missionary program. The new regime, furthermore, was inclined to accede to pressure to do something for the missionaries largely because support of Catholic interests in the Orient would afford a convenient pretext for military action designed to enhance the national glory and the prestige of the dynasty. The French entente with Britain, which found tangible expression first in the Crimean War (1854–1856) and then in the war with China of 1858–1860, eventually afforded Napoleon III an opportunity to transport a considerable armed force to the Far East under cover of co-operation with England. Thus both the Manchus and King Tu-Duc of Annam became the targets of French aggression.[10] It is with the delineation of imperialist French policy in the Far East to early 1853 that the remainder of this chapter is concerned.

Decline and Revival of French Interest in the Far East

The principal effect of the European upheaval of 1848–1849 upon the international situation in the Far East was to relax tension between the British and the Chinese over the Canton entry question. In the face of the uncertainties of the European situation, Lord Palmerston reversed the aggressive trend which he had given to British policy since 1847, concluding that access to Canton was not of sufficient intrinsic impor-

[9] *Ibid.*, 330, 337–343.

[10] The pattern of French action in Annam in 1859 was in many respects similar to that tried in Mexico in the 1860's, combining imperialistic ends with support of church interests. The actions began in both instances in co-operation with Britain and Spain.

92

tance to fight over. The victory achieved by the Cantonese officials in this incident afforded opportunity for conservative interests at the Peking court to reassert themselves. This trend synchronized with Peking's degradation of Ch'i-ying and other champions of appeasement,[11] following the death of the Tao-Kuang Emperor in February, 1850. Anglo-Chinese tension was bound to revive as soon as European affairs again permitted Britain freedom of action. But by the time European affairs were stabilized in early 1852, Palmerston was replaced in the Foreign Office by the more cautious Earl of Granville and by Malmesbury.[12]

During the early years of the Second Republic, French interest in the Far East declined sharply. The suppression of the entire legation establishment in China, as an economy measure, was narrowly averted in 1849, and only because of strenuous protests by post officials and missionary agencies that all previous gains would thereby be sacrificed. Vice-Consul Montigny's request for aid in obtaining permission for missionary access to the interior of China was rebuffed by the French Minister of Foreign Affairs in 1849, on the ground that Catholic missionaries already enjoyed competitive advantage over the less daring Protestant groups by virtue of established tactics and that the question of where and how to intervene to realize Montigny's ends was a grave and difficult question.[13]

Pressure on Paris for aid to missions in the Far East increased during 1850 and 1851. After an abortive correspondence with the imperial commissioner early in 1851 about protection of Christians, Chargé Codrika at Canton submitted for consideration by Paris a long memorial prepared by Bishop Mouly of Hopeh Province asking French aid for the

---

[11] FO, 17, 139, instructions of Oct. 7 and Dec. 30, 1848. Ch'i-ying was recalled to the capital in early 1848, when Peking decided to make a stand on the Canton-entry question. For two years until Emperor Tao Kuang's death he served as President of the Board of War and as Minister of the Inner Council. He was degraded by an imperial decree of Dec. 1, 1850 (Morse, I, 337, 442).

[12] Palmerston on July 5 and Sept. 3, 1850 (FO, 17, 164) authorized diplomatic pressure at Peking (if possible without naval pressure, as Bonham proposed) to obtain commercial access up the Yangtse river. Malmesbury, in June 21, 1852, sent explicit instructions to Consul John Bowring at Hongkong (FO, 17, 186), who had reached his post in 1849 just in time to catch the full brunt of Chinese intransigence (FO, 17, 152, Aug. 18, 1849), to avoid all irritating discussions with the Chinese over entry to Canton, the reception of an embassy to Peking, or even a request to visit the various ports of China.

[13] Dorland, 123–124.

protection of missionaries and for the restoration of ancient church properties.[14] A Catholic missionary assembly held at Ningpo in September, 1851, petitioned the French Foreign Minister for similar ends, and another assembly at Shanghai later in the same year asked the Pope to assign to France the task of protecting Catholic missionaries in China.[15] Paris also received from both its China legation and the Seminary of the Missions Etrangères protests concerning persecutions inflicted under Tu-Duc's anti-Christian decrees of 1851, accompanied by a request for diplomatic pressure to oblige the Annamite King to surrender arrested missionaries to the French consul at Macao.[16] It was at this juncture (October, 1851) that M. de Bourboulon, the first regularly accredited diplomatic official of the new French regime, arrived in China.

Minister Bourboulon's Early Difficulties

Bourboulon and his entourage themselves symbolized the confusion of counsels which characterized the Second French Republic. The newly appointed minister was a Knight of the Legion of Honor and a career diplomat with previous experience in Buenos Aires and Washington. He professed to be a follower of the philosophers and an atheist and boasted of his socialist convictions as a disciple of Fourier. Bourboulon was very small in stature, personally ugly, and reserved in temperament. His gracious and affable American-born wife, a good foot taller than he, dominated her adoring husband and tolerated his radical notions without sharing them. Roussel de Courcy, a young man half Bourboulon's age who had patriotic and pro-Catholic leanings and who joined the legation in April, 1852, was much disturbed over the unorthodoxy of his chief and hardly knew what to make of the Bourboulons. The minister, for example, questioned sharply the accuracy of Courcy's estimate of the Napoleonic *coup d'état* of 1851 as constituting the rebirth of the French state and the means of its salvation from the dire perils endured since 1848. Courcy commented, "I would not try to say how absurd and shocking the opinions and attitude of the Minister of France appear to me, charged as he is before everything to defend

---

[14] AEC, 11, 153–159, 160–161, from Macao, May 18, 1851.

[15] Thomas, II, 325.

[16] AEC, 11, 211, from Codrika, July 18, 1851; Launay, *Histoire Générale*, III, 278–279.

Catholic interests in China."[17] Needless to say, Bourboulon's temperament and religious views also had little in common with those of Montigny, and virtually nothing with those of Father Libois of the Missions Etrangères and the other missionaries.

The initial sketchy instructions which Paris prepared for the new minister indicated that the government was not ready at the time of his departure to make any commitment in the Far East. Both he and Codrika before him were under orders to demand strict observance of treaty regulations as to Christian interests, but they were also to urge the missionaries not to incur unnecessary dangers.[18] Formal instructions prepared after Bourboulon reached Macao ran in part as follows:

Our policy in China does not seek . . . to obtain temporary and precarious advantages by violence or menace or by intimidating this or that Manchu authority; our goals are higher. It is by her very moderation that France wishes to establish her influence; it is in respecting the laws, the usages, the prejudices of the country, up to a certain point, that we will obtain unconsciously the confidence of the indigenes and the national authorities. . . . Our respected priests ought to observe extreme circumspection and . . . manage their resources so that . . . they do not have too frequent recourse to our intervention and support.

The instructions also paid tribute to Consul Montigny's achievements but charged Bourboulon not to emulate the consul's "imprudent zeal."[19]

Bourboulon attempted to apply the spirit of his instructions to the first serious question with which he was obliged to deal. It concerned the death of a French priest, Father Vachal, which occurred while he was being held in prison in Yunnan Province during the summer of 1851. Bourboulon lodged a vigorous protest and affirmed the concern of France for the safety of the missionaries. But he stopped short of threatening a rupture of relations and in other ways took care to save the face of the Chinese authorities. Although the incident concerned the most important clause of the French treaty (Article 23) and the victim had apparently suffered physical violence, the minister elected to distinguish

[17] Henri Cordier, *L'Expédition de Chine de 1857–58* (Paris, 1905), 129–130; Courcy, *Souvenirs*, II, 101–103, 126–129.

[18] AEC, 11, 295, Oct. 24, 1851. Apparently Bourboulon was given no fresh instructions when he left France.

[19] AEC, 11, 340–342, instructions dated Dec. 24, 1851.

between what France claimed as a right by virtue of the treaty and what it sought to obtain from considerations of justice and good will. Along with his protest, Bourboulon transmitted a copy of a memorial defending the Catholic religion which had been prepared by the bishops' assembly at Shanghai.[20] The Frenchman's politeness got him nowhere and only cut the ground from under any later renewal of protests. The affair was firmly deadlocked in the spring of 1852, when Courcy arrived in China.[21]

Needless to say, Bourboulon's inept handling of the Vachal affair did not contribute to his popularity among the missionaries or to his prestige at Paris. Courcy, who was perturbed that interests so sacred as the missionary cause should have fallen to the care of one so unsympathetic as Bourboulon, set himself the task of preparing, with the help of Monsignor Libois, a historical resumé of the work of the missionaries from earliest times for the enlightenment of both Bourboulon the French Foreign Minister. Bourboulon consented to the project, but he did not share Courcy's enthusiasm for missionary heroism or his fascinating idea that France and China were destined to be united in a cultural affinity through the diffusion of Christianity.[22]

The Vachal affair occurred contemporaneously with a triumph of Montigny's characteristic methods in an episode on Chusan Island. Trouble arose on Chusan early in 1852 as a result of the forcible expropriation by Chinese priests, backed by Father Dannicourt, of several pagoda grounds, which they intended for use as Christian chapels. The action was contrary to the wishes of the local authorities and to the non-Christian inhabitants, for it involved the demolition of a tomb and the replacement of traditional Chinese figures by Christian images and the cross. When Bishop Dannicourt resisted the efforts of the authorities to reclaim the pagodas, a tense situation developed, and Consul de Montigny with customary zeal rushed to the rescue. At considerable expense and as the result of his sustained efforts on the spot, Montigny arranged a settlement. He and his translator finally reduced the terms to a formal convention consisting of eleven articles, which were signed by Montigny and by the local mandarins. This remarkably irregular document included explicit pledges by the mandarins to protect Christians against extortion, insult, and false accusation. Not only did Montigny neglect to

[20] AEC, 12, 6–10, from Bourboulon, Jan. 20, 1852.
[21] Courcy, *Souvenirs*, II, 170–174.   [22] *Ibid.*, 137–139, 161–162.

96

obtain M. Bourboulon's approval of his presumptuous undertaking, but he reported on it directly to the Foreign Minister at Paris, boasting of his personal triumph.

Bourboulon was exceedingly annoyed and also embarrassed. He informed Paris that Bishop Dannicourt had acted imprudently and that the misconduct of local Chinese Christians had apparently provoked the hostile reactions. He reprimanded Montigny roundly for his presumption and independence. But in the end, the minister had no alternative to repaying Montigny for his financial expenditures and reporting the affair to Paris as a *fait accompli*. Montigny's success disarmed all criticism, and it contrasted sharply with Bourboulon's own ineffective handling of the Vachal affair. According to Courcy, only the accession of Drouyn de Lhuys, an intimate friend of the Bourboulon family, to the post of French Foreign Minister in July, 1852, as successor to Marquis Turgot, saved M. Bourboulon from being recalled because of the incident.[23] The meaning of the episode was not lost on Bourboulon. Thereafter he did not hesitate to ignore his initial instructions and to give more sympathetic attention to the needs of the missionaries.

Development of an Aggressive French Policy

In mid-1852 eight Catholic bishops resident in the Far East addressed a concerted appeal for increased French protection directly to the Prince-President. Their note attributed the renewal of persecution in China to the impression spread abroad by the enemies of France that China no longer had anything to fear from a country torn as was France by internal dissensions. This false idea of French weakness, they insisted, could not be dispelled by peaceful conciliatory tactics. The honor of France as well as the interests of missions required that the persecutions throughout the Far East be stopped. What was needed was the sending of a prudent, energetic naval captain like Rigault de Genouilly with three or four war vessels under his command for the purpose of re-establishing French prestige. The memorialists cited, in support of their appeal, the Emperor Napoleon's decree of 2 Germinal an XIII (1805) re-establishing the Seminary of the Mission Etrangères. They

[23] AEC, 12, 33, 79–88, 101, 172–175, dispatches dated Feb. 6, March 6, March 26, and June 16, 1852; Courcy, *Souvenirs*, II, 176–181, 223–226. Cordier reported (Henri Cordier, *Histoire des Relations de la Chine avec les Puissances Occidentales, 1860–1900* [Paris, 1901–1902], I, 48) that Bourboulon's recall was actually agreed upon in April, 1852, but was rescinded later in the year.

affirmed that "the Catholic influence in the Far East is and will always be there the measure of French influence" and that "in protecting our missions, the Prince-President will march in the steps of the Emperor." [24]

Bourboulon's change of tactics was signalized in a long dispatch of August 21, 1852, which Monsignor Libois had assisted in preparing. The dispatch set forth the disturbing information that Monsignor Bonnard had been executed at Hué in May, 1852, just a year after the similarly tragic death of Father Schoeffler. Neither of the victims, it was alleged, had been accused of committing any crime. The minister commented as follows:

I know that [missionaries] act at their own risk and peril, [and] that France is not obliged to their care; they do not even demand it. But they are nonetheless French and from the political as well as the humanitarian point of view, France shares in fact the responsibility for injuries committed against its subjects. . . . Civilized nations . . . would applaud unanimously a vigorous act undertaken in the interests of all humanity. [France] has a powerful military marine, which costs almost as much unoccupied as active. . . . Does not the sending of war vessels for mere hydrographic work only advertise by their useless presence the impotence [of France] . . . to avenge the shedding of French blood by wretched and insolent barbarians? . . . How can we hope to support ideas of religious toleration and require, at the least, the strict observance of Article 23 of the treaty, when [China] sees at the two extremities of the empire [the unpunished conduct] of two petty sovereigns, [China's] vassals and nominally, at least, its tributaries, the kings of Cochin-China and Korea? Is it not to be feared that seeing these criminal attempts remain unpunished, the Chinese government will ere long follow the example of its vassals? [25]

A month later Bourboulon sent to Paris a much longer analysis of French relations with the Far East in the preparation of which he again had the assistance of Father Libois. It traced the entire history of French connections with missionary persecution in both Korea and Annam. In a coded portion of the dispatch, Bourboulon suggested that it would not be difficult to put an end to such outrages and insults to French nationality and at the same time to re-establish French commercial and political influence in an area of the world where she once

[24] Cordier, "La Politique Coloniale," *T'oung Pao*, 2d ser., X, 28–30.
[25] AEC, 12, 236–240, from Bourboulon, Aug. 21, 1852; also found in abbreviated form in Cordier, "La Politique Coloniale," *T'oung Pao*, 2d ser., X, 26–27.

held first rank. He surmised that the guilty rulers of Annam themselves expected some day to see the power of France deployed on their shores as punishment for persecutions they had inflicted. Missionary reports from Annam, which Bourboulon admitted might be influenced to some extent by the desire for intervention, indicated that the harbor defenses of Tourane could be easily leveled. Such a blow dealt in isolation, thought Bourboulon, need not necessarily place France in a state of war with the Cochin-China government.[26]

Bourboulon proposed specifically that French intervention take the form of a peaceful negotiation in which the plenipotentiary (Bourboulon volunteered for the assignment) should demand three concessions: (a) religious tolerance in favor of Christian subjects, or at least complete security for French and Spanish missionaries; (b) a treaty which would establish relations of friendship and commerce between the two countries on a new liberal and equitable basis; (c) as guarantee for the execution of the treaty and as reparation due France for the blood of missionaries shed over thirty years, Annam should cede in perpetuity the port of Tourane with adjacent territory, as indicated in the 1787 treaty, or another point offering a similarly useful military position. If Tourane were the point ceded, it could take the place of the indemnity. In the event of a hostile reception or a refusal to accept reasonable conditions, the accompanying French naval force should take possession forcibly of Tourane and the territory adjacent to it. Two frigates accompanied by two steamers and several other light craft would be more than sufficient, according to Bourboulon, to accomplish that objective.[27]

Paris' reaction to Bourboulon's proposal was immediate and affirmative. The newly established use of steamers to facilitate mail transmission via Suez made for prompt communication. In successive instructions of October and November, 1852, the French Foreign Office asked

[26] A communication prepared by Monsignor Forçade and Monsignor Retord, both of Tongking, was included as an enclosure. It contained information emphasizing the necessity of occupying permanently an Annamite port or an island and the measures to be employed to achieve that end.

[27] AEC, 12, 256–279, from Bourboulon, Sept. 23, 1852. Monsignor Forçade's enclosure indicated that although missionaries trusted in God more than in men, they would be proud to have the arm of France, preferably to that of any other, serve them in obtaining better days. In a subsequent brief dispatch of Dec. 26, 1852 (AEC, 12, 309–310), Bourboulon indicated that Admiral Laguerre could undertake the proposed mission to Tourane, but he needed an imposing force for the task.

99

Bourboulon to transmit all possible additional information concerning the military forces required and the results which could be expected from a successful operation. The government indicated its particular interest in "the necessity of establishing with Cochin-China and with Korea such normal relations as would restore our national dignity and the interest of our missions." [28]

Evidence available in the French Foreign Office archives for late 1852 and early 1853 indicates that the entire scope of French Far Eastern policy was under review. A memorandum dated February 10, 1853, from the Minister of Marine, agreed that the information under examination (not identified) demonstrated that with respect to both native Christians and missionaries, France occupied a doubly false position in China which called for correction to one more befitting the dignity of France. If the Foreign Minister would propose the measures required for attaining that end, he could rest assured that the Department of Marine would co-operate loyally and energetically, whether the action called for naval demonstrations in Korea and Cochin-China or for threatening China in order to obtain justice at Peking.[29]

The Foreign Office proposal apparently centered on Annam. A French mission to Hué would demand satisfaction for the murders of Schoeffler and Bonnard and concessions similar to those granted by China with respect to humane treatment of missionaries, as well as the cancellation of Tu-Duc's edicts of persecution.[30] A Foreign Office memorandum dated February, 1853, favoring acquisition of a port in Cochin-China ran in part as follows:

In time of peace, [the post] would be a center of sojourn and of succor for our ships of commerce and an entrepot of great importance for the riches and the population of surrounding countries. In time of war it would be a strategic point admirably chosen for its position in the center of rich commercial traffic; it would replace very advantageously our miserable remnants of Indian colonies, the uselessness of which is so notorious and the position so false that they serve only to . . . perpetuate the memory of our decadence in those seas. Finally, the dignity of France is involved.[31]

[28] AEC, 12, 300, Nov. 24, 1852; Cordier, "La Politique Coloniale," T'oung Pao, 2d ser., X, 27–28.
[29] AEC, 13, 75.
[30] Cordier, "La Politique Coloniale," T'oung Pao, 2d ser., X, 33. Cordier's statement that this policy was decided upon as early as December, 1852, is not, however, corroborated by the archives at the Quai d'Orsay.
[31] AEC, 13, 57. Signed by E. Mouchez, February, 1853.

Just how far the plans of the Paris government for forward action in southeast Asia were developed in 1852 and early 1853, while the French legation at Macao and the missionaries were bombarding the capital with historical memoranda and policy recommendations, it is not possible to say.[32] One factor buttressing the French desire to send a mission to Siam and Indo-China was their concern to balance the British gain in lower Burma arising from the war with the kingdom of Burma in 1852–1853.[33] It was at this time also that the papacy assigned to French Jesuits the task of missionary work in Burma.[34]

Three factors were mainly responsible for preventing the French government from embarking on an imperialistic adventure in Annam in 1852–1853. The first was that France was simply unable to provide the necessary naval facilities for the task. Then the impact of the Taiping conquest of central China in early 1853 imperiled the security of both the European commercial and missionary communities, so that the focus of attention was shifted to Shanghai. A final consideration, which vetoed all European operations in the Orient, whether unilateral or in concert, was the development of the Near Eastern crisis leading to the Crimean War.

The only overt action taken in 1852, and that ill-advised, was to authorize Bourboulon to issue safety cards (*cartes de sûreté*) to French

[32] AEC, 13, 34–57. One enclosure of Bourboulon dated Feb. 1, 1853, covered the history of European relations with Annam since 1619 and stressed the future commercial importance of the Pacific area. Courcy's long *mémoire* entitled "Les Missions Catholique et la Protection Religieuse de la France en Chine," was supposedly sent to Paris as an enclosure of Bourboulon's March 4, 1853, dispatch (AEC, 13, 87–90). It is not in the archives, and Courcy explains elsewhere that Bourboulon balked at the last moment in mailing such a huge tome, and that it was actually carried to France by an obliging American naval officer. It argued that a French attack ought to be made on either Korea, Tongking, or Cochin-China, partly for its local effect and partly for its influence on the prestige of France in China. See Courcy, *Souvenirs*, II, 274–275.

[33] Cultru, 50–51. Admiral Laguerre, in July, 1852, and also in 1853 was authorized to negotiate a treaty with Siam, as was Bourboulon also, in February, 1854. See Cordier "La Politique Coloniale," *T'oung Pao*, 2d ser., X, 42–46.

[34] Launay, *Histoire Générale*, III, 316–318. In March, 1856, Bishop Bigandet was consecrated as administrator of the mission of Pegu and Ava; he became coadjutor of the vicar apostolic of Malacca. A French military adventurer named d'Argoni had previously entered the service of the court at Mandalay, where he exerted influence to obtain a favorable reception for Monsignor Bigandet. The latter made Bhamo the seat of his mission, with the idea of linking up with other Catholic work in south China. Italian Catholic missionaries had previously been active in Burma.

missionaries for travel in China. Bourboulon was obliged to protest strongly the compromising character of this action in view of the formal provisions of the treaty forbidding entry of foreigners into the interior.[35] The proposal was actually tried out unofficially by Consul Edan at Shanghai in the summer of 1853, with unfortunate results, as will be indicated in a subsequent chapter.

This meager accomplishment of the French was a far cry from their declared policy of re-establishing French prestige by a vigorous diplomatic and naval gesture. But the combination of clerical pressure, the need to bolster dynastic prestige, and the possibility of acting for unilateral ends under cover of co-operation with Great Britain was fairly well established by mid-1853. It required some time, however, for this pattern of motivation to find expression in action.

[35] AEC, 13, 21, Bourboulon from Macao, Feb. 1, 1853.

VIII

The Taipings, Treaty Revision, and Shanghai, 1853-1854

THE victorious march of the Taiping rebels northward to the Yangtse River during 1852 and then down the river to their capture of Nanking in March, 1853, presented a situation of overriding importance for all foreigners trading or residing in China. The feeble resistance which the Manchus were able to muster convinced observers that the dynasty was near the end of its military resources. At best, the extended period of economic and political chaos which was in prospect would be a heavy blow to foreign commercial interests, especially the British,[1] while at its possible worst the crisis might entail the liquidation of all foreign establishments at the several treaty ports. Catholic missionaries dispersed widely throughout the interior of China were not only endangered by disorderly conditions but were in many instances caught between the cross fire of rebel forces and imperialists. The pseudo-Christian Taipings reflected certain anti-Catholic prejudices, including opposition to the use of images, while the imperial Chinese officials regarded Christianity as a causal factor in the rebellion and accused the illegally resident Catholic missionaries of fomenting unrest.[2]

[1] British trading profits with China in 1853 were estimated at £9,000,000, much of which accrued to the government of India through its monopoly of production and sale of opium for the China trade.

[2] Swisher, 307–308. Yeh's memorial of Sept. 28, 1855, declared that the confusion

103

Initial French Reaction to the Taiping Rebellion

The attitudes of the various elements of the foreign community in China toward the Taiping movement varied considerably. The most favorable view was taken by British and American Protestant missionaries, who praised the Christian aspects of the rebel regime and its alleged reforming zeal.[3] At the beginning, the mercantile community at Canton and to a lesser degree the same groups at Shanghai were also inclined to favor the insurrection. This was because almost any political change carried the possibility of improving trading conditions, while a prolonged stalemate would certainly ruin commerce. An early victory by the rebels would have clarified the situation.[4] Because foreign traders were exempt from the control of the Chinese government in any case, they could be expected to trade with either or both sides as opportunity was afforded. On the other hand, British, American, and French diplomatic representatives, without collusion and each for reasons of his own, discounted the possible gains to be derived from a rebel victory and weighed the possibility of exploiting the embarrassment of the Peking government as a means of enlarging the commercial, diplomatic, or religious rights of the foreigners.

The Catholic missionary community had a viewpoint all its own.

---

was started by Catholic missionary operations, with the banditti practicing Christian rites and then claiming immunity from arrest. The Emperor's vermillion endorsement declared that when China was able to act, barbarian cunning and spying would no longer be tolerated.

[3] Charles Macfarlane, *The Chinese Revolution* (London, 1853), 95–126; FO, 17, 201, enclosure in Bonham's dispatch of May 11, 1853; Maybon and Fredet, 51–52. Rev. W. H. Meadows, the translator and interpreter for the British consulate at Shanghai, published a number of pro-Taiping articles in the *North China Herald*. His considered views as sent in an official dispatch to London ran as follows: "A considerable knowledge of Christianity exists among the insurgents, and could wise instructors affect a residence among them, the good might be fostered and the evil repressed. . . . The advantages to be anticipated from the success of the insurgents are the opening of the country to religious and commercial enterprise, . . . which will benefit both the giver and the receiver. It would be sad to see Christian nations engaged in putting down the movement, as the insurgents possess an energy and a tendency to . . . reform . . . which the imperialists never . . . can be expected to display. . . . The only policy that appears at present advisable is to keep ourselves from being involved any further in the quarrel and to avoid all governmental connections with either party. Foreigners should be prepared, however, . . . to resist any attack which the insurgents may be induced to make on them."

[4] SD, Canton, CL 98, from Spooner, April 6, 1853.

From the outset the missionaries were hostile to the rebellion. The uprising exposed them to bandit attacks, poisoned their relations with local mandarins who had begun to tolerate their presence, and carried with it scant possibility of religious or diplomatic gain. They also disliked certain Protestant aspects of the Taiping program, such as daily assemblies in the evening for preaching services and the distribution of Bible portions and printed tract materials. Catholic-Protestant rivalry around Shanghai was intense, and many Catholic missionaries shared the suspicion that designing Europeans were actually at the head of the insurrection. The better-informed Catholic Europeans were aware that the upheaval stemmed from long-standing governmental evils and personal resentments, which ran much deeper than the surface influence of Protestant protagonists or Garibaldi-like Western radicals who seemingly wished to exploit the movement.[5] Some French observers even professed to see in certain practices of the Taipings survivals of old Catholic traditions of the seventeenth century among the Maoi-tse peoples of south China. The literature of the rebels was carefully studied by the Jesuits in particular for the purpose of detecting some religious symbolism or creed which might be turned to advantage.[6] The unanimous opinion among Catholic missionaries was that every effort should be made to clarify to Peking the difference between Protestant and Catholic Christianity and to convince the Emperor that Catholics were not the enemies of the Manchus and had no part in the rebellion.[7]

The place of most critical danger for the missionaries as well as for the foreign trading community was Shanghai. The vicinity of Shanghai was the focal point of the most intensive Catholic religious work in

[5] Broullion, 1–3, 9–13. This Jesuit Superior of Zikawei wrote of the Taipings: "A thousand passions . . . push the movement; the discontented and the oppressed invoke it; the people want it, shorn of its disasters; foreigners look forward to it, some of them second it; the devil would like to direct it, but God governs it."

[6] AEC, 14, 51–54, Moresca to Montigny to Bourboulon, dated May 19, 1853, transmitted as an enclosure in dispatch of June 30, 1853; Broullion, 293–296. Courcy in 1861 (*Revue des Deux Mondes,* 8th ser., XXXIV, 1–35, 312–360) summarized the evidence that the rebellion stemmed from anti-Manchu secret societies as old as the seventeenth century and reflected old Catholic traditions. He affirmed that the Taipings possessed a measure of sincerity in their religious pretentions and argued that their doctrines were capable of being developed as the basis for a new civilization in China.

[7] AEC, 14, 51–54, enclosure of Bourboulon, June 30, 1853.

China, and the city was also the administrative center for the vicariates apostolic operating in north and west China.[8] As the rebellion approached the city in 1853, Vice-Consul de Montigny made a futile effort to get the British Consul Alcock to agree that the foreigners should take a firm stand in support of the lawful imperial authorities and endeavor to repel the attack from any rebel quarter. In Montigny's view the policy of treating the antagonists as legal equals would be to "assist by inactivity the ruin of an ally in the hope of profiting from his disaster."[9] He also warned Catholic missionaries outside the city that they faced the possibility of violence and ruin at rebel hands for which the government could give no redress. He invited them to accept the hospitality and protection of the French flag at Shanghai, where the armed steamer *Cassini* was anchored. Many of them refused to leave their posts. When the taotai requested the use of the *Cassini* for the defense of Nanking, Montigny avoided a direct refusal by referring the decision to Bourboulon at Macao.[10] Generally speaking, the worst fears of the missionary community at Shanghai had not materialized by June, 1853, when Montigny departed for an extended leave in France. The lack of embarrassment was due partly to the semblance of immunity from local interference which the French consul's vigorous tactics over the previous four and one-half years had given to the Catholic missionaries and partly to the decision of the Taipings to move northward against Peking before consolidating their control along the coastal provinces of China.

Montigny's views concerning the proper policy for France to pursue in the crisis were explained in detail at Macao prior to the consul's departure for Europe. He believed that France should offer to mediate the civil war and then should align itself against the side which rejected its counsels. As compensation for its mediatory services, France should demand the emancipation of Christians in China, the opening of all of China, and the cession of a portion of territory. England only equivo-

[8] Broullion (218–222) listed thirty-one Jesuit missionaries, two scholastic brothers, and five brothers coadjutor (one Chinese) in the Kiangnan mission alone in 1853. Nineteen of them served in outlying areas, being charged with the care of twenty to forty churches and some 3,500 communicants per priest. The area reported 3,200 baptisms in 1852 and 5,445 in 1853.

[9] Maybon and Fredet, 52–53.

[10] Broullion, 268–271; Maybon and Fredet, 46–51.

cated; the Americans fumbled; the solution rested with France. He concluded:

The moment has come for France . . . to play the first role in the Far East. An occasion more favorable will never be offered us. Faithful to the mission that Divine Providence has confided to us, we will once again show ourselves [to be] the champions of humanity.

Courcy, in reporting the conversation, commented that it would not be easy to pacify 360,000,000 people with one steam corvette.[11]

Bourboulon's estimate of the situation created by the surge of the Taiping movement, based on information from Montigny and Monsignor Moresca at Shanghai, was equally positive but more articulate than that of the vice-consul. It was sent belatedly on June 30, after Montigny had reached Macao, and it reached Europe after major policy decisions had already been made. Bourboulon was convinced that if the weight of France were thrown into the balance, the issue in China could be settled in favor of the imperialists and to the profit of Catholic interests. A coded portion of his dispatch ran as follows:

[France must] destroy at one stroke these unfortunate impressions [of Catholic involvement] in the rebellion . . . and produce a new situation which would assure to the Catholic religion in China a future of peace and to the policy of France an extensive and glorious influence. . . . France should offer to the Chinese government a helpful hand in its distress, [and] prove . . . by a signal service that she is its friend and a very powerful and disinterested friend, while what she would demand of it in return would cost [China] nothing either to its pride or its authority.

He added that Vice-Consul de Montigny was returning to France shortly (he left Macao July 12, 1853) and could explain the situation in more detail.[12] The stroke which Bourboulon contemplated was presumably a naval thrust up the Yangtse to interrupt rebel communications with the south and to destroy the rebel base at Nanking.

[11] Courcy, Souvenirs, II, 310–311; Maybon and Fredet, 15–16. While in France, Montigny was elevated to the rank of first-class consul (October, 1855) and upon his return to the Shanghai post in 1856 was entrusted with the task of negotiating treaties with Siam, Cambodia, and Annam. See Chapter X.

[12] AEC, 14, 29–39, from Bourboulon, June 30, 1853. Across the first page of this dispatch, Foreign Minister Drouyn de Lhuys wrote: "Quelles forces navales avons-nous en Chine? Me representer nos dernier lettres à la Marine et à M. de Bourboulon."

The British Proposal for Joint Intervention, 1853

In March, 1853, Sir George Bonham, Governor of Hongkong and ranking British official in China, responded to the alarming reports coming from Consul Alcock at Shanghai by moving his headquarters to that city and by assembling there all available British war vessels. His objectives were to prepare some defenses for the foreign concession area and to bluff off a rebel attack if possible. During the ensuing months, Bonham made two trips to Nanking, partly to estimate the strength of the Taipings, especially their attitude toward foreigners and partly to threaten reprisals if British property or subjects were attacked.[13] He was unimpressed by the political and religious pretensions of the rebel regime itself but was reassured to discover that the Taipings desired to avoid a clash with Britain at the time. The subsequent thrust of the Taiping armies northward in an effort to capture Peking, which came to a halt short of Tientsin, afforded a needed respite for the foreign community at Shanghai and time for the overseas governments concerned to formulate a concerted policy designed to turn the situation to their account. In this effort London took the lead.

Bonham's estimate of the situation and of its possibilities was in many respects similar to that of Bourboulon. He saw no promise in a rebel victory as far as governmental stability and the future of trade were concerned. He was convinced that the Christian pretensions of the Taipings were fraudulent and that the enthusiasm of Protestant missionary apologists for their reforming zeal was without substantial foundation. His estimate of the decisive influence which a foreign naval intervention up the Yangtse could have in relieving pressure on Peking and in disrupting Taiping communications also agreed with that of Bourboulon. Bonham was encouraged to believe, furthermore, that local requests for naval assistance, made in March of 1853, by the taotai and the Governor of Shanghai presaged not only recognition by the imperialists of the importance of foreign aid but also the possibility that the foreigners might be able to demand a substantial compensation in the bargain.

But at this point the similarity between the English and the French views faded, for Bonham's price for affording assistance was far higher

[13] FO, 17, 201, from Bourboulon, May 11, 1853. He threatened reprisals on the same pattern as in 1842 if British persons or property suffered injury.

108

than that of the French, involving numerous commercial concessions, in which the French had no interest. Bonham's policy was to wait until the appeal for help from the desperate Manchu regime was transmitted by a top-ranking official who would be competent to commit the Peking government to major concessions. The apparent inability of the imperial forces to halt the Taiping advance counseled efforts to avoid strife with the victorious rebels, but the very power of the rebels seemed to guarantee in the end that Peking would have no choice but to accept the terms of the foreigners, who alone could save the regime.[14]

In response to Bonham's suggestion of March, 1853, that the difficulties of the Manchu regime be exploited to obtain additional concessions from China, the British Foreign Office decided to press for a general revision of its 1842 treaty. Provision for reconsideration of treaty terms after twelve years had been incorporated in Cushing's Treaty of Wanghia in 1844, and London now claimed the same right for its 1842 treaty under the most-favored-nation clause. In early May Bonham was ordered, therefore, not only to do his utmost to protect British interests but also to make the most of the anticipated opportunity to obtain commercial access to the ports of Chekiang Province and to those of the river above the walls of Nanking, plus permanent diplomatic representation at the seat of the government of China or at least freedom to communicate directly with it. Minor objectives included legalization of the opium trade, regulation of coolie emigration, and the abolition of interior transit duties for goods involved in foreign commerce. Britain sought no exclusive advantage for herself and welcomed the co-operation of other governments in attaining these objectives.[15]

Shortly after the preparation of Bonham's instructions, London sent invitations to Washington, Paris, and St. Petersburg explaining Britain's intention to seek treaty revision in China and inviting the co-operation of other powers in achieving that end.[16] The British invitations did not

[14] FO, 17, 200, from Bonham, March 10, 11, and 28, 1853; 201 from Bonham, May 11, 1853.

[15] FO, 17, 198, instructions, Clarendon to Bonham, May 7, 1853.

[16] The invitations to Paris and Washington were identical (FO, 27, 957, May 17, 1853, and FO, 5, 561, May 20, 1853). The one to St. Petersburg differed only in suggesting that Russia might wish to exert influence through its mission at Peking (FO, 65, 421, May 17, 1853).

109

specify the particular objectives which Bonham had been authorized to seek or the methods he would employ. Nor was Britain's action made contingent on the co-operation of the invited partners.[17]

Only France responded affirmatively and without qualification. Paris did not even wait to receive Bourboulon's assessment of the situation but jumped at the opportunity to get its own stalled Far Eastern policy moving with British aid. Bourboulon was informed that French naval forces in the Far East would be strengthened and that he should follow Britain's lead in diplomacy and in supporting the authority of the existing dynasty, especially in the coastal provinces. He was promised later instructions concerning the guarantees which he should seek for the protection of missions in China and the means for extending these same safeguards to Annam and Korea. Drouyn de Lhuys expressed regret over the reported friction between British and French marines at Canton and emphasized that concerted action with England was the essential point of Bourboulon's instructions.[18]

Several considerations caused London's plan for joint intervention in 1853 to go awry. The primary one was that the expected appeal for aid from desperate authorities at Peking never materialized. The court apparently distrusted the British quite as much as it did the Taipings, and its armies managed, with the help of the Yellow River floods, to halt the attack of the rebel armies short of Tientsin. The southward retreat of the starving Taiping forces began in February, 1854. But aside from this basic factor, the easy long-distance assumption made by London, Paris, and Washington that the interests of foreign groups in China were roughly identical tended to evaporate as one approached the scene of operations. French and British interests in China were not the same, even though both legations could agree that their respective ends could best be realized by obtaining concessions in return for aiding Peking to put down the rebellion. American and British commercial interests were closer together, but the former had little stake in the main

[17] Secretary Marcy authorized U.S. Minister Marshall to maintain cordial relations and free conference with Bonham, but not to co-operate in any measures involving intervention in the civil war or disregard of treaty regulations (FO, 5, 565, from Crampton, June 13, 1853, and enclosure). Russia responded negatively (FO, 17, 198, to Bonham, June 24, 1853). The British embassy at St. Petersburg was immersed at the time in conversations over Near Eastern matters.

[18] AEC, 13, 322–327, to Bourboulon, May 24, 1853. The Foreign Minister at this time also complimented Courcy on his study of Catholic missions.

item of British-Indian import, namely opium, and the two home governments were currently at odds about the Caribbean area and Central America.[19]

Washington's refusal to accept London's invitation to co-operate in China in 1853 was attributable in no small measure to the influence of Humphrey Marshall, the newly arrived American minister to China. This Anglophobe Kentuckian professed to see in Bonham's activities, especially in his repeated visits to Nanking, corroboration of his own conviction that Britain was planning a vast imperialist coup to unite Taiping-controlled south China to the Indian Empire. He accepted as indicative of official British policy the pro-Taiping articles appearing in the *North China Herald*. He affirmed quite erroneously that the portage between the upper Irrawaddy River and the Yangtse was very short, and he also made much of the mistaken allegation that Governor Dalhousie of India was engaged at the time in conquering the Kingdom of Burma to form a connecting link between India and China. His distrust of the British also found expression in resentment concerning the alleged arrogance of Consul Alcock at Shanghai with regard to the administration of the foreign concession. In the instance of Marshall the human factor was responsible for the collapse of the co-operative project.[20]

Anglo-French Friction: The Canton Flagpole Incident

When Bourboulon in late July received his instructions to collaborate with his American and British colleagues in taking advantage of Peking's embarrassment in order to extend European rights in China, he was understandably bewildered. He pointed out in his reply that the Ameri-

---

[19] The Soulé mission to Spain, the Ostend Manifesto, and Isthmian policies are cases in point.

[20] 33d Congress, 1st sess., House exec. doc. 123, pp. 139–144, 268–269; 33d Congress, 2d sess., Sen. exec. doc. 34, pp. 26–27. As if to corroborate his own distrust of the British, Marshall related that the Chinese had confided to him that they would resist every request of Britain, that they feared for their safety (Marshall thought for good cause), and that they had not been inattentive to British policy in India. He also expressed his belief that "a cold and crafty agitator has revamped the matter contained in the [Taiping] religious tracts . . . which the [British] missionaries have published." Marshall also quarrelled with the American naval officers, Aulick and Perry, for not putting a war vessel at his disposal, so that he could proceed to the Peiho River mouth and take advantage of the rare opportunity to obtain the privilege of diplomatic residence at Peking. How he intended to accomplish this miracle was left to conjecture.

111

can and British agents in China at the moment were themselves in sharp disagreement and that French interests were different from those of the other two powers. Despite assurances from Paris that the British favored the imperialist cause, he noted that Bonham was doing nothing to oppose the efforts of a coterie of English and American Protestants to champion the cause of the rebels. Bourboulon enclosed as evidence an editorial clipped from the *North China Herald* for June 25, which acclaimed the rebellion as a heroic struggle for liberty on the part of the Chinese people and urged that Britain enter promptly into relations with the *de facto* government in the interest of resumption of trade.[21]

The rivalry between the French and British marines at Canton had flared up during the spring of 1853 in a tempest-in-a-teapot controversy over the erection of a French flagpole in the park area adjacent to the factories. When the placing of the French standard alongside the British, American, and Danish flags was opposed in early April, presumably on the ground that France had no trading interest in the city, Bourboulon accomplished the project under the protection of a marine guard. After repeated nocturnal incidents in which the ropes sustaining the French flag were cut, the French posted a permanent guard. Eventually the guards seized two blustering and allegedly inebriated Englishmen who were presumed to have been responsible for the previous incidents and carried them away as prisoners to the French war vessel *Capricieuse*.[22] In the absence of Bonham, who was away at Shanghai, Acting Consul Parkes (regularly the interpreter of the consulate) protested the action of the French commander as a derogation of his own police jurisdiction over British subjects living in the area. The prestige of both parties was involved, and the issue, petty though it was, came near leading to open strife.[23] Opponents paraded along the walks of the park with pistols in their belts.

Tension at Canton eased after the French guard was removed. In August the British accepted the apologies of the French minister and the offending commander. An agreement to arbitrate the claim of the two victims for damages was reached in September.[24]

[21] AEC, 14, 65–70, from Macao, July 20, 1853.

[22] SD, DD, from Marshall, no. 14, May 16, 1853, enclosure B. Americans opposed the erection of the French banner but Commodore Perry and the consul at Canton threatened to punish any Americans involved in the subsequent feud.

[23] AEC, 13, 107–320, April to June, 1853; Courcy, *Souvenirs*, II, 266–267; Stanley Lane-Poole, *The Life of Sir Harry Parkes* (London, 1894), I, 180–183.

[24] FO, 17, 198, from London, Aug. 8 and Sept. 24, 1853.

112

Both Parkes and Bourboulon were criticized by their respective governments for quarreling over such an insignificant matter, especially at a time when important political developments were demanding their co-operation. Bourboulon's instructions from Paris nevertheless approved his measures taken to support French prestige.[25]

The Paris authorities encountered serious difficulty in keeping their performance in the Far East abreast of their declared policy intentions. When in July, 1853, Bourboulon's "full powers" to negotiate treaties with China, Korea, and Cochin-China were transmitted, his accompanying instructions contained no specific directions as to procedure and directed that co-operation with England as authorized in the May instructions be adjourned until the situation had clarified. Bourboulon should nevertheless prepare to profit from any developments affording opportunity "for strengthening and improving our relations with the Celestial Empire." [26] The promised French naval reinforcements added up to one additional vessel only, and on arrival it was placed under immediate orders to return to Reunion Island.[27] As late as October the French Foreign Minister was prodding his Marine colleague at Paris to make available a force which would give moral support to Bourboulon's endeavors to protect Catholic missionary interests in the Far East. When Bourboulon threatened to resign because of lack of naval support, the Foreign Minister pleaded in extenuation the uncertainty of events and the insufficiency of material means available for assignment to distant parts like China.[28] By the early months of 1854, the imminence of war with Russia (the Crimean War began in March) vetoed any possibility of sending material reinforcement to China. Bourboulon was left with one or two steam corvettes and an inexperienced consular staff to do what he could for French prestige and the missionaries. The frigate *Jeanne d'Arc* commanded by Admiral Laguerre eventually arrived in the summer of 1854.

[25] FO, 27, 957, instructions to Cowley at Paris, May 17, 1853; AEC, 14, 63–64.

[26] AEC, 14, 91–92, 159–160, instructions dated July 23 and Aug. 23, 1853.

[27] The wide use being made of the Suez route for transport of mail made possible Far Eastern communication with Europe in less than two months, whereas vessels en route had to circle Africa.

[28] AEC, 14, 253, 258–259, October, 1853. Across the top of Bourboulon's complaining dispatch was scrawled an "urgent" note to the effect that the question of naval support to China must be given serious attention. Other dispatches from Bourboulon were marked for making extracts for publication in the *Moniteur* (*ibid.*, 184–197).

Bourboulon and Bonham did reach agreement in August, 1853, with respect to their low opinion of the Taiping regime and also their conviction that nothing could be done at the moment in support of the demoralized imperialist cause.[29] Thus the first proposal for joint intervention collapsed before it ever got under way. Bonham was relieved of his post in the fall of 1853 for reasons of health.[30] In April, 1854, Sir John Bowring, Bonham's successor and previously the British consul at Canton from 1849 to 1852, arrived with fresh instructions to inaugurate a second phase of joint negotiation.[31] In the meantime Bourboulon and Consul Edan had encountered increasing difficulties at Shanghai.

The French Problem at Shanghai, 1853–1854

Bourboulon's unenviable responsibility to maintain French prestige and to protect French missionary interests in China was made more onerous by the lack of judgment displayed by both his subordinates and his missionary wards. A particularly egregious blunder, committed by Montigny's inexperienced successor at Shanghai, Benoit Edan, in July, 1853, did much to compromise French status unnecessarily with the imperialist authorities. It occurred at a time when Montigny's departure on the *Cassini* had left the consulate with no protecting ship.

In response to the request of the Jesuit Superior, Broullion, two missionaries of that order who wanted to visit Taiping-held Nanking were granted by Consul Edan formal passport declarations stamped with the seal of the consulate and addressed to all mandarin officials civil or military. The declaration specified that the bearers, who were to dress as Chinese, should be allowed to proceed to Nanking on an errand of justice and humanity by virtue of the imperial toleration edicts. The statements also declared that all missionaries were under the protection of France. In a covering letter to Broullion, Edan urged that the two emissaries practice reserve and discretion and also expressed satisfaction that they proposed to travel as Chinese so as to attract as little attention as possible. The objective of this daring trip to Nanking was to re-establish contact with Chinese Catholic Christians, some of whom were reportedly being forced to enroll under the rebel flag.[32]

[29] *Ibid.*, 119–226, from Bourboulon, Aug. 5, 1853.
[30] FO, 17, 198, to Bonham, Aug. 31, 1853.
[31] To be examined in Chapter IX.   [32] Broullion, 282–288.

The two Europeans were stopped repeatedly en route and were severely pressed to explain the nature of their mission and their reasons for wearing the Chinese queue and mode of dress. The obdurate mandarin who finally turned them back denied their right to preach in the interior even if they had been Chinese. He assigned two men to escort the two Jesuits back to Shanghai, where they arrived within less than a month after their departure. The incident was brought to the attention of the imperialist Viceroy, who protested in strong terms the laxity of the taotai of Shanghai. He recalled the treaty provisions forbidding Europeans to travel outside the open ports (a 50-li radius was apparently permitted) and pointed out that the infraction in question was so serious as to threaten to disturb the good relations between the two countries. Edan in a weak rebuttal expressed to the taotai his astonishment that the Chinese government should value the restrictive clause of the treaty above the regard of the French government.[33] But serious damage to relations between the French and the imperialists had been done. It would indeed have been difficult to devise a situation which would have done more to confirm the quite mistaken suspicions of the imperialist officials that the French consul and the missionaries were in league with the rebel cause.

The situation in and around Shanghai suddenly took a turn for the worse when a group of Triad Society rebels from Fukien Province and Canton, not associated with the Taipings and operating from inside the native city, quietly took over control of the walled enclosure on September 7, 1853. The rebel regime was fairly orderly at first, respecting foreign property and churches and attracting considerable sympathy within the neighboring foreign concession community.[34] Consul Edan's bold hoisting of the French flag above the cathedral and adjacent French buildings effectively exempted them from immediate invasion, and a small guard loaned him by the British prevented the French consulate and the house of the merchant Remi from being looted.[35] The danger increased greatly when the armed junks and other riff-raff troops hired by the taotai began to infest the rebel stronghold. Stray shots frequently fell among buildings of the French Concession.

[33] Ibid., 291–292, 297–302.
[34] Eldon Griffin, Clippers and Consuls . . . (Ann Arbor, 1938), Appendix II, 424–426.
[35] Maybon and Fredet, 59–64, 73–75.

In November Bourboulon proceeded northward on the corvette *Le Colbert* to investigate the situation, but there was relatively little that he could do. A small marine detachment rescued two of Bishop Moresca's Chinese catechists from the rebels. Bourboulon conferred with imperialist officials and with leading Chinese citizens, who pressed him to take action to restore peace.[36] He also talked with various missionaries and received an urgent request from Fathers Dannicourt and Guierry that a French war vessel visit Ningpo harbor in order to forestall a threatened attack by rebel forces. The accumulating problems were outstripping Bourboulon's limited means to cope with them.

In early December Bourboulon, accompanied by his wife, Courcy, and two Jesuit fathers, journeyed to Nanking aboard the steamer *Cassini*. The unconcealed hostility exhibited by the entire party toward the Taiping regime was so pronounced that their visit was short and highly inconclusive. Much of the time of the single interview between Bourboulon and the Taiping minister was consumed by a wrangle over why the Frenchman was not provided with the same type of armchair that the minister used. Bourboulon angered the Taiping official further by talking persistently about the protection of Catholic interests and the preservation of the treaties negotiated with the Peking Emperor. Nanking was puzzled over the purpose of the visit and apparently concluded that the French were spies. Bourboulon was back in Shanghai on December 18.[37] There he made an abortive effort to negotiate withdrawal of the rebels from the walled city on the basis of a payment of silver and a promise of safe passage, a proposal probably sponsored by the taotai. The idea was strongly opposed by the British community. Bourboulon finally left for Macao on February 4 aboard *Le Colbert*.[38]

The comic-opera aspects of the early stages of the imperialist siege of Shanghai (there was much din and shouting, but little serious fight-

[36] *Ibid.*, 79; AEC, 15, 79–80, from Bourboulon, Jan. 13, 1854.

[37] Maybon and Fredet, 75–78; 35th Congress, 2d sess., Sen. exec. doc. 22, p. 92, McLane to Marcy, enclosure. Father Broullion, one of the Jesuits in Bourboulon's party (Broullion, 387–389), gave a detailed description of the desolate condition within Nanking (La Servière, I, 276–280).

[38] Maybon and Fredet, 82–83; the *North China Herald* of Feb. 11, 1854, declared: "The French and the English have for the moment too few interests in common to accommodate their respective policies . . . in dealing with the great Chinese revolution."

ing) took on a more serious character for the French in February and March, 1854. Respect for the French flag began to wear thin, and in the absence of any defenders the western section of the French Concession farthest from the river was overrun by imperial troops. When the French consul protested these and later violations, including an attack on his own junk in the river while it was en route to the cathedral site, the taotai urged in reply that Edan and other residents in the vicinity of the consulate retire to the main concession area. He also proposed that the stone bridge across the Yang king pang Creek be destroyed in order to break the contact of the rebels with the British concession area. He wanted to utilize the French consulate area for attacking the walled city from the north.

Although the consulate was in obvious danger of fire from the city, Edan stubbornly refused to abandon his post. By making the question a matter of personal honor, he finally won reluctant support from Alcock to keep the stone bridge intact. There followed in April the battle of Muddy Flats, a quite unpremeditated action between the imperial forces and the British-American defenders of the foreign concession, in which the French took no part. The return of *Le Colbert* from Macao at this juncture eased somewhat the pressure on the French, but there ensued a period of fraternizing and trading in supplies between foreign merchants and the rebels within the city, involving much going and coming across the French Concession area. Such activities compromised French neutrality and gave a justified grievance to the taotai, but the Anglo-American traders were amenable only to the control of their own consuls and conceded even this to an almost negligible degree.[39]

Bourboulon, back at Macao, had meanwhile begun to tire of the importunities of the missionaries, who exposed themselves gratuitously to dangers and then clamored for protection that was simply not available. In mild fashion he complained to Paris that the zeal of the

[39] Maybon and Fredet, 84–93, 96–100. John King Fairbank, ("The Provisional System at Shanghai in 1853–54," *Chinese Sociological and Political Science Review*, XIX [April, 1935], 90–97) relates that both sides hired discharged or deserting foreign seamen at high wages and that foreign traders sold munitions to all buyers at eight times their cost. Consuls Murphy (U.S.) and Alcock (Britain) were obliged to issue a joint notice, as a means of clarifying *pro forma* their official relations with the Chinese authorities, that their respective countrymen were forbidden to aid the rebellion and that consular protection would not be extended to violators who sold supplies or hired their services to the rebels. See SD, Shanghai, CL 3, Murphy to Washington, April 20, 1854.

Lazarist congregation in particular was not always accompanied with appropriate discretion.[40] On the occasion of the imprisonment in distant Shensi of a Neapolitan Lazarist, Father Seraphin, in the summer of 1854, he wrote letters both to Canton and to Peking invoking the terms of the French treaty, but to no effect. To the newly arrived Admiral Laguerre, who apparently questioned why France should concern itself over the safety of a citizen of Naples, Bourboulon explained that since the Chinese themselves could make no distinction between the nationality of the Catholic missionaries, French policy had come to include all of them within the scope of its protection.[41] Meanwhile the question of comprehensive treaty revision had been revived by the British and American governments.

[40] AEC, 15, 77, March 19, 1854.
[41] *Ibid.*, 267, Bourboulon to Laguerre, Aug. 6, 1854.

IX

Ineffectiveness of the
Anglo-French Alliance, 1854

THE British decision in 1854 to press for Chinese acquiescence in a demand for revision of the Treaty of Nanking was based essentially on political rather than legal grounds.[1] The undertaking was rendered more problematical by entrusting it to Sir John Bowring, the new British Governor of Hongkong and Chief Superintendent of Trade. Bowring was a versatile man, a liberal economist, a literary figure, and a linguist. His mind was brilliant, but he was deficient in perception and practical judgment.[2] As a youthful

[1] FO, 17, 198, Clarendon to Bonham, Oct. 3, 1853. Wrote Clarendon: "The articles of the French and American treaties . . . on which the corresponding British right is founded, do not make the revision *necessary* after the specified period of twelve years, but leave it *optional*." Ch'i-ying had interpreted the articles in 1845 (FO, 17, 97, Feb. 7, 1845) as requiring that twelve years elapse before revision would be possible and that changes were then not to be lightly proposed, each party being nevertheless obligated to appoint ministers to determine any new regulations.

[2] Sir John Bowring, *Autobiographical Recollections* (London, 1877), 4–8, 52–57. Bowring's best translation was a *Servian Anthology* (1827). He was a master of six European languages and had a fair book knowledge of seven others, in addition to Arabic and Chinese. In 1829 he was granted the Doctor of Laws degree from Groningen University in the Netherlands. He could list as of 1836 no less than twenty academic citations and membership listings in scholarly societies, eighteen of them being from the continent of Europe. He had edited Bentham's *Life and Works* in eleven volumes and was the author of a number of hymns, including "In the Cross of Christ I Glory."

119

and precocious disciple of Jeremy Bentham, Bowring in 1824 had helped found the *Westminster Review,* of which he served for a time as co-editor. He was a member of Parliament from 1833 to 1837 and again from 1841 to 1849, identifying himself as an ardent free trader and an advocate of repeal of the corn laws. But he exhibited no administrative capacity and no promise of statesmanship.

Bowring's Assignment in China

Bowring became interested in relations between Britain and China in 1847, when he served as a member of a parliamentary commission inquiring into the affairs of Hongkong.[3] In 1847–1848 he became involved in an unsuccessful ironworks venture and lost his entire fortune. Bowring's friend, Foreign Minister Palmerston, came to his financial rescue in 1849 by appointing him consul to Canton.[4] Here he spent three painfully frustrating years immediately following the Chinese triumph over the Canton-entry question. In 1852 he temporarily took over Bonham's post as Superintendent of Trade at Hongkong, but at this time London denied him substantive authority. He returned to England on leave in early 1853.[5]

Bowring's designation in 1854 to Bonham's post, to which Foreign Minister Clarendon added the title of plenipotentiary with power to negotiate treaties with China and adjacent countries, afforded the new appointee a long-awaited opportunity to play a heroic role in world affairs. His sense of destiny was enhanced by his being knighted on the eve of his departure for China.[6] He could also presume on his long-time personal friendship with Foreign Minister Clarendon.[7] Bowring's self-confidence was based not only on his premonition that he was destined to be another Clive or Raffles but also on his unbounded

[3] E. J. Eitel, *Europe in China, the History of Hongkong . . . to 1882* (London, 1895), 295–297.

[4] FO, 17, 152, Jan. 4, 1849.

[5] FO, 17, 186, instructions dated Jan. 19 and July 21, 1852; *ibid.*, 198, instruction of Jan. 20, 1853; Lane-Poole, I, 160–165. Bowring was expressly forbidden in 1852 to legislate, sign treaties, engage in irritating discussions with the Chinese, visit the treaty ports, or reorganize the consular routine, all of which he had proposed to do.

[6] Bowring, *Autobiography,* 8–10, 17–20. Bowring boasted (*ibid.,* 216) that as envoy to China, Japan, Siam, Cochin-China, and Korea he was accredited to "a greater number of human beings . . . than any individual . . . before."

[7] *Ibid.,* 13–15. The two had co-operated on a commercial mission sent to France in the thirties.

faith in the beneficent character of the free trade cause and of British rule in general. The validity of British objectives in the Far East, in his mind, justified his employment of tactics which did not always square with his religious professions and his one-time service as the secretary of the Peace Society.[8] With respect to the China situation in particular Bowring was outspoken prior to his departure from England, in urging that the maritime powers should "profit from the embarrassment of the Tartar dynasty to obtain . . . a better position." [9]

Clarendon's instructions to Bowring, dated February 13, 1854, asserted flatly that Britain had a right to claim a revision of the Treaty of Nanking on August 29, 1854, the twelfth anniversary of its signing. If the Chinese authorities should plead delay by reason of political circumstances, immediate revision should not be pressed, as delay might actually prove advantageous. But Britain's right to claim revision must be acknowledged under any circumstances.[10] Clarendon extended the list of desired changes which had been furnished Bonham the year before. Most of them had no relevance to French interests.[11] As to the methods to pursue, Bowring was admonished to use caution and to maintain the most friendly intercourse with the Chinese authorities. Wrote Clarendon:

While steadily upholding the rights and privileges secured to British subjects under treaty, you will as far as possible avoid occasion of angry discussion calculated to lead to an interruption of friendly relations. . . . If we should press [demands] in menacing language, and yet fail in carrying them, our national honor would require us to have recourse to force; and . . . we might place in peril the vast commercial interests which have already grown up in

[8] *Ibid.*, 213–221, 232–233. Bowring affirmed that a moderate course, practicable at home, would not succeed abroad when faced by the "unreasoning and the unconvincible."

[9] AEC, 15, 4, dated early 1854. Walewski, French Ambassador in London, was here asked to bring Bowring's declared views to the attention of Lord Clarendon for comment.

[10] Clarendon called for "a formal admission that if, out of consideration for the embarrassment of the Imperial Government, we are willing not to insist immediately upon our right, we are not to be precluded by our forbearance from urging our claim at a later period."

[11] FO, 17, 210, to Bowring, Feb. 13, 1854. The proposed changes included such additional items as the following: free admission into additional cities (especially Canton), suppression of piracy along the coasts, and regulation of Chinese (coolie) emigration.

China, and which, with good and temperate management, will daily acquire greater extension.[12]

Finally, Bowring was enjoined to observe strict neutrality in the Chinese civil war and to enforce the rule that foreign participants forfeited any claim they might have to British protection.[13]

As was befitting relations between two nations about to participate as allies in the war against Russia, the British government furnished Paris with a verbatim copy of Clarendon's general instructions to Bowring and also with a transcript of orders to the British Admiralty authorizing reciprocal protection by the naval forces of Britain and France of their respective nationals and interests in all parts of the world. Not transmitted to Paris was Bowring's additional authorization to negotiate standard commercial treaties, including extraterritorial and religious privileges, with Siam, Cochin-China, and Japan. The latter country was to be considered much the most important of the three. Bowring was not to leave China for such negotiations unless and until British interests there were safe.[14] The United States government was also invited to co-operate.

The United States in 1854 was in a position to play an independent role in the Far East. Its two maritime rivals were heavily involved in the Crimean War and were in fact much concerned over evidences of American friendship for their Russian enemy. President Pierce was not prepared to follow Admiral Perry's "manifest destiny" recommendation to establish a territorial foothold in the Orient,[15] but he was not averse to breaking away from London's leading strings and seizing the diplomatic initiative in the Far East as he had in Central America.

---

[12] *Ibid.;* AEC, 15, 38–42.

[13] FO, 17, 210, to Bowring, Feb. 13, 1854; Lane-Poole, I, 217–218.

[14] FO, 27, 996, to Cowley at Paris, Feb. 7 and 13, 1854; FO, 17, 210, to Bowring, Feb. 13, 1854.

[15] U.S. Navy Department, East India . . . Squadron, Perry I, no. 30, Dec. 24, 1853. The Admiral had already made a treaty with the supposedly independent king of the Ryukyu Islands, and he proposed annexing Formosa and the Bonin Islands as well. He wrote: "This is the moment to assume a position in the East, which will make the power and the influence of the United States felt. . . . It is self-evident that the course of coming events will ere long make it necessary for the United States to extend its territorial jurisdiction beyond the limits of the Western Continent . . . as a measure of positive necessity to the sustainment of our maritime rights in the East." See also Dennett, *Americans,* 270–277, 292–293.

He chose as the new American minister to China Robert M. McLane, an able and experienced lawyer, military man, and politician, the son of Lewis McLane, formerly Secretary of State under President Jackson and one-time United States minister to England and France.[16] He was to be supported in the Far East by a substantial American naval force. He was ordered to obtain from China satisfaction for American demands, both commercial and diplomatic, by negotiating either with the Peking authorities if they were amenable or, if they were not, with the victorious insurrectionary faction. The latter alarming alternative was regarded by the French in China as a genuine possibility, not as merely a bargaining threat. Whether Bowring or McLane took the lead, Bourboulon was doomed to play a poor third under the circumstances.[17] McLane reached China shortly after Bowring's arrival in late March, 1854.

Anglo-French Friction Defies Europe's Instructions to Co-operate

Paris welcomed London's invitation to co-operate in the Far East and instructed Bourboulon to maintain a close relationship with Bowring. It would be preferable, if possible, for Bourboulon to adjourn the matter of treaty revision until August, 1857, when the French treaty would itself be subject to reconsideration under its own terms, but Bourboulon should not remain aloof if the British pushed the revision question. In addition to the general British objectives mentioned by Clarendon, France would seek both the right of missionary access to the interior and vigorous enforcement of the edicts for toleration of Christians. Bourboulon was promised later instructions covering the negotiation of French treaties with Siam and Japan.[18]

At the outset the imperious Bowring took the lead, determined to make the most of Clarendon's unconditional orders to obtain Chinese acquiescence in Britain's demand for treaty revision. Diminutive in physique and unprepossessing in appearance, the French minister was short-tempered and in constant friction with his own staff; he was no

[16] Dennett, *Americans*, 191–192; Richard W. Van Alstyne, "British Diplomacy and the Clayton-Bulwer Treaty, 1850–60," *JMH.*, XI (1939), 168–170.

[17] AEC, 15, 145–146, Bourboulon to Paris, May 19, 1854. Dennett's claim (*Americans*, 223–224) that McLane's hints that he would deal with the rebels was only a threat and not seriously considered is not borne out by Bourboulon's reactions.

[18] AEC, 15, 47–50, to Bourboulon, Feb. 23, 1854.

match for the eminent British scholar.[19] Bourboulon's critical account of Bowring's initial communication with Yeh at Canton on April 25, 1854, ran as follows:

I have found the new English plenipotentiary very desirous of signalizing his arrival in China by some important act, and perhaps a little more impatient than policy and circumstances permit to broach all at once the divers questions which are connected with his most complicated mission. He first conversed with me concerning a *démarche* which he had already made (following an intention which he had previously announced to me) with the imperial commissioner [Yeh] at Canton to demand of him an interview at his residence, that is to say in the interior of the city. He assigned as a motive that [he wished] to interview the Viceroy concerning matters of the highest importance, notably that the English Government intended to demand of the Imperial Government . . . revision of the treaty of Nanking. . . . The Viceroy Yeh, in his reply, did not even mention that the English minister had written to him on the subject of the revision of the treaty. . . . The English minister had [also] informed the Viceroy in his first communication . . . "that the instructions . . . from his government had been communicated to those of France and the United States and that the views of those two powers were in entire accord with those of H.B.M. to claim the same changes in existing relations." [20]

Bourboulon objected not only to the precipitate and unilateral character of Bowring's action but also to his involvement of the other powers in his unnecessarily provocative demands. By demanding entry into the city of Canton, he had created new difficulties from the otherwise simple matter of sending a communication. More seriously, Bourboulon complained that Bowring had attached excessive importance to a demand which he had neither the means nor the intention to enforce. Bowring had in fact conveyed a thinly veiled threat: "Nothing would be more painful to me than irritating and unfriendly discussions, the consequence of which might be deplorable." [21] Bourboulon reported to Paris that even in the unlikely contingency that the requested interview should be granted, he would refuse to follow Bowring's lead under the circumstances, which inevitably subordinated moderate French objectives to the sweeping demands of England. When requested to co-

[19] Courcy, *Souvenirs*, II, 378, 381–382. Courcy himself confided: "Sir John intimidated me extremely. I considered myself so little before his eminent superiority."
[20] AEC, 15, 171–173, May 19, 1854.
[21] *Ibid.*, 173–175; Lane-Poole, I, 219–222.

operate in a naval demonstration before Canton, Bourboulon temporized by assuring Bowring only that he would seize the first opportunity to confirm the alleged accord between their two governments. Subsequently, in August, Bourboulon honored his instructions in qualified fashion by informing Yeh that when the time came for the revision of the treaties after twelve years, as provided for in the American and French treaties, he would co-operate with the English in that endeavor.[22]

Receipt of the news at Hongkong at the end of April that war had broken out in Europe diverted Bowring's attention from his gratuitous quarrel with Yeh and sent him off to sea for several weeks on a futile undertaking to locate the Russian Far Eastern fleet.[23] The wartime alliance between Britain and France also changed the general situation materially by making the defense facilities of each ally available for the protection of the interests of the other.

At Shanghai the French and British tended at first to draw closer together in opposition to the divergent prorebel sentiment popular in American circles. This point of difference cleared somewhat after McLane returned on June 4 from his fruitless visit to Nanking, but still no agreement between the three emissaries could be reached on how peace could be restored at Shanghai. The American officials and British Admiral Sterling, who was anxious to proceed to Japan, favored a policy of nonintervention and withdrawal from advance posts. The British consul made a futile effort at mediation.[24] Consul Edan, on the other hand, favored a united effort to force the disbanding of brigades in the imperial pay. Edan was particularly unhappy over the agreement reached with the rebel forces which left the French Concession outside the neutralized area, completely exposed and defended only by a handful of French marines.

French relations with the Americans were not improved when the newly arrived frigate *Jeanne d'Arc,* commanded by Admiral Laguerre, attempted to enter the Woosung River in August, 1854, and ran firmly aground while in the hands of an inept pilot carrying American cre-

[22] AEC, 15, 173–175, May 19, 1854, and 310–311, letter to Yeh dated Aug. 29, 1854.

[23] Eitel, 297–299. Hongkong developed a near panic in early June, 1854, over baseless rumors that Putiatin's fleet was about to attack. Captain Elliott eventually located the fleet at De Castries Bay, opposite northern Sakhalin Island.

[24] Maybon and Fredet, 100–102.

dentials. Here the frigate remained stranded for nearly three months. When a French group from the Concession started to go to the assistance of the admiral, the rebels from the native city threatened to overrun the Concession area thus vacated. The French also had no share in the Anglo-American negotiations of June and July covering the setting up of the foreign customs administration. Thus, despite the insistence from Europe on solidarity between the Anglo-French allies, by the summer of 1854 the local groups at Shanghai had reached the parting of the ways.[25]

Bourboulon Refuses to go Northward to the Peiho

Meanwhile at Macao Bourboulon received fresh instructions, no doubt inspired by Bowring's complaints to London, transmitted to Paris, directing that he co-operate more fully with British efforts to obtain treaty revision.[26] Concurrently Bowring was told by Clarendon to insist that the French representative associate himself with any effort to approach Peking, in order to rebuff Chinese efforts to exploit the jealousy obtaining between representatives of the Western powers.[27] When Bowring and McLane, finally satisfied that nothing could be accomplished at Canton, moved northward to Shanghai in September, Bourboulon accordingly accompanied them. But Bourboulon's exposure to the situation at Shanghai, his talking with Edan, Laguerre, the missionaries, and the resident Chinese Governor, caused the minister to cancel whatever plans he may have had to go along with the Anglo-American mission to the mouth of the Peiho River. His real reasons for the decision were his confidence that no good could come from it and his objection to identifying France with the rabidly anti-Peking mood of Bowring in particular.[28] His ostensible reason was that the *Jeanne d'Arc* was aground and hence not available for his use.

France was therefore represented on the Peiho trip only by the young Polish-born Kleczkowski, the interpreter for the Shanghai consulate,

---

[25] *Ibid.*, 103–112. Bowring was hostile to the rebels at Shanghai, but Admiral Sterling refused to commit forces under his command to an attempt to clear the native city for fear that the action would hamper his intended trip to Japan.

[26] AEC, 15, 211–215, to Bourboulon, July 10, 1854.

[27] FO, 17, 211, to Bowring, July 5, 1854.

[28] FO, 17, 216, from Shanghai, Oct. 4, 1854. Bowring here explains that he gauged the strength of his own desire for any particular course by the amount of Chinese resistance to it.

who traveled with McLane on the *Powatan*. McLane appears not to have been greatly concerned whether the French participated or not, but Bowring was exceedingly annoyed over this second refusal of Bourboulon to follow his lead. He complained again to London about it.[29]

Kleczkowski kept very much in the background during the course of the Peiho conversations, not even being introduced to the Chinese until near the end. His position was both equivocal and highly unimpressive, for although he supposedly was present only "to see, hear, and report," he also indicated formally that France supported the British demands for revision of the treaties. In contrast to the numerous and far-reaching demands made by Bowring, some eighteen all told, Kleczkowski confined his complaints to verbal protests over the lack of courtesy on the part of Chinese officials, particularly their failure to give prompt attention to correspondence and to enforce the toleration edicts for native Christians. Whether his studied moderation impressed the Chinese spokesman is doubtful. Peking took little stock in the alleged French opposition to the Taipings, which was based on Catholic-Protestant distinctions incomprehensible to the Chinese, and continued to regard the meddlesome influence of Christian foreigners in the interior as one of the causes of the rebellion. Bourboulon's own previous visit to Nanking was also a matter of record as was Consul Edan's gauche attempt to aid the two Jesuits to reach the rebel capital.

In the Peiho conversations and in subsequent exchanges, the imperial spokesmen continued their perennial efforts to separate their foreign opponents. Commissioner Tung was not impressed with McLane and directed his reply to Bowring. He pointed out that only the French and American treaties provided for possible modifications after twelve years and that Britain was permitted by the most-favored-nation clause only to share in any additional imperial favors which might be accorded the other two. Most of Bowring's demands he declared to be so prejudicial to the interests of the Emperor that they were not worth discussing. Two items only, those relating to remission of duties and to justice to injured foreigners, could be discussed, but only through the regular channels at Canton.[30]

[29] 35th Congress, 2d sess., Sen. exec. doc. 22, pp. 22–24, 290–292, 340–343, 416–417; FO, 17, 224, to Bowring, Dec. 5, 1854.

[30] FO, 17, 217, enclosure of Bowring, Nov. 10, 1854; AEC, 15, 437–442; Swisher (p. 279) gives the Chinese reaction to Kleczkowski.

Bourboulon's labored effort to justify to Paris his decision to send Kleczkowski but to remain himself officially aloof from the Peiho negotiation did not impress French authorities.[31] The Foreign Minister criticized as damaging to French prestige his sending as the French representative a person so young and so Polish-appearing as Kleczkowski.[32] In December, 1854, Drouyn de Lhuys for the third time committed France to support Clarendon's proposal to demand an extention of the rights of foreigners in China,[33] although he repudiated, as did Washington, the bellicose posture which McLane had assumed.[34] Clarendon himself refused to approve Bowring's recommendation, following the rebuff at the Peiho, to exert naval pressure to force Peking to agree to revision of the treaties; it was "doubtful as a matter of right and very questionable as a matter of policy." [35]

The French Missionary Point of View: Monsignor Mouly's Memorial

That the McLane-Bowring negotiation of late 1854 was ill-advised may be accepted without argument. Its failure stemmed from the fallacious assumption originating with Bonham that the desperate Manchu court would meet whatever demands the foreign powers might make in order to obtain their assistance in suppressing the rebellion. It suffered also from the overbearing presumption of Bowring, who refused to take into consideration any viewpoint but his own and who justified his own tactics by reference to the "enlightened economic principle of free trade" which he was trying to force on the incorrigible Chinese.

That the Paris government was amenable to pressure from London to co-operate in the treaty revision effort indicated, among other things, that it was out of touch with the French situation in China. Bourboulon and other French officials in China operated from a different point of

[31] AEC, 15, 407–414, 430–436.   [32] *Ibid.*, 16, 115–116, Jan. 17, 1855.

[33] *Ibid.*, 15, 427–429, instructions of Dec. 9, 1854.

[34] *Ibid.*, 16, 120, instruction of Feb. 9, 1855. McLane had threatened war if the Emperor did not appoint a commissioner to negotiate revisions. To President Pierce, McLane recommended tactics similar to those used by Perry in Japan calling for delivery of the President's letter for the Emperor in the presence of an imposing naval force, and this to be followed by measures in 1856 calculated to "command the respect and obedience of both parties, and at once extend our intercourse into the interior wherever and whenever the opportunity may offer" (35th Congress, 2d sess., Sen. exec. doc. 22, pp. 286–288, Nov. 19, 1854).

[35] FO, 17, 224, to Bowring, Jan. 24, 1855; SD, China, Instructions 1, 105–108 (1855).

view and a different set of assumptions from those stressed by the British. The prosperity of Catholic missions in China, with which French policy was identified, depended on gaining the friendly tolerance of the official mandarinate. To associate Catholic missionary interests with the Taiping or other rebellions or with the pressure for basic commercial and diplomatic concessions demanded by the hated British was to poison Catholic relations with Peking and to eliminate all chance of gaining voluntary acquiescence in the Christianizing program.

The missionary viewpoint was expressed succinctly in a highly indiscreet document prepared some time in 1854 by Bishop Mouly,[36] apostolic vicar of Hopeh and Mongolia. Monsignor Mouly had risen to a position of some influence and respect among the mandarins in the vicinity of Peking before he was arrested in 1854 on suspicion that all Christians were somehow involved in the rebellion. Although subject to being delivered to the French consul at Shanghai, he was allowed to postpone his departure to suit his convenience. He seized the opportunity to prepare an extended exposition on French policy and the Catholic cause in China, which he attempted without success to send to Peking through the Viceroy of Hopeh. He eventually arrived at Shanghai and persuaded Bourboulon to intercede with Peking in behalf of his cause.[37]

Mouly's statement, ultimately published in the *North China Herald* (November, 1855), was revealing. He presented the history of Catholic missions as a long-time operation in China going back to the ninth century. He cited similarities between the Chinese classics and Christian literature, especially with respect to reverence for parents and superiors, including the Emperor. He told of the work of Ricci and Schaal in the seventeenth century. He cited the honors which K'ang Hsi had accorded the missionaries because of their assistance in the fields of mathematics, diplomacy, and the casting of cannon. He denounced the base slanders which eventually prompted the imperial rulings against the missionaries. He alleged that in more recent times when the

---

[36] For previous reference to Mouly, see Chapter VII, n. 14.

[37] AEC, 16, 251–253, 260–267, 302, May 23, 1855, and July 4, 1855. Bourboulon's letter to the principal Secretaries of State at Peking stressed the friendship of France for China and the fact that Catholics had no sympathy for the rebellion. He also asked that priests be permitted to reside in Peking and that old churches and cemeteries, especially those of the Portuguese, be turned over to the French missionaries so that tombs of the dead could be venerated.

English disputed the Chinese prohibition of the importation of opium, the French had interposed with exhortations of peace. He denounced non-Catholics who preached false Christianity in the name of the "religion of Jesus"; they differed from the followers of the true faith, he insisted, as ice from hot coals. Catholic missionaries, he admitted, entered the interior in violation of treaty terms, but they did not cause trouble, and they alone deserved the indulgence of the government. He concluded as follows:

European propagators of religion . . . have no idea of assuming office or of receiving pay, looking neither for fame nor gain;—but remembering that the Emperor K'ang Hsi . . . allowed them to travel freely throughout the empire . . . , the western scholars of the present day [are] willing to become the arms and legs, the ears and eyes of the government and to aid the Celestial Dynasty in obtaining lengthened tranquillity and perpetual rule.[38]

French Forces Attack the Rebels at Shanghai

While Bowring and McLane were journeying to the Peiho, Bourboulon and Laguerre at Shanghai were visited by Governor Keih, who solicited their aid against the rebels and protested the disloyal conduct of the foreign community at the city.[39] As a result of the conference, French marines began to afford protection to workers sent by Keih to build an earth and timber wall twelve feet high and about three feet wide at the top running north and south through the French Concession and then westward. The object of the barrier was to prevent the rebels within the walled city from using the French Concession as an avenue for purposes of trading with the Foreign Settlement. The British and American merchants who had been furnishing supplies to the rebels in return for clothing, furniture, and other looted articles complained that their liberties were infringed by the action. Since the French consul could not arrest non-French nationals, the latter claimed the right to go and come freely. The French accordingly received no assistance in the wall project from the Settlement authorities, who accused the French of unneutral conduct.[40]

Just prior to Bourboulon's departure from Shanghai on December 4, 1854, he secretly presented to the resident Chinese Governor a labored

[38] AEC, 17, 292 ff., November, 1855.
[39] René de Courcy, L'Empire du Milieu (Paris, 1860, 1867), 591.
[40] Maybon and Fredet, 113–119; Broullion, 452–462.

exposition of the conditions under which the traditionally amicable relations between the French and the Chinese could be continued. He entered three complaints only: difficulty of access to the interior, inability to correspond with the central government, and laxity in the enforcement of the imperial decrees granting toleration to Christians. The particular case cited was that of one Abbé Fann, a missionary arrested in Shensi Province, who had not been escorted to the nearest treaty port as stipulated in the treaty. The letter closed by emphasizing the advantages for China of keeping the friendship of France.[41]

The tension between the Triad rebels and the French at Shanghai came to a head on December 9, only a few days after Bourboulon had departed for Canton. A French marine detachment, accompanied by one hundred or more Chinese coolies and supported by naval gunfire, demolished a rebel battery emplacement outside the north wall of the native city which had been designed to cover the retreat of rebel forays made in the direction of the Foreign Settlement.[42] On December 13 Admiral Laguerre, acting on his own authority, captured a battery at the East (riverside) gate. Full-scale fighting developed on the following day. When Laguerre reproached the British for communicating with certain rebel elements over a non-French section of the protecting rampart, Consul Alcock replied heatedly that the French had not been courteous enough even to consult the other foreigners about Laguerre's action, which the defense council of the International Settlement had never approved.

On the morning of January 6, 1855, the French finally succeeded in breaching the wall of the old city. One detachment of marines held open the breach and another cleared a path to the North Gate, which it opened for the imperialist forces to enter. The several thousand of the latter who poured into the city put on a cowardly performance. They eventually stampeded in a panic over the walls and back through the breach, actually firing on the French who tried to deter them. The only determined rebel resistance came from British and American mercenaries, estimated to number from some thirty to several score men. After three hours of fighting, the ammunition of the French gave out and they retired, sadder and wiser, with casualties numbering approximately

---

[41] AEC, 15, 524–526, from Bourboulon, Dec. 2, 1854.
[42] John Scarth, *Twelve Years in China* (Edinburgh, 1860), 197–206. The author claims that Laguerre wanted to pick a fight.

one-fifth of their force of 250 men.[43] Consuls Murphy (of the United States) and Alcock refused to intervene beyond asking for extradition of the foreigners fighting with the rebels and promising to seize any of them who might venture within the Foreign Settlements.

The unilateral action of the French aggravated tension within the foreign community at Shanghai. Edan reproached Alcock for his passive role at a time when the armies of their respective countries were allied in Europe.[44] French honor was committed and they had no choice but to see the matter through. Alcock co-operated only to the extent of agreeing to refuse to deal independently from the French in arranging surrender terms for the rebels. But the cause of the rebel Chinese was doomed, for they had been thoroughly shaken by the spirited French assault. A tight blockade was imposed by the French and the imperials while waiting until more munitions could be brought up from Macao. On February 7, the rebels, unwilling to face a renewal of the French attack, abandoned the ravaged city. Thirty or more foreign mercenaries, many of them Americans, fled to Ningpo and to Chusan Island.[45]

In actual fact neither Alcock nor the British naval officers at Shanghai were proud of their correct but timorous role during the affair. European as well as French prestige was involved. Consul Alcock admitted to Bowring that the French and the imperialists were justified in complaining about the role of British and American traders in provisioning the besieged city from the Foreign Concession. The consul's personal sympathies were clearly with the French.[46] The *North China Herald* recognized editorially that French honor was involved and counseled no retreat. Privately, Admiral Sterling assured Bourboulon that British marines would assist if the small French force should encounter really

[43] Scarth, 208–218; Montalto de Jésus, *Historic Shanghai* (Shanghai, 1909), 80–82.

[44] Maybon and Fredet, 120–128. The French marines were drawn from the frigate *Jeanne d'Arc* and the corvette *Le Colbert*.

[45] *Ibid.*, 122, 130–132. Consul Murphy reported that the foreigners hired by the Shanghai rebels were mostly deserters from the U.S.S. *Vandalia* and *Hancock*. See 35th Congress, 2d sess., Sen. exec. doc. 22, pp. 548–551, Murphy to Parker and vice versa, Jan. 22 and 30, 1855.

[46] FO, 17, 226, from Alcock, Dec. 19, 1853, and Jan. 6 and 11, 1854. See also correspondence between McLane and Governor Keih at Shanghai in November, 1854, on American participation in supplying the rebels, in 35th Congress, 2d sess., Sen. exec. doc. 22, pp. 418–419.

serious difficulty in a renewal of the assault.[47] The difference in policies stemmed from a divergence of interests. The British officially were willing to aid the imperialists only if Peking would make substantial concessions in a sweeping treaty revision; British traders meanwhile were making money trading with the rebels. Admiral Laguerre and Consul Edan were concerned neither for treaty revision nor for trade. After long provocation they acted unilaterally to end what to them was an intolerable local situation.[48]

The Sequel to the French Attack

Official French reactions to Laguerre's storming of Shanghai varied. Bourboulon conceded that the affair, once begun, had to be pushed through, but he held Consul Edan responsible for not exerting prudent restraint on the actions of the rash Admiral.[49] The news of the affair aroused a sharp interchange at Paris between the Ministers of Marine and of Foreign Affairs. The Marine chief defended Laguerre and echoed his complaint concerning the lack of co-operation on the part of the British forces. Foreign Minister Drouyn de Lhuys conceded that some retaliatory action against the rebels had been called for, but not a foolhardy attempt to storm the city walls with only 250 men. Laguerre's action, he pointed out, constituted a clear derogation of the policy of neutrality adopted in co-operation with England and America, and it had been taken without even consulting the French envoy to China. The Foreign Minister insisted that the instructions being prepared for Admiral Guérin, Laguerre's successor as commander of naval forces in the Far East, charge him specifically not to engage the French flag in similar enterprises in the future in the absence of formal authorization.[50]

Bourboulon naturally tried to make the most of French belligerence in order to gain favor with the imperialists at Shanghai. Even before

[47] AEC, 16, 36–37, from Bourboulon, Jan. 2, 1855. In February, 1855, when the foreign community at Canton was threatened by rebel attack, Bowring acceded to Bourboulon's urgent request that a British force be assigned to protect French nationals at the place.

[48] London reacted (FO, 17, 224, April 19, 1855) to the news of Laguerre's action by approving Capt. O'Callaghan's refusal to take part in the French attack; but Clarendon authorized joint action with the French to repel any attack by Chinese elements, rebel or imperialist, on any European holding in Shanghai.

[49] Maybon and Fredet, 130–132.

[50] AEC, 16, 165–167, exchange of letters dated March 3 and 8, 1855.

the rebel forces abandoned the city, Bourboulon wrote to the taotai asking him to solicit the Emperor immediately for favors in behalf of French religious interests in recognition of the services already rendered by the French to the imperial cause and of other services to be expected in the future. The letter proceeded:

I hope that not only [the taotai] but the Emperor himself will know how to recognize by real acts of reciprocal friendship, the rectitude and the generosity with which the agents of France have not feared to . . . do justice in behalf of the [imperial] cause, even at the cost of French blood and without placing any conditions on the action.[51]

Governor Keih responded by agreeing to bring the names of the fallen Frenchmen to the attention of the Emperor and by entertaining the French and American naval officers and consular agents (the British refused the invitation) at an elaborate "victory breakfast." He also presented to Consul Edan and to the respective commanders of the participating marine detachment and of the two French war vessels inscribed standards, marked with the Governor's seals, eulogizing the loyalty and bravery of the French. But no generally applicable concession to French missionary interests was forthcoming. The episode confirmed the opinion of Chinese observers that the French were strong militarily but interested only in promoting missions.[52]

When in April, 1855, Edan and Laguerre each accepted as personal gifts four bales of silk cloth and also received on deposit a contribution of 10,000 taels (some 70,000 francs), they seriously compromised the status of France by seeming to enter the pay of the Governor. The imperialist authorities informed the court, in fact, that they had "purchased for a modest sum the assistance of the French barbarians, your slaves." Bourboulon's indignation over the consul's indiscretion overflowed all bounds. Courcy commented that the naïve Admiral Laguerre, "indoctrinated by the missionaries to whose advice he listened too docilely," was under the delusion that his action of January, 1855, at Shanghai had established France in the good graces of the Chinese. Admiral Guérin, who replaced the embittered Laguerre soon there-

---

[51] Maybon and Fredet, 418–420.

[52] *Ibid.*, 134–136; SD, Shanghai, CL, Murphy, Feb. 10, 1855. American missionaries whose houses near the wall had been occupied by imperial forces received $18,000 compensation. See Swisher, 285.

after, was by contrast a prudent man, small, courteous, and reserved.[53]

For reasons of health and family considerations, Bourboulon was granted permission in June, 1855, to return to France. He actually delayed his departure until November, expecting that he might be instructed to negotiate a treaty with Siam, only to discover to his chagrin that Montigny had been chosen for the task. He left the twenty-eight-year-old René de Courcy in control of the legation as chargé during his period of leave.[54] A fair estimate of Bourboulon's mission would appear to be that he failed to measure up to the exacting demands of a harrowing and difficult assignment which Paris imperfectly understood.

One significant development in long-range French relations with the Far East was the agreement reached in 1854 between the new pro-French ruler of Egypt, Said Pasha, and Ferdinand de Lesseps establishing the Campagnie Universelle du Canal Maritime de Suez. The Empress Eugénie, a cousin of de Lesseps, became an ardent supporter of the canal project, and Louis Napoleon not only supported it diplomatically but also subscribed personally to some 177,000 shares of stock. The project encountered strong British opposition, so that work on it was not started until 1859. It was 1869 before the canal was in operation. The railway across the isthmus was built between 1851 and 1858.[55]

---

[53] Courcy, *Souvenirs*, III, 12–15, 29.
[54] Henri Cordier, *L'Expédition de Chine de 1857–58* . . . (Paris, 1905), 5–6.
[55] H. L. Hoskins, *British Routes to India* (New York, 1928), 302–320.

X

Competition: Bowring,
Montigny, and Parker

ECAUSE France lacked both a territorial base and substantial
commercial interests in the Far East, Paris experienced considerable difficulty in matching the pace of diplomatic activity in the area set by rival governments during the early 1850's. Political instability at home, difficulties of naval mobilization, and dependence on British diplomatic support were additional handicaps. Then France's self-appointed role as protector of far-flung Catholic missionary operations in the area proved to be a liability to prestige in situations where protests were so frequently made without any sanctions to back them up. During the Crimean War period in particular, British, American, and Russian rivals realized accretions in prestige which tended to reduce the relative influence of France.

The Rising Tempo of Diplomatic Competition

Under Presidents Fillmore and Pierce, United States policy in the Far East was aggressively active. It operated under the impetus of the "manifest destiny" urge which characterized American national psychology following the acquisition of California and Oregon. America had a substantial commercial stake in the China trade and was free from the European international involvements which tied the hands of its Western rivals from 1848 to the middle of 1856. Washington sent

Perry's powerful fleet to pry open the door to Japan, and it also undertook to play a leading role in the negotiations with China from 1853
to 1856. American efforts were handicapped by the use of inexperienced
agents sent for short terms only. Their ambition to achieve significant
results far surpassed their skill as diplomatists or their grasp of the
political realities of the situation. The United States also lacked a territorial holding in the area which could serve as a base of operations.
Finally, the executive branch of the government was unable, because
of constitutional limitations, to act on the recommendations by Commodore Perry, Peter Parker, and others to acquire a needed foothold.[1]
The abortive American mission of Joseph Balestier in 1850 to Tourane,
Bangkok, and the islands of the East Indies was an exhibition of inept
bungling from beginning to end.[2] But in spite of these handicaps, American influence in the Orient was clearly on the increase.

Russian operations in the Far East during the fifties were confined
to northeastern Asia, but they were important because they were concerned with the occupation of territories on the Pacific coast con-
tiguous to China. Using as a pretext the need for supplying Russia's
Pacific coast outposts during the Crimean War, Muraviev occupied the
left bank of the Amur River,[3] while the Russian fleet took refuge at the
De Castries Bay some distance south of the river's mouth. Russia's
encroachment on Chinese territory, combined with its long-established
overland contact through the ecclesiastical mission at Peking and its
active interest in the opening of Japan, stepped up the international

[1] Recommended bases for American operations included the Ryukyu and Bonin
Islands, Formosa, and protectorate arrangements with countries of southeastern Asia.

[2] 32d Congress, 1st sess., Sen. exec. doc. 38, pp. 3–24, Balestier to Webster, Nov.
25, 1851; U.S. Navy Department, East India Squadron, Com. P. F. Voorhees, no.
10–13, Feb. 18 to July 23, 1850. At Tourane, Balestier attempted to establish a basis
for negotiating a treaty with Hué by presenting an apology for violence committed
at the port by Captain Percivall of the U.S.S. *Constitution* in 1845; he succeeded
only in talking to minor officials. At Bangkok, Com. Voorhees, Balestier's naval
escort, refused to approach the cholera-infested city (he remained fifty miles down
the bay) and refused also to provide the frustrated agent with a suitable escort.
Voorhees eventually abandoned his petulant and demanding passenger in Borneo
after the planned itinerary had been only half completed; illness of the crew and
need for provisions were the alleged reasons.

[3] The first Russian barges descended the Amur River in May and June, 1854, a
second fleet of barges in May, 1855, and a third in January, 1856, all without seeking
Chinese permission. See Hoo Chi-Tsai, "Les Bases Conventionelles des Relations
Modernes entre la Chine et la Russie" (University of Paris thesis, 1918), 136–140.

137

competition very materially. French diplomatic officials reported in 1855 that Russian pressure to the north of China appeared to be so great that the Anglo-French allies could expect to obtain no concessions from China unless a solemn embassy could be sent to Peking backed by a naval demonstration which would be capable of inspiring more terror than the Russians could exert.[4]

At the end of the Crimean War, Courcy tried to counter Russia's influence at Peking by sending a copy of the Treaty of Paris to the imperial commissioner at Canton. He wanted to show how effective French arms and policies had been against the not invincible Russians and how France had acted in support of the cause of Christianity in the Near East.[5] Admiral Guérin's report following his visit to Japan at the end of 1855 indicated that Russia, as well as America and Britain, was actively interested in the area, and he recommended urgently that France act to obtain a treaty with the newly opened country.[6]

But it was from the British in southeast Asia that France faced its most formidable competition. Britain operated from a strong commercial and political base in India, combined with a valuable intermediate post at Singapore and a footing at Hongkong on the China coast. British shipping dominated the trade of the Chinese waters, and Britain's naval power everywhere commanded both fear and respect. The British conquest and annexation of the lower Irrawaddy and Sittang valleys of Burma in 1852–1853 had not been matched by any compensatory gain by the French. Englishmen participating in the drama of eastern Asia habitually assumed that they were cast for a primary role, while other residents of the area whether indigenous or foreign were inclined to concede, however unwillingly, that this presumption was

[4] AEC, 17, 83–84, from Courcy, Dec. 28, 1855. The French did not co-operate in Bowring's protest to Yeh in November, 1855, against Russian occupation of some forty or fifty miles of the China coastline south of the mouth of the Amur. Bowring cited this as a grave infraction of international law on China's part in allowing her territory to be so used. Bowring also investigated current rumors that China had ceded Chusan to Russia (FO, 17, 242, 243, instructions of March 1 and Dec. 24, 1856; AEC, 17, 183–184, enclosure, Bowring to Yeh, Nov. 28, 1855, and Yeh's reply, Nov. 29, 1855).

[5] AEC, 18, 17, from Courcy, June 30, 1856.

[6] Ibid., 17, 75–77, 80–87, and 278–279, from Guérin to Minister of Marine, Oct. 9, 1855; from Courcy, Dec. 10 and 28, 1855. Guérin actually negotiated a coaling-station treaty with the authorities of the Ryukyu Islands similar to Perry's earlier one. See also Courcy, L'Empire du Milieu, 596.

correct.[7] The experienced British diplomat or trader in the Far East possessed a degree of self-confidence and aplomb that the Americans could not match at all, and the French could equal only in the personalities of the ablest of the Catholic missionaries. But the missionaries also confronted the officers of France with problems in their endless appeals for aid and protection. France could not match Britain's pace.

The Burden of Missionary Claims on French Policy

The extent to which French policy in the Far East was becoming subordinated to the demands of the missionaries can be illustrated by the items which were the subject of the legation's correspondence with Paris in 1855. With respect to western Tongking, Monsignor Pellerin presented an appeal asking that a French naval demonstration be made along the Annamite coast to halt continuing anti-Christian persecutions and insults to the name of France.[8] Later in 1855 Tu-Duc's decrees added to the tension by outlawing all expressions of Christianity, threatening the execution of all priests European or native, and offer rewards for their arrest.[9] Courcy reported that partisan rebel elements in Tongking, led by disaffected relatives of Tu-Duc, were allegedly awaiting the signal of French co-operation on the coast to rise against the King. They would guarantee to carry out conditions for French aid that were agreed upon in advance. In code Courcy suggested that if France decided to revive the treaty of 1687 and establish a protectorate at Tourane, the enemies of Tu-Duc could create a powerful diversion in favor of such a project.[10]

At Canton Yeh's release of Monsignor Jacquemin, in broken health after a five months' imprisonment, was a topic of dispute between the

---

[7] From Henri de Ponchalon (*Indo-Chine, Souvenirs de Voyage et de Campagne, 1858–1860* [Tours, 1896], 84–86) comes the following: "It is necessary to leave Europe to understand the power of England, the influence which she exercises in the world. . . . One cannot keep from admiring the hardihood, the innate assurance of the sons of Albion, finding themselves at home under all climates and on all points of the globe. . . . In the field of governmental action, she distinguishes herself by the continuity, by the constancy of effort, by her vigilance and especially by her audacity to profit from every occasion. . . . [For] Oriental peoples . . . 'the fear of the English is the beginning of wisdom.'"

[8] AEC, 16, 287–288, Pellerin to Libois, Dec. 14, 1854, sent as enclosure in Bourboulon's dispatch of May 7, 1855.

[9] Launay, *Histoire Générale*, III, 335–341.

[10] AEC, 17, 92–93, from Courcy with enclosure, Dec. 31, 1855.

French chargé and the Chinese. At the same time the Spanish Dominicans in Foochow and Ningpo were asking that a French war vessel visit
those ports for purposes of affording protection.[11] From the Peking area
came Lazarist and Jesuit requests that Courcy support their demand
for the restoration of eighteenth-century Catholic properties located in
the capital and also for permission to use the official seal of the French
legation as a means of authenticating title to such property.[12] In the
vicinity of Shanghai, news of the menace of Triad bands seeking revenge
on the French was relayed to Paris and became the subject of a request by Foreign Minister Walewski to his Marine colleague Admiral
Hamelin that a French naval vessel be stationed permanently at Shanghai. Hamelin replied by submitting a report of Admiral Guérin's extensive current operations against the Russian fleet in Japanese waters.
He could promise only that all possible measures would be taken to
protect French interests along the China coast.[13] From remote Yunnan
came the news that a missionary penetration of Tibet was being planned
via the northern provinces of Burma, whose King had volunteered his
good offices in support of the project.[14] These cases were reported in addition to standing complaints of missionaries in Shensi, Hopeh, and
Kweichow Provinces.

The policy which Courcy embarked upon as chargé, following Bourboulon's departure in November, 1855, increased clerical influence. To
all Catholic bishops in the Far East he sent a circular letter of his own
devising which ran in part as follows:

The vast field of [the missionary] harvest is only opening to the action of the
protective policy of France, and the moment is not distant, I hope, when
she will . . . make a decisive step. . . . In order that these efforts . . .
should produce all the good which one can expect from them, it is necessary
that the government of His Majesty not be ignorant of your needs. . . . It
should know as soon as possible the countries where you reside . . . , their
moral and political situation, their industrial and commercial resources, their
customs, prejudices, tendencies. I dare therefore to ask [you] to submit to
me, without constraint or reserve, your desires and views.[15]

[11] AEC, 17, 24–30, Dec. 3, 1855.   [12] Courcy, *Souvenirs*, III, 122–124.
[13] AEC, 17, 37–40, 65–66, exchanges dated Nov. 7, 12, and Dec. 6, 1855.
[14] AEC, 17, 90–91, Libois to Courcy to Walewski, 1855. A French missionary was
posted at Bhamo, Burma, in 1856.
[15] Courcy, *Souvenirs*, III, 83–84.

As might have been anticipated, the French legation was flooded with missionary advice and demands, which, in Courcy's own words, "attested much more their ardor and zeal than the sagacity of their political views." [16] One can appreciate the readiness with which Fathers Libois, Mouly, and Lemaitre congratulated the enthusiastic chargé on his succession as head of the French legation, even though some of them apparently thought he was taking his role a bit too seriously.[17]

In time Courcy lost much of his enthusiasm for the missionaries. Contrary to missionary predictions at Shanghai, he discovered that in return for the aid which France had given to the imperialist cause in ousting the rebel Triads, French residents received only sterile good wishes instead of real protection.[18] Then he became involved in the furor caused by the discovery and publication by the *North China Herald* of Bishop Mouly's highly indiscreet memorial to the Emperor. As explained above (pp. 128ff.), the prelate falsely claimed that France had interposed its good offices in China's behalf during the Opium War. He also attacked Protestantism and argued that Catholic Christianity alone should be tolerated in China. Courcy wrote to Paris deploring Mouly's lack of any sense of propriety in attempting to communicate directly with the Emperor. Even worse was his imprudence in proposing that Catholic missionaries, who had already given umbrage to the mandarins by clandestine residence in China's interior in violation of treaty prohibitions, should now become the "arms and legs, the eyes and ears" of the imperial government. The Viceroy of Hopeh and the Governor of Kiangsu, Courcy believed, had well served the cause of Catholic missions by refusing to transmit the memorial to Peking. He reported that in reply to the inquiries from the American legation he had declared that the French legation had had no part in the compilation or in the publication of Mouly's memorial. Courcy's dispatch to Walewski closed with the following comments:

Perhaps your Excellency will find it appropriate to communicate the preceding reflections to the General Superior of the Lazarist Mission at Paris. I am convinced on the basis of the conversations which I have had with Monsignor Mouly . . . and the demands which he has addressed to me that the venerable prelate cherishes a false idea of the extent to which the [French] Gov-

[16] *Ibid.*   [17] *Ibid.*, 51.   [18] AEC, 17, 40–41, Dec. 4, 1855.

141

ernment . . . intends to extend its protection to Catholic missions in China;
. . . their sometimes indiscreet zeal ought to be curbed.[19]

It is significant that Courcy's disillusionment developed several
months prior to the receipt at Macao in July, 1856, of the news of the
death of Father Chapdelaine. That event was destined to become a pretext for a French war with China and to set up a train of events leading
to the conquest of Annam.

Bowring's Mission to Siam, 1855

In the spring of 1855 British diplomacy in southeast Asia achieved a
signal victory when Sir John Bowring negotiated a new commercial
treaty with the government of Siam. King Mongkut, who had come to
power in 1851, was receptive to European culture and had decided to
attempt to come to terms diplomatically with the Western powers rather
than to resist their influence. He claimed acquaintance with Bowring's
literary reputation and flattered the Englishman by inviting him in
November, 1854, to come to Bangkok so that they could talk together
personally while their respective agents concluded a commercial treaty.
McLane was also included in the Siamese invitation, but the American
was unable to accept because of ill health and his orders to proceed to
Europe.[20]

Bowring's mission to Bangkok was by far the most gratifying achievement of his checkered diplomatic career. He was there afforded opportunity not only to exhibit his literary talents but also to lecture the
patient Siamese on the advantages that would derive from their adop-
tion of a free trade program. Lane-Poole has commented that the

[19] AEC, 17, 284–288, to Walewski, April 28, 1856. In his *Souvenirs* (II, 163–164;
III, 83–84) written in 1860, Courcy acknowledged his mistake as chargé in encouraging exaggerated missionary expectations of French support. He added: "The propaganda of our missionaries who resided in all provinces of the empire was, then, a
constant and flagrant violation of the treaty; the representative of France . . . not
only permitted [that violation], but also encouraged it, protected it, and was morally
implicated in it. . . . The position of the Minister of France at Macao was essentially
false."

[20] FO, 17, 226, from Hongkong, Jan. 6, 1855; John Bowring, *The Kingdom and
People of Siam* (London, 1857), II, 209–212; Eitel, 299–300. The King's invitation
was dated Nov. 20; previous correspondence between Bowring and the Siamese government took place in August, 1854. James Brooke had made two futile efforts to
improve British treaty relations with Siam in 1850 and 1851, following Balestier's
visit. See FO, 17, 164, instructions to Brooke, May 15, 1850, and September, 1851.

Groningen "doctors gown in which Bowring used to astonish the natives of China had a good deal to do with the success of his Siamese treaty." [21]

But Bowring did not depend entirely on his own powers of persuasion or even on the formidable personality of his negotiator and interpreter, Harry Parkes. Bowring anchored his shallow-draft war vessel, the *Rattler*, opposite Bangkok itself, where it could deliver frequent twenty-one gun salutes with maximum psychological effect. British officers also wore their swords impressively at formal audiences. When the Siamese negotiator resisted British proposals, Bowring threatened to delay the scheduled departure of the *Rattler* downstream. Relations on the whole were nevertheless extremely cordial, for the Siamese were obviously prepared to conclude a satisfactory treaty. They asked repeatedly whether the terms agreed upon would also be satisfactory to the French and the Americans. They were also much concerned that Bowring promise to make a similar visit to Tourane, the port of the government of Annam, archenemy of Siam.[22]

The treaty consisted of twelve articles. The most important items provided extraterritorial privileges for resident Britons, the right to establish a consulate at Bangkok as soon as British trade reached ten ships a year, access to all ports of Siam, and the right to rent land, to construct residences, and to travel a day's journey inland from the capital. The treaty also provided for a single export duty and for a maximum 3 per cent duty on imports.[23] At the conclusion of the mission on April 25, Bowring returned to Hongkong while Parkes departed immediately for Europe to obtain London's ratification of the treaty.[24] Clarendon heartily approved Bowring's work at Bangkok, but he directed Parkes to conclude a complementary convention covering omitted details when he returned a year later (in April, 1856) to exchange ratifications.[25]

Bowring later gave some attention to Cochin-China, although with discouraging results. He sent his aide, T. F. Wade, to Tourane harbor

[21] Lane-Poole, I, 191–192.   [22] Bowring, *Siam*, I, 248–337.
[23] *Ibid.*, II, 214–222.   [24] Lane-Poole, I, 191–195.
[25] FO, 17, 225, to Bowring, July 6, 1855; Cordier, "La France et la Cochinchine," *T'oung Pao*, VII, 484–486. Parkes's additional provisions, obtained only with difficulty, provided for the organization of a custom service, the free export of gold and rice, abolition of the government monopoly on coconut oil, and the right of foreigners to acquire living quarters and warehouses.

aboard the *Rattler* in August, 1855, to deliver a letter from Bowring to King Tu-Duc. Local mandarins refused to accept it, and Wade accordingly departed. Britain's continuing interest in the area was evinced by London's instructions to Bowring six months later to make a second try, this time carrying valuable presents for delivery to the Annamite court.[26] Bowring's move was not without its effect, however, a fact which attested British prestige. Reports from Catholic missionaries in Tongking reaching the French legation at Macao indicated that the *Rattler's* short visit at Tourane had aroused considerable sentiment among high mandarins to moderate the persecution policy of Tu-Duc.[27]

Preparations for the Montigny Mission

Although Paris had long contemplated sending a diplomatic mission to Siam and Bourboulon had reported the favorable prospect for obtaining a treaty at Bangkok immediately following Bowring's return,[28] French authorities were dilatory in pursuing the project. London finally forwarded to Paris a patronizing invitation to follow Britain's example in Siam. Clarendon sent to Foreign Minister Walewski, through Britain's Paris embassy, a copy of Bowring's treaty, with the accompanying information that the Siamese were quite prepared to grant France the same privileges. Only Bowring's lack of positive information as to the wishes of the French government had allegedly prevented him from negotiating simultaneously in its behalf. Walewski thanked London immediately for assistance in preparing the Siamese government for the reception of a French plenipotentiary, but two months elapsed before the Montigny mission was set up.[29] In February, 1856, London again conveyed to Paris Bowring's desire to give every assistance to the French plenipotentiary at Bangkok, including his suggestion that Montigny's

[26] Cordier, "La Politique Coloniale," *T'oung Pao*, 2d ser., X, 674–675; FO, 17, 242, to Bowring, Jan. 2, 1856.

[27] AEC, 17, 289–291; Meyniard, 359. The reports came from Fathers Pellerin and Lefèbvre, Jan. 3 and Feb. 1, 1856, respectively.

[28] AEC, 16, 289–295, to Paris, May 25, 1855. Bourboulon reported that two shallow-draft war vessels would be needed and expected that he himself would get the assignment. Admiral Laguerre, in 1852 and 1853, and Bourboulon also, in 1854, had been given full powers to negotiate with Siam, but developments in the Crimea and Shanghai had intervened (Cordier, "La Politique Coloniale," *T'oung Pao*, 2d ser., X, 42–46).

[29] Cordier, "La Politique Coloniale," *T'oung Pao*, 2d ser., X, 41–42; FO, 17, 225, to Bowring and enclosures, Aug. 6 and Oct. 18, 1855.

credentials as plenipotentiary extend to Hué as well.[30] It was all very friendly but also very patronizing, whether intended to be so or not.

Under these circumstances the Montigny mission developed from modest beginnings into a major diplomatic effort by France to recover lost ground in the competition for prestige in southeast Asia.[31] Evidence of the broadening arena of French competition with Britain for influence in south Asia can also be found in the orders given to Admiral Guérin in 1854 to show the French flag in the Red Sea, the Persian Gulf, and the port of Rangoon while operating in the Indian Ocean area.[32]

The selection of Montigny as head of the French mission to Siam may have been due in part to Bourboulon's prospective return to France on leave,[33] but more importantly it was prompted by the support which Montigny's persistent application for the assignment enjoyed from religious circles at Paris.[34]

Montigny's initial instructions, dated November 22, 1855, concerned Siam alone, despite urging by the Superintendent of the Seminary of the Missions Etrangères that Montigny be directed to touch at various points in Annam also after leaving Siam.[35] A proposed draft treaty of twenty-two articles was prepared for his guidance, but he was instructed to be content, for the most part, with securing acceptance of the terms granted previously to Bowring. Of special importance was the proposed Article 3, which granted to French subjects freedom to practice their religion openly throughout Siam and permission to build churches at

[30] FO, 27, 1109, to Cowley at Paris, Feb. 18, 1856.   [31] Cultru, 51–54.

[32] AEC, 15, 405–406, Drouyn de Lhuys to Minister of Marine, Nov. 5, 1854. A French diplomatic mission to Teheran was also in prospect. The sending of French war vessels to the Red Sea and the Persian Gulf was long delayed because of other demands on the fleet from the war in the Far East, from the Montigny mission, and from the Reunion Island theater. In May, 1856, it was still being planned (*ibid.*, 18, 238–240, 250, April 8 and May 10, 1856).

[33] Permission to return was given to Bourboulon in June, 1855, but he delayed his departure from Macao until November in the hope that he would be asked to go to Bangkok, in accordance with his earlier authorization of 1854.

[34] Courcy attributed his own failure to be chosen for the task to his lack of influential friends near the Emperor. His disappointment developed into a personal feud with Montigny after the latter wrote from Egypt in a patronizing tone to his "young friend" explaining why he had asked for the appointment (Courcy, *Souvenirs*, III, 239–241).

[35] Cordier, "La Politique Coloniale," *T'oung Pao*, 2d ser., X, 50–51, in a letter to Walewski dated Nov. 8, 1855.

places agreed upon with local authorities.[36] In supplementary instructions dated December 21, Montigny was ordered to consult the local bishop in Bangkok concerning other needed guarantees. He was to attempt in particular to devise for Siam, in lieu of official passports, a system of identification cards to be carried by traveling missionaries, authenticated by the local bishop and signed by a Christian mandarin. Walewski's lack of genuine interest in obtaining these additional concessions was indicated by his authorizing return to the simple English text if Montigny encountered any serious objection to French demands.[37]

Montigny was also ordered to stop at Tourane while en route to Shanghai to explain to the Annamite authorities in "an energetic but moderate tone" that France was displeased over the recently published edicts of persecution. But he must not compromise the dignity of France by using menacing language which he did not have the physical power to support. Walewski was under no illusion that a simple remonstrance at Hué would suffice, but he indicated that it was not his intention to divert to Montigny's support French naval forces operating elsewhere in the Far East.[38] Not until months later, while Montigny was en route to the Far East, did Paris provide him with a vaguely tentative authorization to seek a treaty with Annam on the same general terms as the one with Siam. This belated decision apparently was made solely in response to Bowring's suggestion.[39]

Montigny's first stop after leaving France on December 30, 1855, was Rome, where, following a request by the papal nuncio at Paris, he was to consult with Vatican officials with the assistance of the French Ambassador to the Holy See, M. de Rayneval. During a month's delay at Rome, which was occasioned by Rayneval's illness, Montigny explained to Pius IX and Cardinal Antonelli the services which France was rendering to the cause of religion in China. He lost so much time at Rome that he missed the March mail boat sailing from Egypt and had to wait for the next one, which delivered him at Singapore on May 16.[40]

At Singapore another month's delay was entailed because the corvette

[36] Cordier (*ibid.*, 52–65) reproduces the entire instructions.

[37] *Ibid.*, 67–69.   [38] *Ibid.*, 69–70.

[39] *Ibid.*, 185–186. Walewski was not sure that the occasion for negotiation at Tourane was opportune. The disposition of the Annamite government was to determine the extent of Montigny's efforts to negotiate.

[40] *Ibid.*, 70, 183–185; Meyniard, 128.

Capricieuse (a sailing vessel), carrying provisions and presents for the King of Siam, did not arrive until late June. Then the receipt of Walewski's belated instructions to attempt to negotiate at Tourane as well as at Bangkok became the basis of the plenipotentiary's insistent demand on Admiral Guérin that the expedition be escorted not only by the gunboat *Marceau* but also by the two corvettes, *Capricieuse* and *Catinat* (a steamer), as an indispensable condition of the success of his Tourane mission.[41] While waiting at Singapore, Montigny also obtained permission from Bowring at Hongkong to announce to the Hué government that the French visit would be followed shortly by another one on the part of the British.[42]

In further preparation for his Tourane visit, Montigny persuaded the head of the Missions Etrangères at Singapore, Abbé Beurel, to request Monsignor Miche in Cambodia to meet him at the coastal town of Campot at the end of July, in order to accompany him to Hué as interpreter.[43] Father Miche was asked to persuade the King of Cambodia to travel to Campot in order to meet Montigny, and the missionary was also to prepare a suitable house where the prospective interview might be held and Montigny's family be entertained ashore. If a meeting at Campot should prove to be not feasible, the King was to be asked to provide the necessary means for Montigny to proceed to Battambang for the interview. All these arrangements exceeded the terms of Montigny's instructions. Monsignor Miche's reply, which reached Montigny at Bangkok three months later (September 7), explained that the torrential rains made out of the question Montigny's proposed travel into the interior, that suitable quarters were not available at Campot for entertaining the King, and that any meeting would have to be on board a vessel. The Cambodian King, Ang Duong, had declined the invitation on the ground that he could not fathom why the French emissary should

---

[41] Cordier, "La Politique Coloniale," *T'oung Pao*, 2d ser., X, 49–50, 183–185, 192–198; Meyniard, 131, 141. Captain Le Lieur of the *Catinat* was under orders to accompany Montigny, but the *Capricieuse* had to be requisitioned by him. Montigny insisted that the French force must be at least as imposing as the British and American ones, which had preceded him to Siam.

[42] Cordier, "La Politique Coloniale," *T'oung Pao*, 2d ser., X, 310–311. Bowring replied to Montigny on June 9: "Whenever the many demands upon the naval services in these parts will enable the admiral to place at my disposal a becoming maritime force, . . . you may be assured of my . . . co-operation."

[43] A letter from Monsignor Barnabo of the Propaganda at Rome was enclosed, which directed Catholic missionaries to assist Montigny's mission wherever possible.

be so concerned with his tiny country, but Miche would try again.[44]

While at Singapore, Montigny also ordered the Catholic bishop at Bangkok, Monsignor Pallegoix, who was to act as his interpreter in Siam, to ask the Premier of Siam, as an act of courtesy to the British and French sovereigns, to send to King Tu-Duc of Annam a message announcing the prospective arrival of the French mission at Tourane. When Pallegoix replied that Siam and Annam were bitter enemies and that such a request would be both futile and highly inappropriate, Montigny only became the more insistent.[45]

By the time Montigny had completed his elaborate preparations at Singapore, the mood of the Siamese authorities had taken a turn for the worse. This was due primarily to the two months of angry, bullying negotiations on the part of Harry Parkes (from March to May, 1856) to obtain his additional concessions.[46] The mild-mannered American, Townsend Harris, who reached Bangkok just as Parkes was concluding his mission, found the Siamese extremely hostile toward the English and in a difficult frame of mind. They confided to him that they saw in Parkes's attitude portents of a fate similar to that which Burma had suffered, and they asked if Siam could be taken under the protection of the United States.[47]

Montigny at Bangkok and Campot

Except for the successful initial step of negotiating the already-promised treaty with Siam,[48] Montigny's mission was a comedy of errors. His principal mistake was in the matter of timing. He remained at Bangkok from July 10 to September 21. Only ten days of this seventy-three-day period was consumed in the actual process of negotiating the terms of the treaty. He then dallied off Campot, Cambodia, for more than a month, until the onset of the typhoon season in late October vetoed his plan to follow his two major escort vessels to Tourane harbor.

[44] Meyniard, 353–357.

[45] Cordier, "La Politique Coloniale," *T'oung Pao*, 2d ser., X, 306–311 (Montigny to Pallegoix, May 27 and June 19, 1856; Pallegoix's reply, June 9).

[46] See n. 25 above.　　　[47] Dennett, *Americans*, 352.

[48] Cordier, "La Politique Coloniale," *T'oung Pao*, 2d ser., X, 324–329; 34th Congress, 3d sess., House exec. doc. 60, pp. 177–188. The treaty consisted of twenty-four articles and four items regulating commerce. Article 3 on religion contained the only important innovation to the terms of the British and American treaties. It established the freedom of Frenchmen to reside and circulate in all provinces, to exercise their religion publicly, to purchase ground, and to erect churches and residences.

148

His remaining vessel could not face the storms and in November was forced to return for reasons of safety southward to Singapore. Meanwhile the *Catinat* and *Capricieuse,* having overstayed their time at Tourane, were obliged to proceed to Macao in order to obtain needed supplies. Montigny finally reached Tourane on January 23, 1857, but by then he lacked naval support and had no chance to accomplish positive results. When he quit the Annamite port in mid-February, the political prestige of France was at its nadir, and the Christian and missionary communities were more precariously exposed than ever.[49]

Montigny's other mistakes were attributable to his ignorance of the political realities of the area, his complete dependence on missionary advice and assistance, except where he chose to ignore it, and his habit of invoking the threat of British support on every possible occasion. This latter practice simply underscored his own deference to British leadership and did nothing to bolster French prestige.

Montigny's blunders at Bangkok were made, for the most part, after the treaty was negotiated and signed. Instead of entrusting the treaty to a special messenger for prompt transmission to Europe on a war vessel, he sent it unattended aboard a merchantman. When the ratified document was eventually returned to Bangkok, it was delivered to the government without any accompanying presents by a resident Portuguese national whom Montigny, before he left, had appointed as the titular French consul. The Siamese authorities regarded this strange procedure as an intended slight and disdainfully rejected the treaty. Not until the new consul for Bangkok, who was sent directly from France, arrived at Singapore in September, 1857, did the French learn of the treaty's rejection. The consul, M. Heurtier, was so coldly received when he actually reached Bangkok in December, 1857, that he quickly asked for leave.[50]

Another inexcusable mistake was Montigny's unwitting stimulation of the suspicions of the Siamese by attempting through the intervention of Bangkok authorities to prepare for his favorable reception by Cambodia and Annam. The first state was a zealously guarded vassal of Siam, and the second was one of its bitterest enemies. Montigny's long

---

[49] The best accounts of the Montigny mission are by Cordier ("La France et la Cochinchine," *T'oung Pao,* 2d ser., VII, 486–514, and "La Politique Coloniale," *T'oung Pao,* 2d ser., X, 186–189, 311–339, 675–692) and by Meyniard (pp. 359–423). Meyniard's is perhaps the more accurate of the two.

[50] Cordier, "La Politique Coloniale," *T'oung Pao,* 2d ser., X, 669–672.

delay in leaving Bangkok was due in part to his desire to await a reply from Monsignor Miche in Cambodia (it arrived September 7) and in part to Siamese arrangements. Under pretext of carrying out Montigny's request to assist his negotiations with the ruler of Cambodia, Bangkok sent emissaries of its own to Battambang to see what was up and to ensure that the suspicious French machinations with Siam's vassal were defeated. Montigny unknowingly co-operated by giving the Siamese ample time. When the French ships finally departed from Bangkok, the *Capricieuse* carried on board nine spies of the Siamese court in the guise of agents sent ostensibly to assist in the negotiations.[51] At Campot the Siamese representatives did everything possible to wreck Montigny's plans. The *Catinat* meanwhile had been sent ahead to Tourane in early September.

The negotiation at Campot was undertaken entirely on Montigny's initiative. The stop had been intended originally only to pick up Monsignor Miche, who was to act as Montigny's interpreter at Tourane and Hué. At Singapore Montigny had learned of an alleged proposal made to Miche in 1853 by the Cambodian King, Ang Duong, that France undertake to protect him from enemies in Annam.[52] The French plenipotentiary envisaged the prospect of achieving a brilliant diplomatic coup with the aid of Monsignor Miche. Montigny found the Bishop waiting for him when he reached Campot on October 5. The *Capricieuse* stopped at the place on October 7 long enough to put the Siamese spies ashore. It left on the following day for Tourane with orders to

[51] *Ibid.*, 672–674, 677–680. While at Bangkok, Montigny also urged the court to send an embassy to France. He offered the use of a French steamer, which would be available, he thought, in November, after he had concluded his mission to Cochin-China. The offer was politely declined. See SD, Bangkok, CL nos. 4 and 5, Aug 22 and 24, 1856.

[52] Meyniard asserted (pp. 359–360, 372–376) that there existed no proof that the King of Cambodia ever offered to accept the protection of France, as Monsignor Miche alleged. The King sent presents to Napoleon III in 1853, accompanied by a letter written by Miche himself offering friendship and "humble homage," but this letter was not official and had not reached Paris before Montigny's departure. The plenipotentiary learned of it from Catholic sources after reaching Singapore. Miche had written Courcy at Macao, in July, 1856, that Catholic missionaries in Cambodia suffered no persecution from the friendly King but that local mandarins often acted otherwise. He recommended a *démarche* on the part of France to put liberty of the Catholic faith on a treaty basis and to obtain a royal edict to that effect. Meyniard concluded that the subsequent charge that Ang Duong refused to ratify a treaty which he himself proposed was unfounded.

prevent the *Catinat* from leaving that harbor to join Guérin's fleet at Macao until Montigny could arrive. But the northeastern monsoon winds by that time were well started, and the *Capricieuse* ran into a typhoon which greatly delayed and almost wrecked the ship. It did not reach Tourane until October 24.[53]

Meanwhile, a contest had been going on at Campot between the French-transported Siamese representatives on the one side and Montigny and Monsignor Miche on the other. The Siamese threatened the agents of the vassal Cambodian King for entertaining French diplomatic proposals which had not first been cleared with Bangkok. Montigny denounced the conduct of the Siamese group as an insult and a taint on the friendship recently established between Siam and France. The resulting altercation completed the poisoning of French relations with Siam. Father Miche brought a letter from King Ang Duong dated several months back, which told of the King's desire to talk with Montigny and of his elaborate preparations of roadway, bridges, and elephant train for his trip to Campot.[54] But the agents of Siam at Battambang had in the meantime effectively sabotaged whatever plans the King may have entertained to make the journey. On October 12 or 15 news arrived that the King had allegedly suffered a sudden attack of boils (probably a pretext) and would not be able to make the trip after all.[55] Two days later several Cambodian ministers arrived bearing vague assurances that Ang Duong had commissioned Miche to handle the interview.

This event set the stage for the final episode. Four copies of a treaty following the general lines of the one recently signed with Siam were hastily drafted and translated by Montigny and Monsignor Miche without any reference to the newly arrived Cambodian ministers. The treaty included two innovations, both contributed by Father Miche. One was a provision making the Catholic religion one of the religions of the state. It guaranteed that the people of Cambodia would not be intimidated for accepting the new faith and that its adherents would be

[53] Cordier, "La France et la Cochinchine," *T'oung Pao,* 2d ser., VII, 505–507.

[54] Forty leagues of roadway, twenty bridges, and a troupe of two hundred elephants had allegedly been prepared.

[55] Meyniard (pp. 377–399) differs from Cordier's account ("La Politique Coloniale," *T'oung Pao,* 2d ser., X, 677–682) at a number of minor points. Cordier has Montigny reaching Campot on Oct. 1, Meyniard on Oct. 5; Cordier has the news of the nonarrival of the King coming on Oct. 12, Meyniard on Oct. 15.

required to do nothing contrary to their consciences. The other was an annex by which Cambodia ceded the forty-mile-long wedge-shaped island of Koh Doat (Cô Trol in Cambodian and Phu Quoc in Annamite) located off the mouth of the Campot River, to Napoleon III in perpetuity as "a guarantee of admiration . . . for the Emperor of the French . . . to prove his [Ang Duong's] sincere attachment to the loyal French nation." The annex also stated that French control of the island would enable them to intervene to protect Cambodia from attacks by Annam, in accordance with the alleged earlier request of the Siamese themselves.[56]

Because Monsignor Miche was to accompany Montigny to Tourane and the Cambodian ministers refused to act, the delivery of the treaty to King Ang Duong was entrusted to Miche's young assistant, Abbé Hestrest. He also carried a personal letter from Montigny explaining the economic and political advantages of alliance with France and repeating the allegation that the first King of Siam had expressed the desire that France occupy the island in question. Abbé Hestrest had no success whatever at Battambang. The King feigned anger that Montigny had not visited him personally, and he denounced the proposed cession of the island as an action which would involve him in war with Cochin-China authorities. Nor did he concede that his decisions should conform to the supposed wishes of Siam. A relevant factor in the situation was that the two sons of the Cambodian King were being held as hostages in Bangkok, so that he had no choice but to reject the treaty even if he had been inclined to do otherwise.[57]

Although Montigny was prepared to leave Campot for Tourane on October 16, the storm forced him to delay his departure for another week. Even then the seas were so violent that the *Marceau* had to return to Singapore, as stated above. From this point, Montigny wrote optimistically to Admiral Guérin on November 10 that his mission to Cambodia had succeeded perfectly and had ensured that henceforth French interests and those of the Catholic faith would be honorably safeguarded in that kingdom. When the plenipotentiary subsequently learned that the *Catinat* and the *Capricieuse* had already left Tourane

[56] Meyniard, 400–409; Cultru, 54–57; Cordier, "La Politique Coloniale," *T'oung Pao*, 2d ser., X, 681–687.

[57] Meyniard, 400, 410–423; Cordier, "La Politique Coloniale," *T'oung Pao*, 2d ser., X, 688–692.

to rejoin Admiral Guérin's fleet at Macao and also that persecutions had revived in Annam following their departure, he appealed in vain to Chargé de Courcy to intercede with the Admiral to restore the two vessels to his control.[58]

The Fiasco at Tourane

The story of what happened at Tourane while Montigny dallied at Bangkok and Campot can be briefly told. Captain Le Lieur of the *Catinat* reached the port in mid-September carrying as a passenger Abbé Fontaine, who was commissioned to deliver Montigny's letter to the Annamite King. The letter announced the desire of the French to negotiate a treaty of amity, commerce, navigation, and religion; it expressed French sympathy for the peoples of Cochin-China despite the provocations France had suffered and threatened that if this final opportunity to renew ancient relations of friendship were rebuffed, dire consequences would follow. If the mandarins refused to deliver the letter to the King at Hué, Abbé Fontaine was instructed to declare that Montigny and his English colleague, Bowring, would "demand judgment of the ministers responsible, [an action which] could produce the most unfortunate consequences." This letter was written from Bangkok on August 9. Montigny promised to follow Captain Le Lieur to Tourane within fifteen days.[59]

Within little more than a week after Le Lieur's arrival at Tourane, the *Catinat* became involved in combat with the harbor forts. Only after the steamer had pushed some distance up the river was the initial French letter accepted. But it was returned to Le Lieur on September 21 rudely and with one seal broken. Trouble began on September 25 when the French occupied an island in the harbor and undertook to prevent Annamite soldiers from manning the adjacent harbor forts. Eventually the French destroyed the forts with their sixty cannon and occupied the citadel. When local mandarins again appeared and offered to treat for peace, Le Lieur at first dallied by demanding assurances that his letter

[58] Cordier, "La France et la Cochinchine," *T'oung Pao*, 2d ser., VII, 492–493; Courcy, *Souvenirs*, III, 242; AEC, 19, 163. Courcy reported to Paris December 1, on word that came via Manila, that it was regrettable that Montigny had not been constrained to arrange it so that he could have appeared at Tourane within a month at least of the preparation of ground for negotiation.

[59] Cordier, "La Politique Coloniale," *T'oung Pao*, 2d ser., X, 675–676; Cordier, "La France et la Cochinchine," *T'oung Pao*, 2d ser., VII, 493–496.

would be delivered to Tu-Duc. But finally he was forced to explain that negotiations would have to await Montigny's arrival, which he expected within a few days.[60]

Weeks passed without any sign of the plenipotentiary. The *Catinat* ran short of supplies, and Monsignor Fontaine became alarmed lest the opportunity for negotiation would pass and the effects of the French effort be dissipated. Captain Collier, Le Lieur's superior, who arrived on the storm-battered *Capricieuse* on October 24, approved the previous actions of Le Lieur, although admittedly they had exceeded his instructions. But the French commanders still could not negotiate and had no choice but to continue their dilatory tactics. In a final exchange of communications with the local mandarins directly before the two ships departed for Macao on November 10, Captain Collier adopted a more friendly tone, but he could propose nothing in the way of a settlement.[61]

Montigny's eventual arrival at Tourane on January 23, 1857, only underscored the loss of French prestige. Montigny now could do nothing to carry out the threatened retaliation in case Tu-Duc again molested French missionaries. His departure on February 11 signified fearful forebodings for the missionaries.[62] Following his own return to Macao in March, 1857, Bourboulon aptly described the Tourane episode as "badly contrived in principle, commenced by force and terminated after a long interval by an impotent retreat." [63] Monsignor Pellerin, who had escaped from Tourane on the *Capricieuse*, reported that the abortive effort had left the missions in Tongking more desolate than ever. He was returning to France to appeal to the government for aid. The decapitation of the Spanish bishop, Monsignor Diaz, by Tu-Duc's order later in 1857 provided the pretext for the eventual joint Spanish-French intervention in Annam.

Montigny's final act in the fiasco was to address a complaint to the King of Siam concerning the indiscreet, impertinent, and menacing conduct of the Siamese agents at Campot. He attempted also to explain

[60] AEC, 19, 171–179, Le Lieur's report of Oct. 26, 1856.

[61] Cordier, "La France et la Cochinchine," *T'oung Pao*, 2d ser., VII, 504–514.

[62] P. Adrien Launay, *Mgr. Retord et le Tonkin Catholique (1831–1858)* (Lyons, 1893), 371–381.

[63] AEC, 20, 131–132, from Bourboulon, March 9, 1857. Courcy wrote on Dec. 27, 1856: "The ill-will of the Annamite authorities toward our missionaries is disclosed [anew] each day, . . . and there is reason to fear that cruel persecution will follow."

that the religious article in the Cambodian treaty in no way compromised Siam's suzerainty and that the annex calling for the cession of Koh Doat Island was a move of no importance which merely transferred the proposal to Paris for consideration.[64]

French prestige could not have withstood many repetitions of Montigny's performance, which the efforts of his apologists have done little to excuse.[65] The Annamite authorities gloated over the discomfiture of the French, proclaiming after Montigny's departure that the French barked like dogs but later ran away like goats.[66] The *Catinat* did return to the coast of Tongking in September, 1857, to rescue several endangered missionaries, but the next important move was the gathering of Franco-Spanish forces at Hainan Island in the summer of 1858.[67] By that time the question of French prestige in southeast Asia had become involved in much larger plans covering the Far East generally.

French Policy Regarding the Mission of Peter Parker, 1856

The mission of Peter Parker, an American, occupied the center of the diplomatic stage in China during the period of the Montigny mission in southeast Asia. As a long-time medical missionary to China (since 1834), as an interpreter and secretary to both Cushing and McLane, and as five times chargé ad interim of the American legation, Parker was well known in China. He was selected by President Pierce to make a determined attempt in co-operation with Britain and France to obtain a revision of the China treaties. Parker was directed to seek three main objectives: residence of diplomatic officers at Peking, unlimited extension of trade, and removal of restrictions on foreigners beyond those to which the Chinese themselves were subject.[68] To these he eventually

---

[64] Cordier, "La Politique Coloniale," *T'oung Pao*, 2d ser., X, 693–697; Cordier, "La France et la Cochinchine," *T'oung Pao*, 2d ser., VII, 514.

[65] The defense of Montigny's conduct by Abbé Louvet (*La Cochinchine Religieuse*, II, 215–219) is a partisan account which argues that none of the French demands on Hué were exorbitant. He asserts that "as for the missionaries, they . . . did not ask for anything."

[66] H. I. Priestley, *France Overseas* (New York, 1938), 114; Septans, 133–134.

[67] M. Picanon, "La Prise de Saigon en Février 1859 et les Débuts de Notre Action en Cochinchine," *Académie des Sciences Coloniales*, VIII (1926–1927), 386–387.

[68] SD, China, Instructions 1, 121–127, Sept. 7 and Oct. 5, 1855. He was also authorized to give moral support and aid to the imperial government as a *quid pro quo* for concessions, but not to intervene or to wage war, both of which lay outside the limits of U.S. policy and the powers of the executive.

added a fourth of his own, namely, to reform the court system of China by "friendly suggestion." [69] Although Parker was a man of education and intelligence, he was a bumptious type of person who entertained grandiose dreams as to the potential effectiveness of his diplomatic efforts. He was at the same time incapable of getting along with his own legation and consular staff.[70] French and British colleagues in China, who knew Parker best, expected little to come from his efforts.

Parker's conversations with Clarendon and Walewski at London and Paris respectively, which he visited en route to China in October-November, 1855, succeeded in dispelling certain anxieties which the European governments seem to have entertained concerning the intentions of the American agent. Both Foreign Ministers declared that his objectives accorded with their own, and both agreed that it might be possible, as he suggested doing, to assemble the combined fleets in the Gulf of Pohai in June, 1856, in support of joint demands upon Peking.

But neither European Foreign Minister committed himself to anything in the way of active co-operation with Parker. They delayed many months before sending instructions to Bowring and Courcy about the policy to pursue.[71] The conclusion of the Crimean War and the subsequent staging of the Congress of Paris occupied the center of interest in Europe. Bowring was eventually instructed in very general terms on March 7, 1856, to act in concert with the American and French representatives to induce Peking to revise its treaties along lines indicated in previous instructions.[72] Paris did not see fit to send similar instructions to Macao until May 10, too late for Courcy to participate in the formal demands of the other two that negotiations for treaty revision be held

[69] AEC, 17, 162–167. This supposedly "confidential" letter from Parker to Bowring, dated Feb. 2, 1856, found its way to the French archives.

[70] Griffin, 128–130; D. Malone, *Dictionary of American Biography*, XIV, 234–235; Cordier, *1857–58*, 7.

[71] SD, China, DD, from Parker at London, Oct. 26, at Paris, Nov. 8, 1855. Parker was flattered by his seeming success. Clarendon sent a perfunctory reference to Bowring concerning the visit (FO, 17, 225, Dec. 4, 1855) and Walewski merely asked the French Ambassador at London (Nov. 19 and Jan. 30) to inquire what Clarendon intended to do.

[72] FO, 17, 242, to Bowring, March 7, 1856; 35th Congress, 2d sess., Sen. exec. doc. 22, p. 633, from Parker, Feb. 12, 1856. Bowring invited Parker to accompany him to Japan after completing the Chinese negotiation and added: "We ought also to open Korea."

at Peking. The familiar pattern of French lack of co-operation thus re-appeared.

French hesitance can probably best be explained by reference to Courcy's dispatches. Although he maintained cordial personal relations with Parker, Courcy was convinced nothing could be accomplished by making demands which the Chinese were perfectly able to spurn. The liberalizing demands of the West, although possibly capable of justification in terms of China's best interests, had not in Courcy's opinion been sufficiently sustained nor had they been sufficiently based on principle for the Chinese to appreciate their value. He declared that the Chinese government, even though hard pressed by rebellion, would oppose systematically and by all possible means the advances of the West. Since a tentative effort not supported by an imposing array of force would certainly fail and only add more grief and humiliation to the sad story of Western relations with China, Courcy refused to co-operate with Parker in the absence of definite instructions to do so.[73]

Courcy also opposed a contemporary proposal by Bowring to by-pass Parker by basing Anglo-French demands for compensatory advantages from China on Peking's assumed acquiescence in the Russian occupation of the Amur River mouth and De Castries Bay to the disadvantage of Britain and France. The French chargé foresaw that such a move would afford China a welcome opportunity to pit Russia and the United States against Britain and France and that it was calculated therefore to cause endless mischief. Neither Parker's optimistic expectations nor Bowring's overclever legalistic maneuvering would, in his opinion, serve the interests of France.[74] The receipt at Paris of this dispatch from Courcy during the first week of April apparently led to the canceling of the French decision to co-operate, as announced to Lord Cowley at Paris on April 4, 1856.[75] Another reason for the divergence of French and British policies was the revival among the British in China of the idea of promoting trading interests by co-operation with the Taipings. Bowring urged in this connection that the allies establish foreign pro-

[73] AEC, 17, 169–175, 225–226, 269–270; 18, 15–22, 38–42, successive dispatches dated Feb. 8, March 1, April 10, May 22, and June 6, 1856.

[74] *Ibid.*, 17, 169–182, to Walewski, Feb. 8, 1856. Courcy here presents an able and thoroughgoing analysis of the situation.

[75] *Ibid.*, 17, 247–249, to Cowley, April 4, 1856. No corresponding instruction was sent to Courcy.

tectorates over all the open ports in a move to counter Russian gains.[76]

Meanwhile Parker was having a most distressing time. Yeh neglected to acknowledge his first communication in April, and the distraught American could see no signs of the expected concentration of allied naval power to support his demand for treaty revision at Peking. A second note of intention was sent to Yeh on May 2, this time requesting the Emperor to appoint a commission for purposes of treaty revision to meet with Western negotiators at Peking. Bowring supported the request two weeks later, but Courcy confined his action to indicating his close relations with the others and to reaffirming French rights under the most-favored-nation principle. Within less than a month prior to the July 3 deadline, when the twelve-year period since the signing of Cushing's Treaty of Wanghia would expire, Parker found himself with only a single American sloop of war available, itself without orders to aid him, while the rest of the naval forces of England, France, and America were widely dispersed. When it became obvious at the end of June that no joint fleet action was possible for the current year, Parker decided to go northward alone, stopping at successive treaty ports, and, if practicable, proceeding to Peking. He admitted that he entertained little hope of full success. Yeh's replies to the several communications of the three diplomats had consistently denied any obligation on China's part to consider revision of the British treaty and had declared that no changes were necessary in the others.[77] Courcy commented that Bowring now shared his own view that Parker's misguided solo effort would inevitably run aground and would only be the source of new griefs which all would have to share in common.[78]

When Courcy's instructions of May 10 to co-operate with Parker finally reached him on July 27,[79] the American project for revision was already dead, if indeed it had ever shown any signs of vitality. The

[76] FO, 17, 244, Bowring from Hongkong, Jan. 12, 1856, transmitting an enclosure by Consul Robertson of Shanghai.

[77] 35th Congress, 2d sess., Sen. exec. doc. 22, pp. 761, 799–800, 812–817, 834, dated from March 13 to June 30, 1856; Cordier, 1857–58, 7–17. Some of Cordier's dates are wrong.

[78] AEC, 18, 75–76, 80, to Paris, June 30 and July 4, 1857. Bowring referred to Parker disrespectfully as the "official homeopath."

[79] Ibid., 18, 6–13, to Courcy, May 10, 1856. Walewski directed that all other objectives in the French effort should be subordinated to obtaining diplomatic residence at Peking. Admiral Guérin's forces might assist by their presence but could not be assigned any particular role because of their other duties (aiding Montigny,

French chargé had just corroborated the news of the judicial execution of Father Chapdelaine of the Missions Etrangères at Hsi-lin in Kwangsi Province on the previous February 29. This event gave France a tangible grievance against the Chinese authorities for a violation of treaty guarantees.[80] With respect to Parker's forlorn effort, sustained only by his illusions about the possibility of convincing hard-pressed Peking that the foreigners were really sincere and disinterested friends of the Chinese,[81] Courcy was politely tolerant and noncommittal. The nearest the French chargé ever came to actual collaboration was in late October when he accepted Parker's invitation to join him in prospective negotiations at Shanghai, but he accepted only under the unlikely contingency that the Chinese should agree in advance to concede the right of diplomatic residence in Peking. Parker abandoned his hopeless project on November 1, 1856.[82]

By the fall of 1856, the fumbling effort of Washington to take over the diplomatic initiative in the Far East had spent itself (except for Townsend Harris in Japan); the Crimean War had been concluded; France had a *cause célèbre* to justify punitive measures in China; and the famous *Lorcha Arrow* incident in the Canton River (October 8) had provided Britain with a less valid but convenient pretext for carrying out measures already decided upon at London. The deplorable collapse of French prestige in all Annam following Montigny's inept efforts inevitably brought that area also within the purview of French planning. But in the ensuing preparations to enforce demands on China for substantial treaty revision, London and Paris understandably preferred to consult *à deux,* with little concern for Washington's views.

---

for example). The seal of the envelope carrying these instructions had been broken, and Courcy suspected British prying. See Courcy, *Souvenirs,* III, 252–253.

[80] Cordier, *Histoire Générale,* IV, 44; Courcy, *L'Empire du Milieu,* 598–602; *Annales de la Propagation de la Foi,* XXVIII (1856), 461–481. The news first reached the missionaries at Canton on July 7. After verification, Courcy wrote to Walewski, July 17, and sent the first of a long series of protests to Yeh on July 25, 1856.

[81] AEC, 18, 169, to Walewski, Aug. 20, 1856; 35th Congress, 2d sess., Sen. exec. doc. 22, pp. 920–922, Parker from Shanghai, Sept. 3, 1856. Parker apparently entertained some hope that the newly demonstrated strength of the Taipings would moderate Peking's pride and also hinted at the possible alternative of shifting American support to the supposedly more democratic Nanking regime (AEC, 19, 146–147, Parker to Bowring, August, 1856).

[82] AEC, 18, 317–320, 324–325, Courcy to Walewski and enclosures, Oct. 28, 1856; 35th Congress, 2d sess., Sen. exec. doc. 22, pp. 968, 1076.

XI

Origins of the Joint Intervention, 1856-1857

THE vague and sometimes contradictory character of French policy from 1853 to 1856 with respect to the revision of the China treaties can be attributed in large measure to a difference in point of view between the Foreign Office at Paris and French diplomatic representatives in the field. From the broad perspective of the viewpoint of Paris, the advantages of maintaining a close entente with Great Britain in matters relating to the Far East seemed obvious. France by herself was in no position to demand satisfaction for the numerous complaints arising under its self-imposed responsibility to safeguard the interests of Catholic missions, while at the same time the government of Louis Napoleon did not find it politically feasible to repudiate its alliance with the church. Furthermore, considerations of prestige forbade that France be left out of any military or diplomatic action which Western powers might undertake in the Far East. Thus it happened that Paris gave a consistently affirmative response to British and American proposals to collaborate in liberalizing treaty relations with China, even though French policy directives and commitment of material resources to implement such a program were halting and tentative.

French agents in China, on the other hand, were close enough to the actual situation to realize that French interests in the Far East were

160

not identical with those of Britain and America. For one thing, Catholic and Protestant missionary interests were in bitter rivalry. The French missionaries did not share the stake that the Protestant groups thought they might have in the prospective victory of the Taiping rebels. The Catholics were trying to find favor with the imperialist authorities by dissociating themselves from their supposed involvement as Christians in the rebellion. Nor did the French have any commercial stake in the revolutionary situation. They had no opium or other goods to sell, no customs administration to organize, no interests of a resident business community to take into account. Whether the French adopted a program of all-out collaboration with missionary interests, as at Shanghai, or the more reserved policy of Bourboulon at Macao, it was clear from the point of view of the French in the Orient that the interests and prestige of France would not be served by following a pattern of conduct determined by Britain or America. The grievance which all shared was the exasperating difficulty of diplomatic communication, which denied them a prompt and courteous hearing from Commissioner Yeh at Canton and prohibited their direct contact with Peking.

It is significant that Foreign Minister Walewski's instructions to Courcy during the first half of 1856 placed the emphasis not on the promotion of missionary interests, but on the fundamental problem of obtaining diplomatic representation at Peking. The change of emphasis was so striking that Courcy, in his acknowledgment on July 27 of the receipt of instructions going back to March 25, expressed surprise that he found nothing in them concerning patronage of the missionaries, which had so long been the basis of French policy in China. He asked for specific information on how much initiative it was intended that he should exercise on this important matter.[1] Only a few months before, Courcy himself had given vent to his impatience over the presumptuous demands of Monsignor Mouly.[2]

The news of the execution of Father Chapdelaine was a tangible and flagrant challenge to French political prestige as well as an attack on the missionary cause. It served, therefore, to bring about a coalescence of French political objectives and interest in missionary patronage, thus bridging the gap between the viewpoints of Paris and Macao.

[1] AEC, 18, 129–130, from Courcy, July 30, 1856; Courcy, *Souvenirs*, III, 264.
[2] Chapter X, n. 19.

Courcy and the Chapdelaine Affair

Father Chapdelaine was the first representative of the Missions Etrangères in China since 1815 to suffer death by order of a Chinese magistrate. Although he was a man of nearly fifty years, Chapdelaine had been resident in his field of labor in Kwangsi only a scant fifteen months prior to the date of his execution on February 29, 1856. Shortly after his arrival in December, 1854, he had been arrested, but was released after a hearing.[3] He was again denounced in early 1856 on charges of dividing families and causing trouble generally, and was finally apprehended and taken to Hsi-lin for trial on February 25. According to the gruesome reports which reached Canton, Chapdelaine was brutally flogged, imprisoned in chains, exposed publicly in a cage, and otherwise abused; his decapitated head was then suspended publicly until knocked down by stones and given to the dogs; his heart was cut out, cooked, and eaten, and his body hacked to bits. Two native Christians were reported to have died with him and some nine others to have been retained in prison for religious causes only.[4]

Courcy's first report of the affair to Walewski reflected the repressed fury of the French community at Macao. He declared that the bloody hand of a barbarian Chinese had destroyed the French treaty. Timid claims, vain excuses, sterile promises were at an end, for the honor of France was at stake. He would complete his review of the facts of the case, formulate demands that could not be brushed aside through endless delays, and attempt to come to agreement with Admiral Guérin, as soon as the officer returned to Macao, concerning measures to be taken if French demands were refused.[5] But a certain amount of delay was inevitable. Courcy's letter of July 18 to Guérin, asking him to co-

[3] P. Adrien Launay, *Histoire des Missions de Chine, Mission du Kouang-si* (Paris, 1903), 46–59.

[4] *Ibid.*, 66–78, 88–90, 112–121; Cordier, *1857–58*, 19–22. The report was based on information supplied second or third hand by Abbé Lyons (from near Hsi-lin) and Monsignor Perny, the Superior of the Kweichow mission. Informers sent to Hsi-lin gathered the data, which probably lost nothing in the telling. The final report, prepared by Monsignor Guillemin, was dated July 13.

[5] AEC, 18, 90–93, to Walewski, July 17, 1856. In his *Souvenirs* (III, 170–202) Courcy explained that in 1856 the first secretary of the legation, Casimir Troplong, urged immediate bombardment of Canton, while Kleczkowski opposed hasty action. On July 22, Courcy also received reports of renewed persecution of Christians east of Peking and at Soochow, near Shanghai.

operate in energetic measures to obtain satisfaction from China, was not answered until September 20, and then only by the Admiral's promise to return to Macao in November.[6]

In the chargé's initial complaint to Commissioner Yeh he reviewed the reported details of Chapdelaine's execution, asserting that the facts as established by a vigorously impartial inquest admitted of neither doubt nor discussion. The toleration decrees of the Emperor had been flouted and Article 23 of the French treaty flagrantly violated. Yeh must offer *une éclatante réparation* without delay if he wished to maintain amicable relations with France. Courcy reserved the right to decide whether the offer was such that the dignity and honor of France permitted its acceptance. He requested an appointment to meet Yeh at Canton to discuss the issue and asked to be informed a week in advance as to the time and place.[7]

To Walewski, Courcy explained that he did not expect Yeh to grant his request for an interview. The minimum demands he had in mind would include punishment of the guilty official, guarantees against repetition of the incident, assurances that China desired to maintain good relations with France, and the insertion in the *Peking Gazette* of an imperial decree telling of the reasons for the degradation and exile of the guilty mandarin. He decided to hold in abeyance the possible additional demand that French priests be authorized to reside freely in the interior. He explained that China could be expected to oppose bitterly the granting of corollary privileges of equal interior access for both Protestant missionaries and foreign merchants. Since he was confident that the combined military efforts of France, Britain, and America would be required to beat down Chinese objections to unrestricted entry, he would await formal authorization from Paris before advancing a demand for this concession.

Courcy's accompanying analysis indicated to Paris that there was a limited choice of sanctions France could use. To undertake unilateral naval demonstrations at the several treaty ports as a means of impressing Peking with the seriousness of the French demands would imperil com-

[6] Cordier, *1857–58*, 23–26. At this point Montigny's commandeering of the *Catinat* and the *Capricieuse* for use in Indo-China (Chapter X) played havoc with naval efforts to support the legation.

[7] Cordier, *1857–58*, 25–28, Courcy to Yeh July 25, 1856. A letter dated July 26 also asked Yeh to take immediate steps to free the nine Chinese Christians still imprisoned.

merce generally and arouse serious resentment among non-French business elements. To take hostages was beneath the dignity of France. He finally recommended that Guérin's marines be authorized to seize and hold Chusan Island until claims were met. This would be a feasible objective and one both intrinsically and strategically valuable to France. The Catholic missionaries in China, he reported, were less worried over the possible ill effects of such a move on their colleagues in the interior than they were over the results of a display of too much moderation and forbearance.[8]

The French chargé realized little satisfaction from his communications with Commissioner Yeh. The latter conceded at first that Chapdelaine had been treated badly and promised to communicate with Courcy as soon as the results were available from the inquiry which he had authorized. But he pointed out that Chapdelaine had no right under the treaty to be in Hsi-lin, and that Kwangsi Province abounded in bandits who claimed to be Christian. He concluded by saying that it would be impossible, as long as the conditions of rebellion persisted around Canton, where he was personally responsible for directing military operations, for him to fix a time and place for the requested interview.[9]

Courcy replied that Article 23 of the French treaty provided for the safe conduct of foreigners to the nearest consular office, and he insisted that the fact of Chapdelaine's martydom was fully known. He then demanded the degradation and exile of the Hsi-lin magistrate, publication in the *Peking Gazette* of an official dispatch to the French legation about the matter, and the issuance of an imperial decree threatening with the same penalty all magistrates found similarly guilty. When Yeh sent the bland rejoinder that investigation of the affair by the Kwangsi Governor would have to follow the normal procedure, the chargé threatened grave consequences,[10] but he had no choice but to subside and await developments.

In the course of these discouraging exchanges, Courcy's mood became petulant and irascible. To Walewski he gave vent to his pent-up feelings of resentment over the dilatory tactics, ill-will, arrogance, and pride of the Chinese—attitudes which, he declared, only force could

[8] AEC, 18, 121–128, to Walewski, July 30, 1856; Cordier, *1857–58*, 26–28.
[9] Cordier, *1857–58*, 30–31, Yeh to Courcy, Aug. 20, 1856.
[10] *Ibid.*, 31–33, 36–37, to Yeh, Aug. 25 and Sept. 20, and from Yeh, Sept. 9, 1856.

overcome.[11] He outlined the manifold commercial grievances endured by foreigners. He complained of Bowring's lack of frankness and the Briton's unreasoning desire to chastise Canton and open it to foreigners even before any joint policy had been adopted or the necessary forces assembled to carry through such an effort. He resented Britain's presumptuous leadership in the Orient, its lack of rivals in prestige, trade, or naval power. He also complained bitterly of Admiral Guérin's lack of attention to his pleas for naval assistance at Canton and Shanghai. In this connection he tried in vain to detain at Canton Captain Maisonneuve of the *Sybille*, who was on his way to Bombay with orders to visit the Persian Gulf. He even repeated unfounded rumors that Russia had purchased eight hundred acres on one of the islands of the Chusan group, and made these rumors the basis of a plea that France must seize for herself a material security like Chusan, which would reestablish her tarnished prestige and restore her rank abreast of other nations. On September 1, discouraged and homesick, the young chargé finally asked for a year's leave of absence, pleading in justification ill-health, family interests, and the need to attend to private affairs.[12]

The Anglo-French Decision for Joint Intervention

It was a foregone conclusion that once the embarrassment of the Crimean War was passed, the British government under Lord Palmerston's vigorous leadership would push to an issue the question of revising the China treaty. The return of Parkes to his post as consul at Canton in the summer of 1856, following six month's leave in England during which he was in constant touch with the Foreign Office (especially Palmerston, Clarendon, and Under-Secretary Hammond), produced a marked stiffening in the local British attitude. The new view was that a "high tone" must be taken; never give in, never allow a slight to pass unchallenged, and seize on the first opportunity which presented itself to reopen the Canton question. An overt act by the Chinese was sure to occur before long.[13]

However congenial this new mood was to Parkes and Bowring, it appeared ominous to French eyes. Courcy reported on August 20 with

[11] AEC, 18, 143–144, Aug. 5, 1856.
[12] *Ibid.*, 147–166, 172–174, 192, 259–260, Aug. 20 through Oct. 5, 1856; Cordier, 1857–58, 33–34.
[13] Lane-Poole, I, 195, 222–235.

some alarm that in the event the Chinese should again refuse to negotiate, Bowring favored renouncing all restraints imposed by the treaties,
occupying by force all trading centers, and proclaiming by right of conquest the complete opening of China.[14] Even if the Manchu court re-
treated to Manchuria, Bowring maintained that trade could continue
at the treaty ports under the protecting foreign garrisons and without
any necessary involvement of foreigners in the civil war.[15] This new
aggressive spirit on the part of the British coupled with French exasperation over Chinese dallying in making amends for Chapdelaine's execution were the basic causes of the joint intervention of 1857–1858.

Serious consideration of the China situation by authorities at Paris
and London began in September, 1856. Bourboulon, in Paris at the time,
told the French Foreign Office that Courcy had erred in the Chapdelaine
affair by not demanding a monetary indemnity to cover the offense to
the dignity of France, the loss to the Missions Etrangères, and the cost
of any countermeasures that might have to be taken. He felt that Peking
would not hesitate to victimize the offending magistrate. Since the seat
of power of the Viceroy responsible for the two Kwangs was at Canton,
which continued to be the unchastised center of the most virulent
hostility to the foreigners, he argued that the reparation must be sought
at that city by a land and sea force capable of capturing the place.[16]

Shortly after Bourboulon submitted his memorandum, the British
Ambassador at Paris proposed urgent consideration of a new proposal
by Clarendon, namely, that the agents of the two powers, with or without American co-operation, should immediately proceed up the Peiho
River as far as was practicable and there claim from the Emperor of
China fulfillment of his alleged engagement to negotiate for the revision of their treaties. The British document continued:

They [British and French agents] will endeavor to make it evident to the
Emperor . . . that he will best consult the interests of his empire by deferring to the wishes of the Treaty Powers, rather than by turning a deaf
ear to their representations, release them from the moral obligation under
which they now labor to recognize and respect his Sovereign rights . . .

Her Majesty's Government are far from desiring the overthrow of the

---

[14] AEC, 18, 166, from Courcy, Aug. 20, 1856.

[15] *Ibid.*, 19, 148–152, from Bowring to London, Aug. 21, 1856.

[16] *Ibid.*, 18, 220–235, by Bourboulon, Sept. 20, 1856. Bourboulon recalled that
the promised imperial inquest into the Vachal case in 1850 had never been made.

present Dynasty in China. . . . But . . . the time is near at hand when either the Emperor . . . must be made to adopt a more liberal system in his intercourse with foreign nations or some other combination must be acceded to by which the humiliating position in which foreigners still continue to be placed in China must be improved and the vast resources of that Empire opened up to the industrial enterprise of foreign nations.[17]

The alternatives which Paris now faced were set forth in two long memoranda originating within the French Ministry.[18] Should France participate with Britain in the Peiho effort and risk overthrowing the Manchu regime, or should it act unilaterally by seizing Chusan as security for limited reparations, as Courcy had recommended? As usual, the advantages of collaboration won the day. Walewski accepted the British proposal on condition that the French demand for an indemnity for Chapdelaine's death be given precedence in the Peiho negotiations. He also reserved the right of temporary French occupation of Chusan Island as surety for payment. He sent a naval captain (Pigeard) to London to confer about plans for armed collaboration.[19]

London replied on October 31. Clarendon agreed that Britain would make common cause with France over reparation for the Chapdelaine affair, but he thought that at the Peiho meeting any claims for reparations should be accompanied by demands for treaty revision. Clarendon was far from enthusiastic over the French proposal to occupy Chusan. He pointed out that such a move would entail no inconvenience to Peking, and its accomplishment would require a considerable military force. More effective pressure on Peking could be exerted at various points up the Yangtse by naval means alone. He added, "It would be as inconvenient for France as it would unquestionably be for England to employ a large military force on the present occasion." [20]

An archival memorandum indicates that Paris did not credit Clarendon's contentions that Chusan would be difficult to occupy or that naval

[17] *Ibid.,* 18, 243–248, Clarendon to Cowley, Sept. 24, 1856; FO, 17, 261, to Bowring, Sept. 24, 1856. Clarendon's agreement with Bowring's proposed action is clearly implied.

[18] AEC, 18, 286–308, undated and unsigned.

[19] FO, 17, 261, a copy of Walewski to Persigny, Oct. 22, 1856, sent as an enclosure to Bowring, Feb. 9, 1857.

[20] AEC, 18, 337–338, Clarendon to Cowley, Oct. 31, 1856; FO, 17, 261, enclosure to Bowring, Feb. 9, 1857. Cordier's account of this exchange (*1857–58,* 90–93) asserts that Clarendon's statement assumed that British troops would share in any occupation of Chusan. This is not necessarily implied.

pressure up the Yangtse would be effective against Peking, especially since the Yangtse Valley was almost entirely in rebel hands.[21] But in the end Walewski bowed to the obvious British objection to French occupation of Chusan, provided the claim for the French indemnity received priority over other demands made on China.[22] The agreement was confirmed in early December and instructions were exchanged by December 16. An additional item of agreement provided that following the completion of their Peiho mission, the combined squadrons were to proceed to Tokyo, Japan, for purposes of treaty negotiation.[23]

The French instructions to Bourboulon (on December 25) and to Admiral Guérin (on December 23) directed that armed operations be undertaken only into the Peiho and Yangtse River areas. In addition to insistence on the priority demand for compensation for the death of Chapdelaine, Bourboulon was to concentrate his efforts on obtaining diplomatic residence at Peking and the right of unrestricted contact by foreigners with the interior. French missionaries must be guaranteed against further arbitrary interference. Reinforcements under the command of Rigault de Genouilly would include one frigate, two corvettes, four gun boats, and two transports carrying marine infantry.[24]

Because the dismal outcome of Montigny's mission was unknown in Paris at the time of the preparation of these instructions, consideration of the possibility of using Genouilly's reinforcements in Annam was reserved for a later occasion. Genouilly's choice as commander was nevertheless itself significant of French interest in Annam.

[21] AEC, 19, 4–10, a memorandum dated Nov. 4, 1856.

[22] *Ibid.*, 106–110, to Persigny, Nov. 20, 1856; from Pigeard, Nov. 20, 1856. Pigeard's report also registered British opposition to conducting operations at Canton.

[23] FO, 17, 261, from enclosures dated Dec. 5, 11, and 16, 1856, in Bowring's general instructions of Feb. 9, 1857; AEC, 19, 222, 249–252, 259–260, to Persigny, Dec. 16, and from Persigny, Dec. 18, 1856. Clarendon offered to seek the good offices of Holland to facilitate negotiations with Japan.

The British Foreign Office at this juncture also advised Bowring to abandon the customs administrative system at Shanghai, allegedly because of complaints lodged by mercantile firms operating in China and the recommendations of the Lords of Trade. Bourboulon was instructed to acquiesce in this proposal; he and Bowring were to work out the details. If this advice had been followed, direct foreign control of all important ports of China, as advocated by Bowring, might have taken the place of the Imperial Maritime Customs. See AEC, 19, 225–241, 302. Bourboulon's instructions to proceed to Tokyo were dated Jan. 7, 1857.

[24] AEC, 19, 263–277, 304–308; also in Cordier, *1857–58*, 94–101.

French Policy toward the Arrow War

The Arrow War incident was in a sense the result rather than the cause of Britain's determination to force China to revise its treaties, a policy which found expression in the joint expedition of 1857–1858. The news of the fighting at Canton did not reach London until December 1, and the seriousness of the affair was not appreciated until months later. The altercation over the seizure of the *Arrow* crew can perhaps be best understood as the explosion of an accumulation of volatile psychological fuel ignited by the knowledge on the part of Bowring and Parkes that Palmerston was adopting a vigorously aggressive mood in London.

The basic British grievance against China was the exasperating refusal of Commissioner Yeh to deal with resident diplomatic agents in a respectful and co-operative manner. Yeh was, of course, a very busy man, and his obstinacy was probably aggravated by the active smuggling of arms and supplies by foreigners to his enemies, rebel elements operating in the vicinity of Canton.[25] Many vessels engaged in the coastal trade were operating in a twilight of semilegality under sacrosanct Portuguese or British registry. The *Arrow* itself had a very shady past. Its crew included several admitted pirates, and its registry at Hongkong, which gave it the right to carry the British flag, had expired eleven days before the incident of October 8.

The real issue, once the controversy had started, was "face." Consul Parkes and Governor Bowring took the view that the British flag had been wantonly desecrated. They demanded not simply the surrender of the seized crew, pirate members and all, but that it be done in such a fashion that British pride would be assuaged and the prestige of Yeh impaired. When Yeh refused to sacrifice his own "face" by the manner of surrendering the crew, hostilities started in November. Bowring then included in the British demand the long-smoldering question of the right of entry into Canton.[26] British leveling of the fortifications around

[25] Charles S. Leavenworth, *The Arrow War* (London, 1901), 10–11, 29–30. Many of the vessels licensed at Hongkong were engaged in distributing the enormous quantities of opium brought from India. Others were guilty of kidnapping operations and of selling arms and munitions to the rebels. See also S. W. Williams, *A History of China* (New York, 1897), 280–285.

[26] Lane-Poole, I, 228–230, 234–235; Leavenworth, 17–22, 27–29. Yeh promised on Oct. 14 not to seize without reason crews of foreign lorchas, but he denied the right of foreigners to sell registries to Chinese vessels and refused to apologize for his alleged offense to the British flag.

Canton followed in November and December, but without making any dent on the obstinacy of Yeh. The antiforeign Chinese population of Canton backed the commissioner, who pictured the English as in league with the rebels and outlaws.[27]

By the end of the year it was clear that the available British forces were not strong enough to force Yeh's surrender. Nor was the moral case of the British entirely defensible. Yeh argued with some plausibility that hostilities had been begun under false pretenses to obtain a concession (entry to Canton) which the British had renounced in 1849 and which Yeh could in no wise grant on his own authority.[28] The eventual British withdrawal from before Canton on January 14 left the factories burned, Chinese "face" triumphant, and British prestige so heavily impaired that, despite London's contrary views, the capture of Canton became the first objective of the eventual joint expedition.[29]

The initial reaction to the Arrow War by American and French elements at Macao and Canton reflected both their own impatience with Yeh's tactics, which made them sympathize with the British action, and their natural reluctance to become involved in an affair of dubious justification which did not directly concern their interests.[30] Courcy

[27] Leavenworth, 34–38; SD, Canton, CL 4, from O. H. Perry, no. 17, Nov. 14, 1856. Actually, Bowring rebuffed the offer of the Taiping rebels to co-operate with the British.

[28] O. L. Oliphant, *Narrative of the Earl of Elgin's Mission to China and Japan in the Years 1857–58–59* (Edinburgh, 1859), I, 2–7.

[29] Although Parkes was responsible for the initial explosion, Bowring's ambition to "write a bright page" in the history of Britain's foreign relations and his restless desire, as alleged by Admiral Seymour, to have events revolve around the orbit of his personal kudos (see Lane-Poole, I, 244–245) were responsible for broadening the scope of British demands.

[30] Dr. Parker hailed Commodore Armstrong's attack on the barrier forts (Nov. 16–20) as an action "calculated to secure for [the U.S.] important prestige in the mind of this haughty government." He nevertheless treated the American incident as a matter isolated from the British action and capable of prompt and amicable settlement. He predicted that events at Canton would assist in obtaining early resumption of trade at Canton. At this juncture also came his proposal that the foreign powers force China to negotiate for treaty revision by America's seizing Formosa, France Korea, and Britain Chusan, at best a highly uneven distribution. In February, 1857, he authorized Commodore Armstrong to raise the American flag over the building of the recently established American-Japanese firm of Robinet and Company operating in Formosa, apparently as a naïve attempt to set up a presumptive American claim to the island. This topic looms large in Parker's correspondence with the Department of State from December, 1856, to March, 1857. See 35th Congress, 2d sess., Sen. exec. doc. 22, pp. 1020–1043, 1083–1084, 1184, 1208–1215. See also AEC, 19, 112–114, 199–202, from Courcy, Nov. 22 and Dec. 6, 1856.

shared the British exasperation with Yeh, and his first reports were pro-British, tending to justify the British action. On October 23 he assured Bowring that the French legation fully supported his objectives. He also protested Yeh's putting a price of thirty taels on the heads of Englishmen. After Admiral Guérin reached Canton on November 3, the chargé sent a detachment of forty French marines to guard the consulate and flagpole at Canton. But Courcy was not explicitly pro-British in his communication with Yeh. He explained that the altercation about the *Arrow* did not concern the French government, although he held Yeh responsible for protecting French citizens at Canton from violence. Courcy receded from this latter stand on November 17, when Guérin accepted Yeh's suggestion that the French withdraw both consulate and flag from the factory area. The Americans took similar action.[31]

Courcy and Parker both challenged British presumption in early November, when Bowring presented his unilateral demand for the right of entry into the city of Canton as coming from "representatives of all the foreign powers." [32] The Frenchman tried to sugar-coat his polite refusal to be associated with Bowring's demand with an expression of hope that the local success of the British at Canton might later be extended to their joint negotiations on the Peiho.[33] To Paris he explained his hesitance to commit France in more thoroughgoing fashion in support of a purely English issue than he had done in the Chapdelaine affair.[34] After expressing doubt concerning the right of the *Arrow* to claim British protection, he suggested that perhaps "never had one placed more of false pretexts to the service of a cause more legitimate" than had Bowring. Yeh could not on his own authority grant the right of foreign entry into Canton, since the decision would have to be made at Peking. To force the concession, as Bowring proposed to do, would entail the shedding of torrents of blood and would cause immense loss to merchants at Canton.[35] After the burning of the Canton factories in Decem-

[31] Cordier, *1857–58*, 55–68, 73–74, 80–83.

[32] On Nov. 17 Parker declared that current British difficulties at Canton lay outside the range of American co-operative effort and expressed hope that he had been misinformed as to the phrase which Bowring had used. See Cordier, *1857–58*, 77–79.

[33] *Ibid.;* AEC, 19, 16–38, Nov. 10, 1856. Numerous annexes accompanied this dispatch (39–82). All reached Paris on Jan. 1, 1857.

[34] Courcy, *Souvenirs*, III, 301–302, 342. The foreign community at Canton resented the disruption of trade, regarded British reprisals as superior to the offense suffered, and attacked Bowring for his "egotistic views and senile ambitions."

[35] AEC, 19, 203–207, to Walewski, Dec. 6, 1856.

ber, Courcy resisted pressure from Bowring to regard that action as an affront to the French, as well as to the British, flag as a *casus belli*.[36]

Courcy eventually abandoned his strict neutrality when, in January, he sent a detachment of French marines to Hongkong to aid the British in suppressing terroristic activities instigated by the agents of Yeh. He also protested the Chinese attempts to poison the British colony at Hongkong and intervened successfully to prevent the Chinese interdiction of supplies for Macao. But Courcy based his successive protests to Yeh on the argument that it was to China's advantage to maintain good relations with the French Emperor. To Walewski he justified the seeming folly of endangering French interests in China by participating gratuitously in the defense of Hongkong on the ground that since Yeh had not taken umbrage over the far more aggressive move by Commodore Armstrong's American war vessels in November, he would probably also not take a serious view of French actions. Courcy ordered the withdrawal of the French marines from Hongkong as soon as conditions permitted.[37] Thus the initial alliance between Courcy and Bowring at Hongkong was a limited and tentative affair. The harried chargé was happily relieved of his responsibilities in late February by the return of Bourboulon.

The French Join the British in the War at Canton

The British instructions prepared in early February, 1857, for Bowring's guidance showed no appreciation of the gravity of the situation which had developed at Canton. It also exhibited a measure of independence in China matters which virtually ignored London's recent agreement with Paris. Clarendon told Bowring that France would probably co-operate in bringing all aspects of their combined difficulties with China to a simultaneous effort at settlement, while Britain would support the reparation for the Chapdelaine affair. But British action would not be conditioned on obtaining French co-operation. Clarendon ordered that naval pressure should be applied not at Canton but along the Yangtse and Peiho rivers in order to oblige Peking to negotiate a settlement of the Canton situation. Instead of basing Britain's demands, as heretofore, on the alleged Chinese pledge to revise the treaties after

[36] *Ibid.*, 279–284, to Walewski, Dec. 27, 1856.
[37] *Ibid.*, 19, 296; 20, 91–93, 98–99, to Walewski, Dec. 27, 1856, and Jan. 30, 1857; Cordier, *1857–58*, 103–113, to Yeh, Jan. 16, 1857.

twelve years, Bowring should take the position that the recent conduct of Yeh in the *Arrow* affair had dealt so severe a shock to their friendly relations that only a new treaty could restore the foundations for lasting friendship. Toward his American and French colleagues Bowring was ordered to exercise the utmost cordiality, but Clarendon was "not inclined to fetter Bowring's experience and ability" by presenting detailed instructions.[38] The implication was clear that Bowring had so effectively exploited the incident which London had been waiting for that he was being given free rein to follow his own devices in obtaining redress.

For several weeks after Bourboulon returned to Macao on February 28,[39] he resisted the efforts of Bowring to get him to authorize French military participation. Bourboulon explained that his instructions to act in full accord with Britain did not cover the situation at Canton. He argued also that since any successful negotiation would now involve nothing less than war, reinforcements and new instructions would have to be awaited in any case. His neutral position was made more difficult by the publication in early March of Yeh's report to the Emperor that the Americans and the French, aware of the fact that the English barbarians were in the wrong, had chosen not to co-operate with them.[40] Bourboulon's policy was to avoid mentioning to Yeh the controversy at Canton, but to review with him at once in serious fashion the still unsettled Chapdelaine affair, emphasizing the gravity of the issue and asking urgently for information concerning it.[41]

By early April when Bourboulon sent his second communication to Yeh, fresh instructions from Paris had arrived approving Courcy's cautious policy in general but concluding that the situation had now gone so far that France must leave no doubt concerning its full solidarity with Britain. Bourboulon was directed, therefore, to co-operate

---

[38] FO, 17, 261, to Bowring, Feb. 9, 1857.

[39] Bourboulon met Montigny and Father Pellerin at Hongkong en route to Shanghai.

[40] AEC, 20, 120–140, from Bourboulon, March 9, 1857. Parker on March 7 challenged Yeh's statement as erroneous and declared in a counterblast that the cause of China's difficulties was her refusal to recognize the foreign powers as equals and to treat them accordingly. This did not signify Parker's alignment with Bowring, for before the month was out they were quarreling lustily over hypothetical claims to Formosa. See Dennett, *Americans*, 288–291; 35th Congress, 2d sess., Sen. exec. doc. 22, pp. 1245–1249.

[41] Cordier, *1857–58*, 116, Bourboulon to Yeh, March 4, 1857.

with the British at Canton if it appeared that a solution of the affair could be achieved there; if not, he was to proceed to the Peiho for negotiations. Concurrently Admiral Guérin was authorized to use his foces to aid in resolving the British conflict with Yeh. Walewski added that France was asking Washington to adopt a similar course.[42]

For the moment Bourboulon held the local diplomatic initiative. He rejected as inadequate and evasive Yeh's fairly conciliatory reply of March 15, which blamed the eight months' delay in reporting the Chapdelaine affair on impaired communications with Kwangsi. Yeh offered to dismiss the guilty magistrate as soon as the required inquest had been made. Basing the French case squarely on the Chapdelaine grievance, Bourboulon on April 4 presented an ultimatum which gave Yeh fifteen days only to produce a memorial from the Emperor in fulfillment of Courcy's demands of the previous August.[43] Bourboulon explained to Paris that he was confident that no satisfactory reply could be given by April 20, after which date he would be free to act with Bowring.

Meanwhile, at Bowring's request, Bourboulon conferred with Parker about agreement on objectives and the reasons for America's participation with the European allies. It was agreed that all had a stake in seeking indemnity for losses suffered, in the opening of Canton to foreign entry, in access by foreigners to China generally, and in obtaining regular diplomatic representation at Peking. Parker was eventually persuaded to ask Washington to authorize full American participation. Bourboulon then got Bowring to agree to defer the resumption of military operations until Parker's new instructions arrived.[44]

Yeh's reply to Bourboulon's ultimatum was received on April 21. It

[42] AEC, 20, 71–73, 111, to Bourboulon, Jan. 22, 26, and Feb. 10, 1857.

[43] Cordier, 1857–58, 116–118, 137–138; 35th Congress, 2d sess., Sen. exec. doc. 22, pp. 1284–1285, enclosure by Parker, April 10, 1857.

[44] AEC, 20, 162–163, Bourboulon to Walewski, April 9, 1857. Parker wrote Washington that although the United States had never associated itself with the British demand to enter Canton, Americans would have no good basis on which to demand indemnity for property destroyed at Canton unless they participated in the local operation. Success at Canton, furthermore, was now, in Parker's opinion, preliminary to any successful move for treaty revision, and it need not involve a declaration of war. He also argued that American participation could forestall any possible British intent to take over a portion of China, as was being demanded in the India press. See 35th Congress, 2d sess., Sen. exec. doc. 22, pp. 1276–1280, from Parker, April 10, 1857.

expressed astonishment at the French demands, pleaded the usual reasons for delay, promised to address the Throne as soon as a proper memorial could be prepared, and asked what sort of satisfaction the French had in mind. Bourboulon rejected Yeh's communication out of hand and did not even deign to reply.[45] The French break with China was finally made, and the government-controlled press in France began to prepare public opinion for the prospect of war with China.[46]

The French and British Ambassadors at Washington meanwhile had experienced less success with the State Department than Bourboulon had achieved with Parker. In early February Secretary Marcy's instructions criticized as indiscreet Commodore Armstrong's November action before the barrier forts and affirmed that the British evidently had objectives at Canton beyond those of the United States. He wrote to Parker:

The President sincerely hopes that you as well as our naval commander will be able to do all that is required to protect American interests . . . without being included in the British quarrel, or producing any serious disturbance in our amicable relations with China.[47]

With reference to American co-operation in the later proposal made by the French Foreign Minister, Marcy explicitly denied that China had any obligation to negotiate for revision of the American treaty at Peking or in its vicinity, and he declared flatly that no United States naval reinforcements would be sent to the Far East for aggressive purposes.[48]

The same neutral position was reaffirmed in rather equivocal fashion by Secretary of State Cass after the new Buchanan administration took over in March, 1857. Cass approved the objectives of the allied inter-

---

[45] Cordier, 1857–58, 139–141. Evidence of Yeh's genuine desire to avoid a break with France was demonstrated in the careful guarding of a French missionary, Monsignor Muller from Swatow, who was picked up out of bounds in northern Kwangtung Province and escorted through hostile territory to Macao in May, 1847 (AEC, 20, 228–232, from Bourboulon, May 21, 1857).

[46] An inspired article in the *Revue des Deux Mondes* (by V. de Mars, 8th ser., IX [1857], 481–534) of June 1, on "La Question Chinoise," asked whether England alone had interests to protect, dignity to maintain, or objectives to achieve in China? The author commented: "We have in the China seas a naval force large enough to operate efficaciously and I wish . . . that it be further increased."

[47] SD, China, Instructions 1, 145–153, Feb. 2, 1857.

[48] *Ibid.*, to Parker, Feb. 27, 1857.

vention and tended to encourage it while refusing to permit American participation.[49] The aggressive proposal concerning Formosa made by the Parker mission was fully repudiated in June when the State Department, in response to an inquiry from the British Ambassador, denied that the United States had any intention or desire to acquire sovereignty over Formosa.[50] This repudiation by Washington of American participation after Parker's complete conversion to it was discouraging news to the allies in China, where a united front policy was greatly desired. On the receipt of his instructions, Parker aggravated the difficulty by abruptly repelling all suggestions of friendly concert even on matters of common interest falling within the limits of his authorized activity. Parker's successor, William B. Reed was appointed in April but did not reach China until November, 1857.[51]

British Parliamentary Check and a Change of Leadership in China

British plans for armed operations in China suffered a temporary check when Palmerston's government was defeated on the issue by a sixteen-vote margin in the House of Commons on March 3, 1857. The initial approval which the Foreign Office accorded Bowring, even though buttressed by a Law Office ruling that the *Arrow* was an English ship [52] and by an extensive parliamentary paper on the subject,[53] stood up badly in the face of the withering criticism to which it was subjected in both Houses of Parliament. Lord Clarendon saw the issue through the Lords by a thirty-six vote margin on the ground that British lives,

[49] SD, Notes to Legation, Great Britain, Cass to Napier, April 10, 1857; *ibid.*, France, Cross to Count de Sartiges, April 14, 17, 1857. Cass took the position that only Congress could declare war, that the U.S. entertained no political views regarding China (implying that Britain and France did), that while in his view moderation and discretion rather than violence were required for opening China, America had a direct interest in the objectives of the allied venture and its agent would be instructed to "labor zealously" for treaty revision, to "communicate frankly" with the allies, to make "firm representations" to Peking, and to seek no exclusive commercial advantage in any new American treaty.

[50] FO, 5, 672, Napier to Clarendon, June 24, 1857, citing a statement by Acting Secretary Appleton. Acquisition of a foreign territory like Formosa was adjudged to be incompatible with the American order of government.

[51] SD, China, DD, from Reed no. 3, Nov. 10, 1857.

[52] FO, 17, 243, instructions of Dec. 10, 1856.

[53] *Correspondence Respecting Insults in China*, submitted to the House of Lords, February, 1857.

property, and prestige would otherwise be imperiled.[54] But when Cobden's opposition motion of February 26 in the Commons was backed by such a formidable array as Gladstone, Russell, the Manchester liberals, the Peelites, and Disraeli, several of them lifelong friends of Bowring, the conscience of Victorian England was stirred and the government defeated.[55] Palmerston immediately called a general election on the China issue, to be held on March 21. The result was a government victory by a comfortable margin. The public obviously cared little about the legal aspects of the case, but responded to stories of kidnapping and poisoning and appeals to national pride and commercial interests, all buttressed by the popular desire to continue Palmerston and the liberals in control.[56] National honor had been engaged and considerations of prestige demanded its vindication. Throughout the course of the parliamentary crisis an attentive Paris perceived that British preparations of naval and military reinforcements for use in China went steadily forward.[57] British naval reinforcements were actually ordered to proceed to the Far East on March 9.

The government had saved its policy in China, but John Bowring's personal reputation and standing as a diplomat were damaged beyond recovery.[58] Whereas Clarendon, in February, had placed great reliance on Bowring's "discretion and experience in Chinese affairs," the Foreign Office became increasingly critical of Bowring's actions following the parliamentary debates.[59] On March 10 Clarendon notified Bowring that

[54] Leavenworth, 40–45; *Hansard's Parliamentary Debates*, CXLIV (1857), 1194–1196, 1322 ff. The Earl of Derby led the attack.

[55] Leavenworth, 45–46; Hansard, CXLIV, 1385 ff. Perhaps the most interesting argument was that of Disraeli. He declared that energetic British action in China would not necessarily produce the same results as Clive and Hastings had achieved in India. The Orient had changed, he said, because America and Russia wanted a compromise, and jealousies would be aroused if the wishes of other powerful states were ignored.

[56] H. C. F. Bell, *Lord Palmerston* (London, 1936), II, 168–169; Bazancourt, I, 52–55. Clarendon complained that the debate was "most damaging to our national character and representative form of government all over the world." See H. E. Maxwell, *The Life and Letters of George William Frederick, Fourth Earl of Clarendon* (London, 1913), II, 138–139.

[57] AEC, 20, 146, instructions to Bourboulon, March 10, 1857.

[58] Eitel, 314.

[59] FO, 17, 261, instructions of March 6, 10, and May 4, 1857. Bowring was sharply criticized for encouraging Consul Wade to correspond privately on matters

177

affairs in China had assumed so grave an aspect that another plenipotentiary would take over his functions at Canton and direct subsequent military and diplomatic operations for the restoration of peace and the revision of treaties. The name of Lord Elgin, former Governor-General of Canada, appeared in the outgoing instructions of March 25 as the new plenipotentiary. All that was left to Bowring were the routine duties of the governorship of Hongkong.[60]

Paris first learned of Lord Elgin's appointment approximately a month later, on April 24. Britain's action necessitated a quick decision on the part of French authorities to select a plenipotentiary whose stature and reputation were equal to Elgin's. On April 28 they selected Baron Gros, a man considerably older than Elgin, with more than thirty years of active diplomatic experience, as France's Ambassador Extraordinary to China. Bourboulon's activities were fully approved, however, and he was not recalled.[61] At the same time Paris was giving serious consideration to proposals to broaden the scope of French operations in the Far East to include Indo-China.

Paris Considers Action in Annam

The principal protagonist of a forward French policy in Annam was the Abbé Huc, a former Lazarist missionary to western China. During 1856 he had written and spoken volubly on the subject, finally gaining a hearing at court. In a secret memorandum prepared for Louis Napoleon in January, 1857, Huc argued that the Pigneau de Behaine treaty of 1787 gave France an incontestable right to occupy the port of Tourane, an action which could easily become the beginning of a new and glorious role for France in the Far East. The occupation, he said, could be achieved by French forces already in the Far East. The suffering Annamite population would receive the French as liberators and bene-

---

of state with friends in England, for assuring British merchants at Canton that their losses would constitute a special claim on the British government, and for his presumption in appointing one Gringall as British consul to Bangkok without obtaining prior approval from London.

[60] *Ibid.*, instructions of March 10 and 25, 1857.

[61] Cordier, *1857–58*, 113; Cordier, *Histoire des Relations*, I, 1–2. Gros was born in 1793 and Elgin in 1811. Gros had served previously in Portugal, Spain, Egypt, Mexico, New Granada, Argentina, and Greece. Elgin had served in Jamaica before going to Canada.

factors, and only a short time would be required to make them entirely Catholic. France must move quickly, however, because the English already had their eyes on Tourane.[62] This statement was made prior to the receipt of any news at Paris concerning the outcome of the Montigny mission.

Huc's proposal was first submitted to the keeper of the archives of the French Foreign Office, Pierre Cintrat, for examination. On March 20 Cintrat came up with a strongly negative opinion. He reported that France had never fulfilled its part of the 1787 bargain; seizure of Tourane would therefore be an act of war without legal justification and one which could entail for France ruinous embarrassment and cost far exceeding the advantages to be realized. He expressed the opinion that France already had enough interests abroad to engage her energies without throwing itself into a hazardous and largely profitless venture in the center of the China Sea.[63]

Not content with Cintrat's adverse report, Napoleon III next referred the matter to a special commission of which Baron Brenier, French diplomatic agent at Naples and representative of the Foreign Office, was president.[64] The findings of the commission, as reported in late May, were that the sufferings of missionary patriots at the hands of the Annamite ruler justified taking punitive action, but that no rights existed under the unexecuted treaty of 1787. The opportunity to act was afforded France by her association with the movement in behalf of progress, civilization, and commercial expansion for which China was going to be the principal theater. The commission recommended that the three principal ports of Indo-China be occupied as chastisement for the treatment of French missionaries.[65] No decision to act was reached at the time, probably because of widespread misgivings con-

[62] Cordier, "La Politique Coloniale," T'oung Pao, 2d ser., XI, 38–41.

[63] Ibid., 41–44, note by Cintrat dated March 20, 1857.

[64] Other members were Cintrat from the archives; Rear Admiral Fourichon and Captain Jaurés representing the Minister of Marine; Fleury representing the Ministry of Agriculture, Commerce, and Public Works; and M. Mofras as secretary. The commission was formed on April 22 and held seven meetings. See also R. Stanley Thomson, "The Diplomacy of Imperialism: France and Spain in Cochin-China, 1858–1863," JMH., XII (1940) 334–336.

[65] Cordier, "La Politique Coloniale," T'oung Pao, 2d ser., XI, 45–52; Bazancourt, I, 268–269; Thomson, 334–336. Hearings were completed on May 18; the report was submitted later.

cerning the affair. Genouilly himself, who had accompanied Lapierre to Tourane in 1847, questioned the optimistic predictions of missionary spokesmen that the task of coercing Hué would be an easy one.[66]

Pressure from clerical spokesmen at Paris for governmental action in Annam continued unrelentingly. Monsignor Pellerin, whom Montigny had rescued from Tourane, became the principal protagonist. In a succession of notes to Baron Brenier, Pellerin told of the dire consequences to the missionaries that had followed Montigny's abortive effort. Pellerin was finally introduced to Napoleon III himself at Biarritz on August 30, 1857, where he presented a petition declaring that the destruction of Christianity in Annam was at stake. Pellerin declared that whether or not France responded to the political and economic advantages inherent in the undertaking, the benediction of God would come to the Emperor and his dynasty if he gave effective aid. Ten days later Louis Napoleon requested that Pellerin's memorandum be submitted to the office of the Foreign Minister for examination.[67] Louis Napoleon was obviously preparing to use the forces sent to the Far East under cover of joint intervention with Britain in China to gain the long-sought French foothold in Annam. The French Emperor may have been encouraged to make this decision by news which reached Europe in July, 1857, of a formidable mutiny within the Indian army.

[66] Cordier, "La Politique Coloniale," *T'oung Pao*, XI, 2d ser., 49. Genouilly to de Lesseps form Shanghai, June 24, 1857. The Admiral declared that at least 1,000 men, two companies of artillery and one of engineers, would be required to capture Hué.

[67] *Ibid.*, 48–50; Cultru, 58–61. Archbishop Bonnechose of Rouen and possibly Eugénie supported Pellerin's project.

XII

French Policy and the Expedition
of 1857-1858

L ONDON'S realization of the critical situation in which the British
at Hongkong found themselves following the *Arrow* incident,
coupled with the fact that the French had largely held aloof from
the conflict with Canton, created in Britain a mood which was
inclined to pay little deference to French wishes. London's secretiveness
about the appointment of Elgin, its failure to disclose the nature of his
revised instructions, and the haste with which he and much of his expeditionary force were dispatched to the Far East via the newly opened
Suez Isthmus railway all suggested that the British were intending to
act as far as possible without waiting for the co-operation of their supposed French ally. That Elgin was unable to carry out the intended unilateral British program in China was due to contemporaneous developments in India, where the outbreak of the Sepoy Rebellion in May, 1857,
threatened to destroy the entire foundation of British power in the
Orient.

Elgin's Instructions and a Check to British Plans

Elgin's final instructions put no stress on the co-operative aspects of
his mission. He was ordered upon his arrival at Hongkong to arrange
with the French and American representatives for any assistance which
they were authorized to afford and to proceed immediately to the Peiho

181

River with whatever naval force could be spared from Canton. If the French or American representatives accompanied him, he should "act, as far as possible, in conjunction with them." Three basic demands should be made the condition of further negotiations: compensation for personal injuries to British subjects (and to French also if they co-operated); execution of full treaty stipulations at all treaty ports, especially with respect to access to Canton; and compensation for recent property losses to British subjects and others entitled to British protection. If these demands were not met, Elgin would be justified in resorting to force. In the event that Peking sanctioned Yeh's actions at Canton, Elgin should proceed to occupy the roadstead at Chusan Island and, if possible, some points up the Yangtse River. Primary British objectives in any further negotiations would be to obtain the right of direct diplomatic contact with Peking, although not necessarily residence in the capital, the opening of the river ports, and the right of Chinese vessels to come to Hongkong to trade.[1]

Only a shorter and earlier edition of British instructions on the China mission, dated April 6, are to be found in the French archives. The tone differs, but the substance of the two is much the same. Elgin's authorization to resort to war unilaterally and to seize Chusan and the Yangtse ports without reference to the co-operation of the French is absent from the earlier version, as is the implication that British action alone was preferred.[2]

Apart from Elgin's general instructions, London directed that the basis of his demands on Peking should be not the often-asserted legal claim that Britain had a right to insist on revision of the Treaty of Nanking after twelve years under its most-favored-nation clause, but rather the political grounds that recent events required that Britain's relations with the Chinese Emperor be put on a more satisfactory footing. This decision was made in accordance with a recent ruling by the Law Office that items covered under the most-favored-nation clause in-

---

[1] FO, 17, 274, to Elgin, April 20, 1857. Supplementary instructions covered trade regulations and negotiations with Japan.

[2] AEC, 21, 35–40. Part of London's desire to avoid deferring to the wishes of other powers may have been due to the unwelcome rumor that Russia would assist the allied efforts to obtain wider trading facilities in China. This news was confirmed in June, 1857 (FO, 17, 274, to Elgin, July 2, 1857. Morse (I, 487–488) reports erroneously that Elgin was ordered to co-operate with his French and American colleagues in all matters. He was not so limited.

182

cluded only "matters of personal right and enjoyment by the individual subjects of foreign countries" and not provisions concerning the revision or renewal of treaties.[3]

A considerable proportion of the British expeditionary force of some 5,000 men, with staff and equipment for a still larger force, left England for China via Suez on May 9. They crossed the isthmus on the first passenger train to use the new railway and were picked up by British boats waiting in the Red Sea.[4] Only Admiral Rigault de Genouilly's advance detachment of French naval reinforcements left Europe in time to rendezvous with Elgin at Macao in early July, 1857. Baron Gros and the main French naval and marine contingents, expanded in size considerably beyond original plans, left France on May 27 and proceeded via the Cape. They did not reach Macao until October.

The instructions given to Baron Gros, dated May 9, differed from those provided Elgin in three principal respects: the tone was more moderate, the emphasis on objectives slightly different, and the assumption of Anglo-French collaboration much stronger. Gros was accorded wide powers in determining the place, time, and duration of any negotiations he might wish to undertake. He was to avoid useless bloodshed or material damage and to put the objective of the progress of civilization alongside the interests of France. After special French claims for Chapdelaine's death and other losses to nationals had been met, indemnity demands should not be pressed to the embarrassment of achieving more fundamental gains such as direct diplomatic access to Peking and the opening of additional ports, which were Britain's major concerns. British-French collaboration was assumed throughout, as well as the possible participation by America. Russian collaboration was nowhere mentioned.[5]

Instructions of the same date sent to Admiral Rigault de Genouilly, already en route to China, named him successor to Admiral Guérin as commander of French naval forces in Indo-China waters. He was to act under Baron Gros's direction with regard to the initiation and break-

[3] FO, 17, 274, to Elgin, April 20, 1857. The Law Office ruling stated the meaning of the clause as follows: "Whenever additional privileges and immunities are granted by the Chinese Government . . . to the subects of those nations who before the 8th of October 1843 had traded to Canton, the same . . . shall be granted to and enjoyed by British subjects."

[4] Oliphant, I, 15–16.

[5] AEC, 21, 28–29; Bazancourt, I, 386–391; Cordier, 1857–58, 145–151.

ing off of hostilities with China but should otherwise direct all French military operations, subject to the requirement of co-operation with the British forces. Genouilly's naval activities outside of the China mission, particularly in Annam, were not to be subject to Gros's control.[6] These instructions from the Minister of Marine reached the Admiral at Singapore in June, approximately at the time of Elgin's arrival. Baron Gros, by contrast, reached Capetown on July 21, Singapore on September 28, and Hongkong on October 13, some three months later than Genouilly.[7]

Lord Elgin first heard rumors of the outbreak of the mutiny in India on May 13, when he stopped in Ceylon in early June to pick up General Ashburnham. The confirming information reaching him at Singapore later in the same month was so alarming that he immediately sent two regiments (1,700 men) back to Calcutta and issued orders that three additional British regiments en route via Cape Colony should be likewise diverted to India.[8]

Elgin's communication with Genouilly while both were at Singapore indicated that in British eyes the India crisis took precedence over the Chinese campaign and that allied objectives in China might have to be modified to the extent that actual war would be contemplated only as a last resort. The Frenchman was particularly annoyed by a public address by Elgin in which Britain's exclusive patronage over Oriental countries was assumed and the alliance with France in the China affair was not even mentioned. The indignant Admiral regarded the speech as a slur on French dignity both in terms of her position as a European power and of her place as sharing with Britain the right to safeguard the "ensemble of European interests in the Celestial Empire." French interests and the size of her expedition made it intolerable, in his view, that she be made to crawl along in tow of the British in the Chinese waters.[9]

French objections to Elgin's assumption of leadership were intensified after Elgin reached Hongkong in the first week of July. In reply to Elgin's announcement, made in identical notes to Bourboulon and

[6] Bazancourt, I, 59–62.

[7] Cordier, 1857–58, 162. Gros left Toulon, May 27, 1857.

[8] Morse, I, 490–493; Oliphant, I, 16–19. Oliphant reported that the British at Singapore were very nervous, fearing trouble from the 70,000 Chinese resident in the Straits settlements. The ultimate destiny of Elgin's forces following the China campaign was India.

[9] Bazancourt, I, 65–69.

184

Parker, that he intended to negotiate on the Peiho and to his asking if they were authorized to co-operate in the effort, the French minister replied that his instructions fully contemplated co-operative action but that active diplomatic measures must await the arrival of Baron Gros.[10] A much more vigorous and effective protest against premature action in the Gulf of Pohai was registered by Admiral Genouilly. He obtained the support of the British Admiral Seymour for his view that any levying of additional demands upon China at that time, when no effective sanctions could be invoked, would only invite a rebuff and add to the loss of European face already experienced at Canton. Precipitate action taken unilaterally by Elgin prior to the arrival of Baron Gros, Genouilly insisted, would not only encourage China's hope that the concert between the two powers could be destroyed but would also give rise to pained astonishment at Paris, especially in view of Elgin's own action in diverting to India the forces required for the success of their joint effort in China.[11]

Elgin had no choice but to abandon his plan for immediate action in China. To Bourboulon, he claimed not to have been fully informed concerning French arrangements to send out an envoy of equal rank with himself.[12] He also learned during his fortnight's stay at Hongkong that the British colony was in grave danger and could spare no forces from its already weak defenses for a diversionary action elsewhere.[13] The entire local foreign community insisted that the pride of the Cantonese defenders must first be deflated before any satisfactory results could be anticipated from negotiations conducted near Peking.[14]

Rather than remain inactive at Hongkong, Elgin departed for Calcutta on July 16, accompanied by two vessels carrying heavy guns and three hundred marines. The situation in India had improved materially by the time he arrived on August 8, so that his contingent of China troops did not have to be used in the interior. He was back in Hongkong

[10] Cordier, *1857–58*, 157–161.   [11] Bazancourt, I, 70–73.

[12] AEC, 20, 293–295, from Bourboulon, July 22, 1857.

[13] The American chargé, Williams, reported that the British blockade was ineffective, that enough native goods came through the Canton blockade by alternate routes to load ten vessels per day at Macao and Hongkong, and that Yeh's prestige locally was enormous (SD, China, DD, nos. 30 and 31, Sept. 9 and 22, 1857).

[14] Morse, I, 493–496; Oliphant, I, 8–14, 50–56. Oliphant's comment on the situation was that "never . . . [since 1834] had Englishmen made so poor a figure in the eyes of the Chinese populace."

by September 20, although it was November before the full complement of the British expeditionary force reached China. Baron Gross arrived in mid-October and the first batch of French marines landed on October 28.[15]

France Decides to Intervene in Annam

In late August, 1857, Bourboulon and Admiral Genouilly received a plea from the Spanish consul at Macao, Canete y Moral, to rescue a Spanish Dominican missionary, Monsignor Diaz, who had been arrested by the Tongking authorities on May 20 and was under sentence of death. It was decided on August 31 that Kleczkowski, who since 1854 had been legation secretary, should proceed in the company of a hydrographic engineer for an exploration of the coast of Tongking on board the *Catinat*. A light draft commercial steamer, the *Lilly*, was purchased to accompany the *Catinat* for the purpose of approaching the shore.[16] The objectives were to inquire concerning the fate of Diaz, to deliver an entering French missionary, and to gather hydrographic data along the Tongking coast. The expedition left Macao on September 3 and on September 8 reached an unidentified point near Porte d'Annam called by Kleczkowski Boung Quioa. From that point the expedition proceeded at intervals northward along the shoreline.

On Kleczowski's first visit ashore on September 9 he learned nothing, but three days later at the second stopping place (called Lach Quen) native Christians informed him that Father Diaz had been executed at Nam Dinh on July 20. Full confirmation of this news came from one Father André, one of Monsignor Retord's men of the Tongking mission, who came aboard the *Catinat* at a place called Lach-trang on September 13. During the two days' stay at Lach-trang, two Annamite mandarins came aboard the unarmed *Lilly* to inquire concerning the purpose of the French visit and to urge Kleczkowski to abandon his declared intention of proceeding to Nam Dinh. They conversed by exchanging notes in Chinese. Kleczkowski avoided making threats which might aggravate the danger for foreign residents, but protested firmly against Annamite treatment of French and other missionaries.

While anchored at a place named Balat, located at the principal

---

[15] Morse, I, 491–493; Oliphant, I, 61–65, 68.

[16] Bazancourt, I, 272–274; AEC, 15, 364–367, from Bourboulon, Sept. 8, 1857; Remi Bourgeois, *Le Tonkin en 1857: La Mission Cleczkowski* (Hanoi, 1943), 9–12.

mouth of the Red River, from September 15 to 22, Kleczkowski found Christian fishermen off shore very friendly but unable to furnish a pilot capable of guiding the *Lilly* into the river. French reconnaissance established the fact that the water over the bar was only six feet deep and that defense preparations were being made upstream to contest any attempted French passage. While at Balat, Kleczkowski received letters from Monsignor Sanpedro, successor to Diaz, from Monsignor Melchior, and also from Monsignor Retord of Tongking, which told the gruesome story of Diaz's death and of missionary persecutions generally. The latter portion of Retord's letter contained hydrographic and topographic information concerning the coastal areas, rivers, anchorages, cities, and neighboring provinces. The letter concluded by urging the French to abandon half measures which only aggravated the plight of the missionaries; France should either strike hard or abandon the missions to their unhappy fate. Retord's letter of September 19 was later transmitted to Paris by Bourboulon. After Kleczkowski had replied to several missionary letters, prepared a formal protest for transmission to the Governor at Nam Dinh, and explored the river's mouth further in small boats, he departed on September 22. The French ships reached Macao on October 3 and 6. Only then did Bourboulon and the Spanish consul learn of the death of Monsignor Diaz.[17]

Meanwhile Bourboulon had dispatched on September 1 a historical review of French relations with the Hué government based to a considerable extent on a document previously prepared by Monsignor Retord. Bourboulon explained that Montigny's mission to Tourane had been doomed to failure because Annamite agreement to French demands so utterly contrary to the traditional practice of the Hué government could have been obtained only by a major expedition having as its objective the permanent occupation by France of a point of territory on the Annamite coast. Bourboulon cited in support his own coded recommendation made in 1852 to the same effect. Montigny's fleeting visit had only aggravated the evils which the missionaries and native Christians had been enduring since the abortive Tongking rebellion of 1855. Bourboulon also cited Retord's report that the Christians had been falsely accused of instigating the rebellion and that their villages had suffered severely in the aftermath of pillage and massacre. The missionaries had escaped death as ordered by Tu-Duc only by hiding away

[17] Bourgeois, 12–19, 21–39.

or by paying extortionate bribes to the local mandarins for protection. These bribes were as high as 9,000 francs for a single mission. Even so, death was hovering near them continuously. Montigny's imperious manner and his empty threats had confirmed the anti-French suspicions of Hué and also its belief that missionaries could be attacked with impunity.

In a coded portion of his September 1 dispatch, Bourboulon urged that France utilize the presence of its considerable naval and military forces in the Far East to exert such overwhelming pressure on Tu-Duc that he would have to abandon all thought of resisting French demands. He believed that the allied forces could finish with their operations at Canton by the end of the year, so that French forces would be able to proceed to Tourane about the first of January. Their primary objective should be to obtain the cession to France of the port of Tourane, plus enough adjacent territory to afford facilities for its military protection. Possession of the port would guarantee the execution of other terms of the treaty and would also afford commercial advantages. The treaty should provide for protection of missionaries, for commercial concessions, and for a pecuniary indemnity of possibly 1,800,000 francs. The expedition must not hesitate to use force, even to the point of menacing Hué itself in order to enforce compliance with French demands.[18] This dispatch was prepared more than a month before news reached Bourboulon of the death of Monsignor Diaz.

Immediately on the arrival of Kleczkowski at Macao on October 3, Bourboulon forwarded to Paris Monsignor Retord's more recent letter of September 19 brought back by the French emissary. In it Retord declared that after twenty-six years of suffering, during which fleeting visits by French naval units had served only to goad the sleeping tiger and then leave the missionaries to face its merciless fury, he was losing patience with the French government. It was time for France to undertake something grand and durable, worthy of itself and its Emperor. He advocated the displacement of the reigning dynasty of Annam by a descendant of the Lê family, a faction popular in Tongking, Christian in sympathies, and fully prepared to negotiate treaties covering religion, commerce and other essential items. He added that Tongking contained valuable mineral resources, gold, silver, copper, and coal, as well as timber useful for shipbuilding. The Tonkinese, he said, dreamed of be-

[18] AEC, 20, 330–360, from Bourboulon, Sept. 1, 1857.

ing freed from control by Hué. They would prefer a ruler of their own nation under the protection of France, but they would not be discontented if France took over direct control.[19]

Bourboulon's final communication on Annam, dated October 12, cited the presence of a Spanish-led Filipino army in the Philippines, reported to be disciplined, strongly Catholic, and accustomed to the climate, whose help could not be disdained. If an expedition were planned, the Spanish forces, he declared, would be strongly disposed to participate. Several annexes to this dispatch contained detailed information furnished by Monsignor Retord concerning the defenses of Hué. So enthusiastic was Manila for Bourboulon's proposal, that Elgin's secretary, who visited the Philippines in October, learned about the pending co-operative venture a full month before the decision to undertake it was made in Paris.[20] Madrid was able to give Paris an immediate affirmative response as soon as the French Ambassador, on December 1, proposed co-operation by Spain. The Spanish were to furnish some 1,400 troops, a battery, and two steam war vessels.[21]

Louis Napoleon's decision to intervene in Annam was made on November 25, after the receipt of Bourboulon's September 1 dispatch but prior to the receipt of the news of the execution of Monsignor Diaz, which reached Paris on November 28. The new project was to be handled not by the Foreign Office, which was not enthusiastic over the affair, but through instructions sent directly to Admiral Genouilly by the Minister of Marine. At first Baron Gros was informed only that the Admiral was being ordered to proceed to Cochin-China to redress French grievances and to establish closer relations with Hué, following the completion of his services in China. Subsequently, Gros was sent a record of the confidential interdepartmental correspondence on the question, a copy of Genouilly's instructions including his full powers to negotiate with Hué, plus the news that Spain had agreed to participate in the undertaking.[22]

[19] *Ibid.*, 413–418, Retord to Kleczkowski, Sept. 19, 1857, sent as enclosure in Bourboulon's dispatch of Oct. 3.
[20] *Ibid.*, 419–422, from Bourboulon, Oct. 12, 1857; Oliphant, I, 84. Oliphant reported that 3,000 Spanish troops had already been engaged by France.
[21] Cordier, "La Politique Coloniale," *T'oung Pao*, 2d ser., XII, 160–165.
[22] AEC, 20, 486–488; 21, 203, 212, 343–344, to Bourboulon, Nov. 24 and Dec. 4, 1857, and to Gros, Nov. 25, 26 and Dec. 25, 1857. Neither the full text of Genouilly's instructions nor the interdepartmental correspondence referred to appears in the Foreign Office archives. The latter item is not available at all.

Admiral Genouilly was told that the Emperor had decided to put an end to the persecution of Christians in Annam by extending to them the protection of France. To aid him in this task, three additional ships and 500 men would leave soon for the Far East. The French naval forces were to seize Tourane and hold it as a guarantee of the execution of any treaty negotiated with Hué. It was the desire of the Emperor to establish, if possible, a French protectorate over Cochin-China providing for the enjoyment of exclusive privileges internally and control of foreign relations. If this goal seemed impossible to achieve, Genouilly was to settle for a treaty of amity and commerce granting indemnity for French losses in lives and property and provisions for their future protection. The Admiral was told to proceed to Tourane as soon as his presence in China in support of Baron Gros was not absolutely indispensable. Wide latitude was accorded him as to the employment of military procedures and the scope of diplomatic negotiations.[23]

The Franco-Spanish decision to attack Tourane was a badly kept secret. The principal leaks were Spanish, although at one time Genouilly accused Gros of divulging the information. Baron Gros reported at the end of January, 1858, that news of the undertaking had spread throughout the assembled allied forces and that Elgin found no pleasure in the affair. The report was confirmed by London authorities in February on information obtained in Madrid. In order to prevent the issue from disrupting mutual confidence between the allied leaders, Gros flatly rebuffed Genouilly's request that he be released from his China responsibilities for a month or so to accomplish the first step in his special assignment at Tourane before allied operations began at the mouth of the Peiho. Gros insisted that French obligations under agreement with Britain in the China affair came first, that French prestige demanded the presence of their troops near Peking alongside the British, and that the Tourane matter could wait.[24]

Ambassador Cowley at Paris got wind of French plans for the expedition to Annam several weeks before the final decision was reached. On November 6 he reported that the French government would have to take action to redress their loss of prestige in southeast Asia following

[23] Cordier, "La Politique Coloniale," *T'oung Pao,* 2d ser., XII, 157–160; Bazancourt, I, 183–184, 270–271.

[24] Cordier, "La Politique Coloniale," *T'oung Pao,* 2d ser., XII, 166–169, from Gros, Jan. 27, 1858; Bazancourt, I, 184–186, 190–193; FO, 17, 284, to Elgin, Feb. 16, 1858.

Montigny's unfortunate experiences in Siam and at Tourane. The method would depend upon how things went in China and upon the possibility of detaching a French naval force from the larger operation. In view of Lord Elgin's previous action in diverting the British expeditionary forces to care for Britain's special interests in India, there were no good grounds on which London could object. Foreign Minister Clarendon was far more concerned about the perils of denuding England of troops during the Indian crisis than about French designs in Annam.[25]

Cowley also relayed to London Foreign Minister Walewski's rather halting explanation of the prospective visit by a French war vessel at Rangoon, to be made at the alleged request of Burmese ambassador who had recently visited France. It seemed that the presents from France which the Ambassador was carrying back to Mandalay had been destroyed by fire at Rangoon and that the French captain wanted to deliver a letter of explanation addressed to the Burmese King. Cowley was not impressed by Walewski's insistence that France had no ulterior objective in mind.[26]

The possibility of French imperialist interest branching out in still another direction was illustrated by a communication of October 15, 1857, from the Abbé Maistre in Korea which Bourboulon transmitted to Paris some months later. The abbé expressed the hope, based on the presence of a large French force in the Orient, that the ensuing year would be one of glory for France and of grace and deliverance to Korea, a country which could become a center of French influence. The abbé provided, among other things, detailed directions for entering the mouth of the river leading to Seoul by approaching it along the shore to the north. The invading French force could prevent popular alarm and panic by issuing, in Chinese characters, an advance proclamation of their purpose. The forces defending Seoul consisted of some five to six thousand troops armed with bows and matchlocks, which could not withstand the attack of a single French battalion. Once the French forces were master of the capital, the optimistic abbé thought that no further resistance would be encountered.[27]

[25] FO, 27, 1205, Cowley to Clarendon, Nov. 6, 1857; H. R. C. Cowley, *Secrets of the Second Empire*, ed. by F. A. Wellesley (New York, 1929), 122–136. Napoleon III relieved the tension in October, 1857, by sending personal assurances to Victoria.

[26] FO, 27, 1205, Cowley to Clarendon, Nov. 6, 1857.

[27] AEC, 22, 41–42, from Bourboulon, April 20, 1858, and enclosure, Maistre to Bourboulon, Oct. 15, 1858.

The Allied Capture of Canton

Despite Lord Elgin's lack of respect for the British position taken during the Arrow War and his disgust at the bullying conduct of his countrymen at Hongkong toward the Chinese in general, there was clearly no alternative to carrying the quarrel with Yeh through to an issue.[28] Before the time for decision, new instructions from London, taking into account the situation in India, suggested that Elgin postpone the trip to the Peiho, and if the forces available to him were adequate, that he should first conclude the affair at Canton. Gros received similar instructions from Paris.[29] The British at Hongkong were loath to let the French in on their contest with Yeh.[30] A full month of conferences preceded the agreement for French participation (reached on November 18), and almost two months elapsed before the ultimata were sent to Yeh in December.

Baron Gros was concerned lest Yeh attempt to divide the allies by meeting the more legitimate grievance of France with respect to the death of Chapdelaine while refusing to comply with British demands with which the French had never identified themselves. He was spared embarrassment when Yeh replied to Bourboulon's preliminary inquiry of December 10 to the effect that the Hsi-lin inquest had revealed a case of mistaken identity. The executed man was not Father Chapdelaine (in Chinese, Father Ma) after all but one Ma Tzu-nung, a confessed rebel and criminal, and it was therefore useless to discuss the matter further. Yeh's reply to Gros' ultimatum, which followed, was in similar vein, but it reflected grave concern and gave the lie to his previous explanation regarding Chapdelaine. He now complained that Chapde-

[28] To Lady Elgin he wrote: "Nothing could be more contemptible than the origin of our existing quarrel." The Arrow War, he said, was considered a scandal by all except the few who were personally compromised by it. With reference to the bullying violence practiced by Britishers toward the Chinese he wrote: "I have seen more to disgust me with my fellow countrymen . . . among populations too weak to resist and too ignorant to complain . . . than I saw during the whole course of my previous life" (Oliphant, I, 95–96; G. M. Wrong, *The Earl of Elgin* [London, 1905], 102–105).

[29] FO, 17, 274, to Elgin, Aug. 26, 1857; AEC, 21, 79, to Gros, July 24, 1857; Cordier, *1857–58*, 166–168.

[30] Lane-Poole, I, 266. Harry Parkes complained on Nov. 15, 1857: "It has been decided . . . that we are to have allies in the French. I for one am sorry for it. The Canton matter is our particular quarrel, . . . and we ought to have been allowed to fight it out."

laine had not revealed that he was French, else he would have been escorted to Macao as had other missionaries, and Yeh also pointed out that Courcy had been neutral in the English quarrel.[31] Yeh had clearly missed an opportunity to embarrass Gros, for the latter was now on strong legal and moral grounds in rejecting the Chinese note as derisory and not worthy of the high functionary from which it came. Elgin hardly alluded to the *Arrow* incident in his own ultimatum, which Yeh rebuffed with even more derision.[32]

The allied capture of Canton, accomplished from December 28 to January 5, afforded ample opportunity for demonstrating Anglo-French rivalry in the glory-hunt. French cannoniers insisted on being properly placed; their attacking column was the first to storm the wall, actually before their own artillery stopped firing; a daring French marine who had mingled with the Chinese refugees fleeing into Fort Lyn mounted the abandoned wall from the inside and unfurled the French flag just as the allied columns began their assault. The hero was invested with the Legion of Honor on the spot.[33] The British were greatly annoyed at such French antics. Elgin's secretary commented appropriately, "Where so little honour was to be gained by anyone, as at the siege of Canton, it is hardly fair for either party to appropriate the entire modicum." The British also complained that French troops within Canton demonstrated superior taste in selecting the most valuable articles of loot. This thievery was halted abruptly at Elgin's insistence.[34]

Lord Elgin was largely responsible for setting up an effective regime at Canton following Yeh's capture and exile to India. He designated the Manchu Governor, Pik-wei, as ruler of the city, to be assisted and supervised by Harry Parkes as principal advisor, with Captain Martineau des Chenez acting as Baron Gros' representative. The blockade was raised on February 10. Elgin's settlement was regularized from the Chinese point of view by an edict from Peking which reached Canton on March

---

[31] Cordier, *1857–58*, 171–179, 191–213; Swisher (334–346) gives the verbatim translation of Yeh's official memorial of Jan. 17, 1858, covering the Chapdelaine affair. He denied that Gros had cause for complaint and declared that Elgin was egging him on. Yeh's statement to Peking attributed to Kleczkowski earlier actions done by Courcy.

[32] Cordier, *1857–58*, 191–192, 216–217; Oliphant, I, 98–105. Yeh proposed that Elgin imitate Bonham, who had been knighted for deciding not to force the issue of entry into Canton.

[33] Bazancourt, I, 104, 142–155.   [34] *Ibid.*, 158–159; Wrong, 109, 113.

3 confirming Pik-wei's authority. The British community at Hongkong compained that Elgin's policy of permitting an early resumption of Chinese control was too lenient.[35] In this situation and in subsequent trouble which developed at Canton the French were little involved.

Allied Operations in North China

Elgin and Gros were not fully agreed as to the proper procedure to follow in projecting their joint operations to north China. Elgin proposed that they act as belligerents, levying demands on Peking and applying military pressure to force acquiescence. He argued that Yeh had been acknowledged as the responsible agent of the Peking Court in charge of its foreign relations, and that a state of war was already a fact. Such procedure would have eliminated the possible employment of American and Russian influence on the Chinese and would have thrown the balance of control to British hands by virtue of their predominant military and naval power. Baron Gros demurred on the ground that the affair at Canton could more wisely be treated as a local engagement only, brought on by Yeh's mismanagement. He pointed to the fact that at no other treaty port in China did anything approaching a state of war exist. He insisted, therefore, that it would be sounder and much less reckless tactics to pursue a negotiator's approach which would not disrupt trade at Shanghai and would also permit the participation of the American and Russian representatives Reed and Putiatin, up to the point where armed pressure had to be applied.[36]

Elgin's reluctant acquiescence in the proposal of his French colleague, in the face of contrary pressure of the British community at Hongkong, was due in part to the nature of his recent instructions from London. The serious crisis in India, the diversion of many of Elgin's troops to that area, and a sudden worsening of relations between England and France in Europe had weakened the resolve of the British government to carry through the bold program in China which Palmerston and Clarendon had originally envisaged. London still trusted Louis Napoleon but not Walewski and other Anglophobe elements in France

[35] Morse, I, 497–506; Williams, 291–294; SD, Hongkong, CL 4, from Roberts March 12 and May 5, 1858. U.S. Consul Roberts at Canton reported that the English feared that Elgin would patch up matters at Canton too soon (SD, Hongkong CL 4, March 12, 1858).

[36] Cordier, 1857–58, 250–254, 259–260; Oliphant, I, 175–179.

194

Even before the accession of the moderate-minded Malmesbury to the British Foreign Office, in February 1858, it was clear that London was willing to settle, if necessary, for much less than Elgin had been authorized at the outset to seek by his own unilateral action.

The worsening of relations in Europe stemmed from the attempt of Felice Orsini and his associates to assassinate Louis Napoleon and Eugénie on January 14, 1858. The plot had been prepared in England, whence the would-be assassins had journeyed to France. England was also criticized for harboring Napoleon's arch enemies, Mazzini and Victor Hugo. The Emperor was thoroughly frightened, and his half brother, the Duke de Morny, attacked England violently. Relations were seriously strained, especially following the acquittal by an English jury of a Briton allegedly involved in the Orsini plot. For a time, both Cowley at Paris and Clarendon in London were concerned over the alarming fact that England at the moment was virtually denuded of troops and had scarcely a friend in the world. Neither side wanted trouble, however, and a visit of Louis Napoleon and Eugénie to Victoria in the early autumn eventually relieved the tension for a time. Meanwhile, on July 21, 1858, Napoleon and Cavour met at Plombières to lay plans for the Italian war.[37]

Against the background of these alarming developments in Europe, Malmesbury's first instructions to Elgin expressed the hope that an early cessation of hostilities in China could be arranged, which would assure for Britain the modest expectation of satisfactory future commercial intercourse at Canton. He left to Elgin's judgment whether or not the operation on the Peiho as originally planned should be suspended.[38] Elgin was torn between both his personal distaste for browbeating the Chinese and London's defeatist attitude on the one hand, and on the other the now-or-never demand of the old China hands at Hongkong and Shanghai that they humble once for all the insufferable arrogance of Peking and open the country for trade. Elgin's position was certainly difficult enough without begging more trouble by precipitating a break

[37] Cowley, 122–128, 130, 145–149, 162–168. Rumors were rife in Britain that French officers were enlisting to fight with the sepoy mutineers in India. It was at this juncture that Walewski first asked Cowley what England would do if France warred against Austria in Italy. London was also annoyed by French friendliness toward Russia. See Jean Maurain, *La Politique Ecclesiastique du Second Empire de 1852 à 1869* (Paris, 1930), 224–227.

[38] FO, 17, 284, to Elgin, March 25, 1858.

with Gros over recklessly following belligerent tactics in north China.[39]

Baron Gros was also worried over worsening relations between France and England in Europe,[40] mainly because of the possible effect such developments might have on his entente with Elgin. The success of their joint project in China was at stake, as was the presumed British acquiescence in Genouilly's planned adventure in Annam. Only if the entente held, would the precedent of French acquiescence in the diversion of British forces to India be definitive. Gros also had strong reasons for wanting to curb excessive British demands in China which might imperil the achievement of more modest and realizable French objectives. The overthrow of the Manchu regime would not serve French interests, but would create instead a situation from which Britain might profit politically far more than any other Western power. In order to redress the unequal balance between himself and Lord Elgin, Gros decided to make use of the hitherto unimportant American and Russian diplomatic representatives.

Gros's Relations with Reed and Putiatin

William B. Reed, the newly appointed American minister to China, and Admiral Putiatin, the Russian diplomatic agent, had arrived at Macao almost simultaneously in November, 1857. The Russian had waited at Shanghai, following his abortive effort to negotiate with the Chinese off the mouth of the Peiho River, until Reed's arrival at Macao. Neither of the two was authorized to participate militarily in the allied operation, but both expected to take advantage of the coercive measures which France and Britain were prepared to apply in behalf of treaty revision. But there the similarity between them ended. Washington had rejected an invitation to participate in the allied intervention, whereas St. Petersburg had accepted the more or less perfunctory request for Russian diplomatic co-operation. St. Petersburg stated in advance that Russia would support the opening of China to Western contact but not the establishment of resident legations at Peking.[41]

---

[39] W. B. Reed, "Private Diary of His Mission to China, 1857–59," Library of Congress, Division of Manuscripts. For April 20 (298–299), Reed remarked: "Elgin looks and is worried."

[40] *Ibid.*, 338, May 13 entry. Gros confided to Reed his anxiety over "the unpleasant feeling" developing in Europe.

[41] AEC, 21, 77–80, to Gros, July 24, 1857; 20, 390, 483–485, from Bourboulon, Sept. 20 and Nov. 12, 1857; 20, 118, from St. Petersburg, Aug. 20, 1857. Bourboulon

Putiatin was an astute and experienced diplomat who was working for clearly defined objectives and who understood the situation with which he was dealing. He realized that he was unwelcome and suspect in British and French circles and would have to earn whatever influence he exercised. In contrast, Reed was a fellow Pennsylvania Democrat whom President Buchanan had appointed minister to China in payment for political services. He had no previous diplomatic experience, no political sophistication on the international level, and no knowledge of the China situation. In addition, Secretary Cass furnished Reed with instructions which were as confusing as they were belated and uninformed.[42] Reed had been provided with a supposed copy of Putiatin's secret instructions. At Macao he tended to parade his collusion with the Russian agent and assumed naïvely that the Russian was equally guileless. Toward the European intervention he took an openly unsympathetic view. He posed as the peacemaking mediator and friend of China, and when not accepted as such, complained that the Chinese failed to distinguish between their friends and their enemies.[43] Reed contributed nothing to the settlement of the China problems, while his Anglophobe propensities were effectively exploited by both Gros and Putiatin.[44]

The reaction of Elgin and Gros to the presence of American and Russian observer negotiators differed sharply. Elgin was personally cordial to both of them, but in a coldly superior way. He shared with them no

---

distrusted the Russians, but both Gros and the Paris authorities saw in Putiatin an ally in checking Britain in the Far East.

[42] Dennett (*Americans*, 303–305) characterized Reed's instructions as tantamount to saying take along a basket and stand under the tree until the British and French shake down the fruit. An example of the remissness of Cass can be seen in Reed's learning from his British and French colleagues in July, 1858, that Secretary Cass, in a conversation with the British Ambassador on April 19, had approved Reed's decision to co-operate with the allies in China. At that time Reed complained that his own most recent instructions were dated Feb. 8, 1858 (SD, China, DD, 17, from Reed, no. 25, July 2, 1858; FO, 5, 691, Napier to Malmesbury from Washington, April 19, 1858).

[43] SD, China, DD, Reed, no. 11, April 3, 1858.

[44] Reed approved what Consul Forbes at Canton had written to Ch'i-ying at Peking in August, 1857, deploring the war at Canton and arguing that all Elgin wanted was representation at Peking similar to that enjoyed by the Russians (Reed to Cass, Nov. 25, 1857, and enclosure in 36th Congress, 1st sess., Sen. exec. doc. 30, pp. 19–21, 25–27). The British found in Yeh's captured papers at Canton a memo to the effect that American sources had indicated that resort to hostilities was unlikely because of American pressure to reopen trade and French unwillingness to incur the hatred of the Chinese. See Oliphant, I, 143–146.

political confidences and kept his own counsels as to what he intended to do.[45] After his first futile effort in December to dissuade Reed from making an obviously profitless proposal of treaty revision to Yeh,[46] Elgin paid little heed to the inept American. Baron Gros, on the other hand, actively cultivated Reed's confidence by his own unaffected communications. He also made it obvious that the French wasted no love on their English friends.[47] Reed's ability to speak French was a help to Gros.

Gros's relations with Putiatin were more formal than those with Reed, but the two quickly found common ground in their mutual jealousy and suspicion of British pretentions to dominance in the Far East. Both were interested in achieving a prompt settlement with Peking that covered essential demands without risking an armed conflict which might overthrow the Manchu regime and play into Britain's hands. The French had other interests to care for in Cochin-China, and no commercial stake in China. Putiatin wanted to accomplish Russia's assimilation into the Western treaty system with China before the British or French got news of the outcome of Muraviev's concurrent negotiations at Aigun (completed May 28, 1858) for the cession of the trans-Amur territory and could formulate compensatory territorial claims for themselves. Whereas the Russian kept Gros informed of his co-operative diplomatic efforts in north China to effect an early settlement of the treaty question, he was content to let the aloof British worry concerning his role.[48] This was especially true during the negotiations at Taku and Tientsin, where Putiatin enjoyed the advantage of sources of intelligence from within Peking itself via the Russian ecclesiastical mission.[49] When Putiatin completed his remarkable diplomatic performance, he had earned the respect of all concerned. Gros actually favored accepting the Chinese proposal made in early June that Putiatin handle all negotiations at

[45] Williams (302–303), secretary to Reed, recorded that Elgin never confided in his colleagues to learn their views and never invited discussion.

[46] 36th Congress, 1st sess., Sen. exec. doc. 30, pp. 48–49, from Reed, Dec. 15, 1857.

[47] Reed, I, 143, 159, 168, for Nov. 15, Dec. 4, and Dec. 10, 1857. Reed contrasted British justification of their treatment of the rebellious Indian sepoys with their sympathy for the slaves in America. He wrote: "I am beginning to be terribly anti-English."

[48] Cordier, 1857–58, 345–346, Putiatin to Gros, April 29, 1857; Oliphant, I, 270.

[49] Hoo Chi-Tsai, 201–211; Cordier, 1857–58, 349–352, 374–384. From May 26 until the end of the Tientsin negotiations, Gros and Putiatin were in almost daily communication.

Tientsin, but to this he encountered an emphatic negative from Elgin.[50]

All four negotiators participated in the abortive initial communications with Peking via Soochow and Shanghai in February and March, and all moved to the mouth of the Peiho in late April.[51] It was hoped that the appearance so near Peking of such an imposing array of foreign war vessels, mainly British and French but including also two American steam frigates,[52] would produce early Chinese agreement to negotiate in a serious fashion. But a full month passed without the appearance of high level commissioners invested with the "full powers" that Elgin and Gros demanded. Putiatin and Reed meanwhile contacted minor officials ashore with differing results. Where the Russian urged prompt Chinese compliance with the allied demands, Reed again posed as the peacemaker friend of China and made no effort to conceal his dislike of British stuffiness and punctilio. Eventually, on May 8, Gros registered a sharp protest to Reed.[53] It was a trying situation in which tempers grew short and illness took its toll. The entire allied force began to despair of success. Things moved more rapidly after the Taku forts fell with ridiculous ease in late May, and the allies moved up the river to Tientsin for serious negotiations in early June.[54]

The Negotiations at Tientsin

Four separate negotiations proceeded simultaneously between the several Western agents and the harried Chinese commissioners at Tientsin, all taking place under threat of military reprisal. Elgin's secretary aptly described the situation as a state not of war, but of intimidation.[55] Reed's secretary likened the four Western negotiators to whist players, each making inferences from the cards played by the others, with the

[50] AEC, 24, 243, from Gros, June 2, 1858.

[51] Oliphant, I, 185–207; Cordier, 1857–58, 259–266, 321–322. The Chinese concluded at this juncture that the French mercenary troops were in the pay of the English. See Swisher, 403, 409.

[52] Reed made a special trip to Manila to persuade Admiral Tattnall to send the U.S. frigates to China just to demonstrate that it was not want of means that prompted the United States to abstain from hostile acts (SD, China, DD, from Reed, April 10, 1858).

[53] Reed, I, 306–307, 331–344, May 5–11. The British were especially contemptuous of the "peacemaking" effort of their "blessed American cousin." See Oliphant, I, 277.

[54] Oliphant, I, 267–273; Reed (I, 370, 378) recounts that Elgin became ill of "billiousness" on June 5; Reed himself was faint much of the time.

[55] Oliphant, I, 349; Swisher, 430–437, 439–440, 442, 449–456, 467.

Russians and Americans acting as partners and the Englishmen seeing no need to find a partner at all. The Chinese tried desperately hard to isolate Elgin by playing up alternately to Reed and Putiatin.[56]

Certainly Gros and Elgin did not operate as partners, even though their relations as allies remained formally correct. Gros was not in favor of insisting on the right of permanent diplomatic residence at Peking, but he could not persuade Elgin to substitute occasional access to the capital and direct correspondence via special messenger.[57] Elgin proposed, to the annoyance of Gros, that they abandon the objective of free access to the interior for missionaries and for businessmen. Gros had an advantage in that he knew that London had already authorized Elgin to moderate his demands if necessary, and he could count also on the aid of Putiatin and Reed. The situation was largely one of Britain against the field. Peking accorded little respect to Gros, who appeared to them to be completely under Elgin's control.[58]

The primacy of the British in the negotiation was nevertheless unquestioned. It stemmed in part from their preponderance of military strength, but also from their long tradition of political and commercial leadership in the Far East and their determination to re-establish to the full their lost prestige. Despite Elgin's acknowledged disgust at the overbearing conduct of his countrymen in China, he decided that too much was at stake to allow himself the indulgence of his sympathies for the mistreated Chinese. He wrote to Lady Elgin on June 5: "I made up my mind . . . to act the role of the 'uncontrollably fierce barbarian.' . . . These stupid people . . . never yield anything except under the influence of fear." [59]

At Elgin's first meeting with the Chinese commissioners on June 4, he declined their hospitality, terminated the session abruptly, and reserved for written communication his comments on the "full powers" credentials which they submitted. Thereafter he delegated to his assistants, Lay and Wade, the task of bullying and browbeating the Chinese, which Elgin himself probably would have been incapable of doing in person. This deliberate procedure of forcing the Chinese to endure abuse from Elgin's subordinates was calculated to destroy their face. It was not

[56] John W. Foster, *American Diplomacy in the Orient* (New York, 1903), 238–242.

[57] Cordier, *1857–58*, 322. This matter was argued on April 3.

[58] AEC, 24, 193, from Gros, May 19, 1858; Swisher, 480.

[59] John Lyle Morison, *The Eighth Earl of Elgin* (London, 1928), 223.

London or even Elgin speaking at Tientsin but rather the hardened group of old China hands who had a long-standing score to settle with the arrogant authorities at Peking.[60] Lay and Wade proceeded by ultimatum; vehemence displaced argument, which was followed by threats to bombard Tientsin. The attempt of the commissioners to ingratiate themselves with Lay following his brutal humiliation of Ch'i-ying on June 8 had no effect whatever.[61] When Putiatin, thoroughly alarmed over violent British tactics, influenced the incredulous Reed to protest to Elgin, the American was unceremoniously snubbed for his effrontery.[62] The Russian also sent his assistant, von der Osten Sacken, to convey his misgivings to Baron Gros, who remained, however, discreetly mum. Reed's diary describes Putiatin's views as follows:

No one but an insolent English official and a subordinate one at that would venture on such an indecency. . . . It . . . is virtually making a new India out of China. This, Count Putiatin said, he and his government would resist to the utmost and that, if persevered in, it would inevitably lead to a European war.

That this was no idle threat is proved by the revelation that on June 20, Putiatin actually offered to provide the Chinese government with 10,000 rifles, 50 cannon, plus officers skilled in the drilling of troops and in the construction of forts, as a means of strengthening the future defenses of Taku.[63]

The bludgeoning tactics of Lay and Wade forced the commissioners to acquiesce in the British demands, but the incident sowed the seeds of

[60] Oliphant, I, 343–344; Morse, I, 519–524. By this time London had actually acceded to the French proposal not to insist on residence at Peking, which was Elgin's principal demand (AEC, to Gros, June 15, 1858, reporting a statement from London of June 17).

[61] Cordier, 1857–58. The Chinese thanked Lay for his frankness, asked pardon for ever having complained of him, and on the following day made him a present of a horse, bridled and saddled.

[62] SD, China, DD, Reed, no. 21, June 15, 1858, and enclosure 9. Reed alleged that the tactics of Elgin's subordinates were imperiling the entire negotiation and that they "could only be accounted for, if authorized, by a new determination on the part of the English to trample on this defenceless people and seek a pretext for new hostilities." Elgin reminded Reed in reply that America intended to claim for its countrymen whatever advantages the British derived from their effort at negotiation and declared that Lay's "language was entirely comformable to the instructions which he received from me for his guidance."

[63] Reed, II, 370–380; Swisher, 495. Kwei-liang gave full credence to this offer.

future trouble. The items in the treaty most objectionable to the Chinese were Article 3, conferring the right of diplomatic residence at Peking, and Article 9, permitting under passport authorization free British travel in the interior of China whether for trade or for pleasure.[64] Peking's reaction to these two articles in particular was sharply negative. Putiatin learned via missionary channels on June 21 that the Emperor was prepared to accept all the consequences attending the rejection of these demands and that anxiety was growing steadily in Peking.[65] The impasse came into the open on June 24, when it became known that the commissioners had been commanded at the peril of their lives to reject the terms in question.

Meanwhile the three other Western agents had finished their negotiations. Putiatin was the first to sign a treaty, on June 13. The most important items in his treaty accorded to Russians the right to trade at all the open ports, the privilege of sending diplomatic agents to Peking on special occasions, the toleration and protection of Christian missionaries in the interior, and a pledge by China that the northern frontier boundary would be fixed.[66] Putiatin exploited the occasion of his signing by thanking Elgin and Gros separately in almost identical letters for the indispensable assistance of their armed pressure in forcing the Chinese to grant the just demands of civilization and by praising their moderation which had spared the Chinese the sufferings of war. His letters concluded as follows:

It is for your Excellency now to decide on the future fate of the present Government, and it will depend on you to place the necessary check on the stream which might otherwise deluge China. . . . The too great concessions which might be exacted from a Government so roughly shaken would but precipitate its fall. . . . It is repose which is necessary for China.[67]

[64] Hertslet, I, 19–23.

[65] *Ibid.*, II, 396–398, June 21. Reed commented on June 23: "Poor China, the Philistines are upon them!"

[66] Oliphant, I, 409–410; Hoo Chi-Tsai, 182–186. The Amur question was avoided by Putiatin because Muraviev was handling it at Aigun and also because Putiatin did not want to prolong negotiations with the attendant danger of an allied attack on Peking.

[67] Leavenworth, 107–109; Cordier, *1857–58*, 411–415. Both letters were dated June 15. Putiatin also thanked Gros for his frank communications and personal assistance. Gros assured the Russian, in reply, that he had no intention of pushing demands so far as to endanger the Chinese government.

The American treaty (signed June 18) and the French treaty (completed June 21) contained little of a general nature extending beyond the Russian document. Reed's missionary secretaries, Williams and Martin, inserted a phrase granting both freedom from molestation for those preaching and practicing the Christian faith in China and the privilege of interior entry of Protestant missionary families.[68] The French treaty provided for the security of persons and property of missionaries, the permission to conduct characteristic Catholic religious rites, the right of the Chinese to embrace the Christian faith, and the complete abrogation of the imperial anti-Christian edicts. The French treaty included also six supplementary articles providing for the permanent degradation of the guilty mandarin at Hsi-lin and for a two million tael indemnity, guaranteed by the occupation of Canton or by an assignment of a portion of the customs receipts, to cover claims for the death of Father Chapdelaine and the expenses occasioned by the armed action at Canton. The French treaty limited the issuance of viséd passports for interior travel in China to those persons only who offered all desired guarantees.[69] Thus in 1858 the French regularized in a formal treaty virtually all of the privileges which they had sought since the Jancigny mission.

The French negotiation was completed on June 21, but Gros delayed the formal signing out of deference to the British, who were not yet prepared to sign. He explained that he did not want to appear to withdraw support from an ally whose aid he might need later.[70] During the course of the stormy two-day session, June 24–26, following receipt of the news of Peking's rejection of two key provisions of the British treaty, Gros undertook to remonstrate with Elgin after Putiatin and Reed had flatly refused to do so.[71] Gros explained that although his own very satisfactory treaty had been concluded and he did not wish to imperil it, he had deferred formal signing out of loyalty to his colleague. Elgin seemed prepared at one point not to press his extreme demands, but he finally refused Gros's request and decided to go on "fighting and bullying" as before.[72] Elgin reported his reactions as follows:

[68] Morse, I, 526–527; Latourette, 274–275.

[69] Hertslet, I, 270–286; Cordier, *1857–58*, 429–433; Cordier, *Histoire Générale*, IV, 21–39. Reed alone objected to this arrangement for passports to missionaries.

[70] AEC, 24, 306–307, from Gros, June 18, 1858.

[71] Reed, II, 398–402, June 23–26.

[72] Cordier, *1857–58*, 436–438.

I sent for the Admiral, gave him a hint that there was a great opportunity for England; that all the Powers were deserting me on a point which they all, in their original applications to Peking, demanded . . . ; that therefore we had it in our power to claim our place of priority in the East by obtaining this when others would not insist upon it. Would he back me? [73]

The timely arrival of 1,000 men of the Fifty-ninth British Regiment from Canton at this juncture and their summons to enter the Peiho River forced the final capitulation from the terrified commissioners.[74] The British treaty was accordingly signed on June 26 and the French treaty on June 27. The latter event was celebrated by a colorful ceremony after dark, with the procession of French troops lighted by bright blue flares.[75] Elgin kept the military pressure on for a week longer until news of Peking's ratification of the British treaty had also been obtained. He left north China for Shanghai on July 6.[76] As S. Wells Williams has remarked, the Emperor might gain satisfaction from his relief that the foreigners had not kidnapped him or joined the Taipings.[77]

All three European capitals were gratified over news of the success of the Tientsin negotiations, which was telegraphed to Europe across Siberia. The text of the Russian treaty was the first to reach Europe, on August 7, being transmitted overland on horseback via Mongolia and Siberia. It was a double triumph for Russia: the Tientsin treaty arrived only a few weeks after the ratification at St. Petersburg of Muriaviev's Aigun treaty.[78] British Foreign Minister Malmesbury, who had become fully reconciled to the prospects of partial failure in China, was most profuse in his praise of Elgin's firmness and sagacity in accomplishing

[73] Walrond, 253. Elgin's statement is not correct. Putiatin had never agreed to demand entry to Peking, and Gros had not flatly refused to go along with Elgin.

[74] Oliphant, I, 350, 412–417, 432; Bazancourt, I, 253–254. Oliphant presents a fairly convincing apology for Elgin's insistence on the right of diplomatic residence at Peking on the ground that only through European pressure exerted directly at court could mandarins in distant areas be forced to abandon their tactics of resisting all foreign demands and pretentions.

[75] Oliphant, I, 410–412, 419–420.

[76] Morse, I, 527–530. Reed's diary for June 30 (II, 407) reflected the nervousness prevalent at Tientsin over the expected news from Peking and Reed's annoyance at the prospect that English extortion might still result in the scrapping of all the treaties.

[77] Williams, 307.

[78] Cordier, *Histoire Générale,* IV, 51–54.

for all what the others had failed to secure.[79] Walewski was equally pleased with the results and especially with the close co-operation between Elgin and Gros. He also spoke favorably to Lord Cowley concerning the contribution of Putiatin.[80] Little could be said in favor of Reed's performance. Cass complimented him for keeping on friendly terms with the other negotiators and wrote privately to him approving his procedures. But Reed himself harbored some doubts. He referred to himself in a letter to Cass as the most inexpert diplomatist on the Secretary's entire staff and added hopefully, "I have, I suppose, succeeded." He nevertheless urged the President to appoint as his successor in China a man of high position, since England and France were sure to select first-rate men.[81]

But while the mood in Europe was congratulatory, the atmosphere in China between the British and the French reflected intensified rivalry. The entente was under severe strain. This episode can be appropriately concluded by quoting from an article, appearing in the (British) *Daily Press* of Hongkong, which Bourboulon forwarded to Paris in July. It ran in part as follows:

There are unmistakable indications that the French sympathise with the Russians on the subject of our power in the East, where certainly our policy has been . . . aggressive. . . . We know that the French have openly and warmly advocated the project of cutting a canal through the isthmus of Suez. The object of this scheme is apparent. . . . If a canal were cut through the Isthmus it would be within the power of France to forestall us [in sending an army to India]. . . . So palpable is this design of the French . . . that we took the island of Perim in the Red Sea to obtain the mastery of the navigation of those waters. . . . We know that Count de Morny is notoriously inimical to the English, that he certainly was sent upon a mission to St. Petersburg, and, it is said, there made a secret treaty with Russia. It seems that the Persian ambassadors have received the highest honours in Paris, and that they have left for their own country accompanied by a number of

[79] FO, 17, 284, to Elgin, July 2 and Sept. 25, 1858; FO, 27, 1238, to Cowley at Paris, Aug. 9, 1858. Malmesbury here agreed that diplomatic residence at Shanghai would be acceptable if it should prove impossible to enter Peking and that if present operations produced no treaty, some middle course should be outlined which the Chinese would accept.

[80] FO, 27, 1256, Cowley to Malmesbury, July 30, 1858.

[81] SD, China, DD, from Reed (marked private), July 31 and to Reed, Sept. 3 and Oct. 16, 1858.

French engineers, military men, and the like. . . . We confess, therefore, that we feel a little fidgetty about the French alliance in the China dispute. We firmly believe that Russian intrigue has been the cause of the Emperor of China refusing to accede to our demands. We do not like the French claiming territory in Cambodia. They have no legitimate interest in this China quarrel. . . . When priests dabble with politics, aggression and territorial acquisition are sure to become the order of the day. The formation of the alliance was ill-advised, and has justified the French in augmenting their forces in these seas to an extent which with this India affair on our hands, is dangerous.[82]

[82] AEC, 22, 97–98, enclosure from Bourboulon, July 1, 1858.

XIII

British Leadership: Tourane, Saigon, and Taku, 1858-1859

LORD ELGIN'S diplomatic coup at Tientsin re-established Britain's predominance in China beyond the point of challenge by France. It was Elgin who decided that military control should be reasserted over restive Canton; it was with him that the imperial commissioners announced they would confer in Shanghai. He also left for Japan at the end of July, and concluded a new British treaty with Japan on August 26, while Baron Gros tailed along some six weeks later.[1] Upon his return to Shanghai, Elgin acted unilaterally in negotiating a modification of the British right of embassy residence at Peking, and he also acted with a minimum of consultation in formulating the new commercial regulations.[2] During the course of the Shanghai negotiations, Elgin required prior agreement on the part of Peking to remove the troublesome Governor-General Hwang at Canton and to cancel the powers of

[1] Oliphant, I, 445–450; Cordier, *Histoire Générale,* IV, 58–59. Townsend Harris signed the U.S. treaty with Japan on July 31, the Dutch theirs on August 18, Putiatin on August 19, Elgin on August 26, Gros on October 9. Elgin's treaty replaced Admiral Sterling's treaty signed in October, 1857 ("Le Premier Traité de la France avec le Japon," *T'oung Pao,* 2d ser., XIII, [1912], 205–290).

[2] Cordier, *L'Expédition de Chine de 1860* (Paris, 1906), 21–44; Reed (Nov. 9, 1858, dispatch), now completely subdued, meekly accepted the British proposal to legalize opium importation and otherwise did not participate in the commercial negotiations. He justified his role by explaining that "distempered jealousy of English or French progress" was "likely to defeat the true aims of American statesmanship."

the Canton "war committee" to recruit local militia to oppose the foreigners.[3] Baron Gros found that the supplementary negotiations were virtually completed by the time he returned from Japan.

Equally impressive was Elgin's execution of his solo expedition up the Yangtse in late 1858. He obtained permission for the trip from the Chinese commissioners at Shanghai in return for his postponement of the actual enjoyment of the right of residence at Peking. His three objectives in taking British war vessels up the river were to show the British flag and thus establish a presumptive right of access when the treaty terms became operative, to obtain data on river navigation, and to make a preliminary selection of the three treaty ports agreed to at Tientsin. Elgin explained to London that Reed and Gros had been informed of his intentions and that they could have accompanied him if either had had the necessary vessels at hand. The British leader extended them no invitation, however. Baron Gros privately resented Elgin's presumption, and commented bitterly in his journal: "Not a word has he said concerning my presence in the river." [4]

At Nanking, Elgin's gunboats silenced the Taiping batteries which disputed their passage. The British nevertheless refused to co-operate with the besieging imperialist forces, who staged a feeble attack during the course of the naval bombardment. The British penetrated rebel-held territory to the vicinity of Hankow, where Elgin interviewed the Governor-General of the two lake provinces. The expedition was a convincing demonstration of British primacy and power.[5]

Britain's leadership had substantial foundation also in the diplomatic field. At the several treaty ports, British consular courts alone undertook to maintain a degree of order among the turbulent foreign residents, who customarily took advantage of their extraterritorial exemption from Chinese jurisdiction to abuse the Chinese population with impunity.[6] Britain was first to establish a regular embassy in China, the Ambas-

[3] Oliphant, I, 269–271.

[4] Cordier, 1860, 19–21. Reed registered no protest at being left out, and Gros's pride prevented him from asking to go along. After all, the right of access up the river as well as residence at Peking appeared only in the British treaty.

[5] FO, 17, 328, from Elgin, Jan. 5, 1859; SD, China, DD, from Williams, Jan. 14, 1859.

[6] Reed and Williams (dispatches of Sept. 4, 1858, and Feb. 25, 1859) complained of the complete lack of American consular control at most of the treaty ports and acknowledged that only the efforts of British consuls tended to relieve the shortcomings of others.

sador-designate being Frederick Bruce, the brother of Lord Elgin.[7] When Bruce set up his temporary headquarters at Shanghai in 1859, all the foreign agents followed suit. Paris at first offered the French ambassadorship to Baron Gros but later decided to leave matters in Bourboulon's hands until treaty ratifications were exchanged.[8] Other demonstrations of British initiative were London's authorization to acquire possession of Kowloon Peninsula opposite Hongkong Island and the pressure of the British consul at Bangkok for permission to install a telegraph line "from Moulemin on the way to China" and to survey the Kra Isthmus "with a view to a ship canal." [9]

The Problem of French Prestige

The only area in which French prestige could still assert its primacy in China was in the field of religion. Consul Montigny at Shanghai managed to obtain official acquiescence in his long-time policy of maintaining direct relations with local mandarins in places of missionary interest.[10] As a possible further extension of French protection, Baron Gros was asked in November, 1858, to comment on the request of the papacy that a supplementary French diplomatic envoy be assigned to China to care for missionary interests there. Before Gros's reply was received, the proposal was vetoed at Paris in favor of vesting all responsibility in the regular legation.[11]

Even in the religious field, French priority was not left without challenge from the British. The Anglican bishop of Hongkong wrote in the Hongkong *Daily Press* for October 18, 1858, expressing his apprehension that the Roman Catholic missionaries would revive claims to former church property, especially at Peking. He added:

[7] FO, 17, 284, instructions to Bruce, Nov. 25, 1858. John Bowring was relieved of his duties at this time.

[8] Cordier, *1860*, 30–44.

[9] FO, 17, 284, to Elgin, June 2, 1858; SD, Bangkok, CL from Mattoon no. 4, May 26, 1856; SD, China, DI, I, 178–180, to Reed, April 28, and from Reed, Sept. 15, 1858. Elgin asked permission to demand Kowloon in April, but the June 2 permission arrived too late for the Tientsin negotiations. At the same time, Reed explained his reluctance to act on instructions from Secretary Cass to seek for the United States a 99-year lease on Kean Island on the Canton estuary some twelve miles north of Macao.

[10] AEC, 27, 245.

[11] *Ibid.*, 26, 271, to Gros, Nov. 9, 1858; 27, 28, to Bourboulon, Jan. 25, 1859. Withdrawal of this proposal of the papacy coincided with reports reaching Paris

French diplomacy having no commercial interests to foster, may busy itself in efforts to sustain . . . a French Protectorate of Native Romanist converts, [to] be gradually established on this Continent. . . . A powerful French ecclesiastical-political organization . . . [may] be one of the results of the Anglo-French alliance and joint intervention in the affairs of the East.[12]

Bourboulon angrily denounced what he termed the British version of the American "Know-Nothing" mania about the destiny of the Anglo-Saxons to civilize and Christianize the world. He commented acidly that the "predestined race" apparently foresaw "obstacles to its exclusive and predominant influence" wherever France took an active role. The Anglicans, he added, were simply jealous that Catholic successes dwarfed their own. Assuming that an intensification of religious rivalry was inevitable, Bourboulon urged that a uniform policy be worked out co-ordinating the efforts of French missionaries, consuls, and Paris authorities to organize the French religious protectorate in China, a step which the Anglicans apparently anticipated. Bourboulon added that an essential condition of such a program would be that the missionaries submit more completely than heretofore to political direction, either through consulates in the field or through legation-bishop connections, as to their conduct vis-à-vis the authorities of the country.[13]

Admiral Genouilly at Tourane

Admiral Genouilly's expedition to Tourane had been designed as a means of shaking off France's embarrassing inferiority to Britain's dominant position in the Far East. Preliminary press notices in the official *Le Moniteur Universel* at Paris were restrained, but the Ministry of Marine elevated Genouilly to the rank of vice-admiral on the eve of the operation.[14] Once the expedition was actually under way, an inspired article in the *Revue Orientale et Americaine* presented in glowing colors the promise of Annam's ample resources and commercial possibilities. The story reviewed the history of French relations from the Pigneau de Behaine episode to Montigny's recent mission to Tourane, and closed with a peroration declaring that the blood of compatriots and repeated in-

---

concerning Admiral Genouilly's difficulties with Monsignor Pellerin. See n. 30, this chapter.

12 AEC, 22, 198–199, enclosure from Bourboulon, Oct. 26, 1858.

13 AEC, 22, 200–216, from Bourboulon, Nov. 11, 1858.

14 Cultru, 61; Bazancourt, I, 292; *Le Moniteur Universel*, Jan. 25, 1858.

sults to the flag gave France the right to impose conditions on King Tu-Duc. As master of Tourane, the Gibralter of Cochin-China, France would become a naval power in the seas of eastern Asia.[15]

The long-protracted allied negotiation in north China delayed the preparations for the French operation against Tourane until very late in the season. Approximately three months only were available between the conclusion of the negotiations at Tientsin and the onset of the torrential October rains and typhoon winds along the Annamite coast. Supplies of food, coal, hospital facilities, and other essentials had to be assembled. A number of vessels had to be reconditioned. Two French ships were sent to Manila to facilitate preparations for the co-operating Spanish contingent. All French ships except the two assigned to take Baron Gros to Japan and the four which were left at Canton started in August for the point of rendezvous at Hainan Island, about 160 miles distant from Tourane. Here the advance group encountered oppressive heat and bad water. Cholera made its omnious appearance on August 20, so that when the main body of troops arrived on August 27 the men were not allowed to go ashore as previously planned.[16] The initial Spanish force, consisting of only 450 men commanded by Colonel Lanzarote, were transported in a French ship accompanied by a Spanish steam war vessel. French troops available for shore duty numbered less than 2,000 men. The French also recruited several hundred Filipino Tagals into their own forces. The fleet consisted of fourteen ships in all, including five transports.[17]

Accompanying the main French force was Monsignor Pellerin, who had done so much at Paris in the previous year to persuade Napoleon III to authorize the venture.[18] The diary notes of a companion French Colonel reported that the affable Bishop harbored no doubts that the expedition could successfully establish a foothold at Tourane and conquer a portion of the country itself if Tu-Duc refused to give satisfaction.[19] The force entered Tourane bay on August 31.

The occupation of the harbor defenses was accomplished without dif-

[15] Léon de Rosny, "La Cochinchine et l'Occupation Française du Port de Tourane," *Revue Orientale et Americaine* I (1859), 67–72.

[16] Ponchalon, 92–94. The author himself fell ill on August 24.

[17] Bazancourt, I, 274–276; Hanotaux, V, 381–383; Thomson, 350.

[18] Launay, *Histoire Générale*, III, 367–374.

[19] Ponchalon, 88. The author describes Monsignor Pellerin as a charming conversationalist and a great smoker of choice Manila cigars.

ficulty on September 1 and 2. The fort gunners gave only a token response to the initial French volleys and then fled. Apparently no defense preparations had been made at the harbor in anticipation of the attack. The murderous sun took a far heavier toll than did enemy fire.[20] The intelligence furnished to Genouilly by young neophyte emissaries of Monsignor Pellerin on September 5, to the effect that an Annamite force of 10,000 men was prepared to attack, proved to be a false alarm. The core of the Annamite army was reported to be the imperial guard, but troops were allegedly arriving daily from all parts of Tu-Duc's domain. It was not until September 21 that reconnaissance efforts cited an enemy camp of an estimated seven or eight thousand troops assembled several kilometers to the west of the harbor.[21] Meanwhile the river route leading to Hué was examined and a camp site explored. The bar at the mouth of the river blocked entry by the French war vessels and the small boats needed for use in the river were lacking. An attack overland with the necessary heavy guns seemed to call for transport and bridging facilities which were not available. The initial ardor of the idle troops quickly cooled. An additional 550 Spanish troops from Manila eventually arrived.[22]

The first difficulties encountered were heat prostration and widespread dysentery, which began to take a heavy toll in sickness and resulted in some deaths. This was followed shortly by an outbreak of fever and eventually by scurvy and cholera.[23] The much-needed indigenous labor force which Pellerin had promised would be available did not materialize, much less any sign of popular rising against the allegedly oppressive ruler. When the excuse was made that political disaffection and the responsive Christian indigenous elements were centered in Tongking rather than in the vicinity of Hué, Admiral Genouilly detached the war vessel *Primauguet* to skirt the coast of Tongking in an effort to stimulate a co-operative rising of native Christian elements there. The vessel returned on October 15, reporting that no appreciable results had been realized from the effort. A similarly futile trip was made to the Tongking coast by the *Pregent* in December.

[20] Bazancourt, I, 276–284. The guns were of eighteenth-century vintage, made of brass and iron.

[21] Ponchalon, 105–106, 112–120.   [22] Bazancourt, I, 284–288.

[23] Bazancourt (I, 288–293) reported that during October the effective force diminished daily because of illness. A captain of the marines died, then the chief captain of the engineers, a serious loss.

The plausible explanation was then advanced that the Christians feared to expose themselves until they were assured that the French installation was a permanent thing. Colonel Ponchalon began to suspect that Monsignor Pellerin's spies ashore were being fed false information by designing mandarins. He noted that until mid-October all of the reports they brought in proved to be without foundation.[24]

Successive entries in Colonel Ponchalon's diary tell a somber tale. By October 20 the rains were upon the troops, and all hands were busy building shelters, hospitals, and storerooms. Sanitation deteriorated steadily from lack of native laborers, while fever and dysentery steadily reduced the number of effective workers. Colonel Ponchalon's slight arm wound became gangrenous; mere skin infections led to a number of amputations. By November the reinforced Annamite army finally assembled and advanced to within two miles of the French camp. Here it began preparing strong defensive fortifications. Vigorous French action taken on December 21 destroyed several enemy batteries and routed some 1,500 Annamite troops, but it did not halt their buildup of strength or lead to any decisive results. The invading force by this time was too weak to take major risks. Meanwhile a concerted but fruitless effort to assemble boats of light draft capable of navigating the river route leading toward Hué was started; the search extended as far afield as Canton and Manila. By early December, Admiral Genouilly recognized the impossibility of attacking Hué and began to consider a diversion to lower Cochin-China. Nothing further could be attempted at Tourane until the rains subsided around the first of April.[25]

One consequence of the embarrassing situation at Tourane was the development of an unseemly quarrel between Monsignor Pellerin and Admiral Genouilly over who was responsible for the debacle. This controversy was destined to be argued for years thereafter by partisan apologists. The Admiral alleged that the missionaries had misrepresented both to him and to Paris the capacity of the French fleet to inspire terror at Hué, the favorable response to be anticipated from politically disaffected elements and Christian indigenes, the supposed ease with which Hué could be captured or other expeditions under-

---

[24] Ponchalon, 120–127; Bazancourt, I, 291–294; Cultru, 66–67. A detachment sent up the river in October to destroy fireboats reported to be there found none at all.

[25] Ponchalon, 127–131; Bazancourt, I, 291–295, 297; Thomazi, 29–32.

taken into the interior, and the availability of local labor such as the allies had utilized at Canton.[26] Pellerin and his apologists, on the other hand, accused Genouilly of excessive timidity for not attempting to attack Hué, then virtually undefended, prior to the onset of the rains, and for expecting an impossible response from scattered pro-French sympathizers prior to his making a major move of this character.[27] Genouilly recalled that Pellerin's own neophyte intelligence agents brought in the false news that the Annamites were prepared from the very outset to contest in force any move toward Hué. He added that Monsignor Retord's insistence that nothing less than a displacement of the pagan dynasty of Tu-Duc by a Christian King ruling under the protection of France would be sufficient to establish a lasting settlement, glorious for France and for religion, had not explained just how that end would be achieved.

Genouilly's official report to the Minister of Marine of January 29, 1859, maintained that the government had been deceived into thinking that the endeavor was a modest and feasible one. The supposed friendly attitude of the inhabitants, the lax authority of the mandarins over them, the inferior size and character of the Annamite army, the weak defenses of Hué, the alleged salubrity of the climate—all these, he declared, had been misrepresented. Lacking the shallow-draft boats by which alone heavy guns could be transported and brought to bear on Hué, the European troops simply could not withstand the arduous assignment, weakened as they were by disease. The Admiral declared that three thousand effective troops would be needed for the attack in addition to the garrison at Tourane and his largely invalided forces. Genouilly renewed his previous proposal, first made on December 3, that a diversionary attack on Saigon be authorized.[28]

The outcome of the quarrel was the forced withdrawal of Pellerin from the expedition and his eventual retirement to Penang.[29] The

[26] Bazancourt, I, 296–297.

[27] Launay (*Mgr. Retord,* 430–433) best presented the missionary case as follows: "The news of the capture of Tourane . . . had penetrated even into the mountains, which gave exile to the bishop [Retord]. Other more decisive successes were awaited. But silence ensued. The French expedition immobilized itself at Tourane, the Admiral closed his ears to enlightened counsels." Louvet (II, 228–230) denied that Pellerin ever told Louis Napoleon that the Annamite Christians would rise en masse at the approach of the French.

[28] Bazancourt, I, 294–299.

[29] Launay, *Histoire Générale,* III, 375–377, and *Mgr. Retord,* 433; Louvet, *La*

Admiral's determination to make a diversionary attack at Saigon rather than at Tongking, where most of the now completely exposed Christian elements were to be found, was a triumph of political over religious interests and a move to end clerical direction of French military policy in Annam.[30]

It is not necessary to take sides in the Genouilly-Pellerin feud to recognize that the expedition to Tourane had been authorized by Louis Napoleon in response to missionary urging, contrary to the advice of his Foreign Minister and without adequate assessment of the difficulties to be encountered. Most French students of the episode agree that Genouilly might possibly have been able to capture Hué by a quick thrust in September and early October, but that for him to have attempted it without cannon and in the absence of knowledge of the terrain or the nature of the defenses to be overcome would have been at best a dangerous gamble.[31] The ravages of disease, the climate, and the lateness of the season defeated any possibility of a solidly planned attack on Hué.

When the inevitable inquiry came in November, 1858, from the British Ambassador at Paris concerning the intentions of the French government with respect to Cochin-China, Foreign Minister Walewski gave a halting reply. Admiral Genouilly, he said, was in fact master of the whole situation and as Foreign Minister he himself harldly knew what was in prospect. He gave Ambassador Cowley a historical review of the relations between France and Annam going back to the Pigneau de Behaine episode. He said that the objective of the French govern-

---

Cochinchine Religieuse, II, 230–231. Monsignor Retord died during the early stages of the campaign, in October, 1858.

[30] Ponchalon's diary (pp. 133–134) for a January, 1859, date runs as follows: "A lively debate has been taking place between the Admiral and Mgr. Pellerin, at the close of which the bishop will be returned . . . to Hongkong. Mgr. Pellerin would have . . . the admiral go to Tongking in preference to Saigon, alleging that one would find there many Christians disposed to rally to us. The admiral has declared that he could not subordinate important strategic questions to more or less problematical religious interests; that whereas the very reduced effective strength of the expeditionary corps does not permit him to attack Hué, he could take possession of Saigon and thus step on the tail of the serpent."

[31] Cultru, 82–85; SD, China, DD, 18, from Williams, Feb. 25, 1859. Williams tells that two or three French steamers were kept busy plying between Tourane and Hongkong, Macao, and Manila bringing in supplies and reinforcements and evacuating the invalids. See also Thomazi, 38–43.

ment was to obtain reparations for atrocities and guarantees against their renewal, but he could not say what the results would be. Tourane's capture had unfortunately produced no proposal to treat, and an expedition against Hué was therefore in prospect. In reply to Cowley's further inquiry as to whether the religious guarantees to be demanded would extend to all branches of the Christian religion, Walewski said that Genouilly's instructions covered only toleration of Catholics, but that presumably the guarantees would include all Christians. Cowley's conclusions as reported to Malmesbury were: (*a*) that a prolonged if not permanent occupation of Tourane was in prospect, (*b*) that, in the absence of any diplomatic agent, Genouilly could be expected to impose harsh terms if thereby he could enhance French prestige, and (*c*) that in Genouilly's mind the operation in Annam from the beginning had taken precedence over the China War.[32]

Meanwhile, relations between Admiral Genouilly and Colonel Lanzarote at Tourane had become strained because the Admiral refused to consult his Spanish associate regarding current developments and future plans. The unilateral French decision not to undertake an attack on Tongking, where Spanish Dominican missionaries were concentrated, in favor of the alternative objective of Saigon, eventually became the subject of acrimonious exchanges between Madrid and Paris. When in early 1859 the Spanish Ambassador at Paris asked Foreign Minister Walewski what French intentions were, he received a vague and equivocal reply, including the assertion that each ally must preserve its freedom of action. This answer was obviously unsatisfactory to Colonel Lanzarote, since Genouilly gave all of the orders without prior consultation.[33]

The French Shift to Saigon and Back to Tourane

The possibility of realizing some kind of consolation victory at Saigon, a port which was accessible by river and capable of being held by naval forces, prompted the Admiral to make the move before he received formal authorization from Paris to do so. Leaving behind at Tourane a small but strongly armed garrison occupying a reconditioned

---

[32] FO, 27, 1262, to Cowley, Nov. 16, 1858, and from Cowley, Nov. 21, 1858. Cowley asked that a search be made in London for a copy of the treaty of 1787 between France and Annam.

[33] Thomson, 337–338.

fort and supported by three gunboats, Genouilly departed on February 2 for Saigon with the remainder of his force. The expedition was made up of five war vessels, three transports, and the Spanish steamer. The squadron reached Saigon on February 9, subdued the outer forts on the 10th, and entered the inner harbor on the 11th. Determined resistance was encountered at several points, and one vessel sustained considerable damage. The last two forts fell on February 15 and 16, and the citadel itself was captured on the 17th. The principal prize was the capture of a quantity of powder (some 85,000 kilos), 20,000 firearms, and enough rice to feed 6,000 to 8,000 troops for a year.

At Saigon, as at Tourane, the French forces received no active assistance from the Christian villagers in the vicinity, but fortunately in the south auxiliary forces were not needed. Genouilly attributed Annamese popular indifference to fear of the vengeance of the mandarins or perhaps to apathetic inability to respond to "noble and . . . holy causes." The experience convinced him that any dependence on native Annamite assistance at any point was highly unrealistic.[34] The local bishop, Monsignor Lefèbvre, visited Genouilly at Saigon on February 16, and subsequently influenced some of the Christian population to seek French protection by assembling near Saigon. But aside from their furnishing the garrison some supplies of food, there is no evidence that they assisted the French forces.[35]

Genouilly's formal report to Paris covering the capture of Saigon was enthusiastic about its strategic and commercial possibilities. Since the forces under his command did not permit establishing an effective occupation of the surrounding area at the time, he decided to garrison the most durable forts with two infantry companies, one Spanish and one French, under the command of naval Captain Jaureguiberry, supported by three war vessels plus a detachment of engineers and marine artillery. Genouilly would then return to Tourane with the remainder of the force after the cessation of the rains in April to see what, if anything, could be done to salvage that situation. The citadel at Saigon was blown up and burned on March 8, punitive measures were applied to several resisting villages in the area, and preparations

[34] Bazancourt, I, 300–317, 321–324.
[35] Ponchalon's dairy for Feb. 16, 1859; Louvet (*La Cochinchine Religieuse,* II, 236–238) alleged that the Christians came to the aid of the French, eventually forming a kind of protective belt around the beleaguered city of Saigon. He gave no confirming evidence.

were completed for evacuating the main force by the end of March. Contrary winds delayed the departure for several weeks, so that some important units did not leave Saigon until April 18.[36]

The situation at Tourane was far from encouraging, despite the arrival via Suez of almost a thousand infantry reinforcements from France, plus several hundred marines, artillerymen and engineers.[37] The strengthened Annamite forces enjoyed the initiative at the time of Genouilly's return. The French garrison had withstood several determined attacks and were actively engaged at the time in improving their defenses. Periodic counterassaults had to be made by the French to protect their positions. A serious engagement took place on May 8. It was a limited victory for the French, but the Annamite forces demonstrated greatly improved effectiveness in their artillery fire, which inflicted some seventy-eight casualties. Unfortunately, the newly arrived French troops from Europe proved to be particularly susceptible to disease, so that by early June an alarming cholera epidemic had developed among them. As the situation was obviously in stalemate, arrangements for an armistice and negotiations were made.

Meanwhile orders arrived from Paris directing that Genouilly should not undertake to attack Hué unless he was fairly sure of success and asking that a detailed statement of his requirements should be prepared for the Emperor's examination. The Admiral's reports of April 26 and May 16, prepared in reply, indicated that the best campaigning season extended from May to September and that some 3,000 effective troops would be required to capture Hué. Several shallow draft (drawing six to seven feet) gunboats, heavily armed, and a large number of smaller boats would be needed also, since the gunboats available at Tourane at the time could approach no nearer than two miles from the city's walls. Genouilly concluded by saying that in terms of accessibility of vital spots to naval attack and the quality of defenses to be encountered, waging war against Annam was more difficult than against China. Any expectation of assistance from the inhabitants must be completely discounted.[38]

[36] Bazancourt, I, 324–329.

[37] Ibid., 324, 329–331. American Consul O'Sullivan at Singapore reported that 700 French troops passed through in April on their way to Cochin-China, but also that 600 Spanish troops had been evacuated to Singapore from Saigon, presumably the sick and wounded.

[38] Ibid., 331–334, 352–353, from Genouilly, April 26 and May 16, 1859.

News of the imminence of the outbreak of war in Italy between France and Austria reached Tourane in early June, 1859, and full confirmation came on June 26, four days after the opening of Genouilly's negotiations. Thus was added to the ravages of cholera and fever the discouraging realization that no further reinforcement could be expected soon from France. Typhus broke out on July 8. Monthly deaths from illness ran almost one hundred, and a large fraction of the force became incapable of active duty. French morale reached an all-time low.[39] It was an inauspicious time to exact major treaty concessions from the Hué government.

Genouilly's report of July 15 was most discouraging. "Everything here tends toward ruin, men and things," he began. Only twenty to thirty men in entire companies remained active. He admitted that any negotiation with King Tu-Duc would entail loss of face for France because the expedition had been virtually committed to overthrowing the existing dynasty. Genouilly's personal pride, nevertheless, would not permit him to take responsibility for evacuating Tourane. He determined to await orders from Paris, but asked to be relieved of his command. Colonel Lanzarote also refused to quit Tourane without explicit orders from his government.[40]

Liquidation of the Tourane Campaign

Two widely separated political developments in May and June of 1859 vetoed any French plans for an independent policy in the Far East and forestalled a major French effort to conquer Annam at this time. The first was Louis Napoleon's reckless declaration of war against Austria on May 3, 1859. This was the sequel to his fright over the Orsini assassination attempt and his subsequent bargain with Cavour at Plombières. It was a characteristic gamble of an adventurer, taken without adequate calculation of the probable political results in Italy or of what it might do to the position of France in the European balance of power. The move was also made in disregard of warnings that English opinion would be solidly against France. The crisis brought to office at London in June a vigorous new cabinet, including Palmerston, Gladstone, and John Russell, the latter replacing Malmesbury in the Foreign

---

[39] Ponchalon, 164–193.

[40] Bazancourt, I, 354–357; Thomson, 339. Madrid proposed to reinforce Tourane at the very time Paris ordered its evacuation.

Office. The new British cabinet was not unsympathetic to Italian nationalist aspirations, but Palmerston saw in the possible disintegration of the Hapsburg empire the unwelcome elevation of Russia to a dominant position in the lower Danube Valley and the Balkans.

The truce of Villafranca with Austria came on July 11, following Prussia's mobilization on France's Rhine frontier, but this did not stop the surge of Italian unification and the final estrangement of the papacy and the French Catholic party from Louis Napoleon. The blunder of the French Emperor lost for him his coveted freedom of action internationally and made France again almost completely dependent on British support, while at the same time it aggravated the chronic distrust with which English opinion regarded France.[41]

The second factor was the repulse which the allied naval forces, mainly British, encountered from the forts at Taku at the mouth of the Peiho on June 25, when Bruce and Bourboulon tried to force their way upstream to Tientsin as the first step in exchanging treaty ratifications. The French role in this episode will be treated later,[42] but its implications for the French cause in Cochin-China were clear. A major European military effort was required in China to recoup the disaster of Taku and to vindicate the hard-earned allied gains previously realized at Canton and Tientsin. For Paris to leave the matter to Britain alone would be to sacrifice all semblance of French prestige in the Orient. French participation in the new war in China meant certain abandonment of the discouraging expedition against Tourane and Hué. Withdrawal might have been necessary in any case, since the Spanish participants in the Cochin-China affair were losing their enthusiasm.[43]

It was therefore under depressing circumstances, both locally and internationally, that Admiral Genouilly began his treaty negotiations with representatives of Hué on June 22 under truce conditions. The French asked for the selection of an Annamite plenipotentiary with full powers "to negotiate religious liberty for missionaries and for native Christians, freedom of commercial access to Annam, and the cession of a point of land to serve as a guarantee." The Annamite delegates at first feigned acceptance of the proposals in general, but they invariably

---

[41] Cowley, 174–175, 179–185, 189; Cordier, *1860*, 98–100.

[42] See below, pages 225–228.

[43] FO, 72, 955, from Buchanan at Madrid to London, March 31, 1859. Spanish opponents of the Queen's propapal policy were using the profitless Cochin-China affair as a club to belabor the Madrid government.

demurred when it came to executing specific terms. The Admiral had no way of challenging their delaying tactics, for the cholera and typhus epidemics continued to ravage the French forces. At the end of July came the news of the affair at Taku. By August 11 Genouilly abandoned his demand for a point of territory and asked only for permission to establish a resident consulate and for acknowledgment of the French right to protect missions, as in China. The Annamite spokesmen evaded the consular issue and then openly charged that French missionaries were political agents plotting against the dynasty. Thereupon Genouilly issued an ultimatum, to expire on September 7.

During the interim, one entire infantry company had to be evacuated to Canton, while the cemetery continued to expand. The Admiral's pride would not let him withdraw, and yet the operations which he attempted on September 15, following the expiration of the ultimatum, clearly demonstrated the hopelessness of penetrating inland.[44]

In Genouilly's summary report to Paris made on September 21, he explained that the principal barrier blocking his negotiations was the profound Annamite distrust of the political intrigues of the priests and Hué's inability to understand why anyone without ulterior motives would try to force the authorities of Cochin-China to favor a religious movement foreign to the country.[45] The Admiral made it clear that if either of the French holdings in Cochin-China were to be evacuated it should be Tourane, since Saigon was intrinsically more valuable and was capable of being fortified in such a way that it could be made very difficult for France to recapture in the future. On September 25 news that Genouilly would be succeeded by Rear Admiral Page reached Tourane. Page arrived on October 19 and Genouilly departed October 31.[46]

The new commander faced the embarrassing assignment of liquidating the Tourane undertaking. He began evacuating advanced posts on November 3, withdrawing his forces to the perimeter of the forts. On November 18 he staged a corrective attack on Annamite fortifications guarding the entry to the river. But on the very next day he learned

---

[44] Ponchalon quotes Genouilly as saying: "Had I no more than four men and a corporal, the French flag would still float at Tourane" (Ponchalon, 193–209; Bazancourt, I, 357, 376).

[45] AEC, 28, 249, from Genouilly, Sept. 21, 1859.

[46] Bazancourt, I, 364; Thomazi, 40–43. Genouilly returned to Paris, where he championed the cause of permanent French control of Annam.

that the French and British govenments had agreed to collaborate in the China war. Thereafter, Page's forces were placed under the superior command of Admiral Charner. The evacuation of troops and supplies was executed in orderly fashion, but it was not until March 23, 1860, that Tourane harbor was abandoned by the allied forces. The Spanish troops were taken to Manila, except for the single regiment that had been left at Saigon.[47]

Admiral Page was authorized to attempt to negotiate a moderate settlement with Hué, including provision for protecting those missionaries who caused no trouble, the establishment of three French consulates in Annam, one of them at Balat in Tongking, the assignment to France of port dues at Saigon for twenty years in lieu of an indemnity, and the privilege of sending a French diplomatic chargé d'affaires to Hué once in three years. So discouraging was the French situation that Page made no serious effort to negotiate even for these modified terms.[48] Colonel Ponchalon's diary reflects the wounded pride and anger which attended the humiliating episode, especially so in the seeming sacrifice by Paris of French interests in Annam in favor of those of Britain in China.[49]

Even more angry and disgruntled were the Spanish authorities, who emerged from their costly venture empty-handed and with badly damaged prestige after having been ordered about and then virtually abandoned by their French allies. Nothing had been accomplished for the safety of Spanish missionaries in Tongking in whose behalf the expedition had ostensibly been undertaken. Admiral Page admitted the justice of the Spanish complaint in January, 1860, when he recommended secretly to Paris, in conjunction with his urgent proposal that France annex Saigon, that assistance be accorded Spain to obtain equivalent territorial compensation in Tongking. The newly appointed Spanish commander, Colonel Carlos Palanca Gutierrez, was instructed to demand that Spain obtain a point in Tongking if France should decide

---

[47] Ponchalon, 209–219; Bazancourt, I, 376–378; Thomson, 339–341.

[48] Henri Galos, "L'Expédition de Cochinchine," *Revue des Deux Mondes,* 7th ser., LI (1864), 178–180; Cultru, 70–71. Monsignor Louvet's allegation (*La Cochinchine Religieuse,* II, 239–240) that Page could probably have continued his limited success of November 18 and have obtained the desired treaty if Louis Napoleon had not got disgusted with the enterprise and withdrawn his support apparently has very little to sustain it.

[49] Ponchalon, 199, 209–219, Sept. 13 to Nov. 3, 1859.

to annex Saigon. Spanish Foreign Minister Calderon, in March, 1860, made this demand unconditional. The irritation at Madrid increased further when, later in 1860, Admiral Page opened Saigon to trade in the name of France alone.[50] Here emerged the presumption which persisted for more than a decade that Tongking was a sphere where Spanish interests were paramount while those of France prevailed in southern Annam. The problem of Spanish compensation was destined to continue for several years to be a matter of dispute between Paris and Madrid.

The French had no alternative to participating in the military operations in China. While the China campaign proceeded, Captain Jaureguiberry's Franco-Spanish garrison at Saigon, which was left as a holding force from April 1859 until February 1861, faced some serious fighting against heavy odds. Reinforcements eventually relieved the small contingent in 1861, and the French then began to expand their holding.[51]

The Role of France in the Taku Affair

Both at Paris and in China, during the early months of 1859, the French gave every evidence of their desire to maintain in full force their entente with Britain. Every instruction to Bourboulon enjoined close collaboration. At Canton the two forces participated jointly in a series of peaceful naval and overland forays into the adjacent countryside to test out the mood of the inhabitants and to explode exaggerated local estimates of the military prowess of the Chinese "braves" of the area.[52]

Even though French prestige in China was easily eclipsed by Britain's, it was nevertheless clearly on the upgrade. Paris received requests for assistance in China from the Dutch, the Portuguese, and from Saxony.[53] Paris was particularly concerned that in the ceremonies at Peking attending the exchange of treaty ratifications, Bourboulon act in full harmony with the British and that he insist on being accorded

---

[50] Thomson, 340–342. Thomson bases his account on the archival diplomatic correspondence at Paris relating to Spain.

[51] Bazancourt, I, 334–338; Cordier, "La Politique Coloniale," *T'oung Pao*, 2d ser., XII, 175–176.

[52] FO, 17, 328, from Elgin, Jan. 28, Feb. 12, and April 15, 1859. British forces as a rule outnumbered the French five or more to one. One expedition, a sixteen-day trip, proceeded two hundred miles up the West River.

[53] AEC, 27, 43–44, 155–156, to Bourboulon, Feb. 25, 26, May 3, 6, 1859.

223

honors and facilities equal to those enjoyed by his British colleague.[54] The French ratification of the new agreement with London was completed at Paris in late October, 1858, and it was fully expected at the time that the major portion of Admiral Genouilly's fleet would have completed its assignment at Tourane in time to participate in the exchange of ratifications.[55]

It was common knowledge within foreign diplomatic circles in China that elements at the Manchu court were strongly opposed to the right of foreign access to Peking on any basis savoring of equality. Not only did this concession violate all the political traditions of China, the court suspected that foreigners who sought access with such tenacity and at the cost of such expenditure of effort must harbor ulterior designs against the dynasty itself.[56] Lord Elgin had recognized the need for quieting this fear when he agreed in the Shanghai negotiations of 1858 to forego immediate enjoyment of diplomatic residence at Peking, although not the ultimate right. He did this also to gain important commercial concessions, including full access to the ports of the Yangtse River. This concession on Elgin's part strengthened the hands of the two commissioners with whom he negotiated at Shanghai in their controversy with the more conservative elements at the court, and the two kept Elgin posted on their progress. Thus Elgin had reason to believe that Peking was inclined to be conciliatory rather than difficult, and yet he counselled the British Admiral to retain in China waters all vessels suitable for service on the Peiho River and to furnish Ambassador Bruce with a strong escort when he went north to exchange ratifications at the capital as provided in the terms of the British and French treaties. The news that defense preparations were under way on the approaches to Peking, possibly with Russian assistance, was disquieting. In addition both Gros and Bourboulon were concerned over the inevitable Chinese resentment of the treatment they had received from the British at Tientsin.[57]

Foreign Minister Malmesbury's instructions to Ambassador-designate Bruce reflected London's determination to hold the Chinese to their

[54] *Ibid.*, 45–49, instructions of March 9, 1859.

[55] FO, 27, 1260, Cowley from Paris, Sept. 30, 1858; AEC, 26, 94, to Gros, Oct. 24, 1858. Paris wanted ratifications exchanged as soon as possible.

[56] See Reed's dispatch (no. 31) of Sept. 4, 1858; Williams, 290.

[57] Cordier, *1860*, 9–13; Morse, I, 573–575; FO, 17, 328 from Elgin, Feb. 5, March 2, and April 19, 1859; SD, China, DD, from Williams, Feb. 25, 1859.

bargain. He accepted Elgin's ruling that diplomatic access to Peking would be insisted upon only occasionally, but specified that the full requirements of the treaty must be claimed immediately if any impediment should be interposed to prevent direct communication with Peking by the embassy. Any Chinese efforts to dissuade Bruce from going to Peking to exchange ratifications must be "firmly and temperately resisted." Persistent obstruction should cause him to demand full execution of the treaty terms. Bruce was to request that arrangements be made for his reception at the mouth of the Peiho and at Tientsin, where according to Malmesbury, he was, barring unforseen circumstances, to "arrive aboard a warship." Bruce was to accept no inferior status at Chinese hands, and was to act in "cordial concert and union with the French minister." [58]

Because Genouilly's fleet in May and June, 1859, was fully engaged at Tourane and Saigon, the second allied expedition to the mouth of the Peiho was almost entirely a British show. Admiral Hope had nineteen vessels in all and Bourboulon only one corvette and a dispatch ship. The expedition was also accompanied by several American ships. The latter would have preceded the allies to the Peiho if the Chinese commissioners who met the combined squadron at Shanghai had not insisted that the desire of the American minister to effect the exchanges at Peking would not be honored unless he accompanied the British and French, whose treaties alone specified that the exchanges must be made at Peking. The exchange of Russian ratifications had already been accomplished by one Perovsky, and Russia's Ambassador Ignatieff was due shortly to arrive in Peking to negotiate concerning the demarcation of the boundary north and east of the mouth of the Ussuri River, a tributary of the Amur, which had not been covered in the Treaty of Aigun. The presence of the Russians in Peking, duly noted by the Christian Chinese and reported to Bourboulon by Monsignor Mouly, gave plausibility to the probably erroneous rumors that Russian officers were actively assisting in developing the Chinese defenses. [59]

[58] FO, 17, 311, to Bruce, March 1, 1859. Only in places where Yangtse River ports suitable for European trade had been wrested from the Taipings was Bruce to consider acting against the rebels to protect European trading interests. A full copy of Bruce's instructions went to Paris.

[59] Cordier, 1860, 44–45; Bell, II, 240, 457. Mouly's letter of March 27 reported that the Russians were in high favor at Peking. The new American minister, John E. Ward, had been promised in Jan. 12, 1859, the co-operation of Perovsky at Peking

The Chinese commissioners who came to Shanghai to meet the foreigners were Kweiliang and Hwashana, the two with whom Elgin had treated at Shanghai and who had borne the brunt of the struggle at Peking to honor the treaty engagements. Their objective was apparently threefold: (a) to delay for some two months, if possible, the journey to the Peiho in the hope that the exchanges might in the end be made at Shanghai instead of at Peking, (b) to attempt to obtain the allied evacuation of Canton as part of the total settlement, and finally, if unsuccessful in the first two, (c) to request the allies to anchor their vessels outside the bar of the Peiho River and to assure the representatives of the treaty powers that every courtesy would be extended to them at Peking.[60]

Unfortunately, the impatient British and French envoys were so annoyed by the apparent Chinese effort to hamper their mission that they paid little heed to the implied warning contained in the assurance that they would receive every courtesy *if* they anchored outside the bar at the mouth of the Peiho.[61] Bourboulon discounted rumors of the fortification of Taku because he was reluctant to believe that the Chinese would dare oppose so formidable a fleet. A mandarin at Shanghai reportedly told Bruce that he would encounter resistance and that his fleet must be prepared to give Peking a salutary lesson.[62] When the squadron reached the mouth of the Peiho on June 18–20, the British and French leaders were in no mood to accept the Chinese statements that there was no one at Taku to receive them and that the passage up the river to Tientsin was barred to them. Malmesbury's instructions had specified that Bruce should reach Tientsin "aboard a war vessel," and the qualifying phrase was forgotten.

Except for two psychological factors, mutual suspicion and the question of face, the disaster at Taku could have been avoided. The ratifications were waiting to be exchanged at Peking if the foreign emissaries would agree to approach the capital via Pehtang landing, north of Taku,

---

(from Ward, March 17, 1859). Ward was a Georgia politician who had been president of the National Democratic Convention which nominated Buchanan in 1856.

60 Williams (312–319) was convinced that the Chinese commissioners at Shanghai were sincere, and Ward (dispatch of June 13) reported their assurances without expressing any doubt or qualification regarding them.

61 Wei-Tai Shen, *China's Foreign Policy, 1839–1860* (New York, 1932), 165.

62 AEC, 27, 215–222.

with a small retinue. All arrangements had been completed for their accommodation at the capital, including the concession that they might kneel instead of kowtow before the Emperor. But the Chinese did not intend to allow British war vessels again to reach Tientsin for they feared foul play in using the occupation of that key point as a hostage to enforce further humiliating demands. The Chinese were in a defensible position legally in that Tientsin was not an open port, and another route to the capital had been made available.[63] The basic consideration on both sides was face. Peking was out to regain part of the dignity it had lost at Tientsin. The British were equally determined to crown their triumph of the previous year by an impressive ceremony at the capital in which they would be treated with marked deference and respect. This consideration seemed to require that they disregard the Chinese request that they proceed via the Pehtang route attended by a reduced retinue.

Bourboulon fully shared the feelings of his British colleague. When confronted with Chinese objections to approaching Taku, Bourboulon asked what good the treaties would be if at the very outset Peking was allowed to block the first exercise by the Europeans of the privileges accorded by it. Neither Bourboulon nor Bruce expected to encounter formidable resistance from the seemingly deserted forts, even though British reconnaissance on June 21 revealed that boats attempting to enter the Peiho River would be exposed to both enfilade and flanking fire. The final decision to force the entry was made by the British, of course, for they had the fleet, but it was a decision in which Bourboulon fully concurred.[64] Bruce paid little attention to the final Chinese communication directing entry of the ratification parties at Pehtang. The message reached him at 9 A.M. on the day of the attack.

The one French criticism of British Admiral Hope's tactics was that he committed too many of his vessels to the trap between the outer bar and the boom barring the river's entry before testing the intentions

[63] Wei-Tai Shen, 165; Swisher, 31, 558. Peking's edicts dated April 11 and 14, 1859, accepted as inevitable that exchange of ratifications would take place at Peking and authorized preparation of the entry route via Pehtang. Vermillion approval for this arrangement came June 6.

[64] Bazancourt's account (II, 5–32) is based on the June 30 report of Captain Tricault of the corvette *Duchayla*. Cordier (*Histoire Générale*, IV, 60) holds the English responsible for the affair. With less of self-conceit on the part of Admiral Hope, of obstinacy on the part of Bruce, and of weakness on the part of Bourboulon, the disastrous humiliation, he affirmed, could have been avoided.

and effectiveness of the Chinese defenses.[65] When on June 25 the forts opened their deadly regular fire on the first two gunboats to reach the boom, the latter were completely disabled, as was a third one following. The total casualties were four British boats sunk, two others badly damaged, some 434 British killed and wounded, including critical injury to Admiral Hope. One fifth of the crew of the French corvette were casualties. French reports of the affair found consolation in the cold-blooded fashion with which the unequal attack was met and in the sheer audacity of landing groups in attempting to assault the shore through the deep mud, circumstances which allegedly preserved the "honor of the allied forces." [66]

Sequel to Taku

Bourboulon's report of the Taku disaster gave full credit for the Chinese victory to Sengkolintsin, the Mongol Prince commander of the Chinese defenses. He believed that although the defenders may have received some Russian assistance in reconditioning the forts and in training Mongol troops to service the artillery, "the energetic and intelligent resistance, all too ably directed, that we encountered on that sad day of the 25th was due to indigenous not to foreign elements." He also praised the superior qualities of the Mongol soldiery.[67] Harry Parkes put the blame for the episode on Elgin for not having demanded at Tientsin in June, 1858, an immediate audience at Peking, for ever having withdrawn his forces from Tientsin at all, and for his fatal error at Shanghai in retreating from the requirement of diplomatic residence at the capital.[68]

The personal reaction of British Foreign Minister Lord John Russell to the news of the Taku affair, as contained in a secret memorandum initialed by him, differed markedly from the official approval of Bruce's conduct subsequently issued by the London government. Russell remarked that the treaty did not specify the route to be taken to Peking, nor was Bruce particularly prudent to insist upon his demand by forcible means. The internal waterways of a country, Russell added,

[65] AEC, 27, 319, from Bourboulon, July 30, 1859.

[66] Bazancourt, II, 30–34; Morse, I, 576–584.   [67] AEC, 27, 272–274.

[68] Lane-Poole, 310–311; Morse accepts the standard British apologia (I, 583–584) that although Bruce obviously underestimated his enemy, he had no choice other than to attack Taku.

were not open to foreign ships of war in time of peace. He observed that Malmesbury's previous instructions directing Bruce to reach Tientsin on board a war vessel had been qualified by authorizing him to make another arrangement if unforeseen circumstances should make a change advisable. Lord Russell continued:

If we can import into the treaty or attach to its execution what it does not itself contain, do we not have to allow the Chinese to do the same? It is . . . difficult to teach them European manners by Asiatic methods. . . . [It is] doubtful whether [under] the law of nations, however understood or applied, we could be justified in treating the absolute refusal of a particular route (presuming that fact to be established, which it is not) as an absolute refusal of access to the capital and consequently a breach of engagement.

Russell thought that it was doubtful that Peking had been determined, as Bruce alleged, to resist access to Peking if he had accomplished it by an overland route and had been accompanied by a modest retinue. He regarded as still more doubtful Bruce's allegation that the Emperor had intended to refuse ratifications of the treaties.[69]

Russell's private doubts did not affect the characteristic British aplomb in officially approving four days later the firmness with which Bruce had resisted the Chinese attempts to dissuade him "from insisting on the strict fulfillment of the stipulations of the Treaty of Tientsin." The period of a year's time allowed for exchange of ratification would have expired on June 26, the statement continued, so that the shortness of time did not admit of any further delay. Bruce's conduct was found to be in strict conformity with Malmesbury's instructions, and the Foreign Office saw nothing in Bruce's decision to diminish its confidence in him.[70] It would have been politically impossible, of course, to have reported anything else.

The disastrous effects on foreign prestige in China arising from the allied defeat at Taku were clear to all. The war party at Peking was in the ascendancy. Having been given its turn, it had achieved a signal triumph. Observers at Shanghai remarked that the whole manner and bearing of the Chinese population toward the foreigner immediately changed, and they expressed grave apprehension of an attack on the

[69] FO, 17, 311, from a memo initialled "JR," dated Sept. 22, 1859.
[70] Ibid., instruction of Sept. 26, 1859.

foreign settlement. For a time foreign businesses at Shanghai closed up shop.[71]

Bourboulon, far from apologizing for French involvement at Taku, declared that French prestige was at stake, that the check had been experienced in common, and that its correction must also be by joint action. Following the example of Bruce, Bourboulon sent his first secretary, Kleczkowski, to Paris to transmit in person full details of the affair.[72] When Lord Cowley approached the Paris authorities in late September with a view to obtaining French agreement on joint measures for the punishment of the Chinese, Walewski gave a cordial response. The French government seemed, indeed, happy to find a basis for reviving its entente with London, which only a few months before had been so rudely shaken by Louis Napoleon's ill-conceived invasion of Italy. By mid-October the terms of the new joint venture in the Far East were pretty well worked out.[73]

The experience which American Minister Ward encountered in his private journey to Peking in July, 1859, following the Taku affair, although not strictly relevant to the situation of Bourboulon and Bruce, served to confirm the opinions of those who were already convinced that the Taku affair was a clear demonstration of Chinese perfidy. Ward's position was heavily compromised by American Admiral Tattnal's unneutral conduct during the course of the battle [74] and by the fact that the American treaty carried no stipulation that exchange of ratifications must be made at Peking. It seems probable that only Ignatieff's influence at the court enabled Ward to visit Peking at all, amid the confusion and furor which followed the repulse of the British fleet. Ward entered via Pehtang, but he made the mistake of accepting conveyance in a cart, after the fashion of bearers of tribute, instead of in a sedan chair. At Peking, he was refused the privilege of direct communication with Ignatieff and was denied an audience with the Emperor because he would not kowtow. Ratifications of the American treaty were actually exchanged at Pehtang on August 16 under most undignified circumstances. The facile assumption that Ward's humili-

[71] 36th Congress, 1st·sess., Sen. exec. doc. 30, pp. 598, 617–618, from Ward, Sept. 1, 1859; Swisher, 607.

[72] AEC, 27, 316–317, from Bourboulon, July 14, 1859.

[73] Cordier, 1860, 98–103.

[74] 36th Congress, 1st sess., Sen. exec. doc. 30, pp. 585–587, from Ward, July 15, 1859. The Chinese forces took one American sailor prisoner.

ating treatment illustrated what had actually been in store for all the foreign agents prior to June 25 was not borne out by the information furnished Ward by his Russian friends in the capital.[75] The official Chinese documents now available in translation make clear that the conditions required of Ward were determined after the Taku affair and not before.[76]

[75] SD, China, DD, Ward, nos. 15, 16, 17, July 4, 10, and Aug. 20, 1859; Ward's enclosures include exchanges with Ignatieff from July 6 to Aug. 7, 1859. See also Morse, I, 580–582; Foster, 245–252; Dennett, *Americans*, 341–343. Ignatieff confirmed the news that Peking had made full preparations to receive the foreign emissaries prior to the Taku incident.

[76] Swisher, ch. xii.

XIV

Objectives and Preparations for the China War, 1859-1860

HE defeat suffered at Taku in June, 1859, so damaged the prestige of the British that they saw no choice but to humble the defiant war party at Peking. French involvement in the 1858 expedition and, to a minor degree, in the Taku affair itself also made French participation necessary. The military problem of bringing to bear sufficient armed pressure to force Peking to agree to allied demands for an apology, treaty ratification, and indemnity was nevertheless seriously complicated by strained relations between France and England in Europe. Louis Napoleon's intervention in the Italian war, from May to July, 1859, had offended Britain and had undermined the entire balance of power structure in Europe. The aborted Italian campaign, furthermore, had failed to gratify the aroused French craving for military glory, so that France, both morally and militarily, was all dressed up with no place to go when the war with China came along.[1] The decision to fight China coincided with receipt of the news of Admiral Genouilly's tragic failure at Tourane.

[1] In the parliamentary debate of March 16, 1860, Sir De Lacy Evans described the French response as follows: "The French . . . had a very large army without a present European war wherein to employ it, and this Chinese conflict was perhaps meant as a temporary amusement or occupation for the French soldiery till something more serious turned up."

The European Background

Whereas London wearily approached the costly and arduous military effort against China brought on by Frederick Bruce's poor management at Taku,[2] the ambitious nephew of the great Napoleon apparently regarded the China war as offering an opportunity to restore the prestige of his dynasty, recently tarnished by failure in Italy, and to afford a safe outlet, in co-operation with Britain, for the aroused martial spirit of France. The diversion of French activity to eastern Asia might have been welcomed in London as a safety valve for the dangerous tension in Europe, if Britain's own hegemony in the Orient had not been at stake. The British cabinet feared that, at a time when England dared not weaken its island defences in the face of a potential French threat to the peace,[3] Paris would be prepared to send to the Far East a force of such size as to give France temporary military predominance. This would make possible French acquisition of a point of Chinese territory, either by conquest or in lieu of an indemnity, to match the British holding at Hongkong.[4] London's fears seemed to be confirmed when in October, 1859, Paris proposed sending 15,000 men to China and demanding an indemnity of 100,000,000 francs. Britain's military problem was solved by utilizing two divisions of the Indian army plus two regiments of Sikh cavalry as the major part of their expeditionary force of some 18,000 men. Because of a shortage of ships for the long voyage around the Cape, the French force was finally limited to around 7,000 men.[5]

[2] Palmerston on September 14 commented as follows on Bruce's tactics: "I suppose our officers were piqued to do something desperate in the presence of France and America, but the whole operation seems . . . to have been ill-managed." From A. H. G. Stanmore, *Sidney Herbert* (London, 1906), II, 296–297.

[3] *Ibid.*, 304. Herbert to Canning in India, Nov. 26, 1859: "Nothing could be more suspicious than the enormous preparations of every kind making in France. We are going to raise our home force by 25,000 men. . . . What we really want is twenty good battalions from India; we should then have some sense of security in this country."

[4] *Ibid.*, 295–301; Bell, 240–242. Palmerston commented as follows on September 12, with regard to the proposed joint occupation of Chusan Island: "The [French] emperor will be very liberal in sending plenty of his Italian campaigners thither. We should soon be in a minority there and that might in the end be inconvenient." Secretary of War Herbert replied: "Whatever is sent in the way of forces must be sent from India. In the present state of feeling in France, it would be unwise to send a man from [England]."

[5] London did not accept the initial French proposal that part of their 15,000-man army be transported by British vessels (Stanmore, II, 301, 310).

Secretaries Lord John Russell and Herbert in London were also apprehensive that France, having no commerce to sacrifice in China but yearning to publish a military bulletin from Peking,[6] would push military matters so far as to overthrow the Manchu dynasty and thus precipitate a situation of chaos, which would inevitably be a British headache for years to come. Britain's profitable trade with China was particularly important to the revenues of India, which realized handsomely from the production of opium for the China market.

The real danger of upsetting the dynasty was to be found in the belligerent spirit prevailing within British circles at Hongkong and Shanghai (among Parkes, Wade, Lay, et al.), to whose influence Frederick Bruce was susceptible. This danger London eventually reduced by selecting the more moderate Lord Elgin to resume his 1858 role as ranking officer of the expedition.[7] In the choice of military commander, London passed over the more vigorous Sir William Mansfield in favor of easygoing Sir Hope Grant of the Indian army, as a man more capable of getting along with the French and of taking orders from a diplomatic chief of mission.[8]

London's forebodings concerning French intentions were only partially correct. Paris was more concerned to re-establish the French entente with Britain in the Far East than London realized, and had no intention of risking the overthrow of the Manchu dynasty. As matters turned out, the French actually opposed granting permission to attack Peking and acquiesced in leaving that decision to the discretion of the commanders only when Palmerston insisted.[9] But the Paris government was clearly determined to act in eastern Asia no longer as a satellite of Britain. It wanted in particular to make good the lack of a French counterpart to Hongkong in China, as well as to expand the French foot-

[6] Herbert's instructions to General Grant in November, 1859, explained that one of the General's problems would be to contend with the prestige value which the French would put on publishing a military bulletin from Peking. He concluded by saying: "There exists between the two nations a jealous and uneasy feeling" (*ibid.*, 302–304). Palmerston alone in the British Cabinet favored taking the risk of capturing Peking if the allies should be stalled at Tientsin (Bell, II, 242).

[7] Stanmore, II, 298–301. Elgin's appointment in early March, 1860, was also related to British negotiations with Paris.

[8] Cordier, *1860*, 113. The French regarded Gen. Grant as "old womanish," but they got along well with him and acknowledged his ability and courage.

[9] Stanmore, II, 307–308, 314–315.

hold at Saigon. Foreign Minister Walewski insisted in an October memorandum to the French Emperor that France attain in the China area approximate military equality with Britain and that a definite policy be adopted to acquire a point of Chinese territory, preferably Chusan Island, as a commercial and naval base and as a point of leverage for French political influence throughout the Far East. England, he argued, could not be surprised if such a move were made, and in view of England's own possessions in the area, she had no sufficient grounds to deny France the right to take action in her own interest.[10] Walewski's position was based upon a thoroughgoing analysis of French interests in the Far East prepared by Kleczkowski for the Foreign Ministry.[11]

The Chusan policy was determined upon as a result of consultations between Walewski and the French Ministry of Marine. French naval officers agreed that the island was the only point in China suitable for permanent French occupancy, but they felt that in view of its intended use as a staging base for the joint expedition, coupled with England's prejudicial influence, the matter of acquisition could not easily be raised until the conclusion of the joint occupation. The interim period could be utilized for studying the problem. Walewski eventually agreed that confidential instructions to the commanding Admiral be sent by special messenger informing him of the government's desire to acquire a point of land in China and asking that he undertake, whenever opportunity was afforded, to examine Chusan and other possible locations and to report his findings. The actual instructions, sent by the Minister of Marine on November 11, concluded as follows:

I do not need to urge you to exercise great circumspection in that study. You will easily understand how important it is to avoid with care any *démarche*

[10] Cordier, *1860*, 104–107, Walewski to the Emperor, Oct. 17, 1859.

[11] AEC, 28, 126–177, a memo dated Oct. 19, 1859. Walewski quoted verbatim from an early draft of the memo. Kleczkowski declared that France's entire Far Eastern position was imperiled by the Taku incident, that a self-sufficient French army of at least 10,000 men was needed to lift France from its role as a satellite to England. He insisted that London's opposition to the assessment of a large indemnity need not be taken seriously, that a French counterpart to Hongkong should be acquired at Chusan or in Korea, and that a serious effort should be made to expand the potentially valuable holding at Saigon. Kleczkowski favored taking Chusan, but he admitted that its very attractiveness made it the object of extreme vigilance by England. In Britain's hands, Chusan would become, he said, a second Malta to balance the new Russian Sevastopol at the mouth of the Amur.

likely to awaken [British] susceptibilities, before the Imperial Government, enlightened by your reports, has come to a definite decision on that important question.[12]

In Walewski's view, the new expedition was a military rather than a diplomatic mission. Its objective was to inflict punishment on Peking for the injury and insults suffered by the allies and to prepare the way for negotiations of a new settlement supplementing the treaties of Tientsin. He considered the Chinese attack at Taku to have been a deliberate act of war rather than a mere interruption of efforts to exchange ratifications. The commander of the French forces, General Cousin de Montauban, was accordingly ordered to work out plans in concert with the English for the capture of Tientsin, using Chusan Island and Chefoo harbor in northern Shantung as staging points. Hostilities should be confined to the area adjacent to Taku. If, contrary to Walewski's hopes and expectations, Montauban were obliged to march on Peking, he should be sure that all facilities required for decisive action were available. Not until successful military operations made it appear opportune, as determined by the allied leaders, should negotiations be undertaken. Instructions covering diplomatic negotiations would be sent to Bourboulon. Montauban was cautioned to maintain good relations with the English forces and close rapport with French diplomatic agencies. The French cabinet refused to accede to the General's demand to be entrusted with diplomatic as well as military authority, although he was authorized to communicate with Paris in case Bourboulon failed to cooperate.[13]

The *élan* of the French expedition was reflected not only in the embarrassingly large number of volunteers who presented themselves but also in General Montauban's Napoleonesque utterances. His first order of the day (on November 19) informed the troops that under the shield of Napoleon III they had been called to undertake an expedition distant and glorious, not to add new conquests but to display their disciplined courage and martial ardor in the cause of civilization. Their

[12] AEC, 28, 210–213, report of the Minister of Marine, Nov. 3, 1859; *ibid.*, 229, 234–237, Walewski to his Marine colleague, Nov. 7, and Minister of Marine to the Admiral of the China fleet, Nov. 11, 1859.

[13] C. Palikao, *L'Expédition de Chine de 1860: Souvenirs du General Cousin de Montauban, Comte de Palikao* (Paris, 1932), 2–3, 8–9, 9–13; Cordier, *1860*, 108–112.

union with the British was a gage of victory. He concluded: "One day, on returning to *la patrie*, you will say with pride . . . that you have carried the national flag into countries where immortal Rome at the time of its greatness never thought to have its legions go. Vive l'Empereur! Vive la France!" [14]

The major portion of the French caravan, comprising more than three-score ships carrying some 7,000 troops, began leaving France from Toulon, Brest, Lorient, and Cherbourg on December 15, 1859, for the long voyage around the Cape. A number of missionaries and a group selected by the Academy of Sciences accompanied the forces.[15] The higher officers of the expedition, including Montauban, accompanied by two brigades, left for China in mid-January via Suez. Montauban reached Hongkong on February 26, 1860, several months ahead of the main force.[16]

Negotiations between Paris and London

Perhaps the most important difference which developed between Paris and London over plans for the China expedition concerned the degree of belligerence to be assumed. Lord John Russell's first instruction to Frederick Bruce in October expressed the hope that a peaceful settlement could be attained without bloodshed. Once the extent of allied preparations was known, he thought, the Chinese might offer to apologize for the Taku affair, permit Bruce to proceed to Tientsin in a British vessel, and provide for his proper conveyance thence to Peking for exchange of ratifications. Even when it was later learned that these hopes could not be realized, Russell kept the terms of settlement the same, except for the addition of a small pecuniary indemnity. Quite secretly, he also authorized Her Majesty's forces to take possession of the Kowloon Peninsula opposite Hongkong at the first convenient opportunity. The acquisition of Kowloon would be covered by formal cession in any future adjustment of British relations with China.[17] Be-

---

[14] Bazancourt, II, 39–40.

[15] Charles de Mutrécy, *Journal de la Campagne de Chine, 1859–1860–1861* (Paris, 1861), 37–39. Reminiscent of the role played by scientists on Napoleon's Egyptian expedition, the groups of scientists, headed by Escayrac de Lauture, were designated to study geology, geography, arts, literature, commerce and industry, customs and politics.

[16] *Ibid.*; Bazancourt, II, 35–37.

[17] FO, 17, 311, instructions to Bruce, Oct. 10, 29, and Nov. 10, 1859. British

cause Russell feared that France intended to use the assessment of a large war indemnity as an excuse to seize a point of Chinese territory in lieu of payment, it required three months' time (November to February) for London and Paris to agree on the compromise figure of 60,000,000 francs each.[18]

When Russell learned in late December that Paris considered France to be at war with China, he again became alarmed. He took the view that the new joint action to obtain ratification of the treaties was not war but only a resumption of coercive measures which had been temporarily interrupted.[19] It was while this matter was being considered that Walewski retired abruptly as French Foreign Minister (on January 4, 1860) as part of a general French reorientation in the direction of a less aggressive foreign policy. His temporary successor, M. Baroche, admittedly knew nothing about the disagreement over belligerent status but nevertheless promptly accepted Russell's view. He added his own assurances that he wanted complete concert with Britain on China.[20]

Russell had also proposed previously that either party ready to proceed to the attack on the Peiho forts ought not to be required to wait for the other beyond April 25. Walewski had objected so emphatically that Paris had its way on this point. The French Minister insisted that in no case could there be a question of a separate arrival at the Peiho of one flag without the other and that no action should be taken by either apart from the other.[21] Russell agreed that the initial action against the Peiho should be a combined affair, and Baroche later accepted April 25 as merely a date "later than which it would be inadvisable to delay."

---

acquisition of Kowloon at this time was suggested by the Colonial Office. Russell's first suggestion of a £500,000 indemnity was changed to an indefinite figure at Walewski's insistence.

[18] Cordier, *1860*, 123–130; FO, 17, 333, to Bruce, Feb. 8, 1860. Paris indicated that it would divide the indemnity three ways: for war expenses, for reparations for nationals, and for the acquisition of needed properties for legation and consulate premises and for a Catholic church to be erected in Canton.

[19] Cordier, *1860*, 118–120; FO, 27, 1331, from Cowley, Dec. 28, 1859, and to Cowley, Jan. 7, 1860.

[20] FO, 27, 1331, from Cowley, Jan. 9, 1860: Bazancourt (II, 72–73) criticized this alleged French surrender to London's excessive concern for commercial interests, while forgetting the question of wounded honor.

[21] FO, 17, 329, enclosures in Elgin's instructions of April 17, 1860: Russell to Cowley, Dec. 31, 1859, and reply, Jan. 7, 1860.

Baroche expressed the hope that everything would be ready in good time.[22]

Walewski's retirement as Foreign Minister relaxed the tension between France and England, at least temporarily. During Baroche's brief twenty-day tenure (January 4–24) until Thouvenel arrived from Constantinople to take over the Ministry, the famous Gladstone-Cobden free trade treaty was signed (on January 23). This was interpreted on both sides of the channel as a positive contribution to more peaceful relations.[23] On February 22 the two governments signed another convention covering the disposition of captured Chinese merchantmen.[24] Russell's concern to improve relations with France was reflected in his publication of a revised draft of his January 3 instructions to Bruce authorizing the delivery of a British ultimatum to China. In contrast to the earlier version, which scarcely mentioned French participation, the memorandum made emphatic reference to the Queen's august ally, the Emperor of the French, and described all plans for the China expedition in the first person plural.[25]

It was also during the lull between Walewski's retirement and the French annexation of Savoy and Nice by the Treaty of Turin in early March, 1860, that London indicated its intention to nominate Lord Elgin to head for a second time the British expedition to China. Three considerations apparently prompted the move. It would strengthen civilian diplomatic control over the expedition in contradistinction to the French emphasis on its military character. It would also reduce the influence of the excessive belligerency of the British old China hands.[26] Finally, in preparation for the approaching parliamentary debates on approval of the estimates for the China expedition, Elgin's appointment would strengthen the government's position, since it was clear that Bruce's conduct at Taku would be severely criticized.[27] As explained to

[22] FO, 27, 1331, from Cowley, Jan. 9, 1860.

[23] Cowley, 192–196; Cordier, *1860*, 114. Cowley referred to the Cobden treaty as a "keystone to uninterrupted peace."

[24] FO, 27, 1333, Cowley to Russell, Feb. 22, 1860.

[25] FO, 17, 333, to Bruce, Jan. 3, 1860.

[26] See n. 7, this chapter.

[27] Morison (250–252) emphasized London's concern to counteract the aggressive influence of Harry Parkes, who would risk precipitating a cataclysm in China at a time when the state of tension in Europe made such a development too dangerous. Elgin's appointment was announced in early March. See *Hansard's Parliamentary Debates*, CLVI, 922–932; CLVII, 779–786.

Bruce, the entrusting of allied leadership to persons of higher authority (Elgin and Gros) was done because it was feared that some "punctilio or tradition may make the Chinese Government hesitate to make concession to the Ministers whose attempt to ascend the Peiho they [had] successfully repelled." [28]

The French had virtually no alternative to choosing Baron Gros to act again as Elgin's counterpart, not merely because it pleased London,[29] but because otherwise both Bourboulon and Montauban would be outranked and French interests consequently would be subordinated to those of the British. Only Gros could match Elgin's personal authority and his knowledge of the China situation.[30]

The final instructions to Elgin and Gros, prepared in mid-April when news reached Europe of the negative results of the ultimatum served on Peking by Bruce and Bourboulon, were dispatched after the two chiefs had already departed for China. The Chinese reply to the ultimatum proved to be a continuation of earlier efforts to drive a wedge between the allies by blaming the Taku affair exclusively on Britain.[31] France and America, the reply pointed out, had not brought fleets to the Peiho in June, 1859, and the French treaty did not call for diplomatic residence at Peking in any case. The Chinese offered to negotiate a new settlement at Shanghai but declared that the appearance of an allied naval force at Taku would be proof of evil intentions.[32]

The British and French instructions stressed three requirements: an

---

[28] FO, 17, 333, to Bruce, Feb. 27, 1860. Britain's public announcement of Elgin's appointment was postponed until the French had time to reach a decision.

[29] *Hansard*, CLVII, 770–779. In the March 16 debate, Russell praised Baron Gros as a man of peaceful sentiments who had collaborated closely with Elgin in 1858. The two of them, he said, would have authority to halt military operations whenever they thought it advisable to do so. John Bright in particular attacked the ill-defined Anglo-French partnership in China.

[30] Cordier, *1860*, 115–118; Bazancourt, II, 74. The question was analyzed in an extended Foreign Office memorandum dated January, 1860.

[31] Cordier, *1860*, 93–98. In July, 1859, Peking had communicated with Bourboulon through Fathers Lamaitre and Mouly, alleging that the Taku altercation had developed from a misunderstanding, and offering to exchange ratifications of the French treaty at Pehtang. The offer was repeated through Canton officials in September. Chinese officials insisted that they had no valid cause of enmity for France. Bourboulon declined both proposals. The formal allied joint ultimatum of March, 1860, was sent through Governor Ho of Shanghai. See T. F. Tsiang, "China, England, and Russia in 1860," *The Cambridge Historical Journal*, III (1929), 118.

[32] Bazancourt, II, 53–56.

apology for the Taku affair, the exchange of ratifications at Peking, and the levying of an indemnity secured by continued joint occupation of Canton and another coastal point until payment had been made or a portion of the customs receipts set aside for its retirement. It was left to the discretion of the allied commissioners whether they should continue their residence at Peking through the winter. In case the Chinese court should flee to the interior, the allies should return to the coast to levy distress upon the government but not to promote the downfall of the dynasty or to assist the rebellion.[33]

Both commissioners carried secret supplementary instructions covering matters of special interest to their respective governments. Gros was given no responsibility for the investigation of Chusan, which was to be handled through the French Admiralty. He was directed to acquire a suitable site for a church at Canton, to recover seventeenth-century mission-owned property in Sunkiang and Peking, to arrange passports for the use of French missionaries in the interior, as well as to complete unfinished business with respect to the death of Chapdelaine and to treaty guarantees respecting Christianity in China.[34] Elgin's supplementary instructions regarding the acquisition of Kowloon rejected his own proposal that the peninsula be purchased by the return of a portion of the indemnity fund. It was felt that such procedure might be a "convenience . . . too dearly purchased" if it established a precedent for France to follow. Elgin was to determine the means to be employed and was given the alternative of abstaining altogether from making the attempt to acquire Kowloon if it seemed likely "to lead to other demands injurious to China and unfavorable to British interests."[35]

Allied agreement on the China expedition under Elgin and Gros was contemporaneous with the furor of hostile protest in England to the French annexation of Nice and Savoy in early March, 1860, and the answering spate of Anglophobia from the other side of the channel. The Prince Consort was violently anti-French. Palmerston and Russell were thoroughly angered over the French move and talked for a time of siding with the rest of Europe, especially Prussia, against France.[36]

[33] FO, 17, 329, to Elgin, April 17, 1860; Cordier, *1860*, 131–137.

[34] Cordier, *1860*, 123–131.

[35] FO, 17, 329, to Elgin, April 16, 18, and 25, 1860. This decision constituted an important qualification of Britain's traditional "open door" policy.

[36] Cowley, 198–207, 214. The bitterness felt by Queen Victoria and the Prince Consort was mollified somewhat by the visit of Empress Eugénie to England in late

Strained relations between the two forces in China required all of the moderating influence of the two chiefs to ensure co-operation, and, even so, the Elgin-Gros rapport was by no means as close as it had been in 1858.[37]

The French versus the British Points of View

The British and French expeditions differed markedly in composition and point of view. There was a larger element of chauvinism and belligerence in the French participation, partly because Napoleon III's government was riding a wave of militarist enthusiasm and a craving for glory quite divorced from economic considerations. There was by contrast little enthusiasm for the affair in England.[38] The London government, itself much worried, was obliged to defend both the war policy and its implementation before a critical parliamentary minority.

An equally important difference came from the fact that the British army, largely Indian, was a professional, disciplined, balanced force and constituted an impressive projection of British imperialist power into the Far East. Britain financed the army and provided needed supplies and ships, but the show itself was Indian, and militarily it was a creditable one. Elgin commented on the Indian troops located at the Bay of Dairen (Talien-Wan): "The contrast with what I saw when I was in China before, in regard to the treatment of natives, is most remarkable. There seems to be really no plundering or bullying. . . . We have here . . . a truly model army and navy." [39] The horsemanship and fine appearance of the Sikh cavalry brigade, numbering some 1,200 men, impressed all observers, including the French. The British-Indian force was far superior to the French in animal transport for artillery and

---

1860. Both of the debates in Parliament regarding China (February 13 and March 16) were associated with discussions of Savoy and Nice.

[37] Cordier, *Histoire Générale*, IV, 60–61. Chinese accounts from Shanghai (Swisher, 657) reported that French belligerency far surpassed that evidenced by the British.

[38] The following item from *Blackwood's Edinburgh Magazine* (LXXXVII, 525–526) of March, 1860, illustrates the British manifest destiny interpretation: "It is a false humanity to allow an Asiatic despot to suppose that he may insult or slay a Christian with impunity. On the other hand, 'Providence that doth shape our ends' has never caused us to vindicate the claims of Western civilization without our leaving behind us abundant and living proofs of our desire to improve the races we have come in contact with."

[39] Walrond, 335, dated July 14, 1860.

supply purposes.[40] The French vessel, *La Duperré*, transporting most of the horses, was delayed in the Indian Ocean by storms and failed to reach Hongkong until June 24.[41] The French had to send fourteen ships to Japan and Manila to purchase some 1,200 horses, virtually all of which had to be broken to harness before they could be used. The first one hundred of these reached Shanghai on June 12.[42]

London was actually embarrassed by the zeal of India's Viceroy Canning in sending so large an Indian force to China, even though the move did effectively defeat any French expectation of military primacy.[43] To War Secretary Herbert's protest that the army was overlarge for the task to be done, Earl Canning replied that the larger force would guarantee a shorter war and added: "You gentlemen in England have not looked this China affair in the face. . . . I judge you expect to get a short, sharp, decisive campaign done at a low price." To which Herbert replied disconsolately: "We shall spend an enormous sum of money, and get nothing but the seeds of fresh difficulty in return. . . . I heartily wish we were out of this business." [44] From the British point of view, therefore, the war was very much an Indian and old China hand affair.

The evidence of British predominance east of Suez was clearly impressed on French participants in the expedition. Observers reported that the number of British vessels in the Red Sea made it seem like a veritable English lake. Mutrécy commented that for the Frenchman a voyage to China was a great adventure, a kind of madness, whereas the Englishman took it in casual fashion.[45] French observers also talked

---

[40] Mutrécy, I, 308–311; G. Allgood, *China War, 1860* (London, New York, 1901), 49. Allgood commented: "The French play quite second fiddle, as they have no cavalry and their artillery ponies are all done up. Ours is perfection."

[41] Mutrécy, I, 303–304.

[42] Bazancourt, II, 77–92; Mutrécy, I, 219–222. The French task of providing horses and their provender was entrusted to two firms at Shanghai, Soucher brothers and Remi-Schmidt. These firms encountered many difficulties at Nagasaki and Kangawa, and the Japanese horses obtained proved to be ferociously wild.

[43] Stanmore (II, 350) quoted Herbert as follows: "The British forces [were] swelled by the too great zeal of the viceroy of India to a size which neither the British treasury nor the French government had bargained for."

[44] *Ibid.*, 317–325.

[45] Mutrécy, I, 56. The author added: "I regret that my country does not fling itself more into the habit of distant excursions, and I rally . . . to the idea of the Emperor, who wishes to establish the influence of France in the most distant countries . . . where the name of England only is known."

of plans for establishing a branch of the French shipping firm Messageries Imperiales for bimonthly passenger service to the Indian Ocean via Suez in competition with the British "Peninsula and Orient" line. Others favored starting a French colony in Zanzibar and a coaling station at Djeddah (Jiddah) on the Red Sea and another on the Abyssinian coast. Djeddah in particular was destined, in their minds, to acquire importance as a way station to India and Indo-China.[46] But all French plans were for the future, while Britain's activities were present and operative.

At Hongkong, Mutrécy commented on the influence and opulence of the British merchant establishments and concluded: "It is in reality these nabobs of Hongkong who make war against China." The British cargo ship on which he took passage to Shanghai carried from five to six million francs worth of opium, which was picked up like pounds of gold at Woosung by country vessels abundantly armed with lascars and cannon.[47] The presence of an Indian army reinforced French awareness that the East was Britain's domain.

Incidental items reflected the adventurous mood of the French contingent. One of the French vessels carried on board as a kind of sacred fetish the ship's boat which had transferred the remains of Napoleon from St. Helena to the ship which took them back to France in 1840. Of the French troops arriving at Hongkong Mutrécy boasted: "Our soldiers have carried to these distant shores the gaiety, the carefree attitude that they had in the plains of Italy . . . or the trenches of Sebastopol. With such men, the leaders can be sure of success in all military operations." [48] French unfamiliarity with the China coast took its toll. One French frigate was wrecked in Amoy harbor, with serious losses sustained in water-soaked harnesses and shoes. Another ship at Macao caught fire and burned with the total loss of its cargo of arms, medical supplies, surgical instruments, and winter clothing.[49]

The British had nothing good to say about the French army in operation, and their adverse comments carry weight even when discounted on grounds of prejudice. Much of the French force was very late in arriving. The lack of trained artillery transport was the most serious handicap.[50] General Hope Grant complained particularly of the looting by

[46] *Ibid.*, 188–202.   [47] *Ibid.*, 95, 100–102.   [48] *Ibid.*, 233–235, 263, 269.

[49] *Ibid.*, 236–241, 249–251. *L'Isère* was wrecked, and *La Reine-des-Clippers* burned.

[50] *Ibid.*, 148–151, 169–170, 303–305; Bazancourt, II, 41, 62–71. *Le Duperré,*

the French at Pehtang and their refusal to control the activities of their portion of the Chinese coolie brigade.[51] Still more annoying was the French insistence that virtually their entire force be utilized for front-line duty (some 6,500 of the 7,000 total), leaving to the British virtually all of the garrison duty, communications, and supply services. All forward action had to be undertaken jointly, with British troops leading one day and the French the next.[52] This meant in practice that much British effort was expended making good the deficiencies of the French. Characteristic of the British complaints was the following statement of July, 1860:

We are waiting for the French. . . . It is a thousand pities that they were ever allowed to meddle with our affairs out here; they have nothing to do with China, having no interests commercially in the country whatever. They can't colonize, therefore the Saigon expedition is a farce, and setting their missionaries aside, for whom neither Government nor people care very much, I should imagine, they have no business here whatever. There is not a French-man [who] can tell you what they have come here to fight for; the result is they have done nothing but hamper and delay us.[53]

By no means all of the difficulty in relations came from the French side,[54] but the British were better prepared to move than the French and consequently gave less reason for complaint. The deeper meaning

---

bringing the horses, did not reach Hongkong until June 24, after encountering severe storms en route. The transport *Japon* reached Reunion Island on June 27, 1860, and China in August, while the steam frigate *L'Impératrice-Eugénie* did not even leave Toulon, France, until May 19, 1860. One ship stopped at Saigon to supply the garrison there.

[51] Lane-Poole, I, 358–360; Stanmore, I, 325, 328, 331. Parkes complained: "So long as we have to work with the French, it is almost hopeless to look for good management [of coolies]." Wrote Grant from Pehtang: "The robbery and plunder that has been carried on . . . by [the French force] is . . . a dreadful example to our men. The French troops—here at least—appear to me the worst I have ever seen."

[52] Morse, I, 589; Bazancourt, II, 62–65.

[53] F. C. A. Stephenson, *At Home and on the Battle-field: Letters from the Crimea, China, and Egypt, 1854–1888* (London, 1915), 261–262. Parkes complained similarly: "[The French] do us no good and act . . . like a drag upon our coach. They use our stores, get in our way at all points, and retard all our movements" (Lane-Poole, I, 346–347). Bruce, on Jan. 10, 1860 (FO, 17, 133), challenged the wisdom of London's order to act jointly with the French in all undertakings.

[54] Bazancourt, II, 62–71. When Montauban wanted to shift his assembly point to Chefoo in mid-May, Bruce objected that the French force must not precede the British even though no fighting was involved.

of British resentment lay in the difference that they had serious and urgent business to care for in China, while the French, for the most part, had embarked on a combination of glory-hunt and crusade.[55]

[55] Lane-Poole (I, 347) stated: "There was not a man in the [British] army who did not wish the French away."

XV

The French Role in the
War with China, 1860

N EWS of the reappointment of Elgin and Gros as chiefs of mission was not well received in the Far East. The action delayed formulation of plans until the arrival of the newly chosen principals. Bruce and Montauban were miffed at being reduced in importance, and both British and French groups expressed concern that a too conciliatory policy was in prospect which would prevent taking the necessary steps to restore European prestige and end Peking's intransigence. Harry Parkes and other British critics, who had never liked Elgin, declared that if he now kowtowed to please the London cabinet, the British could expect to be bearded in Hongkong itself. They insisted that Peking must be captured and the Manchu court thoroughly humbled if Europeans were to have peace with either China or Japan.[1] Mutrécy declared similarly for the French that a conciliatory approach would never do; the honor of France and England was engaged and powder must speak. He insisted that the Taku forts must be eliminated, strategic points in China occupied, and the full scope of allied demands obtained by prompt and vigorous action.[2] The person who seemed to be least disturbed was General Hope Grant, who worked loyally under Elgin.

[1] Allgood, 20, letter dated April 24, 1860. See also Swisher, 651–652.
[2] Mutrécy, I, 214–216.

Progress of Operations in China

Bruce and his supporters began the occupation of Kowloon Peninsula before Elgin arrived. In mid-March they sent troops to occupy the place and announced that the Governor-General of the two Kwangs had consented to the lease of Kowloon on the grounds that British occupation would aid in suppressing piracy. French critics denounced the action as a new method of territorial aggrandizement. They noted that nothing was said about the terms of the lease, the rent to be paid for it, or the way in which the Chinese would get rid of the tenant at its expiration.[3]

Preparations for the campaign to capture Tientsin began in earnest following the arrival of Elgin and Gros at Shanghai in late May. Some of the allied contingents had already started north to the staging points on the shores of the Gulf of Pohai at Chefoo and Dairen Bay. Between June 16 and June 18 it was decided that the British forces would land at Pehtang and approach the Peiho forts from the north, while the French reserved the right to consider attacking from the south below the Hsin-ho River outlet. The landings were to take place during the third week of July, following a rendezvous ten days in advance of the date.

When it became apparent in late June that the French were not ready to move, mainly because their horses had only begun to arrive, Elgin threatened to act alone unless the French forced the pace of their preparations.[4] Elgin left Shanghai on July 5 and Gros followed him two days later. Not until July 10 did the British agree to cancel General Grant's plan to stage an exclusively British landing. French reconnaissance, checking information furnished by Ignatieff, revealed that the shore line and terrain rendered impossible an attack on the Peiho forts from the south, so that the final arrangement was for a simultaneous joint landing at Pehtang late in July. The allies agreed not to negotiate until their forces had captured Tientsin.[5]

---

[3] *Ibid.*, 210–212.

[4] Cordier, *Histoire Générale*, IV, 61–62; Mutrécy, I, 249; Bazancourt, II, 86–89. Elgin's threat to act alone was strongly supported by Foreign Minister Russell, who expressed extreme impatience with the jealous sensibilities of the French (FO, 17, 329, instructions to Elgin, Sept. 3, 1860).

[5] Lane-Poole, I, 345–346; Mutrécy, I, 314–318, 320–323; Bazancourt, II, 92–101. The Russian, Ignatieff, came to Chefoo on July 20 and gave the French accurate in-

The allied forces left a disturbing situation behind them at Shanghai, for the rampant Taipings were threatening to overrun the city. The rebels had broken out of the imperialist siege of Nanking in early May. By the end of May they had captured Soochow, where the imperialist troops, after looting the place, had opened the gates and enlisted with the rebels. Only Shanghai in the lower Yangtse area remained in the hands of Peking authorities. When the rebel forces approached the vicinity around June 10, the native city went into panic. Fleeing junks jammed the river. The taotai offered at first to hire the British and French forces to defend the city. Subsequently he displayed to the French commander a memorial to be sent to the Emperor asking that Peking make peace with the foreigners in order to get their aid against the rebels.[6] Bruce and Bourboulon issued a reassuring joint proclamation that the allies intended to protect the city against pillage and massacre and to defend it against attack.

The first rebel forces which approached the city demonstrated no inclination to attack, but rather sought the friendship of the foreigners by offering to open up all cities which they controlled to foreign trade.[7] From August 17 to August 20 the Taipings nevertheless overran the Jesuit orphanage at Zikawei, where they killed Father Massa, and they then actually attacked Shanghai. They were driven off by the defending British, French, and Indian troops. When the rebels took refuge within the old city adjacent to the French Concession, the French set fire to the entire area involved. The situation remained critical until September, when a British regiment and some two hundred French marines were sent back from the north to bolster the Shanghai defenses. A kind of truce agreement was arranged by the end of September, 1860.[8]

The actual allied landing at Pehtang took place on August 1, after

---

formation concerning the Chinese defenses along the Peiho. He stressed the difficulties to be faced by any attempted attack from the south. Swisher reveals (651–652, 665) that the Chinese referred to Ignatieff as a "fire-brand' and were fully aware that he was giving military information to the allies.

[6] Mutrécy, I, 215–216, 245–259; Bazancourt, II, 80–84, 104–107. Lane-Poole (I, 345) alleges that Montauban proposed on this occasion that the allies stage a side expedition to oust the rebels from Soochow. The Shanghai taotai had offered to pay the allies, 1,200,000 francs for their aid in defending the city.

[7] Mutrécy, I, 273–282. Mutrécy's reaction ran: "With monsters of this sort [who profane the Christian faith] it is not possible . . . to make an alliance of any kind, not even to enter into friendly relations."

[8] Ibid., 246–247, II, 95–108; Bazancourt, II, 170–171; Morse, I, 593.

having been delayed several days because of bad weather. Led by their generals, four hundred men from each force waded ashore through several kilometers of chest-deep water to find Pehtang a morass of mud but quite undefended. The route from Pehtang southward to the Peiho River was similarly undefended. The reason was that Peking apparently hoped that permitting unimpeded access to Pehtang would encourage the allies to negotiate and avoid fighting.[9]

The spirit under which the French undertook the advance was reflected in the following statement of Montauban on the eve of the attack:

France is a martial nation. The noise of battle intoxicates and enraptures it. . . . France goes to defend the great cause of civilization, and may God watch over that little army so far from native soil. . . . The desire to prove to the Emperor and to France that we are worthy of the mission which we have received will fortify our strength.[10]

This same martial spirit is reflected in Mutrécy's description of the action of August 9–15 against the Chinese forces guarding the Peiho route. He tells how the "smell of powder" pulled all but the seriously ill of the French from their hospital beds into the thick of the fight.[11]

The French complained that General Hope Grant burdened his troops with too much baggage, which rendered their advance overcautious and slow. In order to avoid trouble between the two forces, each side was permitted alternately to select the direction of march to follow and the terrain to occupy. Serious disagreement developed on August 22, when Admiral Hope sent three British gunboats into the mouth of the Peiho River without waiting for orders and without previously consulting Admiral Charner of France. French boats followed immediately, but there was little glory for either country in the action because the guns of the defending forts remained silent. The capture of the first Taku fort by a scaling operation was nevertheless a costly venture, for the Tartar garrison refused to run.[12]

[9] Swisher, 658, 664, 669. As late as August 2 Peking hoped to avoid fighting.

[10] Bazancourt, II, 108–111, 113–120; Mutrécy, I, 328–333. The allies discovered that false cannon made of logs had been set up by the Chinese.

[11] Mutrécy, I, 334–340, 349–351; Bazancourt, II, 125, 130–141. Montauban favored more reckless methods of attack upon the main forts on the south bank of the Peiho River, but Grant's methodical plans were followed.

[12] Bazancourt, II, 146–155, 162–164. Some 3,000 Tartar troops in the second fort surrendered without a blow on August 22.

The French role in the subsequent advance from Tientsin to Peking can be quickly reviewed. Baron Gros opposed Lord Elgin's acceptance of the Chinese invitation of September 11 to send ahead a small un-escorted mission, a move which resulted in the kidnapping of Parkes, Loch, and some forty others. Gros argued that Sengkolintsin's Mongol army was not really under governmental control and therefore could not be depended upon to honor the pledges of the Chinese negotiators. When the kidnapping and ambuscade became known, General Montau-ban was restrained with difficulty from launching an immediate im-petuous attack on the Tartar army.[13] The same reckless spirit of the French leader was demonstrated on September 21, when the advance was actually resumed. The French were in the lead that day, and Gen-eral Collineau boldly attacked the very center of the Tartar army. The small French force was almost overwhelmed by the mass of Tartar cavalry, which cut it off for a time from the British forces. The latter arrived in the nick of time to avert disaster. Montauban refused to attribute the surprisingly few losses suffered by the French to the wild artillery fire and the obvious ineffectiveness of the bows and lances carried by the Tartar cavalry. He claimed that "our soldiers were pro-tected by an invisible hand which warded off balls and bullets which the enemy directed with unequalled profusion." In the end, it was the French brigade which captured the vital bridge that opened the route to Peking.[14]

The Breakup of the Entente at Peking

The Anglo-French entente began to wear thin following the collapse of Chinese resistance. The allied advance was resumed after Prince Kung refused on September 30 to accede to an ultimatum to surrender the European hostages as a preliminary to negotiations. Mutual recrim-ination between the allies began when the French forces reached the Summer Palace area on October 7. General Hope Grant accused the French of looting and destroying many art objects and other valuable contents of the palace prior to any agreement as to the disposition of the booty. The French did not deny being the first to loot, but they

---

[13] Bazancourt, I, 181–185, 193–208; Morse, I, 597–605. According to Wei-Tai (175–176), the ambuscade was deliberately planned, but the kidnapping resulted from Chinese pique at the haughty, demanding demeanor of Parkes.

[14] Bazancourt, II, 224–235.

did claim that they took nothing before the British commander arrived and that both sides shared equally in the end.[15]

During the course of the negotiations with Prince Kung, difficulties between the allies increased. The French were miffed when the British forces failed to await their arrival before entering the gates of Peking for the first time on the morning of October 15.[16]

When the bodies of some twenty murdered victims of the kidnapping were surrendered later on the same day, more serious differences developed. The British demanded the imposition of punitive measures which the French refused to approve. Elgin proposed forcing high Peking officials to accompany the bodies to Tientsin and there to erect a monument in expiation. He also urged the immediate seizure of the imperial palace within Peking and the destruction of the Summer Palace, where the personal effects of some of the dead prisoners had been found.[17] Gros replied, acting in close consultation with General Ignatieff, that the Chinese would never agree to erecting the expiatory monument, which would be a perpetual reminder to their injured pride, and that the destruction of an unfortified palace would be a useless act of vengeance which might cause Prince Kung to break off negotiations and flee. He proposed instead that the allies threaten to destroy the main palace within Peking as part of their ultimatum but that they refrain from doing it unless it seemed probable that they should have to leave Peking without achieving their ends. The French were particularly concerned lest the advent of bad weather should render the roads to the coast impassable and force the two armies to winter near Peking. General Montauban supported Gros and indicated his intention to withdraw his army to Tientsin by November 1.[18]

It was finally agreed to omit the requirement of the Tientsin memorial ceremony, but to augment the indemnity demand by 500,000 taels to

[15] Stanmore (II, 334–339) presents Gen. Grant's complaint, while Bazancourt (II, 243–253, 262–275) and Mutrécy (II, 25–28) present the French defense. French soldiers profited in money to the extent of 80 francs per man as compared with some £2 for each British soldier, and the French apparently got the pick of the loot.

[16] Mutrécy, II, 33–35. British troops were already on the city's ramparts when the French entered the gates. According to Mutrécy, the French marched inside, where their band played "God Save the Queen" in mock homage to the valor of the conquering British army.

[17] Bazancourt, II, 281–286, 294–296.

[18] Ibid., 288–297; Mutrécy, II, 25–28; Morse, I, 608–611.

cover compensation for the families of the victims, and to threaten the destruction of the imperial palace if the indemnity was not paid by October 22 and treaty ratifications fully exchanged by October 23.

When the British persevered in their unilateral decision to burn the Summer Palace, Gros left to Montauban the decision as to whether the French would co-operate. The two commanders argued the matter for two days. According to the French account, Montauban warned that the move might precipitate the fall of the dynasty and defeat the efforts to reach agreement with Kung. Grant replied that exemplary chastisement was due and threatened to make French participation in the affair a condition of any further co-operation between the allied forces. The palace was burned by the British on October 18.[19]

Relations between the allies continued to degenerate. When General Grant proposed to attack the city itself on October 20 despite the fact that the ultimatum had not expired, Montauban declared that he would actively oppose any attack prior to the 23rd. Both Gros and Montauban, who were kept informed by Ignatieff, were convinced that Kung had no choice but to meet the allied demands, and they suspected that the British wanted to overthrow the dynasty. The temperature dipped to a chilling eight degrees centigrade on October 20, a reminder of approaching winter. On October 22 the indemnity sum was duly paid, and exchange of the final ratifications was arranged for October 26.

The British ceremony came first. It was an icily formal affair punctuated by several tiffs over matters of etiquette. It was designed to emphasize the fact that the peace was one of conquest in expiation of accumulated grievances going back, in British memory at least, to the Macartney mission of 1792.[20] Baron Gros's subsequent meeting with Prince Kung was by comparison friendly, a deliberate effort being made to avoid inflicting gratuitous humiliation.

The French performance was capped on October 28 by an elaborate religious ceremony held on the site of the old South Cathedral (*Nan T'ang*) in connection with the burial of the six Frenchmen who had lost their lives in the ambuscade. The locating and clearing of the site had been the first act of the French troops within the city. The low mass

[19] Bazancourt, II, 297–303; Morse, I, 610–612.
[20] Bazancourt, II, 304–312; Mutrécy, II, 38–39. Wrote Bazancourt: "In Lord Elgin's conduct toward Prince Kung was one political thought only: to make China feel that England was signing a treaty . . . of conquest."

performed for the deceased was attended by a large array of troops, the foreign diplomats, the French and Russian bishops, and some twenty priests. One hundred and fifty Chinese catechists dressed in choir robes sang the *Te Deum*. A presiding priest pronounced the cause upon which the French flag had been engaged a just and holy one waged in behalf of Christian civilization.

The church itself was formally reopened on October 29. Monsignor Mouly, the presiding bishop, compared the re-establishment to the return of the Jews from the Babylonian captivity and gave tearful thanks to Emperor Napoleon III for the assistance he had given to religion.[21] On the same date Baron Gros presented the first passports, duly visaed by Prince Kung, for delivery to twenty-eight Catholic missionaries operating in the interior of China.[22] It was a fitting climax to what had been throughout, from the French point of view, a modern crusade. Later developments in the French expedition were anticlimactic in character.

The French Treaty of Peking

In addition to reaffirming the Tientsin Treaty, the French acquired by the new Convention of Peking an indemnity of some eight million taels (as compared with two million in the 1858 treaty) secured by the allocation of a percentage of maritime customs receipts of the Empire. Since nonclerical claimants for the one million taels set aside for settlement of private losses qualified for only 170,000 taels of this amount, the remaining 830,000 taels went to the various Catholic missions.[23]

Article 6 of the convention involved the interesting and often noted discrepancy between the French and the Chinese texts. The French

[21] Cordier, *Relations*, I, 41–42; Bazancourt, II, 320–324; Mutrécy, II, 56–58.

[22] Cordier, *Relations*, I, 60–63; J. B. L. Gros, *Négociations entre la France et la Chine en 1860: Livre Jaune du Baron Gros* (Paris, 1864), 194–199. The passports certified that the bearers were priests of the religion of *T'ien Tchou*, men of virtue and honor, and asked Chinese authorities to protect them as friends and to permit them to preach, to reside in any locality, to rent or purchase ground, and to construct churches and houses.

[23] Morse, I, 615–616. Cordier (*Relations*, I, 3–7, 49–50) presents the full text of the French treaty of Oct. 25, 1860. The occupied coastal areas of China were to be surrendered on the payment of a half million taels, the first installment of the indemnity, due within a month, but the French reserved the privilege of wintering their army in China until the payment of the indemnity was entirely arranged (Articles 7 and 8). The families of the twelve French victims were allotted 136,000 francs each, whereas the twenty-six British got only 86,000 each.

254

version recalled the terms of the imperial edict issued March 20, 1846, concerning the restoration of cemeteries and of buildings for religious and benevolent purposes that had been taken away from Christians in China during the period of their persecution. It also specified that the diplomatic representative of France should serve as intermediary in carrying out such restoration.[24] The Chinese version did not mention the 1846 edict by name and listed specifically the additional privileges which the French missionaries were to enjoy. It specified that an imperial edict to be published should include the following provision:

Catholic temples, colleges, cemeteries, houses, fields and all other possessions confiscated previously during the persecution will be given over to the French ambassador resident at Peking, who will make due restitution of them. Missionaries of France will be free to rent land in all the provinces of the Empire, to purchase and construct houses as they find it desirable.[25]

The final sentence, repeating the exact wording of the passports (see note 22), was entirely new; it was absent from the French text.

It seems clear that Gros connived at the discrepancy in the wording of the two versions of the treaty in order to avoid divulging in the published official French text the full scope of the exactions levied in the passports in favor of the French missionaries. Otherwise British and Americans would claim the same privileges. The Chinese version of the treaty was made to conform with the terms of the passports, presumably in order to make the latter enforceable by diplomatic agencies. The drafting officers who were apparently responsible for the Chinese translation, in addition to Bishop Mouly, were two members of the Missions Etrangères, Monsignor Delamarre and Monsignor Deluc, the interpreters for Gros and Montauban.[26] A beginning was made in restoring mission property on November 5, when Prince Kung turned over the South Cathedral site in Peking to Baron Gros, who gave it in turn to Bishop Mouly. Prince Kung also agreed to search out and restore the site of the old North Cathedral as well.[27]

Subsequent attempts of the mission to take advantage the sweeping

---

[24] Hertslet, 288–291; Latourette, 276–277.

[25] Cordier, *Relations*, I, 53–54.

[26] Launay, *Histoire Générale*, III, 387–388.

[27] The titles to the *Nan T'ang* property had been entrusted to the keeping of the Russian archimandrite, as had been the cemetery and library records. Gros thanked General Ignatieff for Russian assistance in producing the titles.

terms of Article 6, especially in the years following the suppression of the rebellion, aroused intense hostility among the resident population. The sites involved had long ago been purchased and occupied by the Chinese owners. Arbitrary methods of dispossessing the owners of such properties and of turning the sites over to the foreign clergy were eventually abandoned in accordance with a convention signed in February, 1865, by Bourboulon's successor, Jules Berthemy. Berthemy took the view that Article 6 was not intended to facilitate a real estate grab for the profit of foreign priests but rather to provide the land needed for missionary purposes. His convention provided, therefore, that future sales of former mission property should be made to the local mission collectively, without specifying names of recipients, and that each sale should be preceded by a local investigation to see whether local Chinese citizens approved the transfer. The result was to halt such sales, because very rarely was the local response favorable.[28] Popular hostility to the missionaries provided fertile soil for the spawning of wild charges of criminal practices on their part, charges which subsequently inspired such happenings as the Tientsin massacre of 1870.[29]

Important terms of the British Treaty of Peking provided for the right of immediate residence of a British ambassador at the capital, for possession of the Kowloon Peninsula, and for the joint allied evacuation of Chusan Island.[30]

The net accomplishment of the treaties in realizing French political interests was negative. The French were effectively blocked by the watchful British from acquiring Chusan or any other point in China, while Britain itself obtained the important addition of Kowloon. The only important material beneficiary from the French war with China was, therefore, the Catholic missionary interest, whose potential property claims under Article 6 were extensive.

All French hostilities against the Chinese ceased with the ratification of the Peking treaty on October 26. General Montauban and most of the French army departed from Peking on November 1. A battalion and two guns stayed behind with Baron Gros, who, fearful that the British might exact new concessions, decided not to leave the capital until Lord Elgin did. Montauban and approximately half of the French force

---

[28] Cordier, *Relations*, I, 54–60, 69–71; Williams, 335–336. The Bourée Treaty of 1882 relaxed the terms of the Convention of 1865.

[29] Morse, II, ch. xi and xii.   [30] Cordier, *Relations*, I, 10–11.

left Tientsin for Shanghai on November 22. General Collineau and some 3,000 troops remained at Tientsin in winter quarters.[31]

Back at Peking, Frederick Bruce, the brother of Elgin and Britain's Ambassador-designate to China, put in an appearance on November 6 and demanded that Gros concur in the immediate establishment of British and French legations at Peking. Bruce had brought with him fifty boxes of window glass to replace the paper panes in the palace, which he intended to use as embassy. He declared that he would not leave Peking unless forcibly expelled from it. In response to Elgin's embarrassed request for a French opinion on the matter, Gros, acting on advice from Ignatieff, warned that any premature move of this kind would only strengthen the influence of the old Tartar party at the court, which was already seeking to set aside Prince Kung and the treaty settlements. The foreigners had better first allow the Emperor to return to Peking so that he could then receive the new Ambassadors instead of appearing to submit to those who were already occupying his capital. Otherwise the court might elect to remain in the interior indefinitely. Gros announced his own intention to retire to Tientsin and to wait until spring before attempting to establish the French legation.

Partly to save his brother's face, Lord Elgin arranged to present Bruce formally to Prince Kung, on November 8, as Britain's new minister plenipotentiary. An imposing military escort was in attendance. Both brothers and Baron Gros then left Peking on November 9, accompanied by the remaining British and French troops. Elgin embarked from Tientsin on November 26 to take up his new duties as Viceroy of India.[32]

Russian-French Relations during the 1860 Campaign

Five days after Gros and Elgin departed from Peking, General Ignatieff, the Russian emissary, signed with Prince Kung an important treaty granting Russia the Chinese coastal territory lying east of the Ussuri River. This treaty was the successful culmination of a prolonged and devious diplomatic maneuver which had a tangential bearing on French policy.

Russia had not been asked, as in 1858, to participate in the second allied

[31] Bazancourt, II, 324–329; Palikao, 392. General Montauban reached Shanghai on December 12 and immediately departed incognito for a visit to Japan's Inland Sea. Four French war vessels also proceeded to the Inland Sea to obtain satisfaction for an attack on a Frenchman at the gate of the consulate at Tokyo.

[32] Cordier, *Relations*, I, 43–47.

expedition to China. St. Petersburg had sent Ignatieff to China in March, 1859, as head of a military mission to obtain further territorial and treaty concessions and to offer Peking, in return, military aid in crushing the Taiping rebellion. Border contacts indicated that the Chinese were reluctant even to ratify the Aigun treaty and were quite unwilling to negotiate a supplementary convention or to accept the proffered arms.[33] The Russian agent had reached Peking on June 27, 1859, just two days after the Taku incident. He found the victorious war party at Peking more than ever disinclined to accede to Russian demands. At the same time, the Chinese were unwilling to risk driving Ignatieff into the arms of the British and French. Negotiations were protracted from July to September, 1859, and again from December to April, 1860, when they were finally broken off by Ignatieff on orders from St. Petersburg.[34]

At St. Petersburg, in January, 1860, Prince Gortchakoff informed the British and French Ambassadors that General Ignatieff planned to leave Peking during the course of the allied military operations in order to avoid any suspicion that he was trying to seek exclusive advantage from the situation or to encourage Chinese resistance. He would remain near the allied fleet in order to be of any possible assistance as a go-between. Gortchakoff denied rumors that Ignatieff was leaving Peking because he had encounterd serious difficulties in his negotiation but warned that any application of force at Peking would probably result in the overthrow of the dynasty, with resulting chaotic conditions destructive of all commercial activity.[35]

Ignatieff was hindered by the Chinese from making contact with the Western agents. He finally got word to the American consul at Shanghai in April, 1860, through a letter transmitted by a Catholic missionary asking that a Russian vessel be directed to pick him up at Pehtang.[36]

[33] Morse, II, 83. Russia's offer of arms to China was renewed in 1860 and 1862.

[34] Hoo Chi-Tsai, 242–257.

[35] The same information was relayed to Cass in Washington and also to the French. See FO, 65, 551, Crampton to Russell from St. Petersburg, Jan. 25, 1860, and SD, Russian Legation Note, Stoebel to Cass, Jan. 12, 1860.

[36] In 1861, as in 1858, the Russian government made an ostentatious effort to solicit American collaboration. Cass again authorized Ward to assist Russian efforts in arranging an amicable settlement of the Chinese quarrel but ordered him to return to Shanghai if a peaceful solution proved impossible to attain. Actually American influence was nil (SD, China, DI, I, 22–23, Cass to Ward, Feb. 23, 1860). Ward's anger over English ridicule of his humiliating journey to Peking vented itself particularly on Parkes, whom Ward denounced as "one of the most unscrupulous of

Although commanded by the Chinese to return to Russia overland via Kiakta, Ignatieff found his way to Pehtang in the company of the head of the Russian ecclesiastic mission and there made contact with the Russian vessel which brought him to Shanghai on June 15, 1860.

At Shanghai, Ignatieff followed the pattern set by Gortchakoff in denying rumors that he had failed in his efforts at Peking to negotiate additional territorial concessions and in warning that an advance on Peking would imperil the dynasty.[37] He insisted also that Russian arms had been withheld from the Chinese when it appeared that they would be used against the allies. The most convincing part of his performance was his transmission to the allied forces of detailed military information concerning the defenses of the lower Peiho, the character, size, and aims of the Tartar army, and the defenses of Peking itself, all of which proved to be accurate and useful.[38] The extent to which he gained the confidence of the British forces is evident from the following first hand report of September, 1860: "The Russian Ambassador, General Ignatieff, is in our camp. He has lent us the best map of Pekin I have yet seen— better and more detailed than our own. He gives us all the information he can about Pekin." [39]

Ignatieff's relations with Baron Gros were close throughout the campaign, for it developed again as in 1858 that both continental governments feared that precipitate British action, whether deliberate or not, might end the Manchu regime and might conceivably contribute to establishing virtual British control over south China.[40] During 1860 Gortchakoff regularly provided the French Ambassador at St. Peters-

---

. . . English officials, who . . . has been the means of inflicting more misery upon [the Chinese] people than any other living man" (SD, China, DD, Ward to Cass, Oct. 4, 1860).

[37] Mutrécy (I, 291) reported rumors on June 18, 1860, that the Russians were taking possession of the Ussuri and Sungari valleys and were threatening Korea.

[38] SD, China, DD, 15, from Ward, June 29, 1860. Ignatieff was particularly confidential with Ward, but to no particular end (see Hoo Chi-Tsai, 258–269). Swisher (651–652) reveals that Chinese officials at Shanghai learned of Ignatieff's doings and suspected collusion between him and Ward.

[39] Allgood, 54, dated Sept. 29, 1860.

[40] Palikao, 360; T. F. Tsiang ("China, England, and Russia," CHJ., III, 117–121) tells a story of the Russian agent at Ili who proposed, in early 1860, that the Chinese create a diversion by attacking British India via Tibet, Nepal, and Yunnan, arguing that Britain, not France, was the real enemy of China. Peking refused to credit the sincerity of this suggestion.

burg, the Duc de Montebello, with the most recent news from China, stressing repeatedly the dangers which would attend the forcible allied occupation of Peking.[41]

In August, General Ignatieff trailed the allied agents to Tientsin, where he was able to reopen communications with the Russian ecclesiastical mission in the capital and to contribute through this channel additional military information. He secretly refused initial Chinese offers to act as mediator unless they first would meet his 1859 treaty demands. He eventually accompanied the allied forces to Peking itself, which he entered on October 16. Here he was able to exert a considerable influence on the negotiations, co-operating closely with Baron Gros and Monsignor Mouly to oppose extreme British demands. Gros admitted later that the Russian took advantage of his own naïveté. Ignatieff reassured Prince Kung and his associates that their fear of allied treachery was groundless and urged them to remain at the capital and meet the allied demands. At the same time, the Russian required as compensation for his alleged aid in preventing the destruction of Peking and the downfall of the dynasty the unqualified Chinese acceptance of Russia's demands for cession of the trans-Ussuri region. Ignatieff thus arranged peace at the invitation of both the Chinese and the French, and he actually drafted, with the aid of members of the Russian ecclesiastical mission, Kung's final satisfactory reply to the allied ultimatum.[42] The French were profuse in their expressions of appreciation of Ignatieff's timely aid.[43]

Negotiations on the Russian treaty were resumed by Ignatieff and Kung at the Russian ecclesiastical mission quarters on October 27. The Russian recited his services to the Chinese and took full credit for obtaining the withdrawal of foreign troops and for preventing the immediate establishment at Peking of the British and French embassies as demanded by Bruce. He then threatened to remain at Peking all winter if his treaty terms were not met and thus to hasten the return

[41] Cordier, *1860*, 120–123.

[42] Hoo Chi-Tsai, 269–286; Cordier, *Relations*, I, 91–97.

[43] Paul Varin, *Expédition de Chine* (Paris, 1862), 271; Maurice Irisson, Comte d'Herisson, *Journal d'un Interprète en Chine* (Paris, 1886), 380–381. Irisson cites Monsignor Mouly's account of Ignatieff's efforts to persuade Kung and other Chinese officials to remain in Peking and to reach a settlement. He added: "We owed . . . the rapidity of the decisions of Prince Kung . . . to the good offices of . . . General Ignatieff."

of the British and French Ambassadors to the capital, a move which Kung wanted very much to avoid. The treaty ceding the trans-Ussuri area was signed on November 14, 1860. It was accompanied by the issuance of an imperial decree which formally approved the cession. Ignatieff departed for Urga on November 22. An official Chinese document dated November 23 reveals that the Russian settlement included also a secret agreement to provide China with firearms, with training facilities for a Chinese military group at Kiakta where the arms were to be delivered, and with Russian military instructors who were to be sent part way to Peking. Another Russian offer to send several hundred troops by sea to aid China against the Taipings was vetoed by Viceroy Tsêng Kuo-fan.[44]

Thus one of the important and unanticipated consequences of the Anglo-French war on China was to advance the interests of the erstwhile enemy of the allies. By the treaties of Tientsin and Peking, Russia achieved a leading position as an Oriental power, obtaining the left bank of the Amur River and the coastal province extending southward to the northern tip of Korea.[45] The stage was thus set for a major shift of rivalry in the Far East to that of Britain against Russia, which was destined to continue until after the turn of the century. French financial assistance to Russia after 1890 was to weigh heavily against Britain's side of the balance. This potential shift of relationships was immediately perceived in Britain, where commentators attacked the Government for not having acted with energy in 1855–1856 to liquidate the Russian forces at De Castries Bay and for permitting Russia to profit from allied military efforts by advancing its territorial holdings and its trading advantage in China. One worried British writer criticized the London government's policy in the following terms:

[Russia], having been able to dispose of the wealth and might of England, has, at no cost to herself, obtained the permission so long denied . . . of participating in the coast trade of China, and has established the ascendency of her influence at Pekin. She has, besides, gained a territory worth all the rest of her Asiatic dominions together and so situated that it places the Empires of China and Japan at her feet.

The French Emperor has found the pretext he sought for placing a power-

---

[44] Hoo Chi-Tsai, 242–243, 287–290; Tsiang, "China, England, and Russia," *CHJ.*, III, 115; Swisher, 686–687, 689.

[45] Mutrécy, II, 123–125.

ful naval and military force on the further side of the Isthmus of Suez, and in the neighborhood of British India, so as to be ready to pounce upon Egypt from the rear, in case of the expected dissolution of the Ottoman Empire, or to take advantage of circumstances on the outbreak of a new Indian rebellion.[46]

French Evacuation of China

The French evacuation of Chusan Island simultaneous with the British withdrawal in late 1860 and early 1861 was arranged by Baron Gros in the face of strong objections from General Montauban. The latter remembered the position taken by Walewski and the armed services ministries in late 1859 at the time of his own appointment, and he insisted that matters of military occupation and evacuation were not to be decided by Gros without consulting the military. The General insisted specifically on October 28 that French troops must not withdraw from Chusan as contemplated by the Peking Convention, and his first orders for evacuating Chinese territory, issued on October 29, contemplated continued French garrisoning of the island. Montauban wanted Gros to negotiate separately with the Chinese for permission to install French forces permanently on the island, presumably as a counterweight against British influence at Hongkong and Kowloon.

Baron Gros took the position that the French troops were on Chusan solely to prevent its acquisition by England. On October 31, therefore, he ruled that the French must evacuate the island simultaneously with the British in order to put an end to the differences which would inevitably arise if the allies continued to occupy the island jointly. Montauban, on November 9, carried his protest directly to the Minister of War at Paris, Marshall Randon, urging French retention of Chusan at all costs and denying that England had any legitimate grounds for protesting.[47] Whether Gros was fully informed concerning the results of the secret investigation of Chusan by the Marine authorities (which are unavailable in the archives) or whether Paris had simply failed to arrive at a decision on the matter is not clear.

Word reached London from General Grant in early January, 1861, that Montauban was protesting the French evacuation of Chusan. Grant reported also that Lord Elgin was disposed to challenge prolonged

[46] Francis Marx, "The Pacific and the Amoor: Naval, Military, and Diplomatic Operations from 1855 to 1861," *Fraser's Magazine*, XXXI (May, 1861), 1–12, 19–28.
[47] Palikao, 386–392; Cordier, *Relations*, I, 48–49.

French occupation of Canton, which presumably could serve as a base for the prospective French operations against Cochin-China. Lord Russell in London was inclined to be lenient on the Canton question but insistent on the prompt evacuation of Chusan. He wrote to Ambassador Cowley at Paris as follows:

Her Majesty's Government have no wish to press Lord Elgin's views [with respect to immediate evacuation of Canton]. Indeed with the exception of Chusan, Her Majesty's Government are quite content to retain possession of any points in China which the French Government may desire to retain so long as the Treaties admit of such joint occupation.

Ambassador Cowley was instructed by London to remind the French authorities that the allies were specifically bound by the Peking Convention to evacuate Chusan at a given period and to suggest to Foreign Minister Thouvenel that orders covering the matter be sent to both forces at once.[48]

The response which Thouvenel made to Lord Cowley indicated how far the French authorities had abandoned the aggressive spirit in which the expedition had originally been proposed. Thouvenel replied that he had supposed that the French forces had already left Chusan, but promised in any case to send instructions by next mail to Montauban to evacuate the island. M. Thouvenel explained that he would have to speak to the French Ministers of War and Marine before he could reply concerning the proposed continued use of Canton. Cowley's report of the conversation concluded: "When . . . I alluded to the French expedition to be sent to Cochin-China, His Excellency gave me to understand that its only object, if indeed it could be called an expedition, was to bring away the French force which was already there." [49]

These exchanges at Paris were duly reported to Ambassador Bruce in China, who was instructed to govern his policy on the matter of evacuations by reference to the views which French authorities in China might be disposed to take. Russell repeated the view that with the possible exception of Canton, he did not anticipate that the French would want to prolong their occupation of any point in China beyond the time at which Britain was prepared to end its occupation.[50] Later instructions

[48] FO, 27, 1372, instructions to Cowley, Jan. 5, 1861.
[49] *Ibid.*, 1383, Cowley to Russell, Jan. 7, 1861.
[50] FO, 17, 348, to Bruce, June 26, 1861. A copy of this instruction was forwarded to Cowley to show to Thouvenel. See FO, 27, 1372, Jan. 26, 1861.

to Bruce ordered him not to evacuate Canton "so long as the French remain in occupation, but to leave as soon as the French did." [51]

French withdrawal from Canton was almost completed by June, 1861, to the great relief of the British. Before the end of the year, word reached London of the simultaneous striking of British and French flags at the city.[52]

French sources throw a somewhat different light on the problem of surrendering Canton. When Lord Elgin first proposed the early evacuation of Canton in September, 1860, Gros reported to Paris that the basic reason for his refusal was that "I am convinced that shortly after the abandonment of the city by the Europeans, the rebels would be in possession of it." [53] An important reason for Gros's not wanting to remove French influence from Canton prematurely so as to risk its capture by the rebels was that the local French commander was negotiating with Governor-General Lao at the time for the acquisition by the Missions Etrangères of two valuable sites for churches, one of them being the location of ex-Governor Yeh's yamen. A convention was actually signed on January 25, 1861, providing for a perpetual lease of the desired premises at a reasonable rental figure and agreeing that a more systematic recovery of formerly held mission property in the two Kwangs should begin two years later.[54]

The French leaders were for a time far more interested in Shanghai than in Canton. In October, 1860, General Montauban was approached by Prince Kung, through Monsignor Mouly as intermediary, with an invitation to assist the imperial forces in crushing the Taipings. The proposal was declined at the time.[55] It nevertheless seemed clear to French observers that unless Peking was able to obtain foreign assistance, the cause of the imperialists in the Yangtse area was hopeless. The French were not inclined to permit the British to take exclusive advantage of this situation. Montauban anticipated that Peking's bid for foreign aid would be renewed immediately and that the considerable portion of the

[51] FO, 17, 348, to Bruce, April 25, 1861.
[52] Ibid., 349, Dec. 20, 1861; Lane-Poole, I, 451.
[53] Gros, Négociations, 63. Elgin took the view that the control of Canton was no longer any use to the British. By implication, he wanted to deny France the use of it as a potential base for pending operations against Cochin-China. See Stanmore, II, 355.
[54] Cordier, Relations, I, 63–67.   [55] Bazancourt, II, 332.

French army which would remain at Shanghai even after the departure of Admiral Charner's relief expedition to Saigon would find itself engaged in another campaign in the spring of 1861, this time against the Taipings.[56] The British authorities, for their part, were clearly not happy that during the late months of 1860 the French forces at Shanghai actually outnumbered those of the British.[57] Allied distrust and rivalry were thus transferred for a time to Shanghai.

French suspicions of British intentions seemed to be confirmed when the British refused to support officially any moves to oppose the rampant rebel forces, and when Admiral Hope actually entered into a kind of truce agreement, in February, 1861, under which the rebels agreed not to attack Shanghai. The French suspected that their British allies would not regret a rebel victory and that the English intended to exploit the situation by exacting further political concessions, either from the rebels or from Peking, looking toward the partitioning of the Chinese Empire.[58]

Whether by design or by accident, the British delayed their active participation in suppressing the Taipings until the spring of 1862, after almost the entire body of French forces had left the area. Not until August, 1861, did London give Bruce permission to organize British volunteers for the defense of Shanghai. It was in March, 1862, two months after the rebels attacked the city in January, when official British support was finally accorded to both the anti-Taiping Ever

---

[56] *Ibid.*, 331–332; Mutrécy, II, 116–118.

[57] Stanmore, II, 350. Palmerston wrote to Herbert on December 20 as follows: "I do not like . . . Shanghai being in the possession of a French garrison stronger than ours. . . . It is not pleasant to see the welfare of a large and thriving English community so much depending on French good behavior."

[58] Bazancourt, II, 329–332. There is no indication that London ever contemplated such an objective, although General Grant wrote to Herbert from Peking on Oct. 25, 1860, as follows: "It is a pity we did not take possession of [China] . . . when we took India. . . . The Chinese are no soldiers." One French observer at the time advocated that Britain, France, and the other Christian powers seize the opportunity of the rebellion to split China up into three or four separate political kingdoms of relatively equal size. He argued that if such a colossal state should ever find a great leader capable of adapting European methods of warfare, undivided China could become a redoubtable power. He added: "I well know that no one will do it and that these pages will have been written to no end; but a day will come, perhaps, when they will be cited" (D. Sinibaldo de Mas, *La Chine et les Puissances Chrétiennes* [Paris, 1861], I, 249–288).

Victorious Army of Frederick Townsend Ward and to the Chinese forces under Viceroy Tsêng Kuo-fan.[59] The small French naval force and marine contingent commanded by Admiral Protet, which had remained behind, participated so actively in the anti-Taiping operations of April and May, 1862, that Protet lost his life. Subsequently, a small volunteer French-Chinese force, similar to that led by Ward and "Chinese" Gordon, collaborated in the anti-rebel operations until the fall of the final Taiping stronghold in August, 1864. The services of the French leaders of this volunteer force were subsequently recognized by the Peking authorities.[60]

It remains in a final chapter to indicate how the French prosecuted their campaign in Cochin-China in 1861 and 1862, and to trace briefly how the roots of French imperialism in eastern Asia, established from 1840 to 1860, survived to come to fruition two decades later in the final establishment of French Indo-China.

[59] Cordier, *Histoire Générale*, IV, 38–39.
[60] Morse, II, 74–79, 111–112. The leaders of the French volunteers were Neveue d'Aiguebell and Prosper Giquel.

XVI

Imperialism Takes Root
in Indo-China

T HIS concluding chapter, which covers in summary fashion the trends of French imperialist endeavor in Indo-China during the two decades following 1861, is appended as a kind of epilogue to the main body of the study. An adequate treatment of this phase of the story, including the requisite documentation, must await full examination of the archives of the French Ministry of Marine and of Colonies, which material was not available to the author. Only two episodes from this period have apparently been examined on the basis of unpublished official sources. The first has to do with Franco-Spanish relations during the period of the consolidation of the French hold on Saigon, from 1860 to 1863,[1] and the second with the colorful events at Hanoi in 1873.[2] It is nevertheless believed that enough of the continuous story can be put together from published sources and secondary accounts to contribute a clarifying, although

---

[1] R. Stanley Thomson, "The Diplomacy of Imperialism," *JMH.*, XII (1940), 334–356. The French archival materials examined by Thomson included volumes 1350 to 1363 from *Affaires Etrangères, Espagne*, 1857–1863, and *Mémoires et documents, Asie*, vols. 27–29, 1857–1864. He also used some of the archives of the Minister of Marine.

[2] M. Dutreb [Marthe Du Bert], *L'Amiral Dupré et la Conquête du Tonkin* (Paris, 1924). This is an excellent explanation of a confusing incident.

by no means definitive, commentary on the vitality of the traditional roots of French imperialism in eastern Asia.

The Decision to Retain Control over Saigon and Vicinity

The Paris government had considerable difficulty making up its mind during 1860 concerning its policy toward the discouragingly unsuccessful venture in Cochin-China. Louis Napoleon had lost interest in the affair and his cabinet was divided. In February, 1860, Foreign Minister Thouvenel was ready to settle for a treaty with Hué covering only commercial and religious questions. It was after the receipt of Admiral Page's reports recommending the annexation of Saigon that Thouvenel, in the spring of 1860, joined the Minister of Marine in urging the Emperor to retain the port.[3] Genouilly's return to France also influenced the trend. No one questioned the necessity of rescuing the beleaguered garrison at Saigon, consisting of 800 French troops, mainly Senegalese, and 100 or more Filipino Tagals. The garrison had been cut off from outside contacts since July, 1860, when an Annamite army of some 12,000 men infested the city.[4] But Paris was in no mood to authorize offensive action on a major scale looking toward the complete conquest of Annam. Instructions setting forth the objectives and scope of the relief expedition to Saigon did not reach the bewildered Admiral Charner in China until the final week of December, 1860.[5]

The precise nature of the orders sent to the Admiral is not known. General Montauban's instructions, which reached him at the end of the year, following his return from Japan, explained that the Saigon expedition was to be a limited undertaking which would concern primarily Admiral Charner and the navy.[6] Its objective would be merely to consolidate points already occupied by France and to disperse all hostile Annamite bands encamped in the vicinity of the French positions. The General was accordingly directed to furnish an army contingent of some 800 men to co-operate with the Admiral but to retain at Shanghai the main French force to protect the city against possible

[3] Thomson, 341–342.

[4] Bazancourt, I, 334–338; Cultru, 71–73; Priestley, 114. An earlier Annamite attack in the spring of 1859 had been dispersed.

[5] Mutrécy, II, 128. Final orders were still being awaited by the Admiral as late as December 22.

[6] *Ibid.*, 1.

rebel attack. The army contingent sent to Saigon included two detachments of artillery, a detachment of cavalry, a section of engineers, and an ambulance section. Charner's own forces were made up of approximately 1,000 marines, an equal number of sailors, plus several hundred coolies, mainly Chinese. Added to the 900-man garrison already at Saigon, the total French forces numbered under 4,000 men.[7] Here was little to gratify imperialist enthusiasts and nothing to reassure those who were concerned about the safety of the missionaries and Annamite Christians, especially those in Tongking. Colonel Palanca eventually arrived from Manila with a small detachment of Filipino troops sufficient to sustain to the end Spanish participation in the affair.

The policy of the Paris government was not clarified until the very end of 1860, when the aggressive Chasseloup-Laubat took over the post of Minister of Marine and of Colonies. He exerted vigorous pressure to pursue a forward policy in Indo-China and undertook to keep Louis Napoleon in line with it. It was Chasseloup-Laubat who finally obtained authorization for the new instructions of February 11, 1861, to utilize Montauban's entire force in support of Charner's efforts to extend the perimeter of French holdings at Saigon and to exact from the Annamite government formal recognition of French sovereignty over the territory occupied.[8] These orders came too late to accomplish impressive results, and they were not long sustained. The discouraging difficulties which the French encountered at Saigon eventually strengthened influences at Paris contrary to the views of Chasseloup-Laubat. Napoleon III was becoming increasingly interested in the possibilities of national and dynastic aggrandizement in Mexico.

Admiral Charner at Saigon

Admiral Charner's fleet entered the Donnai River leading to Saigon on February 7, 1861. The subjection of the forts blocking entrance to the river required sharp and costly fighting. The final Annamite stronghold fell on February 24–25 after a spirited defense stand. The French victory broke the back of the regular Annamite army, but Charner

---

[7] Bazancourt, II, 335–336; Mutrécy, II, 130–132; Thomazi, 44–47. Bazancourt mentions 1,000 army troops instead of Mutrécy's 800; Thomazi refers to 600 Chinese coolies and 80 Annamite volunteers.

[8] Thomson, 341–343.

made no attempt to follow up the French success beyond the occupation in mid-April of the town of Mytho, located on the near edge of the adjacent Mekong Delta area.[9] For the time being Saigon was secure, for the surrounding area was deserted by the population as well as by organized Annamite forces. Small guerrilla bands left behind to harass the invader were troublesome, but these melted away in the face of serious attack.

As had been the case in 1859, the most serious deterrent to French activity came not from enemy forces but from illness in the ranks. Gaps within the effective forces grew wider with every passing week. General Collineau was among the victims. The discouraging French situation at Saigon was reflected in the following almost gleeful communication by Harry Parkes from Canton in June, 1861:

The French . . . have already had to call off nearly all their troops [in China] to reinforce their expedition in Cochin-China, and yet they have not a sufficient force there . . . and are . . . waiting fresh orders from France. Admiral Page, writing from Saigon, says that their only occupation lies in counting the sick, the dying, and the dead. They have only a couple of hundred men at Canton and less than a thousand at Tientsin, and these will be removed in the course of a few months. . . . The alliance in this part of the world will then have been terminated, which is also desirable.[10]

In the new instructions from Chasseloup-Laubat, General Montauban was ordered on April 21 to transfer almost his entire force from China to assist Charner in establishing a definitive occupation of the vicinity of Saigon. Montauban accordingly left only a small fraction of his army at Shanghai under General Jamin and proceeded to the support of Admiral Charner. With the aid of Montauban's fresh forces and reinforcements from Manila, the French established effective control over key points in the three provinces of Dinhtuong, Giadong, and Bienhoa adjacent to Saigon. In late spring Charner opened peace negotiations with the Annamite government on the basis of the formal cession of the three provinces, freedom for missionary operations, and the payment of a four-million-dollar (Mexican) indemnity. He later agreed as a bargaining move to surrender French claims to Dinhtuong Province outside of the immediate environs of Mytho. In July, 1861, the

9 Cultru, 72–73; Cordier, "La Politique Coloniale," *T'oung Pao,* 2d ser., XII, 175–176.

10 Lane-Poole, I, 451, Parkes to his wife, June 12, 1861.

Admiral announced unilaterally that Saigon was French by right of conquest. But he made no progress in the peace negotiations and was eventually relieved of his responsibilities in the fall of 1861.

One serious embarrassment to the French negotiators came from Colonel Palanca's insistence that Hué be forced to treat simultaneously with both European allies on the basis of a Spanish demand for a similar territorial foothold in Tongking. But Charner was unable to spare the forces to aid any Spanish expedition against Hanoi and was also unwilling to jeopardize his own negotiations by coupling them with support of difficult Spanish claims. The Admiral proposed instead that Spain be granted monetary compensation in lieu of its share of territorial acquisitions. From July, 1861, Madrid supported Palanca's demand under the threat that Spain would otherwise withdraw its forces from Saigon.[11] The quarrel at Saigon became more heated after the French proclamation of annexation. Since Spanish forces had been associated from the outset in the conquest of Saigon, and since France refused to reciprocate by aiding Spain in Tongking, Palanca insisted that the term "Franco-Spanish Cochin-China" be employed.[12] Paris finally conceded that Colonel Palanca should be associated actively in the treaty negotiations with Admiral Bonard, who took Charner's place in November, 1861, but that Spain's claims be covered either by a direct monetary contribution or by a share of an eventual indemnity. Madrid finally acquiesced in this arrangement, thereby withdrawing its support from the demands of the insistent colonel.[13]

General Montauban and all troops under his direct command were recalled to France in the autumn of 1861.[14] This action not only vetoed any prospects for serious offensive operations in northern Annam but it also became the signal for a counteroffensive on the part of the Annamite army. Rebel elements attacked and burned Cholon, adjacent to Saigon. By vigorous action, Admiral Bonard managed before the end of 1861 to clear the province of Bienhoa lying northeast and east of Saigon between the Donnai River and the coast and also to occupy

---

[11] Thomson, 343–344. Palanca's own account of his difficulties is found in D. Carlos Palanca Gutierrez, *Reseña Histórica de la Expedición de Cochinchina* (Cartagena, 1869).

[12] Palanca Gutierrez., 344–346.   [13] *Ibid.*, 350–353, 356.

[14] Bazancourt, II, 336–338. Montauban's forces withdrew before Admiral Bonard took over command from Charner on November 30, 1861. For the military details of this action, see Thomazi, 47–62.

an additional section of the Mekong Delta further upstream at Vinh-long. But the offensive capacities of the reduced French forces were completely spent at the conclusions of these limited operations; incipient rebellion in southern Cochin-China persisted, and Bonard's prospects of obtaining a peace settlement with Hué seemed far from bright.[15]

The Treaty of 1862

Two factors influenced King Tu-Duc to conclude peace with the French and Spanish negotiators in June of 1862. One was the French denial to Hué of the customary rice supply from Cochin-China. More important was the outbreak of a serious rebellion in Tongking along lines so often predicted by missionary intelligence. The pro-Christian pretender belonging to the ancient Lê dynasty started out in the spring of 1862 to conquer all of Tongking. He appealed for active French assistance, and Colonel Palanca pressed for compliance.[16] Bonard knew little of the circumstances of the Tongking rebellion at the time. In view of his own difficult situation which negated the possibility of intervention in Tongking, admittedly a Spanish sphere in any case, the Admiral overruled Palanca and accepted the conciliatory peace proposals brought forward by the head Annamite mandarin, Phan-Than-Giang, in May, 1862.

The Treaty of Saigon was signed on June 5 by Admiral Bonard and Colonel Palanca. The Europeans agreed to evacuate Vinhlong and to limit French territorial holdings to the three provinces immediately adjacent to Saigon, plus the often considered island of Poulo Condore, lying some fifty miles off the Mekong Delta. In addition to the payment of the four million piaster indemnity to France, Tu-Duc agreed to open three Annamite ports including Tourane to foreign commerce, to grant religious liberty within Annam, and to renounce Annam's tenuous claims of suzerainty over Cambodia. Article 4 of the treaty provided a vaguely defined basis for subsequent claims of a French protectorate over Annam. If any foreign nation should attempt to

[15] Henri Blet, *Histoire de la Colonisation Française, 1789–1870* (Genoble, 1947), II, 221–222; J.-L. de Lanessan, *L'Expansion Coloniale de la France* . . . (Paris, 1886), 525.

[16] Thomson, 353–354.

acquire a part of Annamite territory, the government agreed to present the situation for prior consideration by the Emperor of France, who would then enjoy full liberty to come to the aid of Annam or to refrain from doing so. But no cession of Annamite territory to a foreign nation could be made without obtaining French consent.[17]

The Treaty of Saigon contained mostly paper concessions, for it did not provide the French with effective sanctions for ensuring the execution of its terms. Tu-Duc obviously regarded it mainly as a means of preventing collusion between his foreign and domestic enemies while he gained time to put down the rebellion in Tongking.

When civil war again broke out in Tongking in August, 1862, and Hué authorities began to talk of revising the treaty, Colonel Palanca became so embarrassingly insistent on allied intervention that Bonard disassociated himself entirely from the interests of Spain. The Annamite authorities attempted to aggravate the rift between the European allies by citing alleged earlier statements of Palanca that Spain lacked territorial ambitions and by demanding that Palanca himself aid the Annamite authorities in putting down the rebellion as the price of Hué's ratification of the treaty. Thereupon Bonard and Palanca closed ranks and issued a joint ultimatum on November 2, 1862, threatening to aid the rebels unless treaty ratifications were exchanged within a month following the receipt of the drafts from Europe.

Immediately thereafter a formidable insurrection against allied control broke out in the vicinity of Saigon, and for a time the European forces were hard pressed. The timely arrival at Saigon in February, 1863, of the final remnants of the French Algerian and African troops from China, plus an additional 800 troops from Manila, caused the Annamite insurrection to collapse and forced Hué to accept the treaty terms previously agreed to in June. Ratifications were exchanged at Hué on April 14, 1863. The same month witnessed the departure of the Filipino troops on board a French transport for Manila, thus terminating Spanish participation in what had been for Spain a wholly unprofitable venture.[18]

[17] Cordier, "La Politique Coloniale," *T'oung Pao*, 2d ser., XII, 175–176; Ennis, 41–42; Blet, II, 222.

[18] Blet, II, 223; Thomazi, 71–75; Thomson, 350, 354–356. Spain was eventually accorded half of the indemnity collected from Hué.

Policy Conflict over Indo-China, 1863–1865

A controversy over policy objectives in Indo-China developed again in 1863–1864 between Emperor Napoleon III and his Minister of Marine, Chasseloup-Laubat. The Emperor's flagging interest in the costly and unpromising affair at Saigon had been further reduced by reports from Admiral Bonard indicating that additional headaches were in store in administering even the limited area already acquired. Admiral Charner's initial experiment of direct military rule had failed, as had Bonard's alternative plan, based on experience in Algiers, to use native mandarin officials as agents of indirect rule under the supervision of French naval inspectors. The result of this latter experiment was a resurgence of rebellion. It became apparent that the bureaucratic Annamite mandarins enjoyed no authority in their own right but only as they represented the court at Hué and that they lacked both the capacity and the inclination to act as administrators for the French.[19] In addition, an important new factor behind the Emperor's desire to limit French objectives in Indo-China and to cut operational costs was his commitment to the projected adventure in Mexico. The allocation of funds for Indo-China was therefore sharply curtailed.[20] In strong disagreement with Louis Napoleon's decision was the Minister of Marine and of Colonies and Admiral de la Grandière, the newly appointed Governor at Saigon. The navy by this time had developed a kind of proprietary interest in the Cochin-China affair and was determined to vindicate the honor of the service by expanding French influence and holdings.

The controversy eventually came to a crisis over the Emperor's acquiescence in the revision of the Treaty of Saigon proposed by the able and persistent Phan-Than-Giang, who headed an Annamite diplomatic mission to Paris. The agreed proposal was that France should retrocede title to the three provinces previously acquired and should retain direct control over only the three key points of Saigon, Cholon, and Cape Saint-Jacques at the mouth of the Donnai River corridor leading to Saigon. In return, Annam would acknowledge a French

[19] Priestley, 114; Thomazi, 67–71; de Lanessan, 526, 546. Charner replaced Annamite prefects (*Phu*) and subprefects (*Huyen*) by Frenchmen; Bonard restored mandarins to these posts.

[20] Blet, II, 223.

protectorate over all six provinces of Cochin-China proper, would pay France either a quarter-million-franc indemnity or an annual tribute, and would grant full commercial access to all Annam. Lieutenant Aubaret, a former aide of Bonard, supported the new proposal on the ground that the country would be extremely difficult to govern under French laws, that the more valuable Tongking area was properly a Spanish sphere, and that the new arrangement promised to be less difficult and costly to manage and more profitable commercially than that of 1862. Overruling for the time being the protests of Chasseloup-Laubat, Napoleon sent Aubaret to Hué, where the new treaty was actually signed in June, 1864.

The navy's rebuttal to the Emperor's policy was presented with great vigor. It enjoyed support from the clerical press and eventually from opposition deputies Thiers and Duray. One of the ablest opposing brochures, prepared by Vice-Admiral Abel (a pseudonym for Rieunier), stressed the practical difficulty of retaining possession of three isolated points without control over adjacent and intervening areas and also emphasized the potential value of the provinces being surrendered. Lieutenant Francis Garnier and clerical spokesmen also attacked the Emperor's alleged excessive emphasis on commercial aspects to the exclusion of the "civilizing mission" of France to emancipate the heathen from despotic rule. Opposition pressure eventually became so great that the French Emperor, in 1865, reversed his policy and decided to keep the original Saigon treaty after all.[21]

In the meantime, Governor de la Grandière, acting apparently on his own authority but in pursuance of Admiral Charner's earlier claim that France had fallen heir to Annam's alleged suzerainty over Cambodia, sent naval Lieutenant Doudart de Lagrée to Pnompenh in 1863 to conclude a treaty with King Norodom. Lagrée was assisted in the negotiation by Monsignor Miche. In a secret agreement signed on August 11, 1863, France was accorded exclusive control over Cambodia's foreign relations and the right to install foreign consulates within the country. A French Resident would be stationed at Pnompenh and a representative of Cambodia would reside at Saigon to facilitate

---

[21] *Ibid.*, 223–228; Priestley, 115; M. H. Abel [Adrien Barthelemy Louis Rieunier], *Solution Pratique de la Question de Cochinchine, ou Fondation de la Politique Française dans l'Extrême Orient* (Paris, 1864). This book was distributed by the official agent of the Ministry of Marine and of Colonies.

communications. In return, the French undertook to protect Norodom against Bangkok's efforts to exercise Siam's assumed overlordship. Other terms included reciprocal freedom of travel and rights of property ownership for residents of Cochin-China and Cambodia, the right of the French to exploit Cambodian forests, the right of the mission-aries to preach and teach, and the cession to France of a small area around Pnompenh.[22]

When this Cambodian treaty was sent to Paris for ratification, Na-poleon apparently hesitated to approve it for fear that the move would offend the English, who were about to be associated with France in the initial debt-collecting aspects of the Mexican affair. It required all of the pressure which Chasseloup-Laubat and friends could generate, plus strong representations from de la Grandière at Saigon, to obtain eventual French ratification.

During the period of delay, Siamese agents persuaded the pliant Norodom to sign another treaty which would have made the Cam-bodian King the virtual viceroy for Bangkok. Norodom was actually preparing to proceed to Bangkok to receive his formal investiture and coronation at Siamese hands when Doudart, accompanied by an armed escort, arrived at Pnompenh to exchange treaty ratifications in the spring of 1864. The French officer first resisted efforts to exclude him from Pnompenh by threatening Norodom's person with the French-man's own pistol. Doudart's military escort subsequently fired several warning cannon to force Norodom's abandonment of his plans to pro-ceed to Bangkok. The French then obtained the Cambodian crown from Bangkok and arranged their own crowning of Norodom on June 3, 1864. In July, 1867, the French signed a treaty with Siam con-firming their protectorate over Cambodia but delimiting its territorial extent by allocating the three provinces of Mekong, Battambang, and Angkor to Siam.[23]

Lessened Importance of Prestige and Missionary Considerations

Two of the traditional roots of French imperialism in the Far East were dormant during the remainder of the eighteen-sixties. The first

[22] Blet, II, 224–226; Thomazi, 84–89. See also Antoine Cabatan, "Doudart de Lagrée et l'Indochine, 1828–1868," *Revue de l'Histoire des Colonies Françaises,* II (1933), 205 ff.

[23] Blet, II, 226–228; Priestley, 116–117.

was the desire to bolster dynastic popularity and national prestige by achievements in the area. In this connection the French-sponsored venture in Mexico displaced official interest in Annam. When the Mexican project came to its inevitable denouement in 1867, the harried Emperor undertook to revive his sagging popularity by liberalizing the French constitution and, finally by achieving a cheap diplomatic triumph over Bismarck. The end came with the disastrous defeat of France at the hands of Prussia in 1870–1871. During these years, Saigon was a prestige liability for the Emperor rather than an asset. One informed nationalist spokesman in 1864 levelled a trenchant attack against the whole Indo-China venture on the ground that it had not been thought out in advance in terms of defined objectives and the difficulties and sacrifices entailed.[24] News of the assumption of a French protectorate over the remainder of Cochin-China in 1867 aroused no enthusiasm whatever in France.[25] By the end of the sixties there were few French apologists for Louis Napoleon's disastrous penchant for distant overseas undertakings.

The second root of imperialist motivation, the traditional identification of French national interest with the fortunes of Catholic missions in eastern Asia, did not lose its vitality as abruptly as did the prestige issue. But the missionary cause ceased to be a decisive consideration in determining governmental policy. It has been noted that the French authorities at Saigon resisted Spanish pressure in 1862–1863 to exploit the uprising of the pro-Christian Lê pretender in Tongking as an excuse for aggressive support of missionary interests centering in the disaffected area. They used the Tongking rebellion instead as a lever to obtain Hué's recognition of French territorial gains previously realized in southern Annam. The appointment of Admiral Rigault de Genouilly to the post of Minister of Marine in 1867 ended any possibility of the resumption of naval co-operation with missionary interests, mainly because of the Admiral's long-standing feud with spokesmen of the Missions Etrangères.

The only new aggressive move undertaken by naval officers in support of missionary personnel in Asia was an abortive invasion of Korea in 1866. The action was authorized by M. de Bellonet, French chargé

[24] Henri Galos, 173–208.
[25] Agnes Murphy, *The Ideology of French Imperialism, 1871–1880* (Washington, 1948), 12–13.

277

at Peking, following the receipt of news that nine French missionaries had been executed by order of the Korean Regent. A detachment of French marines under the command of Admiral Roze landed on the Korean coast south of Seoul and marched upon the capital. They encountered more resistance than they had been led to expect and were obliged to withdraw without achieving tangible gains. Louis Napoleon repudiated the quixotic undertaking in 1867.[26]

In 1870 French prestige in China and throughout eastern Asia was seriously damaged by the popular rising at Tientsin, which resulted in the killing of a French consul, two priests, ten nuns, and some thirty Chinese servants of the mission, plus the destruction of a Catholic orphanage and a church. Under normal circumstances, this outrage would have called for retaliatory vengeance, but since the arrival of the news was contemporaneous with the defeat of France by Prussia, the sending of a punitive expedition to China was out of the question. Paris had to content itself with the exaction of an apology from Peking and an indemnity of 250,000 taels.

It was one of the ironies of the fading fortunes of the Second Empire that Louis Napoleon's government was never able to take advantage of the strategic potentialities of the opening of the French-controlled canal at Suez in November, 1869. It was certainly the intention of the Department of Marine and of Colonies to do so. A brochure sponsored by the Department appeared early in 1870 which publicized the importance of the canal for the future development of French Cochin-China and Cambodia in particular. It argued that France must improve the opportunity afforded at long last by the shortened distance to the Orient to develop a strong colonial establishment centering at Saigon which would balance Russian and British gains in the Far East and become a French-controlled commercial entrepot rivaling Singapore and Shanghai.[27] If European complications had not intervened, the

[26] Tyler Dennett, "Seward's Far Eastern Policy," *American Historical Review,* XXVIII (1922), 51–54; Priestley, 108. Both British and American representatives in China were alarmed in 1867 over French activities in Korea.

[27] Théophile Bilbaut, *Le Canal de Suez et les Intérêts Internationaux: La Cochin-chine Française et le Royaume de Cambodge* (Paris, 1870), 26–50, 96–103, 134–135. This brochure told the story of French connections with Annam from the seventeenth century; it emphasized the Pigneau de Behaine story, presented a thoroughgoing apologetic for the actions of Rigault de Genouilly in 1858–1859 and explained why positive collaboration between missionary and political agencies for imperialist ends was neither feasible nor desirable. It also described in detail the agricultural, indus-

Tientsin affair would have afforded an excellent excuse for aggressive French action in southeast Asia in conjunction with punitive measures against Peking. During the more than five years of exclusive French control of the canal, from 1869 to 1875, Paris was not able to develop any imperial interest in Asia capable of being served by the favored French position at Suez. Disraeli's purchase for Britain of the Khedive's half of the shares of the canal in 1875 ended the exclusive advantage which France had enjoyed and signaled a revival of French resentment of traditional British leadership in eastern Asia.[28]

Naval Support of Imperialism in Indo-China

The active interest of the Ministry of Marine at Paris and the agressive initiative taken by naval officers assigned to Saigon were almost the sole influences which kept alive the cause of French imperialism in southeast Asia for a decade or more following 1861. It became a question of maintaining the honor of the service and of gratifying the personal pride of naval officers assigned to the area that the French foothold in Indo-China be extended. In pursuing this project with a minimum of support from Paris, naval imperialists on the spot demonstrated an amazing audacity which occasionally took its toll. For several decades, the rule of the colony of Cochin-China was entrusted exclusively to admirals. At Paris, Chasseloup-Laubat served as Minister of Marine until 1867, when he was succeeded by Rigault de Genouilly, the arch-advocate of the Cochin-China cause. Chasseloup-Laubat was also president of the Paris Geographical Society, which sponsored the exploration of the Mekong Valley in 1866–1868 by naval officers Doudart de Lagrée and Francis Garnier.[29]

The most important gain which the Saigon authorities realized during the later sixties was the de facto occupation of the three westernmost provinces of Cochin-China in 1867. The action followed an alleged Annamite effort in 1866 to establish as King of Cambodia a pretender selected by Hué. The Governor of Saigon, Admiral de la Grandière,

---

trial, and commercial resources of Cochin-China and the benefits to be derived from French control.

[28] See Lowell J. Ragatz, *The Question of Egypt in Anglo-French Relations, 1875–1904* (Edinburgh, 1932).

[29] Blet, II, 230–233; Murphy, 50–56. The Paris Geographical Society contributed 25,000 francs to assist the exploring commission. This sum could not possibly have covered the entire cost, however.

went to France on leave shortly thereafter and conferred with Genouilly about the situation. After the Governor returned to his post, he ordered the military penetration of the upper delta of the Mekong and then proceeded to demand that Hué cede to France the three provinces of Vinhlong, Chandoc, and Hatien. Grandière influenced the resident Viceroy of the area, the venerable Phan-Than-Giang, to accept the arrangement. The latter, considering himself disgraced, refused French asylum and took poison.[30] It was not until 1874, under circumstances to be described below, that Hué finally acknowledged *de jure* sovereignty of the French over the disputed region.

The exploration of the Mekong Valley was planned in 1865 by Chasseloup-Laubat, who obtained for it both the blessing of the Emperor and the financial backing of the Geographical Society of which he was president. The actual instructions for the commission, prepared by Admiral-Governor de la Grandière, indicated that the project was being undertaken in the interest of civilization and the future of the infant colony of Cochin-China. The six-man commission included five naval personnel, one a geologist and another a botanist, plus one representative of the Ministry of Foreign Affairs. Doudart de Lagrée was selected leader as reward for his services in establishing the French protectorate over Cambodia. Francis Garnier, second in command, was a naval lieutenant who was serving at the time as Inspector of Indigenous Affairs and as a member of the important agricultural and industrial development committee for Cochin-China. Grandière's instructions included provision for the eventual publication of the findings of the commission.[31] In nearly every detail the planning of the project and its execution was the work of naval sponsors.

The Outcome of the Lagrée-Garnier Exploration

The Lagrée-Garnier exploration of 1866–1868 and the publication of Garnier's magnificent report concerning it in 1873 exerted a lasting influence on French imperialist policy in Indo-China. It brought to light an abundance of interesting information concerning a vast geo-

[30] Cordier, *Le Conflit*, 11–12; Priestley, 116; Thomazi, 89–98; Blet, II, 229–230.
[31] Francis Garnier, *Voyage d'Exploration en Indo-Chine* . . . (Paris, 1873), I, i–ii, 13–17. The other members of the commission were Louis Delaporte, Eugène Joubert, Clovis Thorel, and Louis Carné.

graphical area previously little known.[32] It also demonstrated conclusively the unsuitability of the Mekong River route as a commercial channel into Yunnan and, conversely, the feasibility for that purpose of the Red River (Song Koi) route through Tongking. Garnier discovered that much of the silk, tea, and textiles available in south Yunnan was actually being imported via Tongking rather than along the more difficult bandit-infested routes running up the valley of the West River from Canton. He concluded that if order could be restored on both sides of the frontier and the political barriers to trade along the Red River could be eliminated, Yunnan could provide a rich outlet for French trade and Saigon would eventually rival Shanghai as the great commercial entrepot for eastern Asia.[33]

Following Lagrée's death from illness at a small community named Tong-Thouen in the upper Yangtse River region in March, 1868, Garnier led the surviving members of the expedition out via Hankow and Shanghai. At Hankow Garnier met for the first time Jean Dupuis, the French merchant and explorer who was destined during the succeeding half decade to champion the opening of the Red River route for trade.[34] The publication of Garnier's report was authorized by Admiral Rigault de Genouilly in 1869, but the completion of the project was delayed until 1873 by the Franco-Prussian war.

Garnier was the adventurer-imperialist par excellence. He was especially perturbed over the indifference of the French public to matters relating to national greatness. He complained that the French view was turned inward, that its perspective was limited to Europe's affairs, that it lacked the tenacity of purpose and constancy of endeavor in prosecuting an overseas policy which England had demonstrated so markedly. If France was to avoid national decadence and avert world domination by the Anglo-Saxons, it must be present at all important points of the inhabited globe. France must no longer subordinate its policies in eastern Asia to the wishes of England; France herself must

---

[32] Garnier's first volume is historical and narrative, while the second is descriptive and topical. The de luxe edition of 1873 is handsomely bound, folio size, with gilt-edged pages. Volume I contains 186 illustrations including excellent pictures of the ruins of Angkor. Volume II covers topical interests such as astronomy, meteorology, geology, minerology and mines, anthropology, agriculture and horticulture, and languages.

[33] Garnier, *Voyage d'Exploration*, I, 447–448, 549.   [34] Blet, II, 233.

become the arbiter between European claims and native interests in Indo-China. Overseas projects such as Cochin-China could utilize constructively those abundant energies of the French people which would either remain sterile or else become dangerous if left to concentrate on European feuds and domestic differences.[35]

Garnier entertained considerable respect for the civilization of China and for the good sense of the Chinese people, but he despaired of the progressive capacities of China's backward-looking mandarin leadership. He foresaw for France a co-operative role looking toward the preservation of China's independence, the development of a more honest and progressive government, and the eventual consolidation and fusion of Oriental and Western civilizations.[36] Toward the peoples and cultures of southeast Asia, Garnier paid no such deference. He insisted that the superiority of French culture and its corollary *mission civilisatrice* must not be permitted to be questioned in connection with the opening up of countries like Annam, Laos, and Siam to contact with the Western world. French schools must be established to train men in the languages, history, geography, and customs of countries neighboring to Cochin-China. A French colonial civil service of far superior quality than the *nullités déclassées* currently being employed must be enlisted and trained. Only thus, insisted Garnier, could France recover in Indo-China the empire of which Dupleix had dreamed in India.[37] It is fairly obvious that Garnier fancied himself to be the heir and successor of Dupleix.[38] Economic motivation was not absent from Garnier's mind, but his fiery enthusiasm stemmed from his sense of manifest destiny, his consuming personal ambition, his urge to enhance his country's prestige, and his keen sense of rivalry with Britain.[39]

Garnier's Attempted Coup at Hanoi in 1873

Garnier's imperialistic proposals elicited meager response in the unfriendly political atmosphere of republican France in 1873, but his daring personal adventure at Hanoi in the same year did much to focus French attention on Tongking. After arranging for the publication of his book in 1872, Garnier resigned his naval lieutenancy and returned to

[35] Garnier, *Voyage d'Exploration*, I, 545–547.

[36] *Ibid.*, 551–558.   [37] *Ibid.*, 547–550.

[38] Albert de Pouvourville, *Francis Garnier* (Paris, 1931), 179.

[39] Guy Chastel, *Un Siècle d'Epopée Française en Indochine (1774–1847)* (Paris, 1947), 150–152.

the Far East. He spent the early months of 1873 in China exploring the upper Yangtse Valley as far west as Chungking. He became increasingly concerned lest the French effort to penetrate Yunnan from Tongking be outdistanced by British preparations to accomplish the same feat via northern Burma.[40] When Garnier returned to Shanghai in August, 1873, he found waiting for him an urgent request from Admiral Dupré, the Governor of Cochin-China, that he come immediately to Saigon.

Dupré's summons to Garnier concerned a situation which had developed at Hanoi as a result of the activities of Jean Dupuis, the French trader and imperialist who since 1860 had been located at Hankow, China. Acting on the basis of geographic information obtained by the Lagrée-Garnier expedition and his own investigation of the feasibility of the Red River outlet through Tongking, Dupuis had obtained a contract from Marshall Ma of Yunnan to supply arms to the Yunnan authorities in return for tin and other export commodities. Dupuis had returned to France in 1872 and had put the matter before the Ministry of Marine. The Ministry had agreed that a French naval vessel at the proper time should afford Dupuis moral support by cruising near Haiphong. Governor Dupré, also in Paris at the time, had given the project his blessing. It was clearly understood, however, that Dupuis would have to bear all of the expense, take all the risks, and renounce any liability on the part of the government should he encounter misfortune.[41] The extreme caution on the part of Paris in this instance stemmed primarily from French military impotence but partly also from the presence in the Foreign Office of the Duc de Broglie, a convinced anti-imperialist.[42]

Dupuis' adventure had begun in late 1872. Appearing at Hanoi in December, where he had posed in the dual role of Chinese mandarin official and French national carrying credentials from the Yunnan authorities, Dupuis had utilized local Tonkinese aid to overcome official Annamite resistance to his proposed ascent of the Red River. He had

[40] See H. A. Browne, *Reminiscences of the Court of Mandalay . . . 1859–1879* (Woking, 1907), 134–143, for an account from the Burma side of Margary's ill-fated attempt in January, 1875, to attempt to return from Bhamo to Shanghai. Margary was killed and his escort waylaid as they started to re-enter Yunnan for the return trip.

[41] Murphy, 58–60.

[42] Eustace G. C. Murray, *The Men of the Third Republic* (Philadelphia, 1873), 96–107. De Broglie was a celebrated Catholic scholar, who had been elected to Father Lacordaire's vacant post in the Academie Française.

eventually reached Yunnan city with his arms cargo on March 16, 1873. Although Dupuis had realized that resistance from the Annamite authorities was almost certain to be encountered on any return trip to Hanoi, he had rejected Marshall Ma's profferred escort of several thousand Chinese troops. After he had obtained a new contract for a cargo of salt and formal orders from Chinese officials in Yunnan directing China's supposed vassal, Annam, to permit Dupuis to navigate the river, he had returned again to Hanoi in May, 1873, accompanied by an escort of 150 men. When the local authorities had blocked his second attempted departure upstream with the salt cargo, Dupuis had refused to leave Tongking and had appealed for aid from Admiral Dupré at Saigon. He had promised the Admiral the assistance of disaffected Tonkinese elements and the prospect of any easy conquest of the province if only a small French force could be provided.[43]

Admiral Dupré's primary concern as Governor of Cochin-China since December, 1872, had been to bring to a successful conclusion the long-protracted negotiations with Hué covering the formal cession of the French-occupied provinces of southern Indo-China. He had despaired of succeeding unless some kind of coercive threat could be used. He had accordingly suggested tentatively that the surest means of forcing a decision upon King Tu-Duc was to seize Hanoi, a move capable of execution by a minimal number of troops and designed to involve Hué in serious domestic embarrassment if left uncorrected. But France at the moment was far too vulnerable in Europe to risk offending either Britain or Germany, so that successive ministries at Paris during 1873 had given no encouragement to Dupré's plans. This was true even after the alleged danger of Chinese or German occupation of the desirable Red River trading route was broached.[44]

Just as the Admiral's discouragement was giving way to despair, in July, 1873, a request from Hué asking Dupré's assistance in expelling from Tongking the obstinate Dupuis had given him an idea and a ray of hope. Dupré had outlined his proposal in a long dispatch to Paris dated July 28, 1873. Briefly stated, the plan was to agree to assist Hué, as requested, in obliging Dupuis to leave Hanoi, but to utilize the

[43] Murphy, 60–83; Jean Dupuis, *L'Ouverture du Fleuve Rouge au Commerce, 1872–1877: Journal de Voyage* . . . (Paris, 1879).

[44] Dutreb, 14–25. The Ministers of Marine to whom Dupré's successive appeals were addressed had to bow to the negative views of Foreign Minister de Remusat and Premier de Broglie.

delicate situation as a cover for sending a small armed French force
to Hanoi. Once arrived at Hanoi, the French would find excuse in the
semianarchy prevailing in Tongking arising from chronic unrest and
activities of coastal pirates, coupled with the alleged threat of Chinese
invasion from Yunnan, to invoke the protectorate clause of the 1862
treaty and to affirm the necessity of temporary occupation of the Hanoi
citadel and the coastal provinces of the delta. These strategic points
could then be retained until Hué agreed to conclude a general treaty
covering protection of Christians, freedom of trade, and amplification
of Annam's protectorate status under France. Dupré had advised Paris
that he anticipated little armed opposition and had offered to accept
full responsibility under penalty of disavowal, recall, or loss of rank,
if the results attained did not vindicate his action. He had asked
neither for approval nor for reinforcements, but only to be allowed to
proceed.[45]

Dupré's dispatch was sent by post, and it was not until September 8,
after Dupré had already summoned Garnier from Shanghai, that a
brief telegraphic reply was received from Paris stating that nothing
should be done which would expose France to dangerous complications. The failure of Paris to interpose a flat veto afforded leeway for
Dupré and Garnier to reason that their own failure to act in the crisis,
especially after Hué had requested assistance, would itself expose
French interests to irreparable damage in the future, especially in view
of a possible Chinese or German invasion of the area. Later instructions
from the Minister of Marine also failed to transmit de Broglie's flat
refusal to go along with Dupré's offer to take full responsibility for the
action. The Minister of Marine indicated, instead, the desire to gain
title to all of Cochin-China proper and to extend the terms of the French
protectorate, but without becoming dangerously involved in Tongking.

Dupré and Garnier decided, therefore, to proceed with their plans,
even though the Governor was able to provide only sixty men beyond
the crews of the three small vessels assigned to Garnier for the Hanoi
mission. It was anticipated that French intervention to expel Dupuis
would provoke disorders which would, in turn, afford opportunity for
Garnier to linger on and to press for basic French objectives, including

---

[45] *Ibid.*, 27–34. De Pouvourville (179) gives the total number as eighty-three
men; de Lanessan (525–527) indicates that the eighty-odd men who accompanied
Garnier were re-enforced by some ninety-two who came later by boat.

the opening of the Red River route. Meanwhile, Dupré would redouble his own diplomatic efforts at Hué. Garnier was not authorized to undertake outright intervention, which would impair future liberty of action for France. He was also ordered to stop at Hué en route in order to deliver a letter from Dupré calculated to dispel any anxieties that the court might entertain about the mission.[46]

For a time the plan worked well. Garnier reached Hanoi near the end of October, got in touch with Dupuis, discovered that Annamite defenses were more feeble than he had anticipated, and proceeded to quarrel with the allegedly un-co-operative local authorities over the quarters provided for his men. Garnier asked that his group be quartered in the citadel itself. On November 17, he declared unilaterally that the Red River was open to trade. Two days later he issued an ultimatum, and on November 20 he stormed and occupied the citadel of Hanoi. Popular disaffection spread quickly, and within three weeks' time pro-French elements had taken over control of the coastal provinces of Tongking, displacing Annamite authority. Meanwhile Dupré received encouraging word from Hué on December 1 that King Tu-Duc had appointed commissioners with full power to treat on all points of the proposed treaty. On December 7 M. Philastre, a French subordinate to Dupré in charge of indigenous court administration, was accordingly sent to Hué to facilitate the progress of the treaty negotiations. He also carried orders to proceed later to Hanoi as well.

On December 21 occurred the tragic death of Garnier. He was at the time on the verge of arranging a *modus operandi* with local Annamite authorities at Hanoi. The citadel was attacked by a mercenary band of "Black Flag" coastal pirates. The attack was repelled, but Garnier and several others lost their lives during their reckless pursuit of the attackers. The cause of French imperialism in Tongking suffered a serious check in his death and acquired its most glamorous martyr.[47]

The Treaty of 1874

The collapse of the Tongking coup followed the arrival at Hanoi of the negotiator Philastre on December 29, fresh from his conferences

---

[46] Dutreb, 35–56.

[47] *Ibid.*, 57–81; Murphy, 62–63; André Masson, *Hanoi pendant la Période Heroïque, 1873–1888* (Paris, 1929), 34–35.

with the Court at Hué. Although he apparently lacked specific instructions from Dupré covering the unanticipated situation, Philastre outranked all of his youthful compatriots at Hanoi, so that none was capable of challenging his decisions. He abruptly repudiated the projected local slettlement which Esmez, Garnier's successor, was negotiating. He also denounced Garnier's attack as "odious aggression" and ordered that the citadel be evacuated and French forces withdrawn from Hanoi forthwith. All this was done without exacting any compensatory guarantees regarding any future local settlement or the safety of friendly elements of the population which had rallied to the French authority. Some fourteen neighboring Christian villages were burned on the same day that Nam Dinh was surrendered by the French, and the total eventually reached several hundred. The evacuation, once begun, could not be halted, and once completed on January 2, could not be reversed.

Before the news of Philastre's actions had reached Saigon, Admiral Dupré received telegraphic instructions from Paris dated January 7 ordering the prompt conclusion of the Cochin-China treaty, the evacuation of the Hanoi citadel, and the abandonment of French efforts to take over Tongking. Thus Admiral Dupré's hands were effectively tied; he could not disavow Philastre's authority or reverse his decisions. The resulting treaty with Hué, signed on March 15, 1874, provided for a resident French consul with a guard at Hanoi, but this concession was a far cry from what local French leaders had expected to achieve.[48] The Philastre affair at Hanoi became the subject of bitter protest on the part of French imperialists generally and of Dupuis in particular. The latter suffered not only rebuff of his plans, but also expulsion from Tongking and the sequestration of his property and ships for a period of twenty months thereafter.[49]

The most plausible explanation of Philastre's nonaggressive attitude is threefold. As a long-time student of the Annamite language in close touch with the indigenous courts of law, he had come to look upon such adventures as Garnier's through Annamite rather than French eyes.

[48] Dutreb, 94–101; de Lanessan (527) says that 20,000 Christians were massacred and that 70,000 were rendered homeless.

[49] Dupuis attacked Dupré directly in his *Intervention du Contre-Amiral Dupré au Tongking* (Paris, 1885) and in other books published in 1879 and 1898.

Furthermore, he was doubtless aware of the general nature of the previous instructions from Paris and the limitations as to both objectives and methods which these instructions had enjoined. Garnier had certainly exceeded those instructions. Finally, Philastre came to Hanoi directly from his conferences with the court at Hué, before whom he had been unable to defend the tactics employed by Garnier. He apparently believed, therefore, that a flat disavowal of the French coup at Hanoi was the best means of facilitating the negotiations at Hué of the pending Cochin-China treaty.[50] Not until the relevant archives of the Ministry of Marine were opened to examination during the 1920's was this situation clarified.

The only solid gain which the French realized from the 1874 treaty was Hué's unconditional acknowledgement of French sovereignty over Cochin-China. The articles legalizing the Christian religion and declaring Hanoi and other ports of the Red River Delta open for navigation were not backed up by effective sanctions and never really became operative. The implied protectorate contained in the French promise to help maintain order and to fight off piratical attacks on the Annamite coast was qualified, in that under terms of the treaty France could act only on the request of the Annamite king. Tu-Duc subsequently undertook to evade admitting French overlordship by reviving in 1876 and 1880 the traditional practice of sending periodic tribute missions to China.[51] French consuls at Hanoi, Haiphong, and Quinhon, who were supposed to have exclusive jurisdiction over foreign residents, had in fact little authority and found themselves hampered by the mandarins at every turn. In 1877 Foreign Minister Decazes at Paris informed an outgoing Governor-General that France had renounced its claims of a protectorate over Tongking and was in no position to undertake aggrandizement.[52] Throughout the decade of the seventies French opinion generally was pre-occupied with internal political problems and was not greatly concerned over eastern Asia.

[50] Dutreb, 94–95.

[51] Priestley, 219–222; Murphy, 63, 67–68. The French consul at Hanoi tried in vain from 1875 to 1877 to assert the right of commercial access up the river. Disaffections recurred in Tongking, and Christian villages were destroyed without France being able to provide expected protection.

[52] T. F. Power, *Jules Ferry and the Renaissance of French Imperialism* (New York, 1944), 156–157. China's formal assertion of suzerainty over Tongking dated from 1881. See Lanessan, 547, and Masson, 38–40.

288

The Changed Political Climate of Republican France

The political confusion and military impotence which afflicted republican France throughout the decade of the seventies negated any possibility of reviving imperialist activities in eastern Asia. Defeat at the hands of Prussia was followed by the tragic civil war with the Paris Commune. The succeeding regime headed by President Thiers managed to pay off the Prussian indemnity, to rid France of foreign troops, and to avert further civil strife. Following the fall of Thiers's government in May, 1873, the first two cabinets under the promonarchist President MacMahon were headed by the stanch anti-imperialist, the Duc de Broglie, who had been a follower of Montalembert in Orleanist times and was an inveterate enemy of Louis Napoleon.[53] The bitter contest between republican and monarchist factions continued to absorb most of the political energies of metropolitan France throughout the remainder of the decade. Not until the constitutional issue was resolved in favor of the republicans with President MacMahon's retirement in 1879 could the French government contemplate imperialist activity as a means of restoring national presitge.

Political and economic developments during the seventies not only altered the relative importance of the traditional roots of French imperialism in the Orient but also contributed new factors. Missionary activity continued to be the major preoccupation of Frenchmen in eastern Asia and to give substance to the somewhat overworked *mission civilisatrice* by which the extension of French political influence was rationalized. But governmental support of missionary operations ceased to be a factor in the formulation of policy. The considerable extent to which the French church had aligned itself with monarchial reaction during the political strife of the seventies robbed it of political influence in republican ranks and stimulated anti-clerical sentiment.[54] The new motives for imperialism which developed during the decade were the increasing concern for markets overseas and the intensification of international competition for colonies.

French jealousy of British predominance in Asia revived following

[53] G. Hanotaux, *Contemporary France* (New York, 1905), II, v.

[54] Power, 19–20. In 1879–1880 the republican government curtailed clerical control over education, marriage, funerals, and cemeteries. It also forced the Jesuit order to dissolve.

Disraeli's 1875 coup in acquiring half interest for Britain in the Suez Canal.[55] Anglo-French rivalry became even more compelling as a result of the participation of Italy, Germany, Russia, Belgium, and Japan in the imperialist competition. If France was to maintain its relative position as a world power in a state system dependent for security on the balance of power, it must find outside of Europe some compensation for the loss of Alsace-Lorraine and must also keep pace with the gains being made by other powers. Although economic factors were probably never an important consideration in determining French policy, a growing popular interest in geographical exploration emphasized the importance of finding overseas markets and places to invest surplus capital.[56] French pride would not concede that the calamity of defeat on the continent meant also the abdication of the country's role of political and cultural leadership in the world outside. By 1880 French protagonists of imperialist expansion identified their cause with the recovery of France itself and made it virtually synonymous with patriotism. Republican politicians supported the trend and used it to divert attention from domestic problems.

Expansionist Agitation During the Seventies

The imperialist revival during the seventies derived its most enthusiastic support from the newly spawned geographical societies within France. The parent body was the venerable Geographical Society of France located at Paris, of which the ex-Minister of Marine, Chasseloup-Laubat, continued to be the president until 1874.[57] German-dominated Europe had seemingly become politically too stuffy for French breathing, so that escape had to be sought in fresher air far afield. The first chair of Geography in the Collège de France was set up in December, 1871, and the subject was brought into the schools in 1872. During

[55] See Ragatz, *passim.*

[56] Two important books designed to underscore the importance of colonies economically were Paul Leroy-Beaulieu's *De la Colonisation chez les Peuples Modernes* (Paris, 1874) and Paul Gaffarel's *Les Colonies Françaises* (Paris, 1880). The first author was Professor of Economics at the Collège de France and editor of *L'Economiste Français* (founded in 1873), while the second was Professor of History at Dijon. Both contributed also to the periodical press.

[57] Murphy, 2–19; Donald Vernon McKay, "Colonialism in the French Geographical Movement," *Geographical Review*, XXXIII (1943), 214–222. The Paris Geographical Society dated from 1821; from 1860 to 1873 its membership multiplied six times. It enjoyed the active support of the *Journal Officiel.*

the ensuing decade, no less than twelve new geographical societies were established in France, plus two more in the colonies. Especially active was the one at Lyons, the center of the French Association for the Propagation of the Faith.

In 1873 the Geographical Society of France set up a special commission to study commercial geography in co-operation with Parisian chambers of commerce, from which effort came the Society of Commercial Geography in 1876. The avowed aims of the new group were to encourage voyages that would stimulate commercial outlets, to study world resources and communications, colonization and emigration, and to spread geographical knowledge generally.[58] A similarly specialized group had appeared earlier at Bordeaux in 1874. An International Congress of Commercial Geography met at Paris in 1878. The activities of the geographical societies included the sponsoring of public lectures, the offering of essay prizes, and the publication of maps and monographs. Ministers of State contributed prizes, while leading newspaper editors and members of government participated actively.[59]

The modulation from purely geographical interests to the promotion of colonial imperialism was natural and inevitable. The Society of France in 1874 declared that in the process of the mastery of the globe by the white race "a country jealous of maintaining its rank in civilization will . . . be obliged to gather geographical information." The *Journal Officiel* in early 1875 warned specifically that England would penetrate south China from Burma if France continued to neglect the route available to it through Tongking.[60] In 1876 an International Association for Africa was formed at a conference sponsored by the King of Belgium. Ferdinand de Lesseps became president of the French section of this association in 1877. The *Revue Géographique*, founded in 1877, expressed a definite interest in colonial expansion.[61] In 1878 the Society of Colonial and Maritime Studies was established, and a colonization company on a joint stock basis was planned. A geographical conference at Algiers in 1881 concluded that France must keep pace with the expansion of Germany, England, and Russia if it expected to retain its rank as a world power.[62] Commerce, emigration,

[58] McKay, 214–220. The Society of Commercial Geography prepared a world map showing the location of all French consulates, the areas of French control, and the potential markets for products produced at Paris.
[59] Murphy, 2–19.   [60] McKay, 222, 225.   [61] *Ibid.*, 227.
[62] Murphy, 27–36.

and colony building would re-establish French prestige and open up new fields of opportunity to carry out the nation's civilizing mission. A book published in 1877 by the Abbé Roboisson combined in articulate fashion appreciation for the grandeur of France with the concern of an ardent Catholic for the propagation of the faith.[63] The author argued historically that national greatness was inseparable from the possession of colonies, and he flatly denied defeatist allegations that France lacked the capacity to colonize. He declared that the crux of successful colonization was not the development of commerce and plantations, but rather the cultivation of intellects and wills. If the true objective of transmitting the spirit and soul of the mother country were made central, colonization would become a wholesome exercise of the body politic affording a fruitful outlet for national energies and also a safety value for unsocial restlessness and violence. He declared that there should be not one France but five or six in the world, all knit to the motherland by "a community of . . . love for God and His Church." He concluded that the colonizing genius of France must not be chained by Godless legislation which hampered the transmission of the nation's heart and soul. A pro-Moslem policy in Algiers and a pro-Buddhist one in Cochin-China were not good enough; the church must again be set free.[64]

But despite all of Abbé Roboisson's persuasive eloquence, the time had passed when the French national spirit could be contained in a clerical mold. More convincing to many was the argument that France would find overseas, rather than in Europe, scope for future political and economic development. Colonization projects would revive the adventurous spirit of the Gaul and afford an outlet for surplus population, capital, and national spirit. Decadence could thereby be avoided and France be permitted at the same time to fulfill its sacred duty to elevate the three fourths of the earth's people who were still uncultivated or savage.[65]

[63] Abbé Roboisson, *Etudes sur les Colonies et la Colonisation au Regard de la France* (Paris, 1877).

[64] *Ibid.*, 208–217.

[65] Murphy, 19–36, 148–152. Jules Delabre, Minister of the Navy, published a book in 1877 entitled *Les Colonies Françaises*, emphasizing that whereas French shipping handled only one third of the trade at home ports, it carried nine tenths of the trade with the colonies. The author naturally stressed the need for a strong navy.

Geographical enthusiasts maintained a school for the training of volunteer explorers, obtained for them attaché status at nearby legations, and provided them with a rent-free house for a year following their return from overseas. Sponsored explorers were expected to carry with them samples of French industry and to bring back native products of potential commercial importance.[66]

Tongking came in for its full share of attention following the *"martyrdom"* of Garnier in 1874. Advocates of imperialism affirmed that in Tongking France would find the empire that had escaped its grasp in India. A Société Académique Indochinoise was established to promote studies in "Transganges India" looking toward the development of commercial activity and colonial power in eastern Asia.[67] In 1877 Jean Dupuis told the Paris Geographical Society that French refusal to acquire the valuable colony of Tongking, which would have provided work for all and opportunity for many to gain fortunes, had in effect repudiated the nation's humanitarian obligation to conquer "disinherited peoples" by intelligence and to admit barbaric peoples to the advantages of civilization. The Société Académique Indochinoise honored Dupuis for demonstrating the feasibility of commercial entry into south China via Tongking, and it also denounced the short-sighted policies of the Cochin-China authorities. The value of the commercial route up the Red River Valley was acclaimed in successive meetings (1878 and 1880) of the International Congress of Commercial Geography, which urged France to open up trade with Yunnan.[68]

French interest in Indo-China reached a climax in the late seventies and early eighties. The Rouen geographical society in 1879 coupled the objective of a French commercial monopoly of Tongking, Annam, Cambodia, and Siam with de Lesseps' newly projected scheme for piercing the isthmus of Panama (Darien). Other enthusiasts called for establishing a French protectorate over Siam and for French exploration of the upper Irrawaddy in Burma.[69] In 1880–1881 the leading imperialist contributor to the *Journal des Débats,* Leroy-Beaulieu, demanded that France restore its moral position in Asia by repudiating the weak policy that had left Dupuis and Garnier without support and by recognizing the enormous commercial possibilities in Tongking. The

[66] Murphy, 44–45.   [67] *Ibid.,* 41–46.   [68] *Ibid.,* 67–70.
[69] *Ibid.,* 23, 36.

293

author argued that the Tonkinese harbored no aversion to French control and that the area would fall to others if France did not acquire it.[70]

It does not fall within the province of this study to trace the steps in the actual acquisition of Tongking and Annam by the French during the early 1880's. By that time the domestic controversy between monarchist and republican partisans had been resolved in favor of the latter. Jules Ferry's first ministry, in 1880–1881, decided to reduce Annam to protectorate status; Freycinet, in 1882–1883, revived Garnier's struggle for Tongking; and Ferry's second ministry completed the project in 1883–1885.[71] French imperialism had outgrown the status of political expediency and, for many, had become a patriotic duty of the first order.[72] The case for French interest in the Far East was ably summed up in 1882 by Paul Gaffarel, professor of history at Dijon and founder of the Dijon Geographical Society,[73] as follows:

The future is [in the Far East]. There is no doubt about it. It would be better to renounce absolutely every idea of European annexation . . . and to shift our field of action to the Far East. . . . [The natives] are . . . children who are just being admitted to civilization. . . . Is it not our duty to direct them, to instruct them, to educate them morally? . . . Our most useful auxiliaries will be missionaries and schoolmasters. . . . Let us use them, and we shall have accomplished a useful and patriotic work.[74]

Conclusion

The taproot of French imperialism in the Far East from first to last was national pride—pride of culture, reputation, prestige, and influence. This was the constant factor which ran through the kaleidoscope of episodes of missionary dedication and daring, of naval coups, and of private adventures by such men as Pierre Poivre, Pigneau de Behaine,

---

[70] *Ibid.,* 159–164.   [71] Priestley, 219–220.

[72] Power, 199. The core of Ferry's argument for imperialist expansion was the need to re-establish the national honor and prestige of France as a world power. His global strategy called for colonies and naval bases. France's "civilizing mission" was a supporting consideration to gratify national pride, and Ferry's economic arguments were little more than a debater's rationalization, according to Power.

[73] Murphy, 191–192, 204–205.

[74] Paul Gaffarel, *Les Explorations Françaises depuis 1870* (Paris, 1882), 315, 332.

Montigny, and Garnier. One need not discount the genuineness of the religious zeal which sustained the program of the Société des Missions Etrangères over two centuries or challenge the vitality of the liberal religious revival under Louis Philippe to see in both of them an expression of supreme confidence in the superiority of French spirit and culture. Christian missions were supported, in large measure, because they were French.

Politically, French imperialism expressed itself most frequently in eastern Asia in terms of perennial rivalry with Great Britain. British pretentions of superiority were unendurable and therefore to be opposed whenever and wherever possible. The basic considerations behind French policy in the Far East from the time of Louis XIV to that of Louis Napoleon and Jules Ferry were more political than economic. The story, in fact, constitutes an effective refutation of any exclusively economic explanation of the imperialistic urge. French honor was enlisted to vindicate the inherent superiority of its national culture and could permit no challenge of it to go unanswered. In such a context the imperialist movement became the expression of the very essence of the French spirit, the *raison d'être* of France as a national state.

Developments in French colonial policy after 1880 illustrate this persistent urge to enhance national prestige and to vindicate French cultural superiority. The magnificent scholarly achievements of the Ecole Française d'Extrême Orient, which was established at Hanoi in 1898, attested the genuineness of French devotion to the cultural ideal. For many imperialist apologists in France, no boon to be conferred on colonial protégés in Annam could match their being transformed into brown-skinned Frenchmen, and no higher goal could be envisaged for Indo-China politically than that of its continuing association with France. French politicians after World War II were thus denied any easy rationalization of the eventual surrender of their colonial empire in Indo-China in terms of the vindication of French ideals. On the other hand, Americans could see in the emancipation of the Philippines a vindication of the principle of "government by the consent of the governed," and the British accepted the independence of India as fulfillment of the concept of a commonwealth of equal partners, each equipped with its own parliament and all co-operating voluntarily for common ends. It may prove to be one of the tragedies of the decline of

295

Western influence in Asia that France could not admit the possibility of cultural or political equality with herself, much less the outright surrender of colonial possessions, without seeming to repudiate not only her position as a world power but also the very rationale of her role in world affairs.

Bibliography

I. Guides

Boudet, Paul, and Bourgeois, Remy. *Bibliographie de l'Indochine Française, 1913–1926: Supplement for 1927–1929*. 2 vols. Hanoi, 1929. Useful.

Cady, John F. "The Beginnings of French Imperialism in the Pacific Orient," *Journal of Modern History*, XIV (March, 1942), 71–87.

Cordier, Henri. *Biblioteca Indosinica*. 4 vols. Paris, 1912–1915.

Fairbank, John King. *Trade and Diplomacy on the China Coast*. Cambridge, 1953. Vol. II, 62–74.

Great Britain, House of Commons. *General Index to the Papers* . . . , *1801–1852*. 3 vols. London, 1852–1857.

——. *General Alphabetical Index to the Bills, Reports* . . . *and Papers* . . . , *1853 to 1899*. London, 1900.

Hasse, Adelaide R. *Index to United States Documents Relating to Foreign Affairs, 1828–1861*. 3 vols. Washington, 1914, 1919, 1921.

Ragatz, Lowell J. *A Bibliography for the Study of European History, 1815 to 1939*. Ann Arbor, 1942. *Supplement, 1943*.

Tantet, Victor. *Archives Coloniales, Inventaire Sommaire de la Correspondance Générale de la Cochinchine (1686–1863)*. Paris, 1905. Tantet was "Chef bureau au Ministère des Colonies."

——. *Catalogue Méthodique de la Bibliothèque du Ministère des Colonies*. Melun, 1905.

II. Archival Materials

Callery, J. M. *Correspondance Diplomatique Chinoise Relative aux Négociations du Traité de Whampoa . . . (1844).* Paris, 1879. Supplements Lavollée regarding the negotiations at Canton.

Cordier, Henri. *Le Consulat de France à Hué sous la Restauration: Documents Inédits, Tirés des Archives des Départements des Affaires Etrangéres, de la Marine et des Colonies.* Paris, 1884.

——. *La France en Chine au XVIIIᵉ Siècle. Documents Inédit, Publiée sur les Manuscrits Conservés au Dépot des Affaires Etrangères, avec une Introduction et des Notes.* Paris, 1883.

——. *Les Origines de Deux Etablissements Françaises dans l'Extrême Orient: Changhai-Ningpo; Documents Inédits.* Paris, 1896.

. ——. "La Première Légation de France en Chine (1847): Documents Inédits." *T'oung Pao,* 2d ser., VII (1906), 351–368.

France, Ministère des Affaires Etrangères,[1] Chine (abbreviated AEC). Volumes 1–28, from 1841 to 1860. This material was available at the search room at the Quai d'Orsay. It contains outgoing instructions, incoming dispatches, and policy memoranda both intra- and interdepartmental, plus relevant material touching problems of co-operation with London. Easily the most important single source for French policy.

——, ——, Espagne, Volumes 1350–1363, from 1857 to 1864. These volumes include data on relations between France and Spain during the joint intervention in Annam.

——, ——, Mémoires et Documents, Asie. Volumes 27–29, from 1857 to 1864.

Great Britain, Foreign Office (abbreviated FO), 17, China. The China correspondence covering the period from 1840 through 1860 extends from volume 89 to volume 349. Items from some thirty-five of these are cited in the footnotes. A great deal of this China material, especially from 1854 to 1862, was reproduced in a series of Parliamentary Command Papers, but the basis of selection renders these published papers of little value for the study of French policy.

——, FO, 27, France. Exchanges between London and Paris regarding affairs of eastern Asia from 1842 to 1860 are scattered widely from volumes 701 to 1383. This material can be checked against data in the China series in the Quai d'Orsay depository.

[1] Inaccessible to the author were the archives of the Ministère de la Marine et des Colonies, covering the activity of naval commanders in oriental waters. This lack is particularly serious after 1861, when the Ministry of Marine virtually directed Indo-China policy.

298

——, FO, 5, America; FO, 65, Russia; and FO, 72, Spain. A number of useful items can be found in the American materials, fewer in the Russian and Spanish series. All of the FO material is available at the Record Office in London.

——, *Correspondence Respecting Insults in China*, submitted to the House of Lords, February, 1857.

——, Hansard's *Parliamentary Debates*. 3d ser. Vols. 144, 156, 157. London, 1857–1858. The only important debates relating to French policy concern the Arrow War of 1856 and the subsequent war with China.

Gros, Baron J. B. L. *Négociations entre la France et la Chine en 1860: Livre Jaune du Baron Gros*. Paris, 1864.

Hawkes, Francis L., ed. *Narrative of the Expedition of an American Squadron to the China Seas and Japan . . . under the Command of Commodore M. C. Perry*. 3 vols. New York, 1857. This is also available as Senate documents, serial nos. 769–771, and as House documents, serial nos. 802–804.

Lavollée, Charles. *France et Chine: I, Traité de Whampoa (1844): Correspondance Diplomatique de M. de Lagrené. II, Expédition de 1860 contre la Chine*. Paris, 1900. Part I reproduces the archival material for 1844 covering the Lagrené mission. The editor served the mission as secretary to the customs service representative.

"Le Premier Traité de la France avec le Japon (Yedo, 9 Octobre, 1858)," *T'oung Pao*, 2d ser., XIII (1912), 205–290.

Swisher, Earl. *China's Management of the American Barbarians: A Study of Sino-American Relations, 1841–1861, with Documents*. New Haven, 1953. This important book contains English translations of 546 official Chinese documents relating to foreign affairs.

United States, Department of Navy Archives. Cruise of Captain John Percival of the *Constitution* 1843–1846: Instructions, Book I, Article 68, Oct. 13, 1843; Log Book, Book J 1, Article 46. Disappointing on the whole.

——, ——. East India, China, and Japan Squadron, Commodore M. C. Perry, vol. I, cruise of Dec. 13, 1852, to Dec. 31, 1853.

——, ——. East India Squadron, Captain James Biddle's cruise from Aug. 1, 1845, to May 3, 1847.

——, ——. East India Squadron, Commodore P. F. Voorhees, cruise from March 1, 1849, to Feb. 7, 1857. Fairly useful.

——, ——. Pacific Squadron, Captain Josiah Tattnall, Book J 1, Article 77, Oct. 15, 1857, to Dec. 1859.

Naval Department archives reflect generally the limited perspective and interest of the authors and were of relatively little value.

——, Department of State Archives (abbreviated SD). Outgoing diplomatic instructions (DI) to China for the period 1840–1860 are included in a single volume, number 1. Diplomatic dispatches (DD) to 1860 extend through volumes 1–19. Index volumes for diplomatic correspondence (numbers 53 for China and 57 for France and Britain) are especially useful. Some valuable information can also be found in the Consular Letters (CL), notably from Shanghai, Hongkong, Canton, Bangkok, Singapore, Tahiti, Manila, Amoor River. Notes to and from foreign legations in Washington for the 1840–1860 period have been indexed (Britain, vol. 59, France, vol. 61, and Russia, vol. 63). This material is accessible in the search room of the National Archives in Washington.

House and Senate executive documents covering American activities in eastern Asia during the 1850's in particular reproduce virtually all of the relevant diplomatic material in the archives. The omissions found were few and unimportant. The most useful of these published documents covering the activities of Balestier, Marshall, Ward, Reed, and Parker were the following:

32d Congress, 1st sess., Senate exec. doc. 38
33d Congress, 1st sess., House exec. doc. 123
33d Congress, 2d sess., Senate exec. doc. 34
35th Congress, 1st sess., Senate exec. doc. 47
35th Congress, 2d sess., Senate exec. doc. 22
36th Congress, 1st sess., Senate exec. doc. 30
36th Congress, 1st sess., House exec. doc. 4
36th Congress, 2d sess., Senate exec. doc. 6

III. Accounts by Participants

Allgood, George. *China War, 1860: Letters and Journal.* London, New York, 1901.

Annales de la Propagation de la Foi, XXVIII (1856), 461–481.

Bazancourt, César Lecat Baron de. *Les Expéditions de Chine et de Cochinchine d'après les Documents Officiels.* 2 vols. Paris, 1861–1862. A good account of naval operations of 1857–1858 based on the official papers of Admiral Rigault de Genouilly.

Bellé, A. S. *Programme d'une Mission en Chine, Fait et Addressé . . . à M. Thiers le 19 Mars et le 16 Avril, 1840.* Paris, 1842.

Bowring, Sir John. *Autobiographical Recollections of Sir John Bowring.* With a Brief Memoire by Lewin B. Bowring. London, 1877. John Bowring took himself very seriously.

——. *The Kingdom and People of Siam with a Narrative of the Mission to That Country in 1855.* 2 vols. London, 1857.

Broullion, R. P. *Missions de Chine: Mémoire sur l'Etat Actuel de la Mission du Kiang-Nan, 1842–1855.* Paris, 1855. The author was the Jesuit head of the Zikawei mission.

Browne, H. A. *Reminiscences of the Court at Mandalay . . . 1859–1879.* Woking, 1907. Contains a firsthand account of the Margary tragedy.

Callery, J. M. *Journal des Opérations Diplomatiques de la Légation Française en Chine.* Macao, 1845. A day-by-day account of conferences held with Lagrené and the Chinese negotiators from Aug. 1 to Oct. 22, 1844. The narrative ends abruptly on page 276.

Cécille, Captain M. "Cochinchine et Tonkin, Extrait d'un Rapport de M. Cécille . . . Commandant . . . en Station dans les Mers de Chine en Date du 18 Août, 1843," *Annales Maritimes et Coloniales* LXXXVII (1844), 750–780.

Chinese Repository. 20 vols. Canton, Macao, Victoria, 1832–1851. A monthly journal containing anecdotes, accounts of current conditions, state papers, and a "Journal of Occurrences."

Clerq, Alexandre Jean Henri de. *Recueil des Traités de la France . . . (1793–1906).* 23 vols. Paris, 1861–1919.

Cooke, George Wingrove. *China: Being the "Times" Special Correspondence from China in the Years 1857–58.* London, 1859.

Courcy, Marquis Marie-René Roussel de. *Souvenirs.* 4 vols. Paris, 1900. Vols. II and III especially are informative and important.

Cowley, H. R. C. Wellesley, 1st Earl. *Secrets of the Second Empire: Private Letters from the Paris Embassy.* Ed. by F. A. Wellesley. New York, London, 1929. Lord Cowley's private letters to Clarendon, Malmesbury, and other British Foreign Ministers cover a number of problems of Anglo-French relations, 1852–1867.

Davis, Sir John Francis. *China: During the War and since the Peace.* 2 vols. London, 1852. Davis defends the policy of the East India Company and his own role as plenipotentiary. His narrative of events is highly trustworthy.

Ferrière le Vayer, Théophile de. *Une Embassade Française en Chine: Journal de Voyage.* Paris, 1854. By the secretary of M. Lagrené.

Fishbourne, Captain Edmund Gardiner *Impressions of China and the Present Revolution.* London, 1855. Fishbourne was a partisan supporter of the Taiping cause and commander of the *Hermes.*

Garnier, Francis. *Voyage d'Exploration en Indo-Chine, Effectué pendant les Années 1866, 1867 à 1868. . . .* 2 vols. Paris, 1873.

Genouilly, Admiral Rigault de. *Expédition de Tourane: Relation Empruntée au Journal de M. Ch . . . Ge . . . Ecrit lors du Bombardement de Tourane par le Catinat, 24, août, 1858.* [n. p., n. d.]

Grant, Sir Hope. *Incidents in the China War of 1860: Compiled from the*

Private Journals of Sir Hope Grant. Ed. by Henry Knowles. Edinburgh, 1875. Reflect difficulties with the French.

Harcourt, Bernard d'. "La Première Ambassade Française en Chine," *Revue des Deux Mondes,* 8th ser., XXXVII (1862), 654–673.

Hertslet, Sir Godfrey Edward. *Treaties, etc. between Great Britain and China and between China and Foreign Powers . . . in Force on the 1st Jan. 1896.* 2 vols. London, 1896. Extended to Jan. 1, 1908, in 3d ed. (1908), 2 vols., including "Orders in Council . . . affecting British Interests in China." Maps.

Kergariou, Achille de. *La Mission de la Cybéle en Extrême-Orient, (1817–1818): Journal de Voyage du Capitaine de Kergariou.* Paris, 1914. Edited by Pierre de Joinville and published by the Society of the History of the French Colonies.

La Bissachière, Pierre Jacques Lemounier de. *La Relation sur le Tonkin et la Cochinchine. . . . Publiée d'après le Manuscrit (de 1807) des Archives des Affaires Etrangères, avec un Introduction et des Notes par C. B. Maybon.* Paris, 1920.

La Grandière, Benoit de. *Les Debuts de l'Occupation Française en Cochin-chine.* Paris, 1864, 1888.

La Gravière, Jurien de. *Voyage en Chine et dans les Mers et Archipels de cet Empire Pendant les Années 1847–1848–1849–1850.* 2 vols. Paris, 1854. An able, instructive account by the commander of the French corvette *La Bayonnaise.*

Lapierre, Captain. "Suite des Opérations dans les Mers de Chine et du Japan de la Division Navale sous les Ordres de M. le Capitaine de Vaisseau Lapierre (Extrait d'un Lettre Particulière)," *Annales Maritimes et Coloniales,* C (1847), 862–867, and CI (1847), 56–65.

Launay, Abbé P. Adrien, ed. *Documents Historiques Relatifs a la Société des Missions Etrangères.* Lille, 1890; Vannes, 1905. Launay is the leading historical scholar of the Société des Missions Etrangères.

——, ed. *Lettres de Monseigneur Pallu.* 2 vols. Angoulême, 1905.

Levêque, Favin, "Extrait d'un Rapport de M. Favin Levêque . . . , Commandant de Corvette l'*Héroine,* en Date du 17 Juin, 1843," *Annales Maritime et Coloniales,* III (1843), 869–889. This report covers Tourane, Callao-Cham, and Poulo-Condore.

Loch, Henry Brougham. *Personal Narrative of Occurrences during Lord Elgin's Second Embassy to China in 1860.* London, 1900 (reprint). Loch was private secretary to Lord Elgin and fellow prisoner with Parkes at Peking.

Lucy, Armand. *Souvenirs de Voyage: Lettres Intimés sur la Campagne de Chine en 1860.* Marseille, 1861. Maps and drawings.

Meadows, Thomas Taylor. *The Chinese and Their Rebellions.* London, 1856.

A descriptive account by an Anglican padre who served as interpreter for the British consulate at Shanghai.

Moerenhaut, Jacques Antoine. *The Inside Story of the Gold Rush. . . .* Trans. by A. P. Nasatir. San Francisco, 1935. Moerenhaut served successively as U.S. and French consul on Tahiti.

Moges, Marquis de. *Souvenirs d'un Ambassade en Chine . . . en 1857 et 1858.* Paris, 1860. There is an English translation, *Recollections of Baron Gros's Embassy to China and Japan in 1857–58.* London, 1860. Gros's secretary prepared this standard account.

Montigny, Louis-Charles de. *Manuel du Négociant Français en Chine; ou, Commerce de la Chine Considéré au Point de Vue Française.* Paris, 1846. This is the second part of *Chine et Indo-Chine: Faits Commerciaux no. 10,* published by the Ministère de l'Agriculture et du Commerce.

Mutrécy, Charles de. *Journal de la Campagne de Chine, 1859–1860–1861.* 2 vols. Paris, 1861. An eyewitness account, discursive, valuable.

Oliphant, Laurence, *Narrative of the Earl of Elgin's Mission to China and Japan in the Years 1857–58–59.* 2 vols. Edinburgh, London, 1859; New York, 1860. A brilliant work, almost definitive; statements must occasionally be corrected.

Osten-Sacken, F. T. P., Baron von. "Souvenirs de l'Ambassade du Comte Poutiatine en Chine," *Journal de Saint Petersbourg,* 1876. By the second secretary of Putiatin at Peking in 1857–1858. Not examined.

Pagès, Léon, and Azy, Benoît d'. *Les Droits, les Intérêts et les Devoirs de la France en Cochinchine: Extrait du Correspondant.* Paris, 1857. A brief apology for French policy.

Palanca Gutierrez, D. Carlos. *Reseña Histórica de la Expedición de Cochinchina.* Cartagena, 1869. By the commander of the Spanish contingent during the later phases of the joint intervention.

Palikao, Charles G. M. A. A. [Cousin de Montauban], Comte de. *L'Expédition de Chine en 1860: Souvenirs du Général Cousin de Montauban, Comte de Palikao.* Paris, 1932. Of limited value.

Pallu, François, Bishop of Heliopolis. *Relation Abregée des Missions et des Voyages des Evêques Français Envoyez aux Royaumes de la Chine, Chochinchine, etc.* Paris, 1682. Pallu was one of the founders of the Société des Missions Etrangères.

Pallu de la Barrière, Leopold. *Relation de l'Expédition de Chine en 1860.* Paris, 1863. An account of military operations based on materials from the French Ministries of War and Marine.

Ponchalon, Colonel Henri de. *Indo-Chine: Souvenirs de Voyage et de Campagne, 1858–1860.* Tours, 1896. Valuable diary account by an observing French officer present at Tourane and Saigon in 1858.

Reed, William B. "Private Diary of His Mission to China, 1857–59, with

MS. letters from British Officials and Others in the Orient Inserted." 2 vols. Library of Congress, Division of Manuscripts. Intimate and personal, reflecting Reed's naiveté and homesickness. Almost illegible.

Reinach, L. de. *Recueil de Traités Conclus par la France en Extrême Orient, (1648–1902)*. Paris, 1902.

Scarth, John. *Twelve Years in China*. Edinburgh, 1860. An eyewitness account but pro-Taiping and tainted by anti-French bias.

Stanmore, Arthur Hamilton Gordon. *Sidney Herbert, Lord Herbert of Lea*. 2 vols. London, 1906. Vol. II includes Herbert's correspondence as Secretary of War regarding preparations for the expedition of 1860.

Stephenson, Sir Frederick Charles Arthur. *At Home and on the Battlefield: Letters from the Crimea, China, and Egypt, 1854–1888.* . . . London, 1915.

Villemereuil, M. de. *Explorations et Missions de Doudart de Lagreé, Extraits de ses Manuscrits*. Paris, 1883.

Walrond, Theodore, ed. *Letters and Journals of James, Eighth Earl of Elgin*. London, 1872.

Williams, Frederick W., ed. "The Journal of S. Welles Williams, LL.D., Secretary and Interpreter of the American Embassy to China during the Expedition to Tientsin and Peking in the Years, 1858 and 1859," *Journal of the North China Branch of the Royal Asiatic Society*, XLII (1911), 3–232.

Wood William Maxwell. *Fankwei: or, the San Jacinto in the Seas of India, China, and Japan*. New York, 1859. Wood was an observing fleet surgeon of the American East India Squadron.

IV. Secondary Accounts

Abel, M. H. [Vice-Admiral Adrien-Barthélemy Louis Rieunier]. *Solution Pratique de la Question de Cochinchine, ou Fondation de la Politique Française dans l'Extrême Orient*. Paris, 1864.

Ajalbert, Jean. *L'Indochine, par les Français*. Paris, 1931.

Allison, John M. S. *Church and State in the Reign of Louis Philippe*. Princeton, N.J., 1916.

Baldwin, J. R. "England and the French Seizure of the Society Islands," *Journal of Modern History*, X (1938), 212–231. Based on British archival and French printed sources.

Baudiment, Louis. *Un Mémoire Anonyme sur François Pallu, Principal Fondateur des Missions Etrangères*. Tours, 1934.

Bauksgevden, Baron A. *La Chine Russe: Aperçus des Relations Diplomatiques de la Russie avec la Chine: Le Traité de Peking de 1860*. Port Arthur, 1902. Supposedly based on unpublished sources. Not examined.

Baulmont, Lieutenant [Marie Gilbert René]. "La Prise de Tourane Septembre 1858–9 et Mai 1859 – 15 Septembre 1859," *Revue Indo-chinoise,* XII (1904), 691–703, and XIII (1905), 13–28. Defends Genouilly's policies and reflects the formidable resistance met at Tourane.

Bell, Herbert C. F. *Lord Palmerston.* 2 vols. London, 1936. A definitive biography of a British idol.

Bellecourt, P. Duchesne de. "La Colonie de Saigon—Les Aggrandissements de la France dans le Bassin du Mékong," *Revue des Deux Mondes,* 8th ser., LXVIII (1867), 427–456.

Bilbaut, Théophile. *Le Canal de Suez et les Intérêts Internationaux: la Cochinchine Française et le Royaume de Cambodge.* Paris, 1870.

Blackwood's Edinburgh Magazine, LXXXVII (1860), 525–526.

Blet, Henri. *Histoire de la Colonisation Française.* 3 vols. Grenoble, 1946–1950. Volume II, *Les Etapes d'une Renaissance Coloniale,* 1947, covers 1789–1870 and is well done.

Boeuf, Abel. *Histoire de la Conquête de la Cochinchine, 1858–1861.* Saigon, 1927.

Bourgeois, Remi. *Le Tonkin en 1857: La Mission Cleczkowski.* Hanoi, 1943.

Bourges, Jacques de. *Relations du Voyage de Monseigneur l'Evêque de Beryte, Vicaire Apostolique du Royaume de la Cochinchine.* 3d ed. Paris, 1683.

Brooks, J. M. *International Rivalry in the Pacific Islands, 1800–1875.* Berkeley, Calif., 1941.

Cabatan, Antoine. "Doudart de Lagrée et l'Indochine, 1828–1868," *Revue de l'Histoire de Colonies Françaises,* 1933, no. II, 205 ff.

Cady, John F. *Foreign Intervention in the Rio de la Plata, 1838–1850.* Philadelphia, 1929. Covers the South American phase of the mid-century Anglo-French entente.

Chailley-Bert, J. *Les Compagnies de Colonisation sous l'Ancien Régime.* Paris, 1898.

Chassigneux, Edmund. *L'Indochine.* Vol. V of *Histoire des Colonies Françaises et de l'Expansion de la France dans le Monde.* Ed. by Gabriel Hanotaux. Paris, 1932.

Chastel, Guy. *Un Siècle d'Epopée Française en Indochine, 1774–1874.* Paris, 1947.

Collins, Ross William. *Catholicism and the Second French Republic, 1848–1852.* New York, 1923. Useful.

Collis, Maurice, *Siamese White.* London, 1936. A novel which reflects the atmosphere of early European contacts with the Tenasserim isthmus of Burma and Siam.

Cordier, Henri. "Bordeaux et Cochinchine sous la Restauration," *T'oung Pao,*

2d ser., V (1904), 505 ff. Cordier is the most prolific author on French policy in eastern Asia. He published many of his articles in *T'oung Pao*, of which he was for a long time the editor.

————. *Le Conflit entre la France et la Chine*. Paris, 1883. This is the earliest of Cordier's studies and is an apology for contemporary French policies in Tongking.

————. *Le Consulat de France a Hué sous la Restauration*. Paris, 1884.

————. *L'Expédition de Chine, 1857–58*. Paris, 1905. This study and the companion one on the 1860 expedition are nearly definitive.

————. *L'Expédition de Chine de 1860, Histoire Diplomatique, Notes et Documents*. Paris, 1906.

————. *La France en Chine au Dix-huitième Siècle*. Paris, 1883.

————. "La France et la Cochinchine, 1852–1858: La Mission du *Catinat* à Tourane (1856)," *T'oung Pao*, 2d ser., VII (1906), 481–514.

————. *La France et l'Angleterre en Indo-Chine et en Chine sous le Premier Empire*. Leide, 1903. Also in *T'oung Pao*, 2d ser., II (1901), 201.

————. *Histoire de Relations de la Chine avec les Puissances Occidentales, 1860–1900*. 3 vols. Paris, 1901–1902.

————. *Histoire Générale de la Chine et de Ses Relations avec les Pays Etrangères depuis les Plus Anciens jusqu'à la Chute de la Dynastie Mandchoue*. 4 vols. Paris, 1920. A valuable standard account.

————. "La Mission de Jancigny dans l'Extrême Orient, 1841–1846," *Revue de l'Histoire des Colonies Françaises*, IV (1916), 140–225.

————. "La Politique Coloniale de la France au Début du Second Empire (Indo-Chine, 1852–1858)," *T'oung Pao*, 2d ser., X–XII (1909–1911). Reprinted, Leide, 1911.

————. *La Première Légation de France en Chine*. Leide, 1906.

————. "La Reprise des Relations de la France avec l'Annam sous la Restauration," *T'oung Pao*, 2d ser., IV (1903), 28–51.

Courcy, Marquis Marie-René Roussel de. *L'Empire du Milieu*. Paris, 1860 and 1867. Includes a good brief account of the history of the period.

————. "L'Insurrection Chinois, Son Origine et Ses Progrès. I, Les Sociétés Secrètes, les Premiers Campagnes des Insurgés et les Deux Empereurs du Céleste Empire," *Revue des Deux Mondes*, 8th ser., XXXIV (July, 1861), 1–35.

————. "L'insurrection Chinois, Son Origine et Ses Progrès. II, Triomphe des Insurgés, le Nouveau Roi et Sa Doctrine Religieuse, dernier Partie," *Revue des Deux Mondes*, 8th ser., XXXIV (July 15, 1861), 312–360.

Courtambert, E., and Rosny, Léon de. *Tableau de la Cochinchine*. Paris, 1862.

Cultru, Prosper. *Histoire de la Cochinchine Française des Origines à 1883*.

Paris, 1910. A balanced, objective account, relatively complete, done by a professor at the Sorbonne. A few inaccuracies mar its excellence.

Debidour, Antonin. *Histoire des Rapports de l'Eglise et de l'Etat en France de 1789 à 1870*. Paris, 1898. Well written, comprehensive, strongly anti-clerical.

Delabre, Jules. *Les Colonies Françaises*. Paris, 1877.

Delvaux, R. P. "L'Ambassade de Minh-Mang à Louis Philippe, 1839 à 1841," *Bulletin des Amis du Vieux Hué*, XV (Oct.–Dec., 1928), 257–264.

Dennett, Tyler. *Americans in Eastern Asia*. New York, 1922. Dennett's account is marred by his too great dependence on the biased reporting of Humphrey Marshall.

——. "Seward's Far Eastern Policy," *American Historical Review*, XXVIII (1922), 45–62. Covers the breakdown of allied co-operation after 1853.

Devine, W. *The Four Churches of Peking*. London, 1930.

Dorland, A. A. "A Preliminary Study of the Role of the French Protectorate of Roman Catholic Missions in Sino-French Diplomatic Relations." Cornell University thesis, 1951.

Dubois, Adolphe. *Les Accords Franco-Chinois*. Paris, 1928.

Dupuis, Jean. *Intervention du Contre-Amiral Dupré au Tongking*. Paris, 1885.

——. *L' Ouverture du Fleuve Rouge au Commerce, 1872–1877: Journal de Voyage de l'Expédition de Jean Dupuis*, Paris, 1876.

——. *Le Tonkin de 1872 à 1886*. Paris, 1910.

——. *Le Tonkin et l'Intervention Française*. Paris, 1897.

Dutreb, M. [Du Bert, Marthe]. *L'Amiral Dupré et la Conquête du Tonkin*. Paris, 1924. A scholarly study of the Hanoi episode of 1873–1874 based on the archives of the Minister of Marine.

Eitel, E. J. *Europe in China, the History of Hongkong . . . to 1882*. London, 1895.

Ennis, Thomas E. *French Policy and Development in Indochina*. Chicago, 1936. Contains relatively little on the 1840–1860 period.

En-sai Tai. *Treaty Ports in China: A Study in Diplomacy*. New York, 1918. Contains useful data on Canton.

Fairbank, John King. "Chinese Diplomacy and the Treaty of Nanking, 1842," *Journal of Modern History*, XII (March, 1940), 1–30.

——. "The Definition of the Foreign Inspectorate of Customs at Shanghai, 1854–1855," *Nankai Sociological and Economic Quarterly*, IX (April, 1936), 125–163.

——. "The Legalization of the Opium Trade before the Treaties of 1858," *Chinese Sociological and Political Science Review*, XVII (July, 1933), 215–263.

Fairbank, John King. "The Manchu Appeasement Policy of 1843," *Journal of the American Oriental Society*, LIX (1939), 469–484.

——. "The Provisional System at Shanghai in 1853–54," *Chinese Sociological and Political Science Review*, XVIII (January, 1935), 455–504; XIX (April, 1935), 65–124.

——. *Trade and Diplomacy on the China Coast . . . 1842–1854*. 2 vols. Cambridge, 1953.

Foster, John W. *American Diplomacy in the Orient*. New York, 1903.

Gaffarel, Paul. *Les Colonies Françaises*. Paris, 1880.

——. *Les Explorations Françaises depuis 1870*. Paris, 1882.

Galos, Henri. "L'Expédition de Cochinchine et la Politique Française en Extrême Orient," *Revue des Deux Mondes*, 8th ser., LI (1864), 173–208. An able review of the entire French story. Galos criticizes the too wide diffusion of French efforts in China, Mexico, Cambodia.

G[arnier], Francis. *La Cochinchine Française en 1864*. Paris, 1864.

Gautier, Hippolyte. *Les Français au Tonkin, 1787–1883*. Paris, 1884.

Griffin, Eldon. *Clippers and Consuls*. . . . Ann Arbor, 1938.

Grosse-Aschhoff, Angelos. *The Negotiations between Ch'i-ying and Lagrené, 1844–1848*. Allegany, N.Y., 1950. The documentary appendix includes English translations of the memorials which Ch'i-ying sent to Peking with reference to the Lagrené negotiations. Manuscript French archives are not used.

Hall, John R. *The Bourbon Restoration*. London, 1909.

Hanotaux, Gabriel. *Contemporary France*. 2 vols. New York, 1905.

——. *Histoire des Colonies Françaises*, Paris, 1932. Vol. V.

Harvey, G. E. *History of Burma*. New York, 1925. Covers early French contacts with Burma.

Hoang-van-Thuy. "Introduction à l'Histoire Abrégée de l'Etablissement du Protectorat Français en Annam," *Revue Indo-chinoise*, V (1906).

Hoo Chi-Tsai. "Les Bases Conventionnelles des Relations Modernes entre la Chine et la Russie." University of Paris thesis, 1918. A useful study with a good bibliography.

Hoskins, H. L. *British Routes to India*. New York, 1928. Covers the Suez Canal problem as an issue in Anglo-French relations.

——. "The Suez Canal in Time of War," *Foreign Affairs*, XIV (1935), 93.

Hudson, Nora E. *Ultra-Royalism and the French Restoration*. Cambridge, 1936.

Irisson [Comte d'Herisson], Maurice. *Journal d'un Interprète en Chine*. Paris, 1886.

——. *The Loot of the Imperial Summer Palace at Pekin*. Washington, 1901.

Jancigny, Adolphe Philibert Dubois de. *Japon, Indo-Chine, Empire Birman* (*ou Ava*), *Siam, Annam* (*ou Cochinchine*), *Peninsule Malaise.* . . . Paris, 1850.

Jésus, Montalto de. *Historie Shanghai.* Shanghai, 1909.

Joinville, Pierre de. "Les Armateurs de Bordeaux et l'Indochine sous la Restauration," *Revue de l'Histoire des Colonies Françaises,* IX (1920), 91–128, 197–248.

Kuo, P. C. *A Critical Study of the First Anglo-Chinese War.* Shanghai, 1935. Kuo uses materials from Chinese sources carelessly and ignores pertinent data in English.

Lane-Poole, Stanley. *The life of Sir Harry Parkes.* 2 vols. London, 1894. A useful book, but the hero makes no mistakes.

Lanessan, J.-L. de. *L'Expansion Coloniale de la France: Etude Economique, Politique, et Geographique sur les Etablissements Français d'Outre-Mer.* Paris, 1886. The author was Governor-General of Cochin-China during the 1890's.

La Servière, Joseph de. *Histoire de la Mission du Kiangnan: Jesuits de la Province de France (1840–1899), Zi-ka-wei.* 2 vols. Shanghai, 1914. A valuable book.

Latourette, K. S. *History of Christian Missions in China.* New York, 1929. An excellent account, thorough and objective.

Launay, Abbé P. Adrien. *Histoire Ancienne et Moderne de l'Annam, Tongking, et Cochinchine, depuis l'Année 2700 avant l'Ere Chrétienne jusqu'à nos Jours.* Paris, 1884. A brief review of the conventional story tailored for the situation in 1884.

——. *Histoire des Missions de Chine: Mission du Kouang-Si.* Paris, 1903. *Supplement* . . . (*Négociations Relatives au Martyre d'Auguste Chapdelaine*). Vannes, 1909.

——. *Histoire Générale de la Société des Missions Etrangères depuis Sa Formation jusqu'à nos jour.* 3 vols. Paris, 1894. A scholarly work of importance, especially vol. III. The approach is apologetic, but factual reporting is accurate and balanced.

——. *Mgr. Retord et le Tonkin Catholique (1831–1858).* Lyons, 1893. A substantial book; reports Montigny's Tourane mission in a favorable light.

Lavollée, Charles. "Les Jesuits en Chine," *Revue des Deux Mondes,* 8th ser., II (1856), 523–526.

Leavenworth, Charles S. *The Arrow War with China.* London, 1901. A useful book based on published British sources.

Leroy-Beaulieu, Paul. *De la Colonisation chez les Peuples Moderne.* Paris, 1874. Imperialist propaganda.

Louvet, Abbé Louis Eugène. *La Cochinchine Religieuse.* 2 vols. Paris, 1885. A highly partisan account. Volume II treats the period after 1847.

Louvet, Abbé Louis Eugène. *Les Missions Catholiques au XIXe Siècle.* Lyons, 1896. A general survey containing useful factual information.

Macfarlane, Charles. *The Chinese Revolution.* London, 1853.

McKay, Donald Vernon. "Colonialism in the French Geographical Movement, 1871–1881," *Geographical Review,* XXXIII (1943), 214.

Mars, V. de. "La Question Chinoise," *Revue des Deux Mondes,* 8th ser., IX (1857), 81, 481–534.

Marx, Francis. "The Pacific and the Amoor: Naval, Military and Diplomatic Operations from 1855 to 1861," *Fraser's Magazine,* XXXI (May, 1861), 1–28.

Mas, Sinibaldo de. *La Chine et les Puissances Chrétiennes.* 2 vols. Paris, 1861. The author was Spanish envoy to China. The second volume is historical.

Masson, André. *Hanoi pendant la Période Heroïque, 1873–1888.* Paris, 1929.

Maurain, Jean. *La Politique Ecclésiastique du Second Empire de 1852 à 1869.* Paris, 1930. A capital book, based on archival data, which brings the French church into political perspective.

Maxwell, Herbery Eustace. *The Life and Letters of George William Frederick, Fourth Earl of Clarendon.* 2 vols. London, 1913.

Maybon, Charles B. "Les Européens en Cochinchine et au Tonkin (1600–1775)," *Revue Indo-chinoise* XXV (1916), 49–98, 411–450.

——. *Histoire Moderne du Pays d'Annam, (1592–1820).* . . . Paris, 1919. A very substantial contribution covering the Pigneau de Behaine episode.

——, and Fredet, Jean. *Histoire de la Concession Française de Changhai.* Paris, 1929. An excellent account based on archival research in Paris and in China.

Medhurst, W. H. *The Foreigner in Far Cathay.* London, 1872.

Meyniard, Charles. *Le Second Empire en Indo-Chine (Siam, Cambodge, Annam): L'Ouverture de Siam au Commerce et la Convention du Cambodge.* Paris, 1891. An excellent account of Montigny's mission and of subsequent French policies in the area.

Michie, Alexander. *The Englishman in China during the Victorian Era, as Illustrated in the Career of Sir Rutherford Alcock.* 2 vols. Edinburgh, London, 1900. Well informed and presented in classical English. A few minor errors.

Millac, M. Arthur. "Les Français à Changhai en 1853–1855: Episodes du Siège de Changhai par les Imperiaux," *Revue de l'Extrême Orient,* II (1884), 1–53.

Milne, W. C. *Life in China.* London, 1857.

Morison, John Lyle. *The Eighth Earl of Elgin: a Chapter in Nineteenth-Century Imperial History.* London, 1928. An apology based on the Elgin papers and private correspondence.

Morse, Hosea Ballau. *The International Relations of the Chinese Empire.* Vol. I, *The Period of the Conflict, 1834–1860.* London, 1910. A summation of materials found in published British records, hence pro-British in tone.

Murphy, Agnes. *The Ideology of French Imperialism, 1871–1880.* Washington, 1948. The author reviews an enormous volume of French writing on the subject. Tends to excuse Catholic agencies for the revival of imperialist *Bell* activities.

Murray, Eustace Clare Grenville. *The Men of the Third Republic.* Philadelphia, 1873. By an informed contemporary observer.

Nasatir, A. P. "French activities in California before Statehood," *Proceedings of the Pacific Coast Branch of the American Historical Association,* 1928, 76–88.

Nevelskoy, Admiral Gennadii Ivanovitch. *Les Exploits des Officiers de Marine Russe en Extrême Orient de la Russie en 1849 à 1855.* St. Petersburg, 1878.

Nolde, John Jacob. "The 'Canton City Question,' 1842–1849; A Preliminary Investigation into Chinese Anti-foreignism and Its Effects upon China's Diplomatic Relations with the West." Cornell University thesis, 1950. A thoroughgoing examination of published English and Chinese materials.

Phillips, Charles Stanley. *The Church in France, 1789–1848: A Study in Revival.* London, 1929. A standard account.

——. *The Church in France, 1848–1907.* New York, London, 1936. Excellent.

Picanon, M. "La Prise de Saigon en Février 1859 et les Débuts de Notre Action en Cochinchine," *Académie des Sciences Coloniales, Compte Rendu des Séances,* VIII (1926–1927), 385–394. A good account.

Pouvourville, Albert de. *Francis Garnier.* Paris, 1931.

Power, T. F., Jr. *Jules Ferry and the Renaissance of French Imperialism.* New York, 1944. Useful.

Priestley, H. I. *France Overseas.* New York, 1938. An enormous compilation of data, especially useful for period after 1861.

Ragatz, Lowell. *The Question of Egypt in Anglo-French Relations, 1875–1904.* Edinburgh, 1932.

Revue des Deux Mondes, 5th ser., X (May 31, 1945), 1033–1036. The "Chronique de Quinzaine" for this issue presents an account of the Basilan expedition.

Roberts, Stephen H. *History of French Colonial Policy, 1870–1925.* 2 vols. London, 1929. Vol. II has a chapter on Indo-China. Good bibliography.

Roboisson, Abbé. *Etudes sur les Colonies et de la Colonisation au Regard de la France.* Paris, 1877.

Rosny, L. Léon de. "La Cochinchine et l'Occupation Française du Port de Tourane," *Revue Orientale et Americaine,* I (1859), 57–77.

311

Roy, Just Jean Etienne. *La Chine et la Cochinchine:* . . . *L'Histoire de la Guerre des Français et des Anglais contre les Chinois, depuis 1844 jusqu'au Traité* . . . *1860.* Lille, 1862.

Sallet, A. "Campagne Franco-Espagnole du Centre-Annam: Prise de Tourane, 1858–1859," *Bulletin des Amis du Vieux Hué,* XV (1928), 171–179. An informed account of the activities of both Genouilly and Page at Tourane.

Septans, Albert. *Les Commencements de l'Indo-Chine Française d'après les Archives du Ministère de la Marine et des Colonies.* . . . Paris, 1887. A fair account, some of it borrowed from Galos and others, but with references to the archives of the Minister of Marine.

Stewart, H. F., and Desjardins, Paul. *French Patriotism in the Nineteenth Century, 1814–1833.* Cambridge, 1933.

Thomas, A. *Histoire de la Mission de Pékin.* 2 vols. Paris, 1925.

Thomazi, Auguste Antoine. *La Conquête de l'Indochine: Avec Vingt-deux Croquis.* Paris, 1934. A pro-Genouilly summary account of operations in Indo-China is included in the first half. The study lacks footnotes.

Thompson, Virginia. *Dupleix and His Letters.* New York, 1933.

——. *French Indo-China.* New York, 1937. Valuable for an assessment of French colonial policy and for the native reaction to it. Contains a bibliography of 600 items.

Thomson, R. Stanley. "The Diplomacy of Imperialism: France and Spain in Cochin-China, 1858–1863," *Journal of Modern History,* XII (1940), 334–356. Utilizes French archival sources.

Tsiang, T. F., ed. "China after the Victory of Taku, June 25, 1859," *American Historical Review,* XXXV (1929), 78–84. Translation of three Chinese documents relating to the American Minister John E. Ward.

——. "China, England, and Russia in 1860," *Cambridge Historical Journal,* III (1929), 115–121. Reveals that the Chinese were aware of differences in the viewpoints and designs of foreigners.

Van Alstyne, Richard W. "British Diplomacy and the Clayton-Bulwer Treaty, 1850–1860," *Journal of Modern History,* XI (1939), 149–183.

Varin, Paul. *Expédition de Chine.* Paris, 1862.

Vercel, Roger, *Francis Garnier à l'Assault des Fleuves.* Paris, 1952.

Vial, Paulin. *Les Premières Années de la Cochinchine Française.* 2 vols. Paris, 1874. The preface is by Admiral Rieunier. The author was associated with Governor Bonard and served briefly in 1886–1887 as Resident-General of Cochin-China.

Wei-tai Shen, *China's Foreign Policy, 1839–1860.* New York, 1932.

Williams, Samuel Welles. *A History of China: Being the Historical Chapters from "The Middle Kingdom."* New York, 1897.

Wood, W. A. R. *A History of Siam.* London, 1926. Rev. ed., Bangkok, 1933.

Valuable for the Phaulkon episode and other aspects of the early history of Siam.

Wrong, George M. *The Earl of Elgin*. London, 1905. A general account, clearly presented but without annotation.

Index

322